THE

LYLE

ANTIQUES

IDENTIFICATION

GUIDE

Copyright © 1981 by Lyle Publications
All rights reserved. This book, or parts thereof,
may not be reproduced in any form without permission
in writing from the publisher. Published on the same
day in Canada by Academic Press Canada Limited, Toronto.

Library of Congress Cataloging in Publication Data

Main entry under title:

The Lyle antiques identification guide.

    Revision of: The antique collector's pocketbook.
    Includes index.
    1. Antiques—Collectors and collecting. I. Curtis,
Tony. II. Antique collector's pocketbook. III. Title:
Antiques identification guide.
NK1125.L77 1981   745.1   81-9866
ISBN 0-698-11114-1 (pbk.)   AACR2

Printed in the United States of America
Distributed in the United States by Coward, McCann &
Geoghegan, 200 Madison Avenue, New York, N.Y. 10016

THE
LYLE
ANTIQUES
IDENTIFICATION
GUIDE

INTRODUCTION

With the ever increasing popularity of antique collecting, there is a need for a comprehensive reference book containing detailed illustrations – not only of the items which command the highest prices but also those pieces which, although not antiques in the true sense, are much sought after by members of the trade.

Here, in one handy, pocket sized volume, are about 3,000 clear illustrations to facilitate instant recognition and dating of the host of day to day items which make up the bulk of the antique market.

Compiled primarily with the professional dealer in view, this book makes inter-trade reference simple and accurate. Interior decorators too, will find communication with their clients considerably improved through use of this book, once again ensuring that there can be no confusion resulting from verbal desciptions being inaccurately given or incompletely understood.

We are confident that every user of The Lyle Antiques Identification Guide will find it of invaluable assistance in the smooth running of their business and a useful addition to their works of reference.

ANTHONY CURTIS

CONTENTS

MONARCHS

HENRY 1V	1399 - 1413
HENRY V	1413 - 1422
HENRY V1	1422 - 1461
EDWARD 1V	1461 - 1483
EDWARD V	1483 - 1483
RICHARD 111	1483 - 1485
HENRY V11	1485 - 1509
HENRY V111	1509 - 1547
EDWARD V1	1547 - 1553
MARY	1553 - 1558
ELIZABETH	1558 - 1603
JAMES 1	1603 - 1625
CHARLES 1	1625 - 1649
COMMONWEALTH	1649 - 1660
CHARLES 11	1660 - 1685
JAMES 11	1685 - 1689
WILLIAM & MARY	1689 - 1695
WILLIAM 111	1695 - 1702
ANNE	1702 - 1714
GEORGE 1	1714 - 1727
GEORGE 11	1727 - 1760
GEORGE 111	1760 - 1820
GEORGE 1V	1820 - 1830
WILLIAM 1V	1830 - 1837
VICTORIA	1837 - 1901
EDWARD V11	1901 - 1910

PERIODS

TUDOR PERIOD	1485 - 1603
ELIZABETHAN PERIOD	1558 - 1603
INIGO JONES	1572 - 1652
JACOBEAN PERIOD	1603 - 1688
STUART PERIOD	1603 - 1714
A. C. BOULLE	1642 - 1732
LOUIS XIV PERIOD	1643 - 1715
GRINLING GIBBONS	1648 - 1726
CROMWELLIAN PERIOD	1649 - 1660
CAROLEAN PERIOD	1660 - 1685
WILLIAM KENT	1684 - 1748
WILLIAM & MARY PERIOD	1689 - 1702
QUEEN ANNE PERIOD	1702 - 1714
GEORGIAN PERIOD	1714 - 1820
T. CHIPPENDALE	1715 - 1762
LOUIS XV PERIOD	1723 - 1774
A. HEPPLEWHITE	1727 - 1788
ADAM PERIOD	1728 - 1792
ANGELICA KAUFMANN	1741 - 1807
T. SHERATON	1751 - 1806
LOUIS XVI	1774 - 1793
T. SHEARER	(circa) 1780
REGENCY PERIOD	1800 - 1830
EMPIRE PERIOD	1804 - 1815
VICTORIAN PERIOD	1830 - 1901
EDWARDIAN PERIOD	1901 - 1910

CHINESE DYNASTIES

Shang	1766 – 1123 BC
Zhou	1122 – 249 BC
Warring States	403 – 221 BC
Qin	221 – 207 BC
Han	206 BC – AD 220
6 Dynasties	317 – 589
Sui	590 – 618
Tang	618 – 906
5 Dynasties	907 – 960
Liao	907 – 1125
Song	960 – 1279
Jin	1115 – 1234
Yuan	1260 – 1368
Ming	1368 – 1644
Qing	1644 – 1911

REIGN PERIODS

MING

Hongwu	1368 – 1398	*Hongzhi*	1488 – 1505
Jianwen	1399 – 1402	*Zhengde*	1506 – 1521
Yongle	1403 – 1424	*Jiajing*	1522 – 1566
Hongxi	1425	*Longqing*	1567 – 1572
Xuande	1426 – 1435	*Wanli*	1573 – 1620
Zhengtong	1436 – 1449	*Taichang*	1620
Jingtai	1450 – 1456	*Tianqi*	1621 – 1627
Tianshun	1457 – 1464	*Chongzheng*	1628 – 1644
Chenghua	1465 – 1487		

QING

Shunzhi	1644 – 1662	*Daoguang*	1821 – 1850
Kangxi	1662 – 1722	*Xianfeng*	1851 – 1861
Yongzheng	1723 – 1735	*Tongzhi*	1862 – 1874
Qianlong	1736 – 1795	*Guangxu*	1875 – 1908
Jiali	1796 – 1820	*Xuantong*	1908 – 1911

REGISTRY OF DESIGNS

USED 1842 to 1883

BELOW ARE ILLUSTRATED THE TWO FORM OF 'REGISTRY OF DESIGN' MARK USED BETWEEN THE YEARS OF 1842 to 1883.

EXAMPLE: An article produced between 1842 and 1867 would bear the following marks. (Example for the 12th of November 1852).

EXAMPLE: An article produced between 1868 and 1883 would bear the following marks. (Example the 22nd of October 1875).

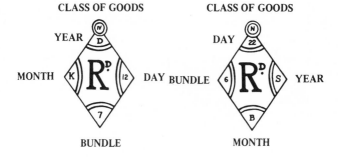

DATE AND LETTER CODE

January	C	1842	X	54	J	66	Q	78	D
February	G	43	H	55	E	67	T	79	Y
March	W	44	C	56	L	68	X	80	J
April	H	45	A	57	K	69	H	81	E
May	E	46	I	58	B	70	O	82	L
June	M	47	F	59	M	71	A	83	K
July	I	48	U	60	Z	72	I		
August	R	49	S	61	R	73	F		
September	D	50	V	62	O	74	U		
October	B	51	P	63	G	75	S		
November	K	52	D	64	N	76	V		
December	A	53	Y	65	W	77	P		

CHINA MARKS

BELLEEK
1857 onwards

BLOOR DERBY
1815-1840

BLOOR DERBY

BOW
1750-1776

1750   1760   1770

CAUGHLEY
1772-1814

imitation
Worcester   in blue   in blue   impressed   SALOPIAN

CHELSEA
1745-1784

Chelsea 1745
incised   in relief   red   gold
1745-1749   1750-1753   1755   1758-1770

COLEBROOK DALE
1785-1820

C Dale   Coalport
1785-1820

COPELAND
1847

1847

COPELAND & GARRETT
1833

1847-1891   NEW FAYENCE
1833-1847

DAVENPORT
1793-1882

Davenport

DAVENPORT
LONGPORT
STAFFORDSHIRE

DAVENPORTS
STONE CHINA

DERBY
1745 onwards

1750   1760   1770-1780

DOULTON
1815

DOULTON
LAMBETH   DOULTON
LAMBETH
pre 1836   1872

FRANKENTHAL
1755-1800

blue   blue   blue   blue
1756   1756-1759   1762-1793   1771

HOCHST
1750-1798

red   blue   impressed
1750-1762   1762-1796   1765-1774   1760-1765

LEEDS
1760-1878

Hartley, Greens & Co
LEEDS POTTERY   LEEDS POTTERY
1760-1783   LEEDS POTTERY
impressed 1864

MARTIN BROS
1873-1915

Martin Bros
London & Southall   R.W.MARTIN & BROS
1873   1900

MASONS
1795-1854

MASONS

PATENT IRONSTONE
CHINA   FENTON
STONE WORKS

MEISSON
1713

1713-1724   1725-1750   modern

MENNECY
1734-1748

DV   D.V.
incised   in blue

MINTON
1793 onwards

MINTON
1800-1836   1851   1860-1880

MINTON B B New Stone   MINTONS
1861 onward   20th century

NANTGARW
1811-1820

Nantgarw   NANTGARW
1811   1813

SWANSEA
NANGARW   NANT GARW
O.W.
1814   1816-1820

NEWHALL
1782-1835

N 332

PETIT JACOB
1796-1862

J.P.   J   P
1800   XX   1820

PLYMOUTH
1768-1772

X 11
21

ROCKINGHAM

ABOMELO
Rockingham
ROCKINGHAM   Baguley
Rockingham Works

early 19th century   red 1824

CHINA MARKS

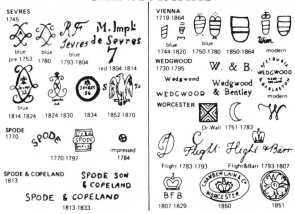

RECOGNITION & DATING
SOME USEFUL HINTS

Obviously the task of committing every china mark to memory is one which will be outside the scope of most collectors and, indeed, most dealers too. For this reason, the following simple guides may prove to be of some assistance in determining the approximate date of a piece without having recourse to long, and frequently involved, lists of the marks used by various manufacturers over the years.

Any piece bearing the words 'English Bone China' or simply 'Bone China' is a product of the twentieth century and the words 'Made in England' also suggest twentieth century manufacture, though they could relate to pieces dating from 1875 onwards.

The word 'England' stamped on a piece suggests compliance with the McKinley Tariff Act of America, 1891 which required all imports to America to bear the name of the country of origin.

In 1862 , the Trade Mark Act became law. Any piece bearing the words 'Trade Mark' therefore, can be assumed to date from 1862 onward.

Following the law relating to companies of limited liability, the word Limited or its abbreviations appears after 1860, though more commonly on pieces dating from 1885 onwards.

When a piece bears a pattern number of name, it can be assumed to date no earlier than about 1810.

Royal Arms incorporated into a small mark indicates a date after 1800.

During the mid 19th century the word 'Royal' was commonly added to the Manufacturer's name or trade name and, consequently, pieces bearing this word can usually be placed after 1850.

HANDLES

1550
Tudor
drop.

1560
Early
Stuart
loop.

1570
Early
Stuart
loop.

1620
Early
Stuart
loop.

1660
Stuart
drop.

1680
Stuart
drop.

1690
William &
Mary solid
backplate.

1700
William &
Mary split
tail.

1700
Queen Anne
solid back-
plate.

1705
Queen Anne
ring.

1710
Queen Anne
loop.

1720
Early
Georgian
pierced.

1720
Early
Georgian
brass drop.

1730
Cut away
backplate.

1740
Georgian
plain brass
loop.

1750
Georgian
shield drop.

1755
French
style.

1760
Rococo
style.

1765
Chinese
style.

1770
Georgian
ring.

1780
Late Georgian
stamped.

1790
Late Georgian
stamped.

1810
Regency
knob.

1820
Regency
lions mask.

1825
Campaign.

1840
Early
Victorian
porcelain.

1850
Victorian
reeded.

1880
Porcelain or
wood knob.

1890
Late Victorian
loop.

1910
Art
Nouveau.

PEDIMENTS

1690
Swell frieze.

1700
Queen Anne.

1705
Double arch.

1705
Queen Anne.

1710
Triple arch.

1715
Broken circular.

1720
Cavetto.

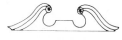

1730
Swan neck.

1740
Broken arch

1740
Banner top.

1750
Dentil cornice.

1755
Fret cut.

LEGS

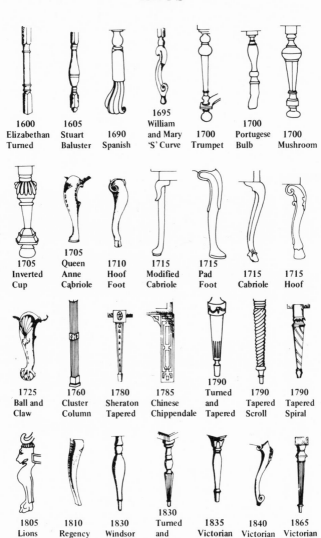

1600 Elizabethan Turned	**1605** Stuart Baluster	**1690** Spanish	**1695** William and Mary 'S' Curve	**1700** Trumpet	**1700** Portugese Bulb	**1700** Mushroom
1705 Inverted Cup	**1705** Queen Anne Cabriole	**1710** Hoof Foot	**1715** Modified Cabriole	**1715** Pad Foot	**1715** Cabriole	**1715** Hoof
1725 Ball and Claw	**1760** Cluster Column	**1780** Sheraton Tapered	**1785** Chinese Chippendale	**1790** Turned and Tapered	**1790** Tapered Scroll	**1790** Tapered Spiral
1805 Lions Paw	**1810** Regency Sabre	**1830** Windsor Baluster	**1830** Turned and Fluted	**1835** Victorian turned.	**1840** Victorian Cabriole	**1865** Victorian Reeded

FEET

1690
Wooden
Wheel

1690
Ball

1700
Bracket

1700
Spanish

1710
Hoof.

1715
Pad

1725
Ball and
Claw

1735
Cabriole
Leg Foot

1740
Stylised
Hoof

1740
Ogee

1745
French
Knurl

1750
Dolphin

1750
English
Knurl

1755
Elaborate
bracket.

1760
Splay

1760
Gutta
Foot

1770
Tapered
socket.

1775
Peg and
Plate

1790
Spiral
Twist

1790
Wheel
Castor

1790
Spade

1800
Fluted
Ball

1805
Decorative
Socket

1805
Paw

1805
Regency

1810
Socket

1815
Lions Paw

1830
Regency

1830
Victorian
Scroll

1860
Victorian
Bun

CHAIR BACKS

1660
Charles II.

1705
Queen Anne.

1745
Chippendale.

1745
Chippendale.

1750
Georgian.

1750
Hepplewhite.

1750
Chippendale.

1760
French Rococo.

1760
Gothic.

1760
Splat back.

1770
Chippendale
ladder back.

1785
Windsor
wheel back.

1785
Lancashire
spindle back.

1785
Lancashire
ladder back.

1790
Shield and
feathers.

1795
Shield back.

1795
Hepplewhite.

1795
Hepplewhite
camel back.

1795
Hepplewhite.

1810
Late Georgian
bar back.

CHAIR BACKS

1810
Thomas Hope
'X' frame.

1810
Regency
rope back.

1815
Regency.

1815
Regency
cane back.

1820
Regency.

1820
Empire.

1820
Regency
bar back.

1825
Regency
bar back.

1830
Regency
bar back.

1830
Bar back.

1830
William IV
bar back.

1830
William IV.

1835
Lath back.

1840
Victorian
balloon back.

1845
Victorian.

1845
Victorian
bar back.

1850
Victorian.

1860
Victorian.

1870
Victorian.

1875
Cane back.

AGATE

Fine Italian agate cameo, 1in. high, late 16th century.

Solid agate silver shaped sauceboat.

Late 19th century Russian figure of a collie carved from milky gray agate, 6.4cm. high.

German agate standing salt, circa 1600, 8½in. high.

Staffordshire solid agate pecten-shell teapot and cover, 7¼in. wide.

Solid agate cream jug, 4in. high, circa 1750.

ALABASTER

Late 19th century alabaster figure of an eagle, by W. Gebler, 17½in. high.

Nottingham alabaster relief of the Assumption of the Virgin, early 15th century, 16in. high.

Coloured alabaster bust of a young woman in a square necked dress, circa 1890, 14½in. tall.

Large Egyptian alabaster jar, early Dynastic period, 11½in. high.

Malines relief in alabaster of Christ and a woman, circa 1600, 7½in. wide.

Italian alabaster group, 1880-1900, 27½in. high.

Very rare passenger pigeon, mounted on branch, 22in. high, in glass dome.

A large tiger-skin 9ft.8ins. long.

Crocodile handbag with stuffed crocodile on the front flap.

A large stuffed moose head.

Stuffed and mounted pelican in glass fronted case, 2ft. 7in. high.

An Indian long-haired black mountain bear.

ARMOUR

Pair of well articulated upper arm defences from the 17th century.

19th century sheet iron articulated helmet of Cromwellian design, circa 1830, 14in. high.

An Allemaine collar of the 16th century from a suit of armour.

A 17th century Cromwellian trooper's helmet, skull formed in two pieces.

19th century Japanese suit of armour.

Italian 17th century suit of horseman's armour with close helmet.

AUTOMATONS

Musical piggy duo auto-maton, 1ft.3in. high, French.

A levitation automaton depicting Snow White lying on a couch, 45in. x 38in., circa 1920.

Late 19th century French musical rabbit automaton, 9in. high.

Late 19th century French musical automaton, 'The Hunter at Rest', 2ft.3in.

Late 19th century French musical seascape automaton, 1ft.8in. high.

19th century clown with dancing midget, musical box inside.

BIRDCAGES

Late 18th century Russian painted birdcage.

Victorian brass birdcage.

Mid 19th century 'Crystal Palace' brass birdcage.

19th century ormolu birdcage with ogee top, 24in. high.

19th century blue and white Delft earthenware birdcage.

19th century brass parrot cage.

Mother-of-pearl in-
laid rosewood baro-
meter, circa 1850,
44¾in. high.

Inlaid mahogany
stick barometer by
Negrety, 1850,
44in. long.

Louis XV
barometer in
boulle case.

Victorian oak
cased baro-
meter.

A circular barometer in
brass case on ebonised
stand.

Late 19th century combined
clock, thermometer, barometer
and barograph , 2ft.3in. wide.

Victorian wall barometer
in an oak case.

Oak barometer
and timepiece,
1880's, 44in.
high.

Early 18th century
walnut pillar baro-
meter, 3ft.3in.
high.

Unusual Dutch
walnut baro-
meter, mid
18th century,
3ft.11in. high.

Very rare George
II column baro-
meter, 2ft.11in.
high.

25

BRONZE

Stylish WMF polished bronze stemmed dish, circa 1910, 19cm. high.

Large Art Deco spelter group, 32in. wide, Paris.

Heyner bronze letter opener, 30cm. long, circa 1900.

Bronze figure of Perseus Arming by Sir Alfred Gilbert, 1880's, 14¼in. high.

19th century bronze figure of an old man, 9in. long.

Late 19th century bronze by W. Szczblewski.

Bronze and ivory figure by H. Chiparus Etling, Paris, circa 1920, 7¾in. high.

Early 20th century bronze group signed T. Campaiola, 24in. high.

Late Ming dynasty bronze figure, 11¾in. high.

Rare North Italian Gothic crucifix figure, 98in. high, circa 1250.

Good Philippe bronze and ivory group, 1920's, 48cm. high.

Bronze and ivory Art Deco figure.

Bronze figure of a jaguar, 22¼in. long, 1920's.

Bronze figure of a grazing ewe, by Rosa Bonheur, circa 1860, 6in. wide.

Gilt bronze group of a Bobsleigh team, circa 1936, 28.5cm. high.

Early 16th century Paduan bronze group of a female satyr and her child, 7¾in. high.

Art Deco metal figure by Rischmann, 22¾in. high.

13th century Pagan figure of the Buddha in bronze, 10¾in. high.

American bronze figure, signed Paul Herzel, circa 1910.

19th century Japanese bronze, 4ft.4in. long.

Bronze figure of a horse, circa 1880, 6in. wide.

Bronze figure of a tribesman, 41cm. high.

A pair of bronze horses, 14½in. high, circa 1900.

Spelter lampstand, after Bouret, circa 1890, 28in. high.

BRONZE

Gilt bronze group of three putti, 1850's, 10¾in. wide.

Early 17th century Florentine bronze figure from the Susini workshop, 6¾in. high.

19th century Japanese bronze group.

Chiparus bronze and ivory figure of a dancing girl, 43.5cm. high, 1920's.

19th century bronze cavalry charger and trooper by J. Willis Good.

Bronze figure of David, circa 1880, 29in. high, signed F. Barbedienne.

Modern bronze bust of an Indian, 14in. high.

Franz Bergmann cold-painted bronze figure, circa 1910, 5in. high.

19th century bronze cavalry charger and trooper by J. Willis Good.

Late 17th century Flemish bronze mortar and T-shaped pestle, 5½in. high.

Bronze group of two dogs, circa 1880, 9in. long, signed Lalouette.

15th century bronze bust of the Buddha by Sukh'o'tai, 28½in. high.

Early 16th century Paduan equestrian group, 16¾in. high.

Hagenauer bronze
vase, circa 1910,
11.5cm. high.

Stylish Guigner Art Deco
gilt-bronze group, 54.75cm
high, 1930's.

Early 17th century
Venetian bronze door
knocker, 16in. high.

Small Egyptian bronze,
10in. high, circa 1090
B.C.

Bronze lion cast in the
T'ang style, 10in. long.

Stylish bronze figure of
a vulture, 20cm. high,
1920's.

Preiss bronze and ivory
figure of a schoolboy,
21cm. high.

Bronze group by Isadore Bonheur,
20¼in. wide.

20th century Italian
bronze figure of a
fawn, 34¼in. high.

17th/18th century Italian
bronze figure of Christ,
9½in. high.

19th century French bronze
group signed L. Longepied,
19in. high.

Splashed gilt bronze vase,
Chinese, 18th century,
29.5cm. high.

George III oval satin-wood tea caddy with hinged lid, 6in. wide.

Victorian coromandel wood games compendium in box, 13½in. wide.

One of a pair of George III canta-loup shaped tea caddies, 4½in. wide.

One of a pair of George III mahogany and satin-wood knife boxes, 22.5cm. wide.

Mahogany 'Duke of York' apothecary cabinet, circa 1780.

Late 19th century oak cased calendar.

Lacquered work box with lift-up lid and four drawers.

Mid 19th century artist's paintbox, 1ft.10in. wide, English.

English box and counters, 1755-1760, enamelled on copper, 6.5cm. wide.

Victorian coromandel-wood box by Baxter, London, 1856, 8½in. wide.

Mid 17th century oak spice cabinet, 15in. wide.

Mahogany and inlaid decanter box with four cut-glass decan-ters, 8½in. high.

Stobwasser box painted with La Toilette.

Small, Victorian tooled leather stationery box with fitted interior.

Late 19th century Indian ivory and ebony box.

An excellent quality late 18th century tea caddy with rolled paper decoration, 5in. high.

Crocodile skin travelling dressing case with gold mounted fittings.

Late 18th century octagonal lacquer Kojubako, signed Zohiko.

19th century Japanese Suzuribako with fitted tray.

Table square spice box with named sectioned interior, circa 1840.

George III woodworker's tool chest in a pine case, 3ft.6in. wide.

Oak candle box, circa 1790, 13in. wide.

19th century English lacquer box by Jennens and Bettridge.

Edwardian C.W.S. biscuit tin.

31

Tortoiseshell and mother-of-pearl inlaid tea caddy.

Regency penwork tea caddy, 9in. wide.

'Intarsia' brass mounted and inlaid wood casket, circa 1900, 14cm. long.

19th century lacquer Suzuribako, 9¼in. wide.

Oak decanter box by H. H. Dobson & Sons, London, circa 1850, 9¾in. long.

Tortoiseshell tea caddy with engraved plate on front.

Reco Capey carved ebony box and cover, 21cm. high.

Unusual 19th century Chinese black lacquer tea caddy.

18th century oak candle box with sliding front, 16in. high.

George III ivory and pewter tea caddy, 5in. high.

Commonwealth carved oak bible box, 1657, 2ft. wide.

Regency mother-of-pearl tea caddy of bow-fronted form, 8in. wide.

Mid 19th century tor-
toiseshell and silvered
metal mounted box.

17th century French red
leather casket, 16in. long.

Circular pollard wood
snuff box, circa 1820,
8.2cm. diameter.

Victorian satinwood
square shaped tea
caddy, 11cm. wide.

Rosewood and satin-
wood portable writ-
ing box, circa 1900,
12in. wide.

19th century mahogany
and brass coal box.

Walnut and marquetry
humidor, circa 1880,
14 x 19½in.

Unusual carved oak
offertory box with
iron lock and chain.

Early 19th century tor-
toiseshell tea caddy, in-
laid with mother-of-
pearl.

Victorian Tunbridge-
ware stamp box.

Rare George II japanned
tea caddy, circa 1740,
10¼in. wide.

Late Victorian pine
specimen chest.

CAMERAS

Fine quarter-plate field camera by Sanderson.

Rare Johnson pantoscopic camera, circa 1860.

'The Telephot' ferro-type button camera, circa 1900, English.

Stirn's small waistcoat detective camera, in brass, second model, circa 1888.

J. Lancaster half-plate 'instantograph' collap-sible camera, circa 1905.

Ensign tropical roll-film reflex camera, circa 1925.

CANE HANDLES

French Art Nouveau cane handle, circa 1900.

English ivory handled walking stick, circa 1830.

Late 19th century Meissen parasol handle, 4.3cm. high.

18th century ivory and Narwhal walk-ing stick, 96.5cm. long.

Rhinoceros horn and silver pique cane handle, circa 1700, 12.5cm. long.

German porcelain cane handle, 2½in. high, late 18th century.

Early 19th century Italian parcel gilt cane handle, 9.5cm. long.

English ivory pique cane handle, 4in. high, 1667.

Carved oak sternboard from the boat of an 18th century Dutch flagship, 33in. wide.

Mid 18th century South German carved wood group.

Early 17th century yew wood mortar, 6¼in. high.

Balsa wood mask made for the 'Goelede' society, Yoruba tribe.

Late 17th century figure of Putai, in lacquered wood, 22in. high.

Lower Rhine oak relief, 19½in. high, circa 1500.

Maori carved wooden house post, before 1840, 4ft.2½in. high.

Large Egyptian wood mummy mask.

Bas relief wood sculpture, by Norman Forrest, 1930's, 93cm. high

17th century Spanish carved wood and painted polychrome religious group, 19in.

Carved walnut figure group of two cavaliers, 41in. high.

Atelier Hagenauer patinated metal and carved wood head, 27cm. high, circa 1920.

35

CARVED WOOD

A pair of carved walnut candlesticks, circa 1900, 18in. high.

19th century Dutch cart-front decorated in poly-chrome.

Maori carved wood present box, 5½in. long.

Fine carved cartouche in the manner of Matthias Locke.

A set of four Tudor oak colonnettes, early 16th century, 25in. high.

Large 18th century lignum vitae cup, 19in. high.

Hawaiian wooden image, 10¼in. high.

19th century Swiss bear furniture.

Wood sculpture on slate base, 1930's, 93cm. high.

Lower Rhine relief in oak, 19½in. high, circa 1500.

Pair of middle Rhine late Gothic oak figures, 35in. high, circa 1480.

Mid 17th century Dutch or German maplewood spoon, 17.5cm. long.

Late Ptolemaic mask, 1st century B.C.

Carved walnut hunting plaque, circa 1870, 47in. high, Swiss.

Fruitwood watch stand, 230mm. high.

Finely carved pinewood cockerel, circa 1820, 18in. diameter.

Turned wood apothecary's jar, late 18th century, 9½in. high, sold with another.

18th century Norwegian polychrome beechwood Skala, 9in. high.

Carved and painted wooden mask from West Africa.

18th century pair of Dutch dummy board figures, 45in. high.

Rowley Gallery giltwood low relief, circa 1925, 71cm. high.

Early 19th century tobacconist's sign of a Highlander.

Painted wood picture frame, circa 1900, 40½in. wide.

Elm bellows with brass center decoration piece, 25in. long, circa 1790.

ALBARELLO

Dated Tuscan albarello, 13.3cm. high, 1600.

A Sicilian albarello, 20cm. high, 17th century

Venetian albarello of dumbbell shape, 1578, 14.2cm. high.

ANSBACH

One of a pair of Ansbach faience wall vases, 8.5cm. wide.

18th century Ansbach faience tankard, with pewter footrim, 1791, 24.5cm. high.

One of a pair of Ansbach equestrian figures, circa 1730, 24.5cm. high.

AUSTRIAN

Austrian glazed earthenware vase, circa 1910, 20.5cm. high.

Turn Art Nouveau ceramic dish, Austrian, circa 1900, 44cm. long.

An Austrian glazed earthenware jardiniere and stand, circa 1905

BAYREUTH

Fine and rare Bayreuth Hausmaler bowl, 18.5cm. diam., circa 1740.

Bayreuth Hausmaler teabowl and saucer, circa 1740.

Du Paquier Bayreuth Hausmaler teabowl, 15cm. diam., circa 1740.

BELLARMINE

BELLARMINE

Early 17th century Frenchen stoneware bellarmine jug, 25cm. high.

Late 16th/early 17th century bellarmine jug, slightly damaged.

17th century armorial Rhenish stoneware bellarmine, 8½in. high.

BELLEEK

Belleek basket, circa 1880, 2½in. high, 5in. wide.

Belleek tea kettle on stand.

One of a pair of Belleek pitchers with scrolled handles and applied floral decoration.

BERLIN

One of a pair of Berlin porcelain cabinet cups and saucers with gilt decoration.

One of a pair of Berlin covered chocolate pots, 7¾in. and 5⅓in. high, circa 1830.

A mid 18th century Berlin dish of chamfered square form, 27cm. across.

BOTTGER

Very rare Bottger jug and cover, circa 1720.

Rare Bottger double-handled beaker and saucer, circa 1720-25.

Rare Augsburg decorated Bottger pagoda figure of a Chinaman, circa 1720-25, 10.5cm. high.

BOW

Rare Bow figure of a gold-finch, 3¼in. high, circa 1758-62.

Pair of Bow figures of a gallant and lady, 6in. high, about 1760.

Bow teapot, painted with a dragon pattern, circa 1760.

BRISTOL

Bristol made cider mug, 1842, 5in. high.

Rare Bristol figure of a goatherder, 10¾in. high, about 1775.

Fine Bristol teapot and cover, 6in. high, about 1775.

BRITISH

Victorian jug and basin set.

A pair of Cauldon vases, circa 1910, 9¾in. high.

Victorian brown glazed pottery cheese dish.
$125 £55

Dawson and Co. creamware cylindrical tankard, 4¾in. high.

One of a pair of early English porcelain square dishes, 6½in.

Rare Glasgow saltglazed stoneware salt-kiln and cover, 14in. high.

BURMANTOFT

Burmantoft vase, about 1885, painted by 'L.K', 8½in. high.

Burmantofts jardiniere and stand, 50½in. high.

BURMANTOFTS

Burmantofts dish, circa 1885, 16in. diam.

CAPODIMONTE

Capodimonte tureen, circa 1750, 11in. diam.

Extremely rare Capodimonte Commedia Dell'Arte group of the Harlequin and two other figures, by Guiseppe Gricci, dated around 1750.

Rare Capodimonte figure, by Guiseppe Gricci, circa 1745.

CARDEW, MICHAEL

Michael Cardew stoneware bowl with tapering foot rim, 1960's, 7¾in. diam.

Michael Cardew large slipware dish, circa 1930, 16½in. diam.

Michael Cardew stoneware bowl, 14in. diam., 1960's.

CASTEL DURANTE

Mid 17th century Castel Durante bottle, 22.5cm. high.

Castel Durante dated wet drug jar, 1644, 22.5cm. high

Rare documentary Castel Durante drug jar, 35cm. high, 1562.

CASTELLI

18th century Castelli plate, 24.2cm. diam.

Late 18th century Castelli plaque, 26.8cm. long.

18th century Castelli majolica plaque.

CAUGHLEY

Caughley teabowl and saucer painted in underglaze blue, circa 1785.

A Caughley cylindrical mug printed in blue, 6in. high, circa 1780.

Caughley shell-shaped dish, circa 1778-82, 8in. diam.

CHALKWARE

Mid 19th century chalkware sitting cat, Pennsylvania, 13½in. high.

Mid 19th century chalkware rooster, Pennsylvania, 11in. high.

Mid 19th century chalkware sitting dog, Pennsylvania, 13¼in. high.

CHAMPIONS BRISTOL

Fine Champions Bristol bell-shaped mug, 5in. high, about 1775.

One of a set of four Champions Bristol figures of the Elements, 10in. to 11¼in. high.

Rare Champions Bristol teabowl and saucer, about 1775.

Chantilly figure of a Chinese man, 7in. high.

Mid 18th century Chantilly porcelain jug with floral decoration, 16.5cm. high.

Chantilly two-handled bowl, 11in. wide.

CHELSEA

Chelsea candlestick group of birds, circa 1762, 7in. high.

Chelsea white figure of a musician, 8in. high, about 1755.

Attractive Chelsea fluted teabowl and saucer painted in Kakiemon palette, 1749-52.

CLARICE CLIFF

Clarice Cliff 'bizarre' vase, 21cm. high, 1930's.

Attractive Clarice Cliff 'bizarre' teapot and cream jug, 1930's.

Clarice Cliff Toby jug.

COALBROOKDALE

Coalbrookdale pot pourri vase, cover and stand, 6¾in. high.

19th century garniture of three Coalbrookdale style porcelain bottle shaped vases.

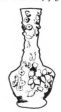

One of a pair of Coalbrookdale baluster vases, 10in. high.

COALPORT

Henrietta, circa 1750, china figure by Coalport, 7in. high.

A Coalport plate from an attractive set of twenty-four, each painted with a scene of game birds, by P. Simpson, signed, 9in.

Coalport flower-encrusted ewer, 10¼in. high, circa 1830.

COMMEMORATIVE

Commemorative mug, 1838, made for Victoria's coronation, 3¾in. high.

Rare British commemorative polychrome posset pot and cover, 1668, 21cm. high.

A rare commemorative Bragget pot of large size, possibly by Ralph Simpson, circa 1700, 7¼in. high.

COPELAND

Copeland Edward VII memorial vase, 1910, 7in. high.

Part of a Copeland tea and coffee service of eighty-two pieces, circa 1900.

Copeland Parian figure of Sir Walter Scott, circa 1860, 11¾in. high.

COPELAND & GARRETT

One of a pair of Copeland & Garrett Japan pattern New Stone plates, 21.5cm. diam.

Copeland & Garrett tureen and stand, circa 1860.

Copeland & Garrett figure of Narcissus by John Gibson, 1846, 31cm. high.

44

COPELAND SPODE

COPELAND SPODE

Part of a Copeland Spode seventeen-piece dessert service.

Mid 19th century Copeland Spode teapot.

Copeland Spode tureens and dish, circa 1850.

COPENHAGEN

Part of a Copenhagen porcelain botanical fruit set.

One of a pair of Copenhagen vases, circa 1870, 38cm. high.

Copenhagen snuff box and cover modeled as the head of a dog, circa 1793, 6.5cm. wide.

COPER, HANS

A stoneware vase, by Hans Coper, the flattened bowl with slightly swelling sides, 16cm. high.

Hans Coper spherical stoneware vase, 1960's, 8½in. high.

Good Hans Coper black stoneware vase, circa 1970, 8in. high.

DAVENPORT

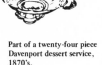

Part of a Davenport tea and coffee service, circa 1870, sixty-one pieces.

Davenport cup and saucer, circa 1870.

Part of a twenty-four piece Davenport dessert service, 1870's.

DECK, THEODORE

Theodore deck faience dish, circa 1870, 14¼in. diam.

Late 19th century Theodore Deck duck, 12in. high.

Theodore Deck dish, 13¼in. diam., circa 1880.

DELFT

A rare 18th century delft Unguent pot, 2¾in. diam.

Late 18th century delft dish, 13in. diam.

Rare delft mug, mid 18th century, 4½in. high.
$745 £330

DELFT, BRISTOL

Bristol delft blue and white two-handled jar, 6¼in. high.

English delft posset pot, 3½in., circa 1680-90, either Bristol or Brislington.

Bristol delft polychrome blue dash portrait charger, circa 1710, 34cm. diam.

DELFT, DUTCH

Fine Dutch Delft tea kettle and cover, 25cm. high.

Dutch Delft bottle, early 18th century, 22.2cm. high.

Dutch polychrome Delft charger, 13¾in. diam.

English delft dry drug jar,
7in. high.

DELFT, IRISH

Small English delftware
cistern and cover, 1644,
14in. high, probably by
Christian Wilhelm.

English delft blue dash charger, portraying King William
III, 13¾in. diam.

Late 18th century, rare,
delftware strainer bowl,
8½in. diam.

DELFT, LAMBETH

One of a pair of rare
Dublin delft vases, late
18th century, 3¾in. high.

Rare Irish delft plate, 9¼in.,
about 1760.

Mid 18th century Lambeth
polychrome delft plate,
33.3cm. diam.

DELFT, LIVERPOOL

Early Lambeth blue and
white apothecary's pill slab,
1687.

Early 18th century Lambeth
delft globular jar, 5¼in. diam.

Very rare late 18th century
Liverpool delft leaf dish,
5½in. high.

Late 18th century rare
Liverpool delft feeding
cup, 3in. high.

Liverpool delft jug, circa
1760-70, 7¾in. high.

DELFT, LONDON

Late 17th century London delft fuddling cup, 3¼in. high.

Late 17th century London delft posset pot and cover, 5¾in. high.

17th/18th century London delft barber's bowl, 10in. diam.

DE MORGAN

William De Morgan lustre bottle vase, 17cm. high.

William De Morgan lustre saucer dish, Fulham period, 36cm. diam.

A De Morgan amphora, by Halsey Ricardo, 14¾in. high, 1888-97.

DERBY

Rare Derby figure of a monkey playing the double-bass, 5in. high.

Pair of Derby 'mansion house' dwarfs, 6¾in. high, about 1820.

Fine Derby bell-shaped mug, 4in. high, about 1760.

DERBY, BLOOR

One of a pair of Bloor Derby sauce tureens, covers and stands, 8½in. wide.

Bloor Derby figure of a lady seated in a chair, 5½in. high.

One of a pair of Bloor Derby ice pails, circa 1830, 12in. high.

Royal Crown Derby slender two-handled oviform vase and cover, 14½in. high.

Part of a forty-piece Royal Crown Derby tea service, dated for 1898.

One of a pair of Royal Crown Derby vases and covers, dated for 1903.

DOCCIA

Volkstedt 'Doccia' tankard and cover, circa 1910, 31.2cm. high.

Rare Doccia bust of the Roman Emperor Augustus, 1750-60, 51cm. high.

One of a pair of Doccia blue and white moutardieres, 11.5cm. high, circa 1760.

DOULTON

Doulton silver mounted stoneware tyg, 6¼in. high, circa 1900.

Doulton stoneware teapot, 6¾in. high, dated 1878, with silver lid.

Unusual Doulton 'Dickens' jug, after a design by Noke, 10½in. high, circa 1936.

DOULTON, ROYAL

One of a pair of Royal Doulton vases, by Emma Shute, 21cm. high.

Royal Doulton jug of a Regency beau.

Royal Doulton Chang vase, by C. Noke and H. Nixon, circa 1930, 9¼in. high.

DRESDEN

A large pair of Dresden figures of a gentleman playing bagpipes and his companion with a hurdy-gurdy, 47cm. high.

Part of an early 20th century Dresden coffee service of forty-three pieces.

One of a pair of Dresden lemon ground ovoid vases and covers, 24½in. high.

DUTCH

Large Tournai dish decorated at The Hague, circa 1780, 40cm. diam.

Early 18th century Dutch tin glazed bird cage, 39cm. high.

19th century faience inkwell, 7½in. long.

EARTHENWARE

Massive Liberty & Co. earthenware jardiniere, 76cm. diam., circa 1905.

One of a pair of unusual earthenware vases, circa 1880, 36.8cm. high, on jardiniere style stands.

Red earthenware globular flagon, probably West African, 20cm. high.

EUROPEAN

Saintonage oval dish, 17th century, 31cm. long.

18th century faience vase, 29.5cm. high, probably Scandinavian.

Swiss tin glazed chest of drawers, 17.5cm. high.

Early 16th century Faenza drug jar, 22.5cm. high, restored.

Italian Faenza dish, dated 1537, 47cm. diam.

Faenza drug jar, circa 1500, 29.3cm. high, decorated in blue, green and ochre.

FRANKENTHAL

Frankenthal coffee pot, circa 1760, 10¼in. high.

A pair of Frankenthal figures of Harvesters, 4in. high.

A Frankenthal figure of a fruit seller, 14cm. high, 1759-62.

FRENCH

Mid 17th century Nevers double-handled urn, 33cm. high.

Boulogne crackle glazed pottery figure, 61cm. high, 1920's.

French biscuit porcelain and gilt metal casket, 3½in. diameter, circa 1900.

FULHAM

Mid 18th century Fulham stoneware mug with foliage encrusted decoration.

One of a pair of C. J. C. Bailey Fulham pottery stoneware vases, 16½in. high, dated 1880.

Rare Fulham stoneware posset pot, 17th century, 6¼in. high.

FURSTENBERG

Furstenberg shaped oblong gold mounted etui, circa 1760, 11cm. long.

Late 18th century Furstenberg figure of a fisherman, 12.5cm. high.

Part of a ten-piece Furstenberg dessert service, circa 1900, each piece painted with fruit.

GERMAN

German faience Hanau blue and white two-handled octagonal jardiniere.

South German faience pewter mounted tankard, circa 1744, 20cm. high.

A finely modelled German faience asparagus tureen.

GOLDSCHEIDER

A Goldscheider terracotta wall mask, the young woman with bright orange hair and lips, 1930's.

A Goldscheider terracotta wall mask of a young woman holding a Scottie dog, 1930's.

A Goldscheider terracotta wall mask of a young girl with flowers in her hair, 1930's.

GOSS

Early 20th century Goss model of John Knox's House, 4in. high.

A fine and rare Goss model of a polar bear.

Goss model of 'A Dangerous Encounter', 4¼in. high, circa 1900.

HOCHST

Hochst tea caddy and cover possibly painted by Heinrich Usinger, circa 1770, 14cm. high.

ITALIAN

Late 18th century Italian group, 18.5cm. high.

JONES, GEORGE

Small, late Victorian pottery butter dish by George Jones.

LEACH, BERNARD

Bernard Leach stoneware bottle vase, 1960's, 7¾in. high.

Rare Hochst figure of Hearing, circa 1755, 14cm. high.

Late 18th century Marcolini part coffee service.

Good 'majolica' camel vase, probably George Jones, circa 1870, 9½in. high.

Bernard Leach stoneware 'Pilgrim' dish, 1960's, 12½in. diam.

HOCHST

Hochst teapot and cover, circa 1765-70, 10.2cm. high.

Large Italian majolica platter, circa 1750, 14¾in. diam.

George Jones 'majolica' jardiniere, 19½in. high, dated 1876.

Stoneware rectangular bottle by Bernard Leach, 7½in. high.

LEEDS

A figure of a Leeds pearlware stallion, 16¼in. high, circa 1790.

Leeds creamware ship-decorated plate, circa 1800-1820, 9¾in. diam.

Rare creamware stirrup cup, possibly Leeds, about 1780, 5in. long.

LIMOGES

Limoges enamelled pot and cover, 1920's, 11.5cm., by Sarlandie.

Limoges painted Grisaille panel, 4¾in. high, circa 1550.

Pair of octagonal based Limoges candlesticks, 6¾in. high.

LIVERPOOL

Liverpool blue and white shell-shaped pickle dish, 4¼in. wide.

Liverpool blue and white pear-shaped coffee pot, 8½in. high.

Fine Liverpool polychrome dish, 13in. diam.

LONGTON HALL

One of a pair of Longton Hall figures of seated nuns, chipped, circa 1775.

Longton Hall leaf-shaped bowl, 3in. diam., about 1755.

Longton Hall jug decorated with bouquets of flowers, 8in. high.

LOWESTOFT

Rare Lowestoft saucer painted with Oriental figures, circa 1785, 4¾in. diam.

Lowestoft porcelain figures of musicians, circa 1780-90, 17.8cm. high.

LOWESTOFT

Lowestoft jug with kick-back handle and pink border, 3¼in. high, circa 1785.

LUDWIGSBURG

Ludwigsburg group of dancers, circa 1765, 14.5cm. high.

Ludwigsburg group of a river god, circa 1770, 20cm. wide.

Late 19th century Ludwigsburg group of figures, 25.5cm. high.

LUSTRE

Good Clement lustre charger, circa 1900, 48cm. diam.

Victorian lustre ware goblet with fern decoration, 6in. high.

Rare pink lustre jug, 13cm. high, circa 1800-1810.

MACINTYRES

Unusual Moorcroft Macintyre jardiniere, circa 1900, 7in. high.

Florian vase made at Macintyres, circa 1893.

A Moorcroft Macintyre Florianware tyg, 25.3cm. high, circa 1898.

MAJOLICA

Large late 19th century
majolica jardiniere with a
stand.

One of a pair of majolica
ewer jugs, 19in. high.

Interesting early majolica
dish, mid 13th century,
19cm. diam.

MARSEILLE

A fine Marseille faience
plate, with fish and lob-
ster design.

A Marseille faience two-
handled tureen and cover
painted in colors with
bouquets of flowers, 36cm.
wide.

A large early 18th century
Marseille charger decorated
with a biblical scene.

MARTINWARE

Martin Brothers jardin-
iere, 7¼in. high, dated
11-1900, incised signature

Martin Brothers bird, 9¾in.
high, incised signature, dated
7-1892.

One of a pair of early Martin
Brothers wall plates, 13¼in.
diam., incised signature and
dated 1876.

MASON'S

Large Mason's ironstone
blue and white platter,
circa 1820.

Impressive Mason's porce-
lain vase, circa 1810,
25½in. high, small repair.

One of a pair of Mason's
ironstone campana-shaped
flower vases and ewers,
10in. wide, circa 1815.

Meissen milk jug, in the manner of C. F. Herold.

Meissen group modelled by J. J. Kaendler, 1744, 8½in.

A large late 19th century Meissen group of Count Bruhl's Tailor, 43cm. high.

MENNECY

Rare Mennecy snuff box in white, mid 18th century, 4.5cm. high.

Mid 18th century Mennecy pomade pot and cover, 8.6cm. high.

One of a fine pair of ormolu mounted Mennecy figures.

METTLACH

One of a pair of German Mettlach jardinieres, 23in. wide, signed Warth.

Mettlach plaque decorated after J. Stahl, circa 1900, 46.8cm. diam.

Mettlach vase, circa 1900-10, 40cm. high.

MINTON

Mid 19th century Minton majolica teapot, 5in. high.

One of a pair of Minton pate-sur-pate vases, 7in. high.

Minton reticulated teacup and saucer, impressed marks.

MOORCROFT

Moorcroft bowl, 9in. diam., circa 1901-13.

Part of an eleven-piece Moorcroft coffee service in Hazeldene pattern.

Moorcroft vase in 'Moonlit' Blue' Hazeldene pattern, 9¼in. high, 1920-30.

MORTLAKE

A Mortlake saltglazed stoneware tankard with a panel showing Hogarth's 'Midnight Modern Conversation', late 18th century, 8¼in.

A Mortlake stoneware goblet applied on either side with a rectangular panel, circa 1800, 7in. high.

A Mortlake stoneware jug with hinged silver cover by Wm. Key, London, circa 1790, 9in. high.

MOTTO WARE

A Dartmouth pottery jug, inscribed 'No road is long with Good Company'.

An Aller Vale pottery hatpin stand, decorated with ship design.

A tile from the Watcombe pottery, decorated with leaf and flower swirls.

MURRAY, WILLIAM

A stoneware oviform vase, by Wm. Staite Murray, 21.5cm. high.

A stoneware flared bowl, by Wm. Staite Murray, 21cm. diam.

Wm. Staite Murray vase with ovoid body, circa 1930, 12¼in. high.

Nantgarw deep dish, 10¼in. diam., 1817-20.

Rare Nantgarw pedestal dish, 5¾in. high, 1817-20.

One of a pair of Nantgarw plates, 8¾in. diam., 1813-22.

NAPLES

One of two Naples armorial wet drug jars, 1690, 22cm. high.

19th century white porcelain Naples figure, 10¾in. high, signed.

Dated Naples bottle, 1701, 25.5cm. high.

NEWHALL

Newhall jug, circa 1787.

Part of a Newhall tea and coffee service.

Part of a Newhall tea service, twenty-eight pieces, 1795-1805.

NIDERVILLE

One of a set of four Niderville figures of Summer and Autumn, 13cm. high.

One of a rare pair of Niderville covered vases, 15¼in. high, circa 1780.

A Niderville Parian figure of a shepherd boy with dog, 67cm. high.

NOVE

A finely modelled Le Nove figure group.

Large Nove Monteith, circa 1780-90, 49.2cm. wide.

Majolica dish made at Nove da Bassano, circa 1770, 15½in. diam.

NYMPHENBURG

Porcelain ice-bucket from the Nymphenburg factory, 6½in. high.

One of a pair of Nymphenburg cabinet cups and saucers, 9cm. high, circa 1830-40.

Nymphenburg model of a parrot, circa 1850-62, 18.7cm. high.

PARIAN

Robinson & Leadbetter colored Parian figure, 12¼in. high, circa 1890.

Samuel Alcock & Co. figure of the Duke of Wellington, 11in. high, circa 1852.

Jug showing the famous brass quintet of the Distin father and sons, in Parianware, about 1850, 14in. high.

PARIS

Paris raspberry ground cache-pot, circa 1870, 18.5cm. high.

Pair of 19th century Paris porcelain figures, 24½in. high.

One of a large pair of Paris vases, 49.5cm. high, mid 19th century.

PETIT, JACOB

PETIT

One of a pair of Jacob Petit vases, circa 1860.

One of a pair of Jacob Petit urn-shaped porcelain wine coolers, 12in. high.

One of a pair of Jacob Petit vases, circa 1840, 21.6cm. high.

PILKINGTON

Unusual Pilkington Royal Lancastrian plate, 12¾in. diam., dated for 1906.

Small Pilkington Royal Lancastrian ovoid jar and cover, 1926, 12cm. high.

Pilkington Lancastrian copper lustred twin-handled cup.

PLAUE

Late 17th century Plaue centerpiece with pierced flared bowl, 30.5cm. high.

Pair of late 19th century Plaue fruit stands, 3.5cm. high.

Late 19th century Plaue centerpiece with pierced bowl, 40.5cm. high.

PLYMOUTH

Pair of Plymouth figures depicting a gardener and his companion, 1768-71.

Rare Plymouth vase with polychrome decoration, circa 1770.

Rare Plymouth teapot and cover, 6½in. high, about 1768-70.

61

POOLE

Poole pottery unglazed jug, 8in. high, 1930.

Poole pottery fish glazed in green with a black base, 17in. high.

Carter, Stabler & Adams Poole pottery vase, circa 1930, 9¾in. high.

POTSCHAPPEL

One of a pair of late 19th century Potschappel pot-pourri vases and covers, 15cm. high.

A pair of Dresden vases, by Carl Thierne of Potschappel, 22½in. high.

Potschappel porcelain fruit basket on stand, circa 1860.

PRATTWARE

A Prattware tea caddy depicting George III, 6¼in. high, 1780-90.

Rare Prattware Toby jug, circa 1780-90, 10in. high.

One of a pair of Prattware fox and swan sauceboats, 6½in. high, about 1780-90.

RIDGWAY

Large Ridgway parian group of Venus and Cupid, 1858, 18¾in. high.

Part of a twenty-one piece dessert service, circa 1825-35.

One of a twenty-six piece apple-green ground dessert service, by Ridgway, circa 1830.

A stoneware vase by Lucie Rie, covered in cream gray glaze, 30cm. high.

A porcelain bowl, by Lucie Rie, of wide conical form, 23.5cm. diam.

Asymmetrical stoneware vase, by Lucie Rie, 8¼in. high.

ROCKINGHAM

One of a pair of Rockingham plates, 9in. diam.

Unusually plain Rockingham swan.

One of a rare pair of Rockingham coffee cups and saucers, circa 1830.

ROMAN

Early 19th century circular Roman mosaic plaque, 7.3cm. diam.

Roman mosaic plaque, circa 1825, 3¼in. wide.

Early 19th century Italian circular mosaic plaque, 2½in. diam.

ROOKWOOD

Rookwood pottery vellum vase, signed A. R. Valentien, 1905, 12in. high.

Rookwood pottery standard glaze cornucopia vase with swirl rim, Cincinnati, Ohio, 1892, 6in. high.

Rookwood pottery matt glaze vase decorated with fish, 12¾in. high, Cincinnati, Ohio, circa 1901.

ROSENTHAL

1930's Art Deco female figure.

Interesting old Imperial German porcelain desk ornament, by Rosenthal, Bavaria, 7½in. high.

Rosenthal porcelain group of a young woman and a fawn, 34cm. high, 1930's.

ROYAL COPENHAGEN

A Royal Copenhagen porcelain vase of double gourd shape, 21cm. high.

A Royal Copenhagen group of St. Paul slaying the Lie, circa 1925, 24½in. high.

A Royal Copenhagen porcelain oviform vase and cover designed by Ch. Thomasen, 21cm. high.

ROYAL DUX

Royal Dux group of a peasant and a bull, circa 1910, 33cm. wide.

Pair of 20th century Royal Dux figures, 41.5cm. high.

Unusual pair of Royal Dux 'clown' figures, 23.4cm. high, circa 1910.

ROZENBURG

Rozenburg pottery vase with twin loop handles, circa 1900, 26.5cm. high.

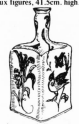

Rozenburg eggshell porcelain bottle vase.

Small Rozenburg vase, circa 1900, 11cm. high.

Ruskin high-fired vase, 8¾in. high, dated 1922.

Ruskin high-fired bowl, 4in., dated 1915.

Ruskin high-fired vase, 8in. high, dated 1924.

RUSSIAN

One of a pair of Russian armorial plates with pierced borders, circa 1870, 25.5cm. diam.

Porcelain group of 'The Barrister's Judgement' by Gardner, Moscow, circa 1860-70, 13.1cm. wide, on octagonal base.

Part of a late 19th century seventy-nine-piece dinner service by M. C. Kuznetsov.

SALTGLAZE

Rare small saltglaze bear mug, 3½in. high, about 1740.

Attractive saltglaze teapot and cover, 4in. high, about 1760.

Coloured saltglaze cream jug, 3in. high, about 1760.

SAMSON

A Samson pear-shaped coffee pot with domed cover, 21cm. tall.

Samson group of the Levee du Roi of five figures, 38cm. wide.

Pair of Samson parrots on tree-stumps, repaired, 42cm. high.

SAVONA

One of a pair of 18th century Savona cisterns and covers, 52cm. high.

Early 17th century Savona tazza, 25.5cm. diam.

Late 17th century Savona drug jar and cover, 34cm. high.

SEVRES

An unusual 18th century Sevres bleu du roi ewer, 25.2cm. high.

A Sevres cabinet plate painted by D. Ceniers, late 19th century, 24cm. diam.

Sevres pattern ormolu mounted bleu nouveau oval casket, 32cm. wide, on four paw feet.

SITZENDORF

Sitzendorf table centerpiece with pierced basket, 29cm. high.

Late 19th century Sitzendorf clockcase, 38cm. high.

19th century Sitzendorf candelabra.

SLIPWARE

Slipware baking dish with typical notched rim.

An early Staffordshire slipware cradle, 9in. long.

Late 17th century slipware charger, by Wm. Talor, 17½in. diam.

Spode pink ground oviform vase with loop handles, circa 1820, 18.5cm. high.

Spode cup and saucer, pattern 967, circa 1810.

Spode pastille burner and cover, circa 1830, 4in. high.

STAFFORDSHIRE

Staffordshire figure of Sir Robert Peel, circa 1850, 12¼in. high.

Staffordshire jug with pictorial decoration.

Staffordshire portrait bust of George Washington, 21cm. high.

STONEWARE

19th century stoneware quart jug with embossed scenic decoration.

Stoneware square two-handled vase, 9½in. high.

Quimper Art Deco decorated stoneware vase, 1920's. 18cm. high.

STRASBURG

One of three Strasburg shaped circular soup plates, circa 1765, 24.5cm. diam.

Strasburg faience white figure of Gilles, after Watteau, circa 1765, 30.5cm. high.

One of three Strasburg shaped circular soup plates, circa 1765, 24.5cm. diam.

67

SUNDERLAND

Mid 19th century Sunderland lustre frog mug.

Sunderland lustre jug, circa 1840, 7¼in. high.

Large Sunderland lustre-ware bowl depicting Newcastle's High Level Bridge.

SWANSEA

Swansea plate painted with a view of Pembroke Castle.

Attractive Swansea cup, coffee cup and saucer, 1813-22.

Swansea tea cup and saucer.

TERRACOTTA

Italian polychrome terracotta bust of Pope Leo X, early 16th century, 37.5cm. high.

South Italian terracotta modello, 10in. high, circa 1680-1700.

Etruscan terracotta 'plastic vase' in the form of an ape, early 6th century B.C., 3¾in. high.

TOURNAI

Tournai barrel-shaped mustard pot with scroll handle, circa 1770, 6.5cm. high.

A rare pair of Tournai figures of gardeners, 17cm. high, circa 1765.

Tournai 'Drageoire' or sweetmeat bowl, circa 1760, 15cm. high.

Large Turner biscuit jug,
circa 1800, 8¼in. high.

URBINO

Turner blue and white
jasper rectangular pla-
que, 8 x 5½in.

Blue transfer pottery shaped
oval dish, possibly Turner,
circa 1780, 12¼in. long.

Urbino 'Istoriato' dish,
25.5cm. diam., circa 1537,
painted by Francesco
Xanto Avelli.

VENETIAN

Urbino majolica dish showing the story of Pluto and
Proserpine, circa 1530,
12in. diam.

Urbino 'Istoriato' dish,
about 1540, 30.3cm. diam.

Early 16th century 'majo-
lica' vase, Venetian.

VIENNA

A rare Venice Vezzi teapot
and cover.

16th century Venetian wet
drug jar, 20cm. high.

Late 19th century Vienna
decorated Eaas and Czjzcr
Schlaggenwald plaque,
50.3cm. diam.

A Vienna group of an old
man and a young girl, 13cm.
high, circa 1765.

One of a pair of late Vienna
bleu du roi ground oval two-
handled vases, covers and
stands, 14in. high.

VINCENNES

Vincennes porcelain covered supper dish, circa 1755, 8¼in. wide.

Vincennes white chinoiserie group, circa 1745, 19in. wide.

One of a pair of Vincennes porcelain baskets of flowers, 14in. high.

VOLKSTEDT

Late 19th century Eckert & Co. Volkstedt group, 22cm. high.

Pair of Volkstedt figures of a Gallant and his Companion, circa 1900, 41cm. high.

Pair of Volkstedt porcelain candlesticks, circa 1800, 14in. high.

VYSE, CHARLES

Charles Vyse figure of 'Barnet Fair', circa 1933, 10¼in. high.

Stoneware foliate bowl, by Charles Vyse, 7¼in. diam.

Charles Vyse stoneware vase, 1930, 5in. high.

WALFORD, JAMES

20th century James Walford stoneware model of a head of a shoebill, 7¼in. high.

20th century James Walford stoneware model of an hippopotamus head, 6¾in. wide.

James Walford stoneware nude, 1950's, 11in. high.

WEDGWOOD

A Wedgwood copy of
the Portland vase.

One of a pair of Wedg-
wood candlesticks mod-
elled as dolphins, late
18th century, 10in. high.

WEDGWOOD

19th century Wedgwood blue
jasperware circular jardiniere,
9½in. diam.

WEMYSS

Small Wemyss conserve pot
and cover, painted with
cherries, 7.5cm. high, with
matching stand.

Wemyssware molded jug,
circa 1910, 8in. high.

Part of a Robert Heron
& Son Wemyssware
toilet set, 20th century.

WESTERWALD

Early 18th century Wester-
wald saltglaze stoneware
jug, 25cm. high.

Early 18th century Wester-
wald salt cellar with saltglaze, 17cm. high.

Late 17th century Wester-
wald stoneware 'humpen',
13cm. high.

WHIELDON

Whieldon green glazed rectangular tea caddy, circa
1760, 11.5cm. high.

Whieldon cow creamer
and cover, circa 1760,
5¼in. high.

Whieldon type Toby jug
circa 1750, 6¼in. high.

WOOD, ENOCH

Enoch Wood figure of a parrot with brown breast and beak, circa 1785, 22.5cm. high.

Massive Enoch Wood pearlware jug, late 18th century, 17in. high.

Rare Enoch Wood figure of John Liston, 6¼in. high, about 1820.

WOOD, RALPH

Ralph Wood elephant spill vase, circa 1770-80, 8in. high.

An inscribed and dated Ralph Wood jug of large size, modelled by Jean Voyez, 9½in. high, 1788.

Ralph Wood group of the 'Vicar and Moses', 9½in. high, circa 1770.

WOLFSOHN

Late 19th century Helena Wolfsohn liqueur set, stand 28cm. wide.

Late 19th century set of Helena Wolfsohn monkey bandsmen.

Late 19th century pair of Helena Wolfsohn bottles and covers, 33cm. high.

WORCESTER

Worcester straight-sided mug with transfer-printed border, circa 1770.

Worcester 'Beckoning Chinaman' teapot and cover, 6in. high, about 1755-58.

A Worcester fluted coffee cup and saucer, 1765-70.

WORCESTER, CHAMBERLAIN

Chamberlain Worcester vase and cover of baluster shape, 46cm. high.

Chamberlain Worcester card tray with painted center.

Chamberlain Worcester figure of one of the Rainer Brothers, 6in. high, about 1830.

WORCESTER, DR. WALL

A Dr. Wall period hot water jug complete with cover.

One of a pair of Dr. Wall First period Worcester porcelain plates, 8¾in. diam.

Dr. Wall Worcester teapot, 6in. high, with scale blue base.

WORCESTER, FLIGHT, BARR & BARR

One of a pair of Worcester Flight, Barr & Barr period lidded vases, 11in. high.

One of a pair of Flight, Barr & Barr claret ground plates, circa 1820, 22.5cm. diam.

Worcester teapot marked Flight, Barr & Barr, 1807-13.

WORCESTER, GRAINGERS

One of a pair of Grainger sauce tureens, circa 1810.

Grainger, Lee & Co. part dinner service, twenty-four pieces, 1812-20.

One of a garniture of three Grainger Worcester pot pourri vases, circa 1815, 13½in. and 10¾in. high.

WORCESTER, ROYAL

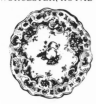

Royal Worcester plate, dated for 1912, 9in. diam.

Royal Worcester teapot and cover, 6in. high, dated for 1882.

Royal Worcester vase and cover, 1899.

WROTHAM

A Wrotham tyg, by George Richardson, dated 1649.

Wrotham pottery jug, by George Richardson, 6½in. high.

Wrotham slipware inscribed and dated tyg, by Henry Ifield, 13cm. high, 1644.

YORKSHIRE

Late 18th century Yorkshire 'squat' Toby jug, with caryatid handle, 7¾in. high.

A rare Yorkshire equestrian figure, 8¾in. high, circa 1780.

Yorkshire pottery group, 9in. high, circa 1780-90.

ZURICH

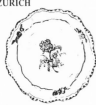

Mid 18th century Zurich plate, 23cm. diam.

Pair of 18th century Zurich porcelain figures representing Autumn, 8½in. high.

Zurich porcelain figure representing Painting, 6½in. high.

Fine 18th century Arita blue and white hexagonal lobed bowl with floral design, Fuku mark, 21.2cm. diam.

17th century Japanese Arita blue and white lidded porcelain jar, 13in. high.

Late 17th century Arita dog decorated in black, iron red and turquoise green, 23cm. long.

BLUE & WHITE

A late 18th century Chinese blue and white porcelain tankard, 5¼in.

Mid 17th century Chinese blue and white porcelain vase, 8¼in. high.

Mid 19th century Japanese blue and white porcelain dish, 14½in. diam.

CANTON

Late 19th century Canton teapot with floral decoration.

One of a pair of Canton famille rose vases, mid 19th century, 35cm. high.

Canton dish, typically painted and gilt, 35cm. diam., circa 1870.

CHENGHUA

Chinese porcelain jar of the Chenghua period, decorated in underglaze blue, 10.3cm

Chenghua stem cup decorated in iron-red and underglaze blue, with various fabulous animals, 4in. high.

Doucai wine cup decorated in blue, red, yellow and pale green, with six character mark of Chenghua.

CHINESE

Chinese white porcelain ewer of the Liao dynasty with a simulated cane work handle.

Chinese Jizhou teabowl with brown glaze, 11.5cm. diam.

One of a pair of apple-green Chinese porcelain vases, 13¾in. high.

DAOGUANG

Small, Daoguang period, famille rose ruby ground bowl with floral decoration and scenic views in panels.

Chinese porcelain orchid vase of the Daoguang period.

Daoguang blue and white circular sweetmeat dish and cover, 13½in. diam.

EDO

Mid Edo period Tamba 'moxa' chaire with ivory lid, 11cm. high.

Early Edo period seto chaire with ivory cover, 5.5cm. high

Early Edo period pottery chaire with ivory cover, 7cm. high.

EXPORTWARE

18th century Chinese export porcelain Masonic tankard.

18th century Chinese export porcelain documentary punchbowl.

Oriental export porcelain chocolate pot, late 18th century, 10in. high.

FAMILLE NOIRE

Mid 19th century famille noire vase with waisted neck, 53.5cm. high.

One of a pair of large Chinese famille noire pear-shaped vases painted with dignitaries and immortals, 21¾in. high.

FAMILLE NOIRE

Famille noire tapering square vase, 20¾in. high.

FAMILLE ROSE

One of a pair of mid 19th century Chinese famille rose jars and covers.

18th century famille rose fish tank, 23in. diam.

Famille rose porcelain plate, 8¾in. diam., decorated with blossom, insects and plants, late 18th century.

FAMILLE VERTE

Pair of famille verte Immortals, 18½in. high.

One of a pair of famille verte brushwashers and water droppers.

Late 19th century famille verte vase and cover with baluster body, 43cm. high.

FUKAGAWA

One of a pair of lobed Fukagawa bowls, circa 1900, 10¼in. long.

Late 19th century yellow ground Fukagawa vase, 18in. high.

Fukagawa bowl, circa 1900, with incurved rim, 15½in. high.

GUAN

Guan compressed jar with crackleware glaze, 4¼in. high.

One of a pair of attractive 18th century gray crackle-glaze Guan vases with French ormolu mounts, 19¼in. high.

18th century Guan type vase, 6in. high.

HAMADA

A stoneware circular dish, by Shoji Hamada, 32cm. diam.

A stoneware flared vase, by Shoji Hamada, 19.5cm. high.

A stoneware shallow circular dish, by Shoji Hamada, 34cm. diam.

HAN

Han dynasty unglazed pottery triceratops, 10½in. long.

Rare green glazed model of a stove of the Han dynasty.

Unglazed pottery head from the Han dynasty, 4in. high.

HICHOZAN

One of a pair of Hichozan Shinpo vases, circa 1870, 17in. high.

One of a pair of Hichozan Shinpo bottle vases, late 19th century, 10in. high.

Late 19th century Hichozan Shinpo vase, 49.5cm. high, with pierced neck.

HOZAN

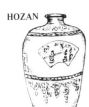

HOZAN

One of a pair of Hozan earthenware vases, circa 1900, 6¼in. high.

Late 19th century Hozan Satsuma dish with fluted rim, 10in. diam.

One of a pair of Hozan vases, circa 1900, 7½in. high.

IMARI

Fine Japanese Imari charger, 23¼in. diam.

Late 17th century green ground Imari wine ewer, 15.5cm. high.

Imari porcelain goldfish bowl with floral decoration, 20in. diam.

JAPANESE

Japanese plique a jour vase with gold wire framed enamel decoration.

19th century Japanese tureen and cover in the form of a roosting crane, 26.5cm. wide.

Japanese whisky set with five bowls.

KAKIEMON

Late 17th century Kakiemon wine-pot and cover of ovoid form.

Late 17th century Kakiemon ewer, painted in red, blue and green enamels.

A fine teabowl and saucer painted in the Kakiemon palette, circa 1770.

KANGXI

One of a pair of Kangxi period famille verte Buddhistic lion joss stick holders, 20.5cm. high.

Kangxi rare underglaze blue and red jardiniere, 8¾in. diam.

Kangxi blue and white stem cup, 5½in. high.

KINKOZAN

Japanese Kinkozan bowl with wavy rim, circa 1870.

Kinkozan earthenware vase, 17in. high, circa 1870.

Kinkozan vase of spheroid form, circa 1900, 4½in. high.

KOREAN

Korean inlaid celadon bowl from the Koryo dynasty, 18cm. diam.

12th century Korean celadon wine ewer, 7in. high.

Korean Yi dynasty blue and white globular vase painted with peony sprays.

KUTANI

Japanese Kutani plate decorated with birds and foliage, 14in. diam.

A Kutani vase and cover, a young sake tester modelled on one side, 27cm. high, late 18th century.

Late 19th century Kutani drummer boy, 9½in. high.

MING   **MING**

16th century Ming jar in blue and white porcelain, 15in. diam.

Chinese wine ewer made in the 14th century and painted in copper red, 12¾in. high.

Early Ming blue and white porcelain flask, 10in. high.

MISCELLANEOUS

Mid 16th century Isnik pottery stemmed dish, 12in. diam.

Ban Chiang gray pottery jar with globular body and flared neck, 2nd/1st millenium B.C., 12in. high.

16th century Annamese saucer dish, painted with underglaze blue.

NANKIN

Nankin tureen, decorated in polychrome with Oriental garden scenes and with a domed cover.

One of a pair of round blue and white Nankin vases, 24in. high.

One of a pair of Nankin style blue and white porcelain vases, 10¾in. high.

PERSIAN

Early 18th century blue and white hookah, probably Persian, 8½in. high.

Persian dish 12th/13th century, made in Rayy, 9½in. diam.

18th century Persian blue and white baluster scent bottle, 7½in. high.

QIANLONG

Qianlong period blue and white pilgrim vase, 51cm. high.

Qianlong blue and white charger decorated with a hunting scene, 17in. diam.

Qianlong incense burner and cover surmounted with a Dog of Fo.

QING

Large late 19th century enamelled dish, 59.2cm. diam.

Chinese porcelain cockerel, circa 1800.

Celadon vase with central floral panel, circa 1870.

RYOZAN

Late 19th century Unzan Ryozan vase, 12in. high.

A Ryozan earthenware dish enamelled and gilt with child acrobats, 15.5cm. high. circa 1900.

A Ryozan Satsuma vase painted with travellers in a bleak snowy landscape, 24cm. high, late 19th century.

SATSUMA

One of a pair of Satsuma baluster vases decorated with heads, 24cm. high.

19th century Satsuma decorated teapot, 7½in. high.

Outstanding Japanese Satsuma bowl with a gilt encrusted pictorial scene of the arrival of Chinese envoys, dated 1804.

Song dynasty jar decorated with three stylised leaf sprays, 5¼in. high.

Chinese Cizhou vase of the Song dynasty painted in dark brown and with a leaf green glaze, 26cm. high.

Chinese white glazed jar from the Song dynasty, 10.5cm. high.

TANG

A Tang dynasty figure of a horse, 28in. wide.

Tang dynasty rare unglazed figure of a camel groom, 16in. high.

Tang dynasty dark green globular storage jar, 7¼in. high.

WANLI

Wanli blue and white saucer dish, 15in. diam.

Wanli blue and white pear-shaped bottle, 27cm. high.

Kraak porcelain dish, Wanli period, circa 1600, 11in. diam.

WEI

Wei dynasty unglazed pottery hound, 6½in. wide.

Wei dynasty gray pottery tomb attendant, 16in. high.

Early Wei dynasty pottery figures of four tomb attendants, 8in. high.

WUCAI

Wucai transitional period jar, circa 1650, 10½in. high.

Very rare Turkish market Wucai bottle in Iznik palette, Kangxi, 23.1cm.

Fine Wucai baluster vase and cover, circa 1650-70, 14in. high.

YIXING

18th century Yixing teapot and cover.

Rare Chinese export Yixing figure, 19th century.

Early 19th century Yixing teapot and cover.

YONGZHENG

One of a pair of Yongzheng famille rose fish bowls.

One of a pair of Yongzheng famille rose dishes, 12½in. diam.

Yongzheng or early Qianlong famille rose square vase on short feet, 5in. high.

YUAN

Yuan dynasty celadon incense burner, 3¾in. wide.

Early 14th century pale blue wine ewer from the Yuan dynasty, 13¼in. tall.

Rare 14th century Yuan dynasty stem cup stand, 7½in. diam.

Quarter repeating oak bracket clock, circa 1900, 16in. high.

George III mahogany bracket clock by William Cozens of London, 1ft. 3½in. tall.

19th century bracket clock, 14in. high, in mahogany and brass case.

Mid 17th century bracket clock in an ebony veneered case by Pieter Visbagh, 10in. high.

A Japanese striking bracket clock, 170mm. high.

Late 18th century musical bracket clock by Robert Ward, London, 61cm. high.

Walnut bracket clock by Daniel Quare, London, 14in. high.

Regency mahogany striking bracket clock by Panchaud & Cumming, London, 16in. high.

Bracket clock by Thos. Tompion, London, circa 1700. 40cm. high.

Late 18th century mahogany quarter repeating bracket clock by William Dutton, 14in. high.

Dutch ebony gilt mounted bracket clock, 17in. high.

Japanned quarter repeating bracket timepiece, 13½in. high.

19th century carriage clock in the Japanese manner, 6¾in. high.

Porcelain mounted carriage clock, 6½in. high.

Gilt metal oval brass striking carriage clock by Drocourt, 5½in. high.

19th century petite sonnerie carriage clock by Joseph Berrolla, Paris.

Late 19th century carriage clock by Nicole Nielson & Co., in silver case, 11.5cm. high.

English gilt metal carriage timepiece by Viner & Co., London, 4½in. high.

French brass cased grande sonnerie carriage clock, 7in. high.

Elaborate gilt metal striking carriage clock, 8¼in. high.

Clock attributed to Mucha, circa 1900, 9in. high.

Gilt spelter carriage clock, circa 1890, 6½in. high.

French brass striking carriage clock by Maurice & Co., 6½in. high.

Early French gilt metal pendule de voyage, dial signed Dubois, Paris, circa 1780, 7½in. high.

Gilt spelter clock garniture, circa 1880, clock 14in. high.

Victorian china clock set with transfer decoration.

Gilt bronze clock garniture, clock in the form of an owl, circa 1890.

Gilt bronze and Dresden porcelain clock garniture, circa 1880, clock 14in. high.

Gilt bronze and Sevres clock garniture, circa 1880.

19th century French style clock garniture.

Late 19th century painted spelter and onyx clock garniture.

Ormolu and marble clock garniture, circa 1900, dial signed Camerden and Foster, New York, Made in France.

Stylish modernistic clock, 1930's, 112cm. high.

Wrought iron long-case clock, circa 1920, 65½in. high.

Wickerwork long-case clock.

Mahogany longcase clock, circa 1830, 93in. high.

Small longcase clock in a walnut marquetry case by J. Wise, circa 1680, 6ft.8in. high.

French provincial longcase clock with elaborate brass pendulum.

Regency longcase clock with brass dial by N. Barwise, London

Early 19th century longcase clock signed Robin aux Galeries du Louvre, 6ft.10in. high.

Early 19th century mahogany longcase clock, 94in. high.

Mahogany longcase clock by Jn. and Wm. Mitchell, Glasgow, mid 19th century, 83in. high.

Small George III mahogany regulator, 6ft.11in. high.

Large marquetry chiming clock, circa 1900, 105½in. high.

Small brass lantern time-piece with alarm, circa 1700, 170mm. high.

Wing alarm lantern clock, 1ft.3in. high.

Provincial lantern clock by E. Bilbie, circa 1675, 10in. high.

Balance wheel lantern clock by Baker, complete with doors.

Lantern clock by John Knibb, Oxford, circa 1690, 17½in. high.

18th century Japanese lantern clock, 280mm. high.

Miniature travelling verge lantern clock by Charles Groode, London.

Alarm lantern clock by Wm. Kipling, London, 1ft.3in. high.

17th century brass lantern clock with one hand.

English brass quarter striking lantern clock, 12¾in. high.

Louis XV provincial wall timepiece, 14½in. high.

Small lantern clock, signed Robert Dingley, London, 9in. high.

Lalique frosted glass clock, 16cm. high, circa 1920.

20th century walnut cased mantel clock.

Louis XVI ormolu and white marble mantel clock, 1ft.2in. high.

Late 19th century clock, with ormolu mounts, 16in. high.

Mid 19th century bronze and marble mantel clock, 21½in. high.

19th century white marble calendar mantel clock, 1ft. 4in. high.

Gilt bronze and porcelain mounted mantel clock, circa 1870, 16in. high.

Small Liberty & Co. pewter and enamel clock, 19.75cm. high, after 1903.

Mid Victorian mantelpiece clock in brass and bronze mounted case.

Gilt and patinated bronze mantel clock, circa 1860, 18in. high, surmounted by a group of a Turk and his Horse.

French gilt and patinated bronze mantel clock, circa 1850-75, 1ft.10in. high.

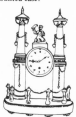

Louis XVI white marble and ormolu timepiece, enamel dial signed Schmit a Paris, 1ft.3in. high.

Mahogany cased clock with tulipwood banding, 25in. high.

Art Deco bronze and marble clock, 26cm. wide, 1920's.

Preiss clock with marble base, 1930's, 37cm. high.

Late 18th century Flemish painted mantel clock, 2ft. 4in. high.

Victorian barometer, clock and thermometer in oak case, 13in. high.

Regency period mahogany cased mantel clock, 13in high.

Late 19th century ormolu and bronze mantel clock with urn surmount.

French 19th century mantel clock.

Gilt metal and marble mantel clock, circa 1880, 13in. high.

Clock case in green marble surmounted by a bronze figure, circa 1900, 39cm. high.

Viennese giltwood David and Goliath grande sonnerie mantel clock, 19in. high.

French Empire mantel clock in mahogany case, 50cm. high.

91

SKELETON CLOCKS

Brass cathedral skeleton clock signed C.Fiedemann, Liverpool.

Unusual early 19th century skeleton clock of 'rafter' construction.

Good quality original Victorian skeleton timepiece, circa 1860.

Mid 19th century silvered brass skeleton timepiece, 12½in. high.

Rare epicyclic skeleton clock, 10in. high, with a glass dome.

Rare chiming calendar skeleton clock, 1ft.7in. high.

Early skeleton clock by Hubert Sarton, 1ft. 5½in. high.

Unusual timepiece skeleton clock, 20in. high, with glass dome.

Skeleton clock by Smith & Sons, Clerkenwell, 1ft. 4½in. high.

Brass skeleton clock with enamel dial, circa 1890, 15¼in. high.

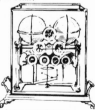

Astronomical skeleton clock, by James Gorham, 19th century.

Unusual long duration Dutch skeleton clock, 2ft. 5in. high.

Stained oak wall clock, Austrian, circa 1880, 38in. high.

Unusual mahogany wall time-piece by James McCabe, London, 8½in. high.

18th century French wall clock, 10½in. high.

Dutch Friesland clock with painted dial, 27in. high.

Early 20th century oak cased wall clock.

Elaborate Victorian mahogany framed wall clock with brass pendulum.

Japanese weight driven wall timepiece, 16in. high.

German Zappler clock, lacking pendulum, 11½in. high.

Vienna regulator in dark walnut, 60in. high, circa 1900.

Bristol example of an Act of Parliament clock by Wm. Preist.

Victorian papier mache wall clock by E. Fixary.

Inlaid American eight day clock, circa 1890, 2ft. 4in. high.

Mid 18th century silver pair cased verge watch by Markwick of London, 73mm. diam.

Silver pair cased false pendulum verge watch by Marke Hawkins, 53mm. diam.

Silver pair cased verge watch, signed Thos. Gorsuch, Salop, 56mm. diam.

Silver gilt and enamel duplex watch, 56mm. diam.

Large silver pair cased verge watch, signed Wm. Smith, 81mm. diam.

Silver pair cased verge watch by Markwick, London, circa 1710.

Gold quarter repeating cylinder watch, by Ellicott of London, 1766, 49mm. diam.

Cartier gold breast pocket clip watch, 1930's, 5.3cm.

Swiss gold quarter repeating Jacquemart verge watch, 56mm. diam.

Oval silver watch for the Turkish Market, with Turkish numerals and subsidiary lunar dial, 63mm. long.

Pedometer watch signed by Spencer & Perkins, London, 52mm. diam., circa 1780.

Swiss silver keyless mystery watch signed A. S. & P. Mysterieuse, Brevete S. G. D. G., 53mm. diam.

Cloisonne enamel quail, 5in. high, Qianlong period.

Two-handled cloisonne bowl, early 15th century, 8in. wide.

20th century cloisonne enamel box, 5in. wide.

Early 19th century cloisonne enamel incense burner.

A good late 18th century cloisonne enamel teapot.

19th century Japanese cloisonne enamel vase, 7in. high.

One of a pair of Japanese cloisonne enamel vases, 36in. high, circa 1900.

19th century Japanese cloisonne dish, 14in., diam.

Fine 19th century cloisonne two-handled vase, 22in. high.

One of a pair of cloisonne enamel pricket candlesticks, 19in. high.

One of a pair of iron-bodied cloisonne enamel and gilded metal vases, 22cm. high.

One of a pair of 19th century ormolu mounted cloisonne enamel vases.

Early 18th century copper wine flagon.

Set of three Victorian brass fire implements.

Late 19th century oak framed gong.

Victorian brass trivet with screw on legs.

19th century brass fireguard.

One of a pair of Christopher Dresser brass candlesticks, 1880's.

W. Benson copper and brass kettle and burner, 11½in. high, 1890's.

Unusual copper and wrought iron illuminated heater, 30in. high, circa 1900.

Late 16th century Venetian brass charger, 19½in. diam.

One of a pair of early 17th century brass candlesticks, 12in. high.

Late 19th century brass fire grate, 38in. wide.

Copper jar with a silver cover, surmounted by a lapis lazuli finial.

Late 18th century pierced brass footman with shaped front legs.

19th century brass chamberstick with drip pan.

Pair of Victorian iron and brass dogs.

A gallon copper measure.

20th century pressed brass magazine stand.

Horse brass on leather.

One of a pair of Liberty & Co. brass candlesticks, 13.5cm. high, circa 1900.

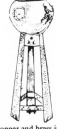

Copper and brass jardiniere on stand, Austrian, circa 1910, 53in. high.

Early 17th century North German brass candlestick, 8¼in. high.

Victorian brass watering can.

Brass and lacquer vase by Jean Dunand, circa 1925.

Late 19th century brass coal scuttle.

CORAL

Chinese necklace of finely pierced hollow coral prayer beads, interspersed with silver gilt beads.

Coral maiden immortal, 4½in. high, on wood stand.

19th century peach-stone necklace, carved with flowers and with a coral bead.

Coral figure of a goddess, 6½in. high, on wood stand.

Carved coral group, 6½in. high, on wood stand.

Coral Kuan Yin, 8in. high, on wood stand.

CORKSCREWS

Late 18th century example of the first patented corkscrew.

Unusual brass Victorian corkscrew.

Victorian brass and ivory corkscrew.

Steel rack and pinion hand corking device, 6¼in. high.

Unusual Victorian brass corkscrew.

19th century Plum's patent ratchet corkscrew with ivory handle, brass barrel and steel screw.

Early 17th century
kid glove.

Rare pair of shoes
made in 1780.

Embroidered linen
coif, circa 1580-
1610.

19th century lady's
Imperial Court dragon
robe.

A pair of 19th century
blonde Chantilly stock-
ings with side lacings,
78cm. long.

North American Athapaskan
Indian softskin embroidered
jacket.

18th century suit
of orange velvet
with fine embroidery.

Pair of Queen Victoria's
bloomers.

Hand woven linen
smock frock or
round frock used by
a shepherd.

Fine Hawaiian feather cape,
'ahu'ula, decorated with red
and black on a ground of
yellow, 39in. wide.

Stovepipe bearskin hat
belonging to Abraham
Lincoln.

Melanesian tunic of woven panels
of Job's Tears, probably from
New Guinea, 18in. x 13½in.

Armand Marseille bisque headed doll, 17in. high.

German doll made by Herm. Steiner, 1912, 16in. long.

Bisque headed doll with composition body and limbs stamped Thuringa, Germany.

A bisque headed character doll by Simon & Halbig.

American Ives & Co. clockwork walking doll, circa 1880, 9½in. high.

Kammer & Reinhardt celluloid character doll.

French bisque Bru doll with paperweight eyes and kid body, 22in. tall.

Jumeau phonograph doll.

A bisque headed child doll with jointed composition body, marked S.F.B.J. Paris 10, 23½in. tall.

Jumeau bisque doll impressed Paris Fr.A.7, 15in. high.

Simon & Halbig Japanese character doll.

Victorian doll impressed 'Fabrication Francaise al and Cie Limoges Cherie 5' 19in. high.

Small Bilston enamel box, circa 1760.

Rectangular enamel snuff box, German, circa 1760, 8cm. wide.

Bilston spaniel bonbonniere, circa 1770-75, 5cm. wide.

Berlin enamel double snuff box, 3in. wide, circa 1750-56.

One of a pair of silver and enamel candlesticks, 6in. high, circa 1770.

13th century Limoges Champleve enamel pyx, 3½in. high.

Fine and large Limoges Champleve enamel plaque of the crucifixion, 13th century, 10¾in. high.

French enamelled brush set, mirror, 24.25cm. high, maker's mark 'JM', 1930's.

An enamel triptych 'The Bridge of Life' by Alex. Fisher, before 1904, 35cm. high.

Large enamel pug dog bonbonniere, 2½in. wide, circa 1830.

German enamel snuff box, circa 1757, 3¼in. wide.

Russian enamelled egg with pull-off top by Pavel Ovtschinnikov, Moscow, circa 1900.

ETUIS

Continental gilt metal etui with some fittings.

George II etui, circa 1745, in green shagreen case.

Gilt metal etui on a chatelaine with dark and light brown agate pendants.

Rococo etui, chased and embossed and with gilt fittings.

Gold mounted shagreen and enamel etui, late 18th century, Swiss, 4in. high.

Chelsea etui of cylindrical form, circa 1756.

FANS

Fan with collection of forty signatures of composers, authors, etc., 1895.

18th century fan, painted after Lancret and with carved and pierced ivory sticks.

French fan set with mother-of-pearl panels, circa 1760, 10in.

Hand-painted fan on fine silk, lace and bone, circa 1880, 1ft. high.

Faberge lace fan with blond tortoiseshell sticks.

Victorian lace fan with embroidered flowers.

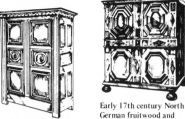

18th century Spanish oak armoire with doors centered by roundels, 55½in. wide.

Early 17th century North German fruitwood and oak armoire.

Late 18th century French provincial walnut armoire, 4ft.10in. wide.

Dutch walnut and marquetry armoire with arched molded cornice, 74in. wide.

Mid 18th century French provincial oak armoire, 172cm. wide.

Mid 18th century Louis XV walnut provincial armoire, 4ft.9in. wide.

Early 18th century Anglo-Dutch walnut armoire, 65in. wide.

Late 18th century North German or Scandinavian elm armoire, 84in. wide.

19th century Dutch mahogany and marquetry wardrobe.

Good late Louis XV provincial Bas'Armoire, circa 1765, 4ft.2in. wide.

Mid 18th century Dutch walnut armoire, 67½in. wide.

17th century Dutch oak armoire, 220cm. wide.

103

Mahogany and burl walnut double bed by Louis Majorelle, circa 1897, 68½in. wide.

One of a pair of Biedermeier beds in golden burr and straight cut elm, 6ft.5in. long, circa 1840.

Brass half-tester bed, circa 1900, 76in. wide.

Unusual Regency mahogany folding campaign bed, 7ft. 4in. high.

18th century French bed, circa 1780, with shaped ends, canopy and bedspread, 8ft. 6in. high.

17th century tester bed with contemporary crewel work hangings.

George III four-poster bed.

Louis XVI carved walnut bed, 3ft.7½in. wide, circa 1790.

Italian painted pinewood bed, 4ft.8in. wide, circa 1690.

Mid 20th century softwood and simulated bamboo tester bed, 72¾in. long.

Victorian mahogany double bunk set.

Victorian mahogany bed with quilted headboard.

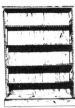

Victorian pinewood bookshelves, 3ft. wide.

George III mahogany bookshelves supported on a central column with quadruple splayed feet.

A walnut square revolving bookcase, with pierced brass gallery, 3ft. high.

19th century mahogany bookcase, 5ft.8in. wide.

William IV pedestal bookcase in rosewood, 19½in. high.

A tortoiseshell bamboo bookcase with glazed doors.

Late 18th century mahogany bookcase in the Chippendale style.

George IV library bookcase, circa 1825, 6ft.2in. wide.

19th century walnut open bookshelves with white marble top.

Oak bookcase with glazed upper half and carved doors.

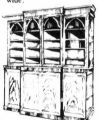

George III breakfront mahogany library bookcase.

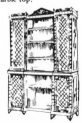

Regency mahogany bookcase by G. Oakley, 78½in. wide.

105

20th century oak bureau with oxidised handles.

19th century Oriental carved teak bureau.

Rosewood and marquetry French bureau de dame, circa 1870, 65cm. wide.

18th century Dutch marquetry double bureau, 4ft. 9in. wide.

Italian walnut marquetry bureau, circa 1780, 4ft.1in. wide.

English Queen Anne period oak bureau veneered with walnut, 94cm. wide.

Georgian mahogany bureau of good color , 3ft. wide.

An Edwardian mahogany inlaid bureau with satinwood banded borders and four long drawers, on bracket feet, 2ft.6in. wide.

An attractive bureau in golden ash crossbanded in walnut with a fine patina, 36in. wide, 41in. high, 20in. deep, circa 1740.

Heavily carved Victorian oak bureau of four long graduated drawers with lion mask handles, 3ft. wide.

Louis XV provincial walnut bureau, circa 1750, 3ft.7in. wide.

Early George III mahogany bureau on stand, 3ft. wide.

Edwardian mahogany bureau bookcase on cabriole legs.

Mid 18th century walnut and floral marquetry bureau cabinet.

20th century oak bureau bookcase with H stretcher.

Mid 18th century Sicilian bureau cabinet in walnut and marquetry, 1.07m. wide.

18th century German walnut bureau cabinet.

Oak cylinder bureau cabinet, possibly German, circa 1780, 4ft.1in. wide.

George I walnut bureau bookcase with broken circular pediment.

Walnut bureau cabinet, circa 1715, with mirrors on the outside of the doors, 47½in. wide.

Late 19th century satinwood bureau cabinet, 24½in. wide.

Victorian bureau bookcase with glazed upper half.

A 19th century floral marquetry bureau bookcase on cabriole legs.

George III mahogany bureau bookcase, 3ft. 11in. wide.

Mid 19th century mahogany side cabinet, 40in. wide, with hinged top.

Late 19th century carved oak coal cabinet with brass handles.

George III satinwood side cabinet, 3ft.2in. wide, circa 1770.

Charles II black and gold lacquer cabinet on stand, 50in. wide.

17th century German carved walnut cabinet, 64in. wide.

Edwardian rosewood music cabinet with a fall front and glazed door.

Art Nouveau style beechwood music cabinet.

Partly 17th century Dutch oak cabinet, 64in. wide.

Fruitwood marquetry display cabinet, by Majorelle, circa 1910, 64cm. wide.

Fine Oriental hardwood cabinet, gold panels with ivory carvings, 48in. wide.

Walnut dental cabinet, circa 1890, figured in burr-wood, 29¼in. wide.

George III mahogany cabinet on stand with marquetry panels on the doors.

Early 19th century Regency
black-painted and gilded
canterbury, 23in. wide.

Victorian ebonised canterbury
on short turned legs.

Burr-walnut music canterbury
with nicely shaped partitions.

Regency rosewood
canterbury with
drawer, 48cm. wide.

Late George III mahogany
plate canterbury, 1ft. 9in.
long, circa 1805.

Victorian mahogany
canterbury in excellent
condition.

Victorian bamboo can-
terbury with lacquered
panels.

Mid Victorian walnut stand
with canterbury below, 2ft.
6in. wide.

Victorian burr-walnut
music canterbury with
fretted partitions and
drawer in the base.

Early 19th century mahogany
music canterbury on short
turned legs.

George III mahogany canterbury
on slender turned tapered legs.

Reproduction mahogany,
flat splat canterbury.

DINING CHAIRS

19th century child's chair in elm.

One of a set of six painted and giltwood chairs, late 19th century, partly upholstered in petit point.

One of a pair of Art Deco giltwood chairs, 94cm. high.

One of a set of seven George III mahogany dining chairs.

Late 18th century carved mahogany Chippendale style dining chair.

One of two rush-seated spindleback dining chairs.

One of a set of six William IV dining chairs.

One of a set of six mahogany dining chairs, circa 1840.

One of a set of seven Regency beechwood chairs, with an X-shaped splat.

One of a pair of oak chairs, by Charles Rennie Mackintosh, circa 1900, 112cm. high.

One of a set of seven Dutch walnut marquetry chairs, mid 18th century.

Queen Anne solid walnut single chair, circa 1710.

Large Art Deco giltwood tub chair, early 1920's.

Victorian oak rocking chair.

One of a pair of Victorian mahogany tub chairs on cabriole legs.

Late Victorian oak easy chair with padded arms.

Beechwood armchair, circa 1680, with padded back and seat.

Fine George III mahogany saddle wing chair, 81cm. wide.

A Victorian waxed rosewood spoon back easy chair on turned legs.

Regency mahogany bereger, circa 1810.

Mahogany armchair, 1860's, on cabriole legs with castors.

George III mahogany library armchair of Chippendale style, arm supports carved with foliage.

19th century highly carved hardwood easy chair.

George III mahogany chair, circa 1775.

ELBOW CHAIRS

One of two carved and ebonised Oriental chairs.

One of a set of eight George III mahogany dining chairs, circa 1780.

Victorian elm smoker's chair.

One of a pair of George III mahogany armchairs, circa 1765.

One of a set of eight mid 18th century Dutch marquetry chairs.

One of a pair of heavily carved oak chairs.

Queen Anne walnut armchair with solid vase-shaped splat and needlework seat.

Yew-wood high back Windsor elbow chair.

George III mahogany armchair, circa 1785.

18th century mahogany lattice back armchair, with upholstered seat.

Charles II open armchair, 1662, with curved arms.

One of a set of eight early George III mahogany ladderback chairs, circa 1765.

19th century walnut military chest of drawers, 99cm. wide.

An Edwardian walnut chest of drawers with pierced brass handles.

Early 19th century Empire style chest with a figured marble top.

George III mahogany chest of three drawers, 92cm. wide.

Victorian figured mahogany bow-fronted chest on bun feet, 3ft.6in. wide.

English oak chest of drawers, 39in. wide, circa 1930.

Dutch marquetry and mahogany chest.

George II mahogany linen press and chest, 3ft.1in. wide, circa 1760.

Victorian Wellington chest veneered in rosewood.

Late 16th century Italian walnut chest, 3ft.8in. wide.

Jacobean oak chest with a pair of geometrically molded doors, 3ft.3in. wide.

William and Mary marquetry chest of drawers.

CHEST ON CHEST

George III mahogany tallboy on ogee feet with an arched pediment.

George I walnut tallboy, base with secretaire drawer, 42½in. wide.

17th century oak chest in two sections, decorated all over, 38in. wide.

A fine quality 18th century walnut tallboy with fluted pilasters and a shaped apron.

18th century Queen Anne burr-walnut cabinet on chest, 109cm. wide.

Late 18th century bow-fronted mahogany chest on chest on splayed feet.

George III oak tallboy, circa 1780, 3ft.10in. wide.

Late 18th century mahogany chest on chest with a secretaire drawer.

18th century mahogany chest on chest fitted with brushing slide.

Late 18th century flame mahogany chest on chest on ogee feet.

Late 18th century Irish mahogany tallboy on claw feet.

18th century walnut tallboy chest on bun feet.

Late 17th century Flemish ebonised and decorated chest on stand.

William and Mary chest on stand, 3ft.5in. wide, circa 1690.

George I walnut chest on stand, 3ft.3in. wide, circa 1720.

A Queen Anne mulberry wood chest on stand with onion shaped feet.

George III oak chest on stand.

Portuguese rosewood chest on stand, 40¾in. wide.

American fruitwood highboy on cabriole legs.

Walnut chest on stand, circa 1710, 3ft.7in. wide.

George I oak and walnut tallboy on cabriole legs.

Small oak chest on stand with molded drawer fronts, 52in. high, circa 1780.

Chippendale walnut chest on stand, 42in. wide, circa 1760.

A fine William and Mary oyster veneered cabinet on stand with barley twist legs and cross stretchers.

CHIFFONIERS

Edwardian walnut chiffonier with carved cupboard doors.

Victorian mahogany chiffonier with arched panel doors.

Fine quality rosewood chiffonier, 45in. wide.

Regency rosewood chiffonier with inlaid cut brass, 43in. wide.

William IV rosewood side cabinet, 5ft.6in. wide, circa 1835.

Late 19th century mahogany chiffonier.

One of a pair of 19th century satinwood chiffoniers with Wedgwood jasper plaques.

One of a pair of Regency brass inlaid rosewood chiffoniers, by Louis Gaigneur.

Regency rosewood and parcel gilt chiffonier with two shelves, 43in. wide.

Early 19th century figured mahogany chiffonier with paneled doors.

Solid satinwood chiffonier, circa 1830, 45in. long.

Regency marquetry and brass inlaid chiffonier.

Late 18th century dark green leather hide covered coaching trunk, 36in. long.

Old elm chest, possibly 14th century.

18th century German oak marriage trunk, 56in. long, dated 1767.

17th century carved oak coffer, 120cm. wide.

George II walnut and mahogany chest with hinged lid, circa 1740, 3ft.9in. wide.

A highly carved 19th century camphor wood chest.

Rare 17th century oak domed top ark of plank construction, 97cm. wide.

Late 18th century pine coffer on bracket feet.

17th century Spanish iron chest, 31in. wide, with floral painted panels.

George II black japanned chest, mid 18th century, with later stand, 4ft. 1½in. wide.

117

COMMODE CHESTS

18th century Danish walnut and parcel gilt bombe commode, 78cm. wide.

Black lacquer and parcel gilt commode, 44in. wide.

A Louis XV kingwood parquetry commode of serpentine shape with ormolu mounts.

Louis XIV marquetry and ormolu mounted commode, 122cm. wide.

Louis XV commode in marquetry decorated with fire gilt bronze, after Duplessis Pere.

Marquetry commode with serpentine top, 46¼in. wide.

Late 18th century Italian rosewood and marquetry commode.

18th century Dutch walnut and floral marquetry commode with shaped top.

Louis XV/XVI transitional ormolu mounted marquetry commode, stamped C. Wolff.

Edwardian satinwood commode with convex center section.

North Italian serpentine commode, late 18th century.

Empire mahogany commode with black marble top, 51½in. wide.

Early 19th century mahogany night commode, 25½in. wide.

Victorian mahogany one step commode on short turned legs.

19th century French walnut pot cupboard on shaped legs.

Victorian mahogany pot cupboard with fluted sides.

A fine early 19th century traveling commode with sunken brass carrying handles and a Spode basin.

Edwardian inlaid mahogany bedside cupboard.

Victorian mahogany commode complete with liner.

George IV mahogany bedside commode with fall front, 67cm.

Late 18th century mahogany, tambour fronted, night commode, with carrier handles.

19th century mahogany lift-up commode with ebony inlay.

Late 18th century Chippendale style mahogany night table, 23in. wide, with tray top.

Late 18th century satinwood bedside table on square tapering legs.

119

CORNER CUPBOARDS

George I black lacquer
hanging corner cabinet,
36½in. high.

Late 18th century pine corner cupboard of good
color

George III walnut venee-
red corner cupboard
with swan neck pediment.

One of a pair of late 18th
century mahogany cabinets
with shaped marble tops.

19th century carved oak
corner cupboard.

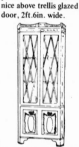

A mahogany wall corner
cupboard, with swan neck
pediment and dentil cor-
nice above trellis glazed
door, 2ft.6in. wide.

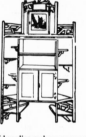
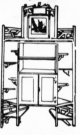

George I mahogany corner
cupboard, 4ft. wide.

Edwardian mahogany corner
cabinet, 40in. wide.

Late 18th century inlaid
mahogany corner cupboard.

Carved and painted corner
cupboard with pierced
cornice, circa 1760, 2ft.
5in. wide.

George III stripped pine corner cupboard with shaped
shelves.

18th century Dutch marquetry corner cupboard.

Mid 19th century oak court cupboard, 51in. wide.

Mid 17th century oak court cupboard with carved frieze, 4ft.6in. wide.

Commonwealth oak court cupboard with molded rectangular top, 44½in. wide, inlaid with bone and mother-of-pearl.

Late 17th century Welsh oak court cupboard.

17th century oak court cupboard, 61in. wide.

Continental oak court cupboard, heavily carved and of good size.

Charles I oak court cupboard, circa 1630, 3ft. 8½in. wide.

Late 17th century Welsh oak duodarn, 48in. wide.

Bleached oak court cupboard, 57in. wide, circa 1860.

Queen Anne oak court cupboard, circa 1710, 4ft.3in. wide.

17th century French oak dressoire with geometric inlay and blind fret decoration, 52in. wide.

Stained oak court cupboard, made in the mid 19th century.

Mid 19th century painted cradle, 38½in. long.

Kidney-shaped Empire style child's cradle, circa 1800, 39in. long.

Dutch child's cradle in the form of a sledge, 22in. long.

17th century Continental oak crib.

19th century Breton style cradle, with turned finials, 90cm. wide.

17th century oak cradle with pointed hood, 3ft. long.

Victorian wickerwork cradle.

Late 18th century mahogany crib.

A 19th century painted wood boat cradle.

19th century mahogany crib with carved end, 97cm. long.

A Victorian brass crib.

Victorian cast iron cradle on castors.

Early 19th century parcel gilt mahogany cradle, 3ft.11in. wide.

A 19th century Indian cradle.

Oak cradle with carved lunettes and lozenge decoration.

122

Victorian burr-walnut breakfront credenza with canted corners, 5ft.7in. wide.

Victorian walnut credenza with concave ends and a glazed center door.

Marquetry kingwood porcelain mounted side cabinet, circa 1870, 82in. wide.

19th century French red Buhl breakfront cabinet, 6ft. 9in. wide.

Walnut side cabinet, circa 1870, 4ft.9in. wide.

Ebonised porcelain and gilt bronze mounted display cabinet, 1860's, 72in. wide.

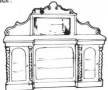

19th century rosewood breakfront credenza.

Italian Renaissance walnut credenza, circa 1580, 4ft. 9½in. wide.

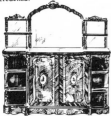

Good burr-walnut side cabinet, 1860's, 72in. wide.

Mid 19th century walnut side cabinet, 67in. wide.

Charles I oak food cupboard.

Late 19th century oak side table with cupboard.

Regency walnut cupboard with molded top, circa 1730, 4ft.7in. wide.

'Mouseman' oak cupboard, 36in. wide, circa 1936-40.

Late Victorian carved oak buffet.

George III mahogany clothes press, 51in. wide.

17th century Flemish oak cupboard, 68¾in. wide.

Fine Art Nouveau mahogany sideboard cupboard, French, circa 1900, 59in. wide.

18th century oak settle with paneled cupboard doors.

German walnut parquetry cupboard, circa 1740, 6ft. 2in. wide.

Mid 18th century Dutch marquetry cupboard, 5ft.8in. wide.

Mid 19th century carved oak cupboard, 145cm. wide.

Mid 19th century walnut Davenport, 21¼in. wide.

Unusual walnut Davenport writing table, circa 1870, 20¾in. wide.

Victorian rosewood Davenport, 53cm. wide.

Burr-walnut inlaid ebonised Davenport, 22in. wide, circa 1860-80.

Satinwood crossbanded mahogany Davenport, 1ft. 9in. wide, 1900's.

Walnut Davenport, circa 1860, 37½in. wide, with central turned balustrade.

Regency rosewood Davenport surmounted by a brass gallery, 17in. wide.

Walnut harlequin Davenport, 1860's, 23in. wide.

Mid 19th century walnut Davenport, 32 x 23½in.

Walnut and burr-walnut Davenport, 1870's.

Late 19th century walnut Davenport, 24in. wide.

William IV rosewood Davenport, circa 1830, 1ft.9in. wide.

DISPLAY CABINETS

19th century mahogany specimen table on cabriole legs with ormolu mounts.

19th century heart-shaped specimen table, inlaid with marquetry.

19th century burr-walnut display cabinet with brass escutcheons.

Mahogany vitrine, circa 1895, 68in. high.

Louis XV silver display cabinet with gilt bronze mounts.

Early George III mahogany display cabinet, 4ft. wide.

Early display cabinet, by Charles Rennie Mackintosh, circa 1895.

Early 18th century Dutch mahogany and marquetry display cabinet, 5ft.6in. wide.

Chippendale mahogany display cabinet with a blind fret cornice, 57in. wide, circa 1890.

19th century Chinese hardwood display cabinet.

An Edwardian mahogany display cabinet, with mirror backed central and lower scroll backed glazed side cupboards.

Fine quality 19th century carved mahogany display cabinet.

126

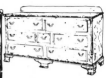

Georgian oak low dresser with molded rectangular top crossbanded in mahogany, 73½in. wide.

Mid 18th century oak dresser base, 5ft.6in. wide.

Victorian carved oak dresser with pot cupboard.

18th century Lancashire oak and pine dresser.

Late 17th century oak dresser with open shelves.

18th century French provincial oak dresser.

Early 20th century oak dresser with brass handles.

George III oak dresser with plate racks, 5ft.7in. wide.

18th century oak clock dresser, dial signed Nathaniel Olding, Wincanton, 96in. wide.

Louis XV decorated cartonnier in fruitwood.

Flemish 17th century oak dresser fitted with three drawers, 7ft. long.

Victorian 'Dog Kennel' dresser, circa 1850, 63in. wide.

DUMB WAITERS

A small Edwardian mahogany serving table on a tripod base.

George III three-tier mahogany dumb waiter on a tripod base with ball and claw feet.

19th century two-tier dumb waiter with marquetry and ormolu mounts.

HALL STANDS

Late 19th century oak hall stand with brass fittings.

Edwardian oak hall stand.

Victorian carved oak hallstand, 7ft. high.

JARDINIERES

Rosewood marquetry jardiniere, circa 1900, possibly French.

19th century black lacquer and gilt jardiniere. $280

Mid 19th century japanned jardiniere, 2ft. 1in. wide.

LOWBOYS

An 18th century mahogany lowboy, 29in. wide.

18th century Dutch marquetry lowboy, 84cm. wide.

Early Victorian walnut lowboy with claw and ball cabriole legs, 30in. wide.

One-piece mahogany pedestal writing desk, circa 1760, 81cm. wide.

19th century oak pedestal desk with tooled leather top.

Small oak kneehole desk of nine drawers, 45in. wide.

George II mahogany kneehole desk with serpentine top, 44½in. wide.

Early 20th century oak tambour top desk.

Late 19th century mahogany desk with tooled leather top.

George II mahogany kneehole desk, 3ft.2in. wide, circa 1760.

Victorian mahogany cylinder top pedestal writing desk.

Late 18th century Sheraton inlaid and decorated satinwood kneehole desk.

Late 18th century inlaid mahogany cylinder desk, 44in. wide.

George IV mahogany kneehole desk, top inset with leather, 3ft.5½in. wide.

William and Mary period walnut kneehole desk with ebony arabesque marquetry inlay.

SCREENS

Early 20th century oak firescreen.

Giltwood and stained glass screen, circa 1900, 62in. wide.

Late 18th century giltwood firescreen with needlework panel.

Mahogany pole screen on tripod supports with tapestry in rococo frame.

Early 19th century six-leaf screen, 70½in. high.

Late 19th century hardwood four-fold screen, 73in. high.

Jennens and Bettridge papier mache firescreen, 41in. high, circa 1850.

Lacquer paneled two-fold screen with carved ivory ornamentation.

Late 19th century brass and glass firescreen.

Mahogany and leather five-fold screen, circa 1900, 85in. wide overall.

Three-fold painted screen, circa 1910, panel signed Jules Vernon-Fair.

John Pearson bronze and wrought iron fire-screen, circa 1906, 27½in. high.

130

Mahogany secretaire of the Sheraton period, interior with concave drawers and inlay, 43in. high, circa 1800.

Victorian rosewood secretaire Wellington chest.

Hepplewhite mahogany secretaire inlaid with rosewood and satinwood.

George III mahogany secretaire chest, 42in. wide.

Writing cabinet of dark stained wood, by Charles Rennie Mackintosh, 37¼in. wide.

Oak secretaire, by M. H. Baillie-Scott with pewter and marquetry inlay, 46in. high.

Walnut veneered fall front cabinet of William and Mary design, 40in. wide.

16th century Spanish walnut vargueno, 4ft.2in. wide, later stand.

Empire ormolu mounted mahogany secretaire a abattant, circa 1810, 3ft.2¼in. wide.

French secretaire a abattant in oak veneered with tulipwood and kingwood, 58cm. wide, by Jean-Francois Dubot.

American 'Wells Fargo' desk by Wootton & Co., 42½in. wide.

South German mahogany secretaire, 1840's, 39in. wide.

131

SECRETAIRE BOOKCASES

Ebonised secretaire book-case, circa 1880, 42¾in. wide.

George III mahogany secre-taire open bookcase, 81cm. wide.

Satinwood secretaire with scalloped gallery, circa 1900, 27½in. wide.

Empire secretaire book-case with fold down flap.

Late 19th century carved mahogany secretaire book-case with astragal glazed doors.

Early Victorian figured maho-gany breakfront secretaire bookcase, 230cm. wide.

Queen Anne walnut secre-taire cabinet, 2ft.5in. wide, circa 1710, on later bun feet.

George III mahogany break-front secretaire bookcase.

Unusual American maho-gany secretaire, 40in. wide, circa 1860-80.

Chippendale period maho-gany secretaire bookcase with ogee feet.

English secretaire cabinet, circa 1780, veneered with sycamore, rosewood and fruitwood, 1.2m. wide.

Early 19th century secretaire bookcase with carved pilasters and vase shaped feet.

Edwardian inlaid mahogany settee on cabriole legs.

Chippendale mahogany chair-back settee, circa 1880-1900, 72in. wide.

A carved oak hall settle, 56in. long.

Ash settle, designed for Liberty & Co., circa 1900, 51in. wide.

An early Victorian walnut framed settee.

Victorian rosewood framed chaise longue on turned legs.

Louis XV beechwood canape on molded cabriole legs, 5ft.1in. wide.

Russian amboyna wood chaise longue with gilt enrichments.

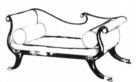

A nicely proportioned Regency mahogany framed couch with brass inlay, splay feet and claw castors.

Charles II walnut day bed, circa 1660, 5ft. long with caned back.

SHELVES

 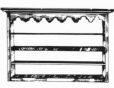

One of a pair of mahogany corner shelves, mid 19th century, 34in. high.

Late 18th century oak two-shelved hanging plate rack.

One of a pair of late 19th century mahogany hanging shelves, 36¼in. wide,

Mahogany Regency set of hanging shelves with carved cresting, circa 1820, 26½in. wide.

One of a pair of late George III giltwood eagle wall brackets, circa 1800, 1ft.3in. high.

19th century mahogany hanging book-shelves with ornate 'S' scroll supports.

STEPS

George III antique oak steps, circa 1790, 17¼in. wide, original bracket feet.

A set of early Victorian mahogany library steps which convert to a small arm elbow chair.

A set of fine Regency mahogany bed steps, 26in. high, 28in. deep, 19in. wide.

George III mahogany library steps with brass fittings.

Mahogany eight tread library steps with handrails, converting to a rectangular top table, on chamfered legs, 40in.

George III oak and satinwood library steps, 7ft.8in. high.

Large sideboard in pale walnut, 1930's, 175cm. wide.

18th century mahogany chest sideboard inlaid in the Sheraton manner.

19th century painted satinwood sideboard.

An Edwardian bow-fronted sideboard, on cabriole legs, with a gadrooned edge.

Late 18th century padoukwood pedestal sideboard.

George III satinwood breakfronted serving table, 71in. wide.

George III bow-fronted sideboard.

Mid 19th century oak sideboard, heavily carved, 90in. wide.

Small 20th century Jacobean style oak sideboard.

Attractively figured Sheraton serpentine fronted sideboard.

STOOLS

Small Regency rosewood footstool.

An Edwardian, rush seated, oblong footstool.

Small Victorian upholstered footstool on bun feet.

Sheraton style mahogany box strung and upholstered lyre shaped window seat.

20th century beech framed piano stool.

One of a pair of folding stools by Jean-Baptiste Sene, circa 1786.

Late 19th century ebonised stool on turned legs.

Unusual stained walnut stool, circa 1890, 43in. high.

Second Empire mahogany stool with drop-in seat, 19½in. square, circa 1870.

A Queen Anne oak close stool with simulated drawers.

Charles II walnut stool, 3ft. 3in. wide, circa 1680.

James I oak joint stool, circa 1610, 1ft.6in. wide.

A superb Regency stool with carved gilt rope feet.

Victorian rosewood revolving top piano stool.

A mahogany inlaid oblong piano stool on square tapered legs.

Part of an Edwardian inlaid seven-piece mahogany suite.

Part of a late 19th century walnut nine-piece suite with upholstered seats and backs.

Part of an Art Deco drawingroom suite, late 1930's, upholstered in velvet.

Victorian carved walnut **parlor** set of seven pieces.

Part of a French giltwood chateau suite of Louis XV design, comprising a canape, four fauteuils, banquette stool, firescreen and three-fold screen.

137

Burr-walnut card table, 1860's, 35in. wide.

Victorian rosewood inlaid envelope card table with drawer and undershelf.

Rosewood card table, 1840's, 36in. wide.

Victorian burr-walnut folding top card table on cabriole legs.

Hepplewhite mahogany card table, 3ft. wide, on French cabriole legs.

Regency mahogany card table.

Late George II mahogany card table, circa 1755, 2ft. 11½in. wide.

Compact rosewood card table, circa 1860.

George II red walnut tea or games table, circa 1740, 2ft.8in. wide.

19th century marquetry and kingwood swivel top card table.

Late 17th century walnut games table with fold-over top, 33in. long.

George IV satinwood card table, circa 1825, 3ft. wide.

Italian painted consol table on hoof feet, circa 1790.

Early 18th century German carved oak consol table.

Victorian cast iron consol table with marble top.

Mid 18th century Genoese painted consol table, 4ft. 1in. wide.

Charles X mahogany consol table, circa 1825, 4ft.4in. wide.

One of a pair of 18th century gilt consol tables attributed to T. Johnson.

Giltwood consol table, circa 1765, by Robt. Adam.

Early 18th century George I giltwood consol table, 48in. wide.

Louis XV giltwood consol table with brown and white marble top, 40½in. wide.

George II giltwood consol table with an eagle support and figured marble top.

Wood and perspex consol table, 1930's, 91.25cm. high.

William IV consol table in rosewood, 3ft.2in. wide.

Early Victorian marquetry center table, 64in. diam., circa 1840.

Walnut breakfast table, circa 1860, 53½in. wide.

19th century oak dining table with carved frieze.

20th century oak draw-leaf table on twist supports.

18th century satinwood table inlaid with bog wood.

18th century mahogany breakfast table on reeded legs, 4ft.6in. x 3ft.4in.

Burr-walnut circular breakfast table, 1860's, 48in. diameter.

19th century mahogany snap-top table on tripod base.

Regency rosewood tilt-top table inlaid with brass.

English walnut dining table, 60½in. diam., circa 1935.

Regency mahogany center table, circa 1815, 4ft.1in. diam.

Ebonised center table, circa 1870, 51in. wide.

Part of a suite of Betty Joell satinwood bedroom furniture, circa 1930.

Liberty & Co. oak toilet table, 38½in. wide, circa 1900.

Small late 18th century bow-fronted mahogany dressing table.

A fine quality Victorian mahogany dressing table.

Georgian mahogany dressing and writing table, 36in. wide, 23in. deep, 31in. high.

Fitted satinwood kneehole dressing table, 35in. wide.

Bamboo and rattan dressing table, circa 1880-1900, 37in. wide.

High Kitsch dressing table, 161cm. high, 1930's.

Queen Anne black and gold lacquer union suite with bureau base, 21½in. wide.

Georgian red walnut dressing table with rising top, 2ft.7in. wide.

Dressing table, by Emile Jacques Rhulmann, circa 1920, 43½in. wide.

Sheraton period mahogany 'D' table, 36in. wide, circa 1780.

DROP-LEAF TABLES

17th century oak well table on turned legs.

Regency mahogany extending dining table, circa 1815, 8ft.4in. long.

George III rectangular mahogany and cross-banded drop-leaf spider gateleg table.

George II mahogany drop-leaf table, 3ft. high, circa 1750.

Italian walnut drop-leaf table, circa 1610, 3ft.11½in. long.

17th century Italian walnut center table.

19th century Cuban mahogany drop-leaf table.

George II period red walnut drop-leaf table, 30in. wide.

George III mahogany dining table, circa 1810.

Country made oak drop-leaf table, circa 1820.

Rare yew-wood envelope table with flap supported by a loper, circa 1730.

Late 18th century mahogany drop-leaf dining table with six legs.

Victorian carved oak gateleg table on barley twist supports.

Mid 17th century oak credence table with carved frieze.

A large 18th century gateleg table with drawer, 5ft.2in. wide.

Late 17th century oak oval gateleg dining table, 4ft.8½in. opened.

An 18th century oak gateleg table, with turned legs.

Louis XIV walnut double gateleg table, circa 1680, 4ft. 11in. open.

Rare 17th century oak gateleg table with plain gate supports, 27½in. high.

Mid 17th century carved oak gateleg table, 72in. wide, open.

Charles II oak gateleg table, circa 1670, 3ft.2in. wide.

William and Mary oak gateleg table, circa 1690, 4ft. 6in. open.

A Victorian oval gateleg table, with two leaves, on turned legs, full width 3ft. 2in.

17th century oak gateleg table, circa 1670, 26½in. diam.

Late George III figured mahogany
twin pedestal dining table, turned
columns and splayed supports.

Early 17th century oak drawleaf
dining table, 133in. wide.

19th century mahogany extending
dining table on claw and ball feet.

Solid mahogany dining table which
makes two breakfast tables, circa
1830.

Fine mahogany dining table with
lattice underframing, George IV,
circa 1825, 7ft. 6in. x 4ft. 5in.

George III mahogany three pedestal
dining table, 51 x 152in. extended.

George III D-end mahogany dining
table, 9ft. 9in. long extended.

Oak dining table by J.J. Joass, 66in.
long, circa 1940.

Mid 19th century American pitch pine
refectory table, 96½in. long.

A fine, semi-circular, Irish drinking
table, with additional flap.

Late 18th century walnut cricket table.

Circular Victorian table in prime condition.

Late George II mahogany tripod table, 2ft. high.

19th century Burmese carved teak wood circular table with pierced apron, 68cm. diam.

Small George II marble topped red walnut table, 1ft. 10in. wide.

George III mahogany circular supper table, 29½in. diam.

Marquetry center table, stretchers edged with bone and ebony, 45in. wide.

A circular garden table on three cast iron legs, 2ft. diam.

Chippendale period mahogany architect's table.

George III mahogany drum top table, 3ft.7in. diam.

George III mahogany architect's table, circa 1765, 2ft. 11½in. wide.

Rosewood coffee table by Jacques Rhulmann, circa 1925, 26½in. diam.

145

PEMBROKE TABLES

George III faded mahogany and crossbanded rectangular Pembroke table, 77cm. wide.

George III satinwood 'Harlequin' Pembroke table, 36¼in. wide, open.

Late Victorian stripped pine Pembroke table with drawer, on turned legs.

19th century satinwood Pembroke table, 32½in. wide.

George III mahogany supper table, with wire grills to the lower section, 39¾in. wide.

George III mahogany 'butterfly' shaped Pembroke table, 37½in. wide, open.

SIDE TABLES

Fine oak side table, circa 1830, 31in. wide.

18th century giltwood side table on square tapered legs.

James I oak side table with bulbous supports, circa 1610.

Stained oak side table, circa 1880, 38in. wide.

19th century boulle side table with ormolu mounts.

Empire simulated rosewood side table, 49in. wide.

146

Regency brass inlaid rosewood sofa table, circa
1815, 3ft.7in. wide.

Edwardian mahogany sofa
table, 58in. wide.

William IV rosewood
sofa table, 88cm. wide.

Regency mahogany sofa
table, 5ft. wide open, circa
1810.

Regency mahogany sofa table,
circa 1815, 5ft.10in. wide.

Regency rosewood sofa
table/games table with
satinwood crossbanded
top.

SUTHERLAND TABLES

Victorian burr-walnut
Sutherland table with
shaped feet.

A rosewood inlaid
oblong two-tier table
with folding leaves
and satinwood banded
borders, 2ft. wide.

Sutherland table in
mahogany with brass
inlay.

A mahogany Sutherland
tea table with two fold-
ing leaves, on turned supports, 3ft. wide.

Solid mahogany Sutherland
table on turned legs, circa
1840.

Walnut Sutherland table,
22¼in., circa 1880.

Victorian chinoiserie lacquer work table, 28in. high.

20th century Carine parquetry games table, 37in. wide.

Victorian rosewood work table with sliding bag.

19th century work table with marquetry decoration, on fine turned legs.

17th century South German games table complete with games.

Victorian rosewood needle-work table.

Good quality early Victorian burr-walnut work table with a chess board top.

Russian ebony and boulle games table, late 18th century, 30½in. wide.

Victorian fitted burr-walnut work table.

Rosewood work table, circa 1850, 30 x 22½in.

Late 18th century mahogany games and writing table, 75 x 109 x 56cm.

Sheraton period tulipwood tricoteuse of French influence, 27 x 16in.

Art Deco galuchat and ivory, lady's writing table, circa 1930.

Late 19th century oak folding desk.

Rosewood writing table, circa 1900, 32 x 24in.

Louis XIV floral marquetrey bureau-plat.

Good bamboo writing desk.

Art Nouveau mahogany writing table with drawer.

Library table with finely marked rosewood veneers, 58in. long, circa 1840.

Victorian pine and cast iron school desk and chair.

Edwards and Roberts fiddle-back mahogany Carlton House writing desk, circa 1900, 3ft.9in.

Louis XV style rosewood bonheur du jour.

Edwardian inlaid rosewood writing table with inset leather top, 2ft.6in. wide.

George III satinwood bonheur du jour on square tapering legs, 2ft.3in. wide.

149

TEAPOYS

A Victorian mahogany teapoy on a carved base.

Regency simulated rosewood teapoy, lid inlaid with cut brass scrolling, 15in. wide.

Georgian period teapoy in mahogany, 20in. wide, circa 1825.

Regency mahogany teapoy with ebony inlay, 29½in. high, circa 1810.

Early 19th century rosewood teapoy on platform base with vase feet.

William IV mahogany teapoy with octagonal hinged top, 14in. wide.

TORCHERES

William and Mary walnut candle stand, late 17th century, 3ft.3in. high.

One of a pair of oak Solomonic torcheres, 75in. high.

One of a pair of George III mahogany torcheres, 38¾in. high.

TOWEL RAILS

Victorian mahogany framed towel rail.

Victorian mahogany towel rail on twist supports.

Edwardian oak towel rail with spiral supports.

150

Late 18th century Dutch faded mahogany wardrobe, 70in. wide.

A large, good quality, Victorian pine wardrobe.

Victorian carved oak hall wardrobe.

Late George III mahogany wardrobe, 4ft. 4in. wide.

Solid walnut breakfront wardrobe by Peter Waals.

Rosewood armoire, by Louis Majorelle, 103in. high.

An Art Nouveau marquetry oak wardrobe, 137cm. wide.

Early 1920's walnut and ivory wardrobe, designed by Leon Jallot, 183cm. high.

Rare painted wardrobe by Wm. Burges, 1870's, 53in. wide.

Satinwood and painted wardrobe, 97in. wide, circa 1880-90.

Wardrobe designed by Gordon Russell, circa 1930, 72in. high.

Heal's wardrobe of 1898.

Victorian marble top wash stand.

Sheraton period corner toilet stand, circa 1790. 43¼in. high.

Victorian marble top washstand.

Victorian marble topped walnut washstand.

19th century marquetry corner washstand.

Late 19th century marble topped mahogany washstand with satinwood inlay.

Victorian mahogany washstand on turned legs.

Victorian marble topped washstand.

George III colonial padouk-wood toilet table with divided hinged top. 2ft.1in. wide.

A mahogany powdering stand, with two drawers and undershelf, on cabriole legs, 3ft.10in. high.

Regency bow-fronted toilet cabinet with divided hinged top, 3ft. 7½in. wide.

George III mahogany square toilet stand, circa 1790, 32in. high.

William IV rosewood whatnot with barley twist supports.

Victorian inlaid walnut whatnot with barley twist supports.

Late 19th century oak whatnot.

Regency whatnot with two drawers, 26½in. wide, 15in. deep, 29½in. high.

Oriental three-tier hardwood display stand.

19th century rosewood whatnot, stencilled Taprell Holland & Son, London, 49cm. wide.

Victorian walnut whatnot of serpentine form.

Late 17th century Japanese lacquer Shodana.

Regency period mahogany whatnot of kidney shape with brass string inlay and a pierced brass gallery.

Mahogany whatnot, 1840's, 55½in. x 21in.

A Victorian walnut serpentine front three-tier whatnot with a drawer in the base, and spiral pillar supports, 1ft.11in. wide.

Carved oak square four tier whatnot with drawer in base, 1ft. 8ins.

153

WINE COOLERS

Large solid rosewood Anglo-Indian wine cooler, circa 1840, 30in. wide.

Early 18th century Sinhalese hardwood and ebony wine cooler, 2ft.7in. wide.

Regency mahogany open wine cooler, 28in. wide.

George III brass bound mahogany wine cooler with twin carrying handles, 11in. wide.

Georgian dome shaped tambour shuttered wine cooler.

Early George III octagonal mahogany wine cooler with brass bands.

A Victorian oak hexagonal cellarette on six legs, 23in. high.

George IV mahogany wine cooler, circa 1820, 2ft.5in. wide.

Late 18th century Dutch marquetry oval wine cooler, 1ft.8½in. wide.

George III mahogany wine cooler with brass liner and brass bound body, 23in. wide.

George III mahogany and brass bound wine cooler, 60cm. wide.

19th century Dutch marquetry wine cooler on cabriole legs, with brass carrying handles.

ALE GLASSES

Dwarf ale glass, circa 1750, 4in. high, bowl with wrythen molding.

Balustroid engraved ale glass with slender funnel bowl, circa 1740, 18cm. high.

Unusual cut ale wine glass, 7in. high, circa 1770.

APOTHECARY BOXES

Brass bound George III mahogany apothecary's box by Cox & Robinson.

Georgian mahogany and brass bound apothecary's box, complete with bottles.

George III shagreen cased apothecary's chest, circa 1760.

BELLS

Victorian cranberry glass bell, 12in. high.

Late 16th century silver mounted latticinio bell, 5½in. high.

Latticinio bell mounted in silver gilt, circa 1600, 9½in. high.

BEAKERS

19th century Mary Gregory beaker depicting a young girl.

North Bohemian lithyalin flared beaker by F. Egermann, circa 1830, 13.5cm. high.

Facon de Venise flared beaker, 16th/17th century, 6in. high.

BOTTLES

Good red overlay Pekin glass bottle, with decoration of birds in flowering prunus trees, circa 1800, 19.1cm. high.

Sealed wine bottle inscribed John Luke 1721, 9in. high.

German enamelled pharmacy bottle, circa 1740, 9.5cm. high.

BOWLS

English cut glass orange bowl, 12in. wide, circa 1790.

Victorian mauve carnival glass bowl.

19th century Lalique glass bowl of clear and opaque white glass, 10in. diam.

Early 18th century glass bowl, 11¼in. diam.

16th or 17th century Façon de Venise Latticinio shallow bowl, possibly Venetian, 13.5cm. diam.

An Orrefors deep bowl by Edvin Ohrstrom, 18cm. diam.

BOXES

19th century ruby glass circular box and cover, 4in.

Victorian purple slag glass tea caddy of sarcophagus form.

Late 19th century ruby glass casket, 9cm. wide.

CANDLESTICKS

Rare glass candlestick, circa 1710, 7½in. high.

Bronze and Favrile glass candlestick, by Tiffany, 8in. high.

CANDLESTICKS

Victorian ruby glass candlestick.

CANDELABRA

One of a pair of Lalique four-light candelabra, 9½in. high.

One of a pair of glass and gilt metal candelabra.

One of a pair of Regency plaster, marble and glass candlesticks.

CAR MASCOTS

Lalique glass car mascot, 1920's, 14cm. wide.

Lalique frosted glass mascot, circa 1920, 17.5cm. high.

Lalique 'Dragonfly' mascot.

CENTERPIECES

19th century cut glass and silver plated centerpiece with a glass bowl.

Coffee and cream glass centerpiece by Webb, 10¼in. diameter.

Large silvered metal Art Nouveau centerpiece, with a glass bowl, circa 1900, 45cm. high.

CHANDELIERS

Fine glass ceiling fixture by Rene Lalique, circa 1925, 10¾in. diam.

Highly colored Belgian chandelier by Muller, 61cm. high.

Superb Adam style chandelier, circa 1785.

CLARET JUGS

Victorian cut glass claret jug with silver mount, Sheffield, 1871, 28cm. high.

Victorian silver mounted clear glass 'Lotus' claret jug, 7¼in. high, by E. H. Stockwell, London, 1880.

An exceptionally fine Webb cameo glass claret jug.

CORDIAL GLASSES

Opaque twist cordial glass with funnel bowl, circa 1765, 17cm. high.

A Facon de Venise cordial glass, 17th century, 4¼in. high.

Opaque twist cordial glass, with funnel bowl, circa 1765, 14.5cm. high.

CRUETS

Late 19th century four-bottle plated cruet.

Georgian cruet bottle, complete with stopper, circa 1810.

Early George II two-bottle cruet frame by Paul de Lamerie, London, 1728, 5½in. wide, 14oz.13dwt.

158

One of a pair of unusual Punch or Custard Cups, circa 1790, 8cm. high.

Galle cameo glass stemmed honeycomb cup, 11.75cm. high, circa 1900.

New England peach blown punch cup with ribbed handle. 2¼in. high.

DECANTERS

Early 19th century ship's decanter.

19th century cut glass decanter.

Lalique glass decanter, 12in. high.

Fine and very rare Giles opaque-white decanter, 11½in. high, circa 1775.

DECANTER BOXES

Victorian, green, Mary Gregory decanter.

St. Louis decanter, 21.5cm. high, with dark blue and opaque white bands.

'Directore' mahogany decanter box, 19½in. high, circa 1912.

Traveling decanter case with glasses and decanters.

Mahogany and inlaid decanter box with four cut-glass decanters, 8½in. high.

DISHES

Mid 16th century Venetian gilt and enamelled dish, 5¾in. diam.

Victorian mauve carnival glass dish.

Webb cameo shallow circular dish, 8½in. diam.

Late 19th century gilt and enamelled glass dish.

Victorian cranberry glass jam dish in a plated stand.

Daum cameo glass dish, 14.5cm. wide, circa 1900.

DISHES, SWEETMEAT

Sweetmeat dish with three base collars, 6¼in. high, circa 1730.

Fine Anglo-Venetian sweetmeat dish, circa 1700, 3¼in. high.

Cut glass sweetmeat glass, with double ogee bowl, 6in. high.

DRINKING GLASSES

Engraved composite stemmed water glass, circa 1745, 14cm. high.

German puzzle glass, 11in. high.

Biedermeier drinking glass in Bristol blue and pink with etched banded panel, 6in. high.

EPERGNES

Unusual Victorian cranberry glass epergne with plated mounts, 11¾in. high.

EWERS

Victorian cut glass ewer.

FIGURES

Lalique opalescent glass figure 'Suzanne au Bain', 1920's, 23cm. high.

FIRING GLASSES

Masonic firing glass of drawn trumpet shape, 3¾in. high.

George III four-branch epergne by Matthew Boulton, Birmingham, 1811, 8½in. high, 64oz.2dwt.

Late 16th century Venetian amethyst baluster ewer, 9½in. high.

Rare 18th century Venetian figurine, 6in. high, in opaque white glass.

Color twist firing glass with small ovoid bowl, circa 1760, 4in. high.

EPERGNES

Victorian three-branch opaline glass epergne.

Central European gilt milchglas ewer, 5½in. high, circa 1740.

Lalique glass bracket shelf, 1930's, 26.25cm. wide.

Scottish Jacobite opaque twist firing glass, 3½in. high.

FLASKS

Manganese purple glass flask of cylindrical form, 3rd-4th century A.D., 4¼in. high.

Early flattened oviform flask, circa 1690, 5½in. high.

Central European flask with enamelled decoration, circa 1740, 17.5cm. high.

GOBLETS

Rare engraved Presentation goblet, 1824, 24.5cm. high.

Rare two-handled coin goblet, circa 1710, 6in. high.

Green goblet of bright emerald color, plain stem on spirally-molded foot, circa 1760, 13.5cm. high.

Baluster goblet with flared funnel bowl, circa 1700, 17.5cm. high.

Large fox-hunting goblet, 7¼in. high, circa 1760.

Late 16th century Facon de Venise goblet, 10¼in. high, possibly Venetian.

HUMPENS

Late 19th century enamelled humpen, 21.4cm. high.

Bohemian enamelled humpen, circa 1590, 11½in. high.

17th/18th century 'Ochsenkopf' humpen with enamelled body, 6in. high.

A rare Tiffany inkwell depicting four frogs.

Art Nouveau glass inkwell depicting a lizard emerging from a pond.

Lalique amber glass inkwell and cover, 1920's, 15.75cm. diam.

JARS

Rare red Pekin glass covered jar, decorated in relief with a dragon among clouds, 12.5cm. high.

Mount Washington Royal Flemish covered jar, 7in. high.

A large apothecary's jar, made of crude bottle glass with enamel splatter.

JUGS

Victorian cranberry glass jug with ridged decoration, 6½in. high.

Mary Gregory glass jug, 8in. high.

Victorian white slag glass jug with thistle decoration.

4th century A.D. pale green glass jug with strap handle, 3¾in. high.

Enamelled milchglas jug, Spanish or Bohemian, circa 1780, 19.3cm. high.

Mid 16th century Venetian gilt and enamelled jug, 8¾in. high.

163

Art Deco bronze table lamp, French, circa 1925, 38cm. high.

Lalique lamp in frosted glass, 1920's, 10½in. high.

Art Deco lady lamp, 15in. high.

Cut glass 'Gone with the Wind' lamp, signed L. Straus & Sons, 18½in. high.

Gilt bronze and Favrile glass three-light lily table lamp by Tiffany, 13in. high.

Le Verre Francais cameo glass lamp with shouldered domed shaped shade, 1920's, 40.5cm. high.

Tiffany spider web lamp with bronze baluster base.

Rare Webb's Burmese glass nightlight stand, circa 1887, 28cm. high

Tiffany Studio bronze table lamp, circa 1900, 63cm. high.

Lithophane desk lamp with five panel shade, 15in. high.

Mid 18th century French lacemaker's lamp, 25.5cm. high.

Tiffany Studio wisteria lamp.

LAMP SHADES

Daum cameo glass lamp-shade, 31cm. diam, circa 1900.

20th century painted glass hanging shade.

LAMP SHADES

19th century Lithophane lamp shade on brass frame, 7¼in.

LIQUEUR SETS

19th century Bohemian gilt drinking set, jug 33.5cm. high.

Etched liqueur service in glass, 1930's.

Glass decanter and six glasses with silver mounts and silver overlay, circa 1920.

LUSTRES

One of a pair of ruby glass double lustres, about 1880.

One of a pair of Bohemian overlay glass lustres, with cranberry glass body, 25cm. high.

Mid 19th century overlay lustre, one of a pair, 29.8cm. high.

MATCH-HOLDERS

A Daum match-holder of rectangular form, the pale blue frosted glass body enamelled with an Alpine scene, 4cm. high.

Glass match striker with silver container, Mappin Bros., 1896.

Small Victorian glass shoe match-holder.

One of a set of six black and white glass buttons.

Rare ormolu mounted cameo glass wall flower-bowl, 13in. diam.

Victorian clear glass jelly mold, 6in. wide.

One of a rare pair of 18th century enamelled opaque white tureens, 4½in. high.

One of a pair of St. Louis fruit door handles, 2in. diam.

One of a pair of glass butter coolers, covers and stands, 7in., circa 1790.

One of a pair of large cut urns and covers, 12½in. high, circa 1790.

Large Lalique frosted glass figure of a pigeon, 14.5cm. high, 1930's.

Rare mead glass, 4¾in. high, circa 1700.

A Tassie glass paste portrait medallion on frosted glass over blue paper, 4¼in.

Lalique glass hand mirror, 1920's, 29.75 cm. high.

16th century Italian verre eglomise picture, 4¼ x 3¼in.

166

Central European opaque opaline globular teapot and cover, mid 18th century, 16cm. wide.

Rare internally decorated textured Galle glass horn, circa 1900, 42.5cm. long.

Victorian glass ship under a glass dome.

Glass vessel, possibly Roman, 2nd century A.D., 8¾in. high.

Pair of Walter pate-de-verre bookends, 1920's, 17cm. high.

Imperial German glass beerstein with soft metal mounts.

Bohemian rose water sprinkler, circa 1850, 30.5cm. high.

L'oiseau du Feu by Lalique molded in relief with a bird woman in exotic headdress.

Pedestal stemmed stand, circa 1745, 12.5cm. high.

Pale green Roman glass vessel in the form of a bucket, 13.7cm. high.

Dated St. Louis pen-holder, 1973, 13.6cm. high, set on a paperweight base.

Pedestal stemmed champagne glass with double ogee bowl, circa 1745, 14.5cm. high.

MUGS

Rare Jacobite mug, 4¼in. high, with ribbed applied handle.

Bottle glass beer mug with white enamel splatter.

Engraved coin ale mug of bell shape, 6¾in. high.

PAPERWEIGHTS

Rare, St. Louis magnum crown paperweight, 4in. diam.

Lalique glass frog paperweight, 6.1cm. high, circa 1930.

Rare, Clichy convolvus weight, 3in. diam.

St. Louis marbrie salamander weight, 8.5cm. high.

Rare New England glass fruit weight, 3½in. wide.

St. Louis double clematis weight, 7.5cm. diam.

PIPES

Rosewater pipe with wicker overlaid glass stem.

Nailsea pink and white pipe, 12in. long.

Cranberry glass pipe with white overlay rim to bowl, 16in. long.

Cased wheeling peach blown pitcher, 5¼in. high.

Galle carved glass pitcher in smoked glass, 1890's, 15.5cm. long.

4th century pale green glass pitcher, slightly cracked, 12¾in. high.

PLAQUES

Sulphide glass cameo plaque of General Lafayette, 8.5cm. wide.

Cameo glass plaque by George Woodhall, circa 1885.

Baccarat sulphide glass cameo plaque of Charles X, 10cm. long.

PLATES

Late Victorian frosted pressed glass plate, 8in. diameter.

Early 20th century Libbey Glass salesman sample cut-glass plate, Toledo, Ohio, 6in. diam.

Venetian diamond engraved Latticinio plate, late 16th century, 16.5cm. diam.

Victorian plate commemorating Gladstone.

Late 19th century Eastern United States cut-glass plate in cornucopia and crosshatch patterns.

19th century light blue slag glass plate with basket weave edge.

POTS

Lithyalin pounce-pot with pewter mount, 2¾in. high.

Daum etched and applied cameo glass pot and cover, 12.5cm. high, circa 1910.

Unusual Pekin glass brush-pot, thinly cased in red, engraved mark of Qianlong, 17.5cm. high.

RATAFIA GLASSES

Ratafia glass with a narrow straight sided funnel bowl molded to two thirds of its height, circa 1745.

Rare Jacobite opaque twist ratafia glass with ogee bowl, circa 1765, 18cm. high.

Ratafia wine glass, circa 1750, 7¼in. high.

ROEMERS

17th century Rhenish roemer of light green metal, 14cm. high.

17th century Netherlandish green tinted roemer with cup-shaped bowl, 20.5cm. high.

17th century large Roemer, Rhenish, 10in. high.

RUMMERS

Large engraved rummer, early 19th century, 8¼in. high.

Battle of the Boyne commemorative rummer, 1690, 6in. high.

Sunderland bridge rummer, 6½in. high, circa 1820.

Daum scent bottle and stopper, 5in. high, signed.

Guerlain 'Mitsouko' glass bottle and stopper.

Webb double overlay globular scent bottle and silver screw cover, 4in. high.

Rare sulphide scent bottle of flattened circular form, 7cm. diam.

Delvaux enamelled scent bottle and stopper, 1920's, 11.25cm. high.

Decorated clear glass perfume bottle and stopper, 13.75cm. high.

SNUFF BOTTLES

Late 19th century interior painted glass snuff bottle.

Red overlay glass bottle with jade stopper.

Interior-painted rock crystal snuff bottle and coral stopper, 2¼in. high.

Interior-painted snuff bottle by Ten Yu-t'ien.

Chinese opaque white glass overlay snuff bottle, red overlay, with coral glass and pearl stopper.

Rare enamelled glass snuff bottle by Ku Yueh Hsuan.

TANKARDS

Central European enamelled milchglas miniature tankard, 3½in. high, circa 1750.

Large glass tankard with scalloped foot, 6in. high, circa 1750.

Ruby glass tankard with silver hinged cover, 8in. high.

Mid 18th century German engraved pewter-mounted tankard, 9½in. high.

Central European enamelled tankard and cover, circa 1750, 24cm. high.

Rare Bohemian enamelled blue-glass tankard, 6¼in. high, circa 1608.

TANTALUS

Plated tantalus frame with two decanters.

Small Victorian tantalus.

Oak decanter box, circa 1880, with Bramah lock, 13¾in. wide.

TAPERSTICKS

Pedestal stemmed taperstick, 5½in. high, circa 1730.

A rare taperstick, the nozzle set on inverted baluster air twist stem, 6½in. high.

Glass pedestal taperstick, 6½in. high, circa 1745.

16th or 17th century Facon
de Venise tazza, 22.5cm.
diam.

Venetian filigree tazza,
circa 1600, 6¾in. diam.

Ormolu mounted amethyst and
opaline tazza, circa 1830, 11cm.
high.

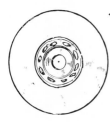

17th century Venetian tazza,
8in. diam.

**Late 16th century
Facon de Venise enam-
elled glass tazza, 5.9in.
high.**

17th century Venetian
tazza, 2in. high, 6¼in. diam.

TUMBLERS

Baccarat armorial tumbler
with enamelled coat of
arms, 9.5cm. high.

Engraved glass tumbler,
4¾in. high, circa 1790.

Venetian enamelled tumbler,
18th century, 4½in. high.

Bohemian amber-flashed hexagonal tumbler, circa 1850, 14cm.
high, with engraved sides.

Bohemian tumbler engra-
ved with cupids and alle-
gorial scenes, circa 1730,
10.2cm. high.

Austrian armorial cut-glass cylindrical tumbler, circa 1835, 9cm.
high.

VASES

Pate de verre small oviform vase, 3¼in. diam.

A Brocard enamelled cylindrical vase with stylised cornflower sprays, 16.5cm. high.

Very rare miniature opaque white globular vase, 2½in. high, circa 1770.

Victorian orange carnival glass vase, 10in. high.

Orrefors engraved glass vase, 18.75cm. high, 1940's.

J. F. Christy oviform vase designed by Richard Redgrave, 1847, 15cm. high.

De Vez glass landscape vase, circa 1900-10, 22.25cm. high.

Pate-de-cristal vase by Francois Decorchemont in deep blue glass, 25.5cm. high, circa 1910.

One of a pair of portrait overlay green glass vases, circa 1850, 33.8cm. high.

Degue overlaid and etched glass vase, 1920's, 40.5cm. high.

Burgun and Schwerer wheel carved vase in bluebell purple and gilt.

Very rare Staffordshire opaque white enamelled glass vase, 5in. high, circa 1760.

One of a pair of Art Nouveau silver overlay blue vases.

Signed Sabino vase, circa 1920, with fish motif, 8in. high.

An escalier de cristal ormolu mounted cameo vase, 16.5cm. high.

Large Mary Gregory vase of pink glass.

One of a pair of flower encrusted bottle vases.

Edelzinn pewter mounted vase, circa 1900, 25cm. high.

Durand blue iridescent glass vase, 18.8cm. high, circa 1910.

Pate de cristal Argy Rousseau vase, 10in. high.

Stevens & Williams cameo oviform vase, 7½in. high.

18th century pale blue ground bottle vase, 8¾in. high.

Good gilt and enamelled Marcel Goupy vase, 24.5cm. high, 1920's.

German blue overlay vase by F. Zach, circa 1857, 22cm. high.

175

BOHEMIAN

One of a pair of Bohemian overlay trumpet shaped vases.

Pair of 19th century red colored Bohemian glass vases.

One of a pair of Bohemian ruby overlay glass vases, 10in. high.

DAUM

Daum cameo glass vase of teardrop form, 30.25cm. high. circa 1900.

Daum etched, carved and enamelled glass vase, circa 1900, 13.5cm. high.

Signed Daum Nancy vase in orange, cream and green, 6½in. high.

GALLE

Mounted Galle cameo glass vase, circa 1890's, 7.75cm. high.

Galle, etched and carved cameo glass vase, 19.5cm. high, circa 1900.

Small Galle cameo glass vase, 7.75cm. high, circa 1900.

LALIQUE

Lalique frosted glass vase, relief molded, 1930's, 13.5cm. high.

Heavy Lalique frosted glass vase, 1930's, 25.5cm. high.

Good Lalique 'grasshopper' vase, 27cm. high, 1920's.

176

LEGRAS

A Legras cameo glass vase of quatrefoil shape, the frosted glass body overlaid in purple, 13cm. high.

Legras etched and internally decorated glass vase, 39cm. high, 1920's.

VASES

Legras etched and internally decorated glass vase, 1920's, 31.5cm. high.

LOETZ

Loetz iridescent glass vase, 14.25cm. high, circa 1900.

Loetz iridescent glass vase, 18.5cm. high, circa 1900.

One of a pair of Loetz iridescent vases.

MULLER FRERES

Muller Freres cameo glass vase, circa 1900, 19.5cm. high.

Large Muller Freres cameo glass landscape vase, circa 1900, 55cm. high.

Muller Freres carved cameo glass vase, circa 1890, 18.5cm. high.

PEKIN

Pekin overlay glass vase of bottle form from the Qianlong period.

Unusual translucent white Pekin glass vase, carved with landscape panels, 21.2cm. high.

Well carved Imperial yellow Pekin glass vase of beaker form carved with blossom, 20.5cm. high.

VASES STOURBRIDGE

Late 19th century vase attributed to Joshua Hodgetts, Stourbridge, white on amethyst glass, 27.5cm. high.

Stourbridge ovoid vase enamelled on a crackle ground, 10in. high.

Stourbridge cameo glass vase, 5in. high, central band with turquoise 'jeweling'.

TIFFANY

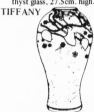

Tiffany Favrile iridescent millefiori oviform vase, 6in. high.

A rare Jack-in-the-pulpit Tiffany peacock iridescent glass vase, 1900.

Gold and yellow iridescent vase by Louis C. Tiffany, 38cm. high, circa 1900.

WEBB

Cameo glass vase by Thos. Webb & Sons, 10.8cm. high.

Webb three color cameo glass vase.

Late 19th century Webb cameo glass vase, 9.5cm. high.

WINDOWS

15th century English stained glass roundel, 4½in. diam.

Early 20th century stained glass window depicting a peacock, 22in. high.

French stained glass panel showing the Risen Christ, dated 1542, 66 x 56cm.

Baluster wine glass with funnel bowl, circa 1710, 14cm. high.

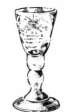

German Royal commemorative glass, engraved with a horseman.

Engraved color twist wine glass in the Jacobite taste, circa 1770, 14.5cm. high.

Unusual Lynn wine glass, 5¾in. high, circa 1750.

17th century Facon de Venise wine glass, 6¼in. high.

Multi-knopped air twist wine glass, circa 1750, 6¼in. high.

Beilby enamelled glass with bell bowl, 6½in. high, circa 1765.

Incised twist bright emerald green wine glass, 1750, 13.3cm. high.

Canary twist wine glass with hammer molded bowl, circa 1760, 6in. high.

Very rare wine glass, circa 1740, 7½in. high.

Dutch engraved whaling glass, 7¼in. high, circa 1750.

Facon de Venise winged wine glass, Low Countries, 17th century, 18cm. high.

19th century Swiss gold musical box, 2¼in. long.

George II gold five guineas young head, 1729, uncirculated.

Mid 16th century Italian gold relief of the Entombment, 2¾in. high.

Gold watch key in the form of a five draw spy glass, circa 1810.

Mid 18th century shell and gold snuff box, Paris, unmarked.

Qajar gold and enamel Qalian bowl, 6.7cm.

English gold vinaigrette, early 19th century, ¾in. high.

Faberge two color gold engine turned box.

Continental gold and enamel pill box.

18 carat gold presentation flask given to General Buller.

Continental gold and enamel box, mid 19th century, 2½in. long.

18th century gold brooch with ruby eyes.

Gold vinaigrette with citrine cover.

Two of a set of five 17th century gold buttons, 1¼in. long.

Mid 18th century gold box by Francois Marteau, France.

K'ang Hsi rhinoceros libation cup, 4¼in. high.

One of a rare pair of hornbill skulls, 7½in. long.

Early 18th century rhinoceros horn libation cup, 3½in. high.

A fine commemorative silver-mounted horn beaker.

Carved horn, gold, enamel, and mother-of-pearl hair ornament by Lalique, circa 1900, 17.5cm. wide.

Early 19th century horn snuff mull, 5in. long.

Victorian brass and horn gong complete with hammer.

Good brass mounted cowhorn powder flask, 10¼in. long.

One of a fine pair of buffalo horn armchairs.

Tiny Ozaki Kokusai study of an owl in staghorn.

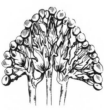

Good carved horn, enamel and moonstone hair comb, circa 1900, 13.1cm. wide.

Bohemian carved staghorn powder flask.

19th century three case red lacquer inro.

Fine 19th century Japanese five case gold lacquer inro.

Late 17th century four case inro, unsigned.

Two case wood inro.

19th century three case red lacquer inro, inlaid with pewter.

19th century four case inro, inlaid with pewter and aogai.

19th century four case lacquer inro.

18th century gold lacquer four case inro, signed Toyo.

A good five case black lacquered inro signed Inagawa.

19th century four case lacquer inro, 7cm. high.

19th century four case lacquer and ivory inro by Shomosai, 8.25cm. high.

19th century lacquered ivory inro, 9cm. high.

Single valve radio, circa 1925, with original valve and tuning coil.

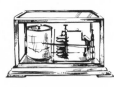

Barograph by Short and Mason.

18th century French brass nautical compass and folding sundial.

Danish magneto desk telephone, circa 1920, 1ft.1in. high.

English Imperial model 'B' typewriter, circa 1915, 1ft. wide.

Victorian cased set of scales complete with weights, 11½in., high.

Ship's binnacle by Hughes & Son, London, 125cm. high.

Magnificent microscope made by Alexis Magny, circa 1750, for Madame de Pompadour.

Columbia printing press, with distinctive golden eagle crest.

Brass equinoctial dial by Pizzala, London, 13.5cm. diam.

Dollands chest type brass monocular microscope, circa 1840.

Early 19th century set of drawing instruments, 5in. long.

INSTRUMENTS

Mahogany 19th century compass.

Late 19th century American J.H. Bunnell & Co., brass recording telegraph.

Eastman Studio scale by Kodak, New York, 9in. wide.

Early Culpeper microscope, 14in. high, with drawer of objectives and slides.

Unusual London Stereoscopic Co. double stereoscopic viewer, circa 1880, 1ft.8in. high.

Early 19th century George Adams waywiser, 4ft.4in. high, with cast iron handles.

Unusual jockey's scale, circa 1880, with mahogany seat.

Early 20th century orrery, 3ft.5in. wide, with sectioned diagram.

Ship's Bridge Telegraph in brass, 105cm. high, signed 'Bloctube Controls'.

Good brass theodolite, 350mm. high.

Two-day marine chronometer by Breguet et Cie, dial 8cm. diam.

Late 19th century galvanometer.

184

Late 19th century sextant with brass frame.

19th century portable orrery by W. Jones, 195mm. diameter.

Beechwood and brass plough plane by J. Mosele, Bloomsbury, London.

Brass surveying instrument by George Beck, late 18th century, 150mm. radius.

Late 19th century English Walters brass recording telegraph.

Sheraton mahogany terrestial globe, circa 1825, 18in. high.

19th century brass astronomical telescope on a steel stand by Jas. Parker

Early 19th century two-day marine chronometer by Parkinson & Frodsham, London, 4¾in. diam.

Early 20th century English Griffin & Tatlock wimshurst machine, 1ft.3½in. high.

Silver letter balance, Birmingham, 1949, 3¼in. high.

A. Abrahams & Co. brass binocular microscope, 1ft. 6in. high, 1873.

Bronze sundial of horizontal pedestal type.

Cast iron fronted painted wooden Mail Box, circa 1910, with brass lock, 29in. high.

19th century Iranian steel cat with silver and gold harness.

Black-lacquered metal coal bin.

Fine cast iron figure of a classical woman, circa 1810, on 5½in. square walnut base.

Victorian cast iron cooking pot with a medallion on the side.

Late 19th century articulated iron crayfish, 9in. long.

Victorian cast iron stove in working order.

Unusual 18th or 19th century iron Buddhist traveling shrine.

Victorian cast iron footman, with shaped feet.

Good strong iron box, circa 1670, 2ft. 8½in. wide.

A large pair of 19th century sheep shears.

Early 20th century inlaid Komei iron dish showing a warrior, 8¾in. diameter.

A pair of German iron candlesticks, circa 1910, 21cm. high.

Fireside crane with two hinges, 26½in. long, circa 1730, initialled S. W.

Iron hand-held fish harpoon, circa 1720.

Pair of Japanese damascened metal stirrups.

A large 19th century polished steel griddle.

One of a pair of Iranian steel doves, damascened in gold, 9½in. high.

Wrought iron gate, 1860's, 78 x 40in.

A wrought iron rushlight and candleholder on a wooden base, 17th century.

Unusual painted, gilded and enamelled coal container.

English cast-iron, walnut and marble occasional table with diamond registration mark for June 1845.

Wrought iron fire basket.

One of a mid 19th century pair of cast-iron garden urns, 45¾in. high.

**Early 17th century
South German ivory
relief, 2¾in. high.**

**16th century Flemish
or Northern French
ivory memento Mori,
2¾in. high.**

One of a pair of carved
ivory sphinx candlesticks,
11½in. high, early 19th
century.

**Early 18th century Italian
ivory oval plaque, 4¼in.
long.**

18th century Dieppe car-
ved ivory group, 3½in. high.

Turned ivory mortar,
6in. high, circa 1800.

**German silver colored
metal and ivory tankard,
8½in. high.**

An ivory fowl, 16.5cm.
high.

South German ivory group,
4½in. high, circa 1600.

**Late 19th century
ivory tusk vase,
25.5cm. high.**

Japanese carved ivory sectional takarabune, 52cm. long.

One of a pair of Ch'ien
Lung ivory lanterns and
stands, 15¼in. high.

19th century Japanese carved ivory figure.

Mid 18th century English ivory relief, 2¾in. high.

19th century Rajasthani in ivory, 3½in. high.

17th century Flemish or Dieppe ivory relief, 1¾in. high.

Japanese carved ivory group of fisherman and child, 13½in. long.

One of a pair of ivory bottles with heads as stoppers.

Carved ivory female head by Julien Dillens, 55cm. high, circa 1900.

Harpoon support in walrus ivory.

Carved ivory figure of Hsi Wang Mu, 34cm. high, Chinese, circa 1900.

Japanese ivory Okimono sectional group, signed Kyokumei, late 19th century, 7in. high.

18th century Italian carved ivory jug, 48cm. high.

Large German jeweled and ivory group of a camel led by a blackamoor, 16½in. wide.

Rare ivory bottle carved in the shape of a reclining lady.

Walther carved ivory figure of a young girl, 8.76cm. high, 1930's.

Late 19th century Japanese sectional ivory sword, 127cm. long.

Fine Nobuaki ivory group, circa 1900, 18.5cm. high.

Interesting ivory casket, partly 15th century, partly 19th century, 10in. long.

Preiss carved ivory figure of a little boy, 14.75cm. high, 1930's.

Early 9th century Carolingian ivory plaque from the cover of a manuscript gospel, 7½in. high.

18th century Italian ivory devotional relief, 7½in. high.

Japanese ivory figurine, 6¾in. high.

Louis XVI ivory carnet de bal.

Pair of ivory tusks decorated with mother-of-pearl, ivory and hardstone, on carved wood stands.

19th century mid European ivory tankard with silver mounts, 12½in. high.

Mottled white and brown jade bottle.

Qianlong mottled white jade koro and cover, 6¾in. wide.

Pale gray jade hexagonal vase, 4¼in. high.

Chrysanthemum dish in dark green jade, 10in. wide.

One of a pair of jadeite parrots, 7in. long.

18th century Chinese celadon jade bowl, 23.5cm. wide.

Celadon jade Ting, 8¾in. high.

Ch'ien Lung grayish white jade globular jar and cover.

Fine quality 18th century jade brush washer.

One of a pair of jade Phoenixes.

Pale gray foliate dish in jade, 7¾in. diam.

Pale green jade figure of a lady, 12½in. high.

Cornflower blue sapphire surrounded by diamonds.

Pair of antique diamond earrings.

Platinum set single stone diamond ring, main diamond weighs 1.70 carats.

Mid Victorian diamond and emerald brooch.

Oval hardstone cameo, signed Verge, circa 1800, 7cm. high.

Victorian diamond and pearl brooch-pendant.

Hexagonal silver brooch, 2.5cm. high, circa 1900.

Art Nouveau hair ornament set with rose diamonds and beryls.

Diamond three row crescent brooch, late 19th century.

A pair of silver and enamel cufflinks, 2.25cm. high, circa 1900.

Mirror locket in Art Nouveau style in yellow gold set with turquoise matrix.

Dunand eggshell lacquer pendant panel, 13.8cm. long.

18ct. gold diamond cluster ring.

Victorian diamond, gold and enamel necklace.

Lady's diamond set dress ring, centre stone 1.49carat.

Elegant bow brooch of circular cut diamonds.

Lalique gold and enamel brooch, 3.4cm. wide, circa 1900.

Pair of antique pear shaped diamond pendant earrings.

Fine antique diamond pendant surmounted by a ribbon bow on chain.

Gold and enamel Lalique brooch, 4cm. high, circa 1900.

Liberty & Co. plique-a-jour enamel pendant, circa 1905, 4.5cm. long.

Platinum set diamond pendant on a fine chain.

Louis XVI rose diamond and enamel necklace.

Gold and enamel diamond set watch and chatelaine, 1790, 43.5cm. diameter.

Late 19th century octagonal lead jardiniere cast with mice and other field animals, 21½in. diam.

18th century lead cistern, dated 1764, 39in. wide.

One of a pair of garden urns of lead, 2ft.6in. high.

Naja by Jean Dunand in patinated lead.

One of a set of four circular lead plaques of classical scenes, 70cm. diam.

18th century English lead figure of a putto with one hand on his head, 81cm. high.

White marble and ivory figure, signed E. Seger, circa 1920, 16½in. high.

One of a set of four 20th century lead peacocks, 24½in. high.

19th century lead figure of Pan, 49in. high.

One of a set of four mid 19th century lead garden figures, 25in. high.

Lead plaque of Napoleon Bonaparte on horseback, circa 1810, 9½in. high.

18th century English lead figure of a naked youth holding cymbals, 135cm. high.

One of a pair of ormolu mounted verde antico marble urns, mid 19th century, 16½in. high.

Late 18th century neoclassic Italian marble trough, 26¾in. wide.

One of a pair of late 17th century baroque Italian white marble seated lions, 10½in. high.

Marble bust of a lady by Sir John Steell, 23in. high.

White marble group of Leda and the Swan, probably French, mid 19th century.

17th century North Italian marble negro head, 14in. high.

Black conglomerate marble head from the T'ang dynasty, 9½in. high.

Venetian/Byzantine 14th century Verona red marble cistern, 64cm. wide.

One of a large pair of white marble seated Buddhistic lions, 44in. high.

Mid 19th century marble bust of a lady by Joseph Mitchell, 20½in., high.

Italian marble group of the Virgin and Child, circa 1400, 24½in. high.

Marble portrait bust of Helen Boucher, 42cm. high, circa 1930.

Rare George III satinwood toilet mirror, 1ft.5½in. wide.

Black lacquer toilet mirror with chinoiserie decoration

Early 18th century Venetian giltwood mirror, one of a pair, 4ft.5in. high.

Guernardeau patinated metal Art Nouveau mirror frame, circa 1900, 41.5cm. high.

Large Art Deco mirror frame, early 1920's.

George II walnut and parcel gilt mirror, circa 1740, 2ft.7in. wide.

Good George II parcel gilt walnut mirror, 2ft.3in. wide.

Walnut cheval mirror, 1850's, 78in. high.

Early George IIi giltwood mirror, 47¾in. high.

Late 17th century Florentine giltwood mirror, 3ft.7in. high.

Good Regency gilt wood convex mirror, 2ft.2in. diameter, circa 1810.

George II giltwood mirror, 2ft. 6in. wide, circa 1730.

Victorian mahogany dressing table mirror.

Copper and enamel mirror, circa 1900, 40in. wide.

Toilet mirror by Gordon Russell, circa 1930, 26½in. high.

One of a pair of Chinese Chippendale giltwood miniature wall mirrors, painted with an Oriental scene.

One of a pair of Thuringian mirror frames, circa 1880, 99cm. high.

Satinwood cheval mirror, 57½in. high, circa 1900.

Sue and Mare Art Deco gilt bronze mirror frame, 1923, 25.6cm. high.

Rare North Italian painted and giltwood mirror, 2ft.1in. wide, circa 1700.

Italian Art Nouveau mirror with carved pearwood frame, 92½in. high.

William and Mary oyster veneered walnut wall mirror, 2ft. high, circa 1685.

Good Regency giltwood mirror, circa 1810, 3ft. 2in. high.

Rosewood and mahogany mirror by Louis Majorelle, 67in. high.

MISCELLANEOUS

Victorian heart shaped
pin cushion, 7in. long.

Rare George III feather
picture, 28in. x 33in.

Rare postcard
depicting a
balloon flight.

One of a pair of doors by Jean
Dunand for a Normandie liner.

One of a rare pack of
French playing cards,
about 1819.

An Indo Persian saddle
of mauve velvet covered
with gold bullion.

19th century hip
bath with brass
fittings.

Stevengraph, complete
with original titled
mount 'Iroquois'.

Very fine Sand Bell,
Victorian, 9½in.
high.

17th century Venetian
sedan chair with carved
gilt wood frame and
leather panels. $1,750

Preserved human head
with tattoo ornament,
7½in. high.

Victorian carved mahogany
fire surround with mirrored
overmantel.

Fine early Bing gauge '0' live steam tank engine no. 3410.

Early gauge 'Three' Ernst Plank live steam boxed train set, circa 1905.

Fine apprentice made model of a ship steam engine, 10 x 15in.

Good 19th century model of a coal-fired horse drawn steam fire engine, 14in. long, in a glass showcase.

Gauge '0' clockwork 4-4-0 locomotive no. 1924, sold with tender and coach, circa 1920.

French prisoner-of-war bone ship model, circa 1800, 10¾in. long.

Coin-operated working model of Stephenson's 'rocket' in glass case.

Unusual spirit-fired live steam launch, 18¼in. long.

A well constructed six wheeled show-man's mobile workshop trailer, 2ft. 2in. wide.

An American cold painted cast iron 'Bucking Mule' money box, 8½in. long.

Unusual musical tinplate money bank, 4¾in. high.

A cold painted American cast iron money box 'always did 'spise a mule', 10in. long.

Late 19th century American owl cast iron money bank, 7¾in. high.

Late 19th century cast-iron 'Swiss Chalet' money box, 7in. high.

Late 19th century American cat and mouse money box, 8½in. high.

20th century English cast iron Artillery bank in the form of a cannon which fires coins into a pill box.

Late 19th century American Punch and Judy money box, 7½in. high.

A late 19th century American cold painted cast iron money box in the form of a soldier who fires a penny into a tree stump.

Late 19th century American monkey and barrel-organ cast iron money bank, 6½in. high.

Unusual German 'Royal Trick' elephant tinplate mechanical money bank, 6in. long.

A 20th century English cold painted cast iron 'Stumps Speaker' money box, 10in. high.

Ebonised musical box
which plays ten tunes.

English 'Puck' phonograph,
circa 1905.

19th century singing bird
box.

Interesting Robeyphone
gramophone, English,
1915-25, 10in. turntable.

Swiss flute basse, voix celeste, inter-
changeable cylinder musical box by
Langdorff et Fils, circa 1850.

Operaphone gramo-
phone, circa 1925-
30, 3ft. high.

Mini record player
with case, circa
1910, 8in. high.

Early 20th century Swiss Britannia
disc musical box, 1ft.9½in. high.

Good Edison Amberola
VIII phonograph, Ameri-
can, circa 1913.

Early 20th century sym-
phonium disc musical box,
1ft. wide, German.

Edison Home phonograph
with Bettini attachment.

Early 20th century German
symphonium disc musical
box, 10½in. wide.

MUSICAL INSTRUMENTS

Small cornet by Boosey & Co., London, circa 1880, 7½in. long.

Symphonium by C. Wheatstone, London, circa 1830, 2¾in. high.

Late 19th century Faience model horn decorated in green, orange and blue on a white ground, probably French.

French Hurdy Gurdy by Caron, Versailles, circa 1770, with S-shaped iron handle, 26in. long.

Rare Salterio Tedesco by Gion Zino, Brescia 1692, maximum length 3ft. 11in.

French pedal harp by Cousineau, Paris, circa 1775, 5ft. 3¼in. high.

English serpent by D'Almaine & Co., London, early 19th century, length 7ft. 7in.

Attractive Dital harp by Edward Light, London, the simulated rosewood body in seven sections, circa 1815, 34½in. high.

Edinburgh made set of bagpipes with the Gordon tartan.

Late 17th century Italian virginals in a leather bound case.

Late 17th century Cor de Chasse, 165½in. long.

202

Japanese ivory netsuke of a puppy pulling a string, signed.

Carved ivory netsuke of a monkey in a shell.

Mid 19th century ivory netsuke, signed Mitsusada.

Unsigned 19th century wood netsuke.

Netsuke of Tamamo No Mae and the Fox with Nine Tails, 2in. high.

19th century ivory netsuke of a rat-catcher, signed Hansaku.

Netsuke group of a bearded man and an ox, 2in high.

Ivory netsuke of Longarms, 3in. high.

Superb horse and foal netsuke by Rantei.

19th century trick netsuke by Tomomasa.

Carved ivory netsuke of a cow lying down.

Ivory mask netsuke.

PEWTER

One of a pair of William and Mary capstan salts, 2¼in. high, circa 1690.

Liberty & Co. 'Tudric' pewter and enamel biscuit box and cover, 14cm. high, after 1903.

Fine late William and Mary posset pot in pewter, 9½in. wide, circa 1695.

Large Maurel Art Nouveau patinated metal jardiniere, circa 1900, 29cm. high.

Pewter cornucopia chariot with Cupid, circa 1880, 10in. high.

Large WMF pewter jardiniere, 32.5cm. wide, circa 1900.

Late 18th century German flask, 8¾in. high, in pewter.

WMF pewter candlestick, 26.25cm. high, circa 1900.

Early Georgian pewter tankard by Richard Going, 6½in. high, circa 1725.

A fine wavy-edged plate by Thomas Chamberlain, 9⅛in. diam., circa 1760.

Rare, William & Mary pewter candlestick, 6½in. high, circa 1690.

Queen Anne plate with gadrooned border by John Shorey, 9in. diam., circa 1710.

A rare trencher salt of bulbous type with incised reeding around waist, 1¾in. high, circa 1700.

Charles II porringer of booged type, 7.1/8in. diameter, circa 1680.

Small, pewter Continental lidded tankard.

Fine, small, Charles II 'wriggled work' tankard by L.A., 6in. high, circa 1680.

Liberty & Co. 'Tudric' pewter stand with glass liner, circa 1905, 16.5cm. high.

An attractive strawberry dish, the booge fluted into eighteen petal-shaped panels, 5in. diam., circa 1720.

Polished pewter water jug with cane handle by Liberty & Co., circa 1905.

A Bernese stegkanne by Daniel Hemman from the first half of the 18th century, 31.5cm. high.

Silvered metal plaque 'The Spirit of Christmas', by John G. Hardy, circa 1895, 41cm. long.

Deep-welled 'Mount Edge-cumbe' bowl with broad rim, 14in. diam., circa 1640.

Set of seven waved-edged pewter dishes, 9½in. across, by George Beeston.

Deep-welled 'Mount Edgecumbe' bowl with broad rim, 14in. diam., circa 1640.

PEWTER

Porringer with finely pierced and shaped ear by Adam Banckes of Chester, 7½in. diam., circa 1700.

German silvered metal box, circa 1905, 16cm. wide.

Large metal tazza, 44cm. high, WMF marks, 1900-1910.

A slit top spoon with maker's mark ?L. stamped in bowl, 6in. long, 16th century.

Gilbert Parks pewter charger, 20¼in. diam., dated 1899.

Edelzinn pewter jug, circa 1901, 33.5cm. high.

Liberty & Co. 'Tudric' pewter tea and coffee service, circa 1910.

Rare Saxon pewter tankard, probably by Hans Wildt the younger, 6¼in. high, circa 1590-1600.

Bud baluster measure of half pint capacity, by John Carr, touch dated 1697, 5¼in. tall.

A Queen Anne tankard by Adam Banks of Milngate, the drum encircled by a single fillet at waist, 17.5cm high, circa 1710.

Kayserzinn pewter jug, circa 1905, 26.75cm. high.

Rare lidless pewter tavern pot, by IG, 5in. high, circa 1720-30.

Upright oak Broadwood
'Manxman' piano, circa
1900, 56½in. wide.

Upright iron framed
piano by John
Brinsmead, London.

Square piano by John
Broadwood, London,
1795, 5ft.2½in. long.

Important spinet by
James Scoular, London
circa 1765, length of
back 73in.

Strohmenger painted
satinwood baby grand
piano and duet stool.

20th century red lacquer
chinoiserie baby grand
piano by Bluthner.

PIPES

Early 19th century block
Meerschaum pipe with
silver mounts, bowl 9½in.
long.

Erotic Meerschaum pipe
holder, about 1885,
10½in. long.

Carved Meerschaum
in the form of a tiger
and a snake in com-
bat, 6in. long.

Oriental metal table
opium pipe with
cloisonne decorated
body, 9in. high.

Meerschaum pipe with
negro head bowl and
top hat extension,
cased.

Edwardian pipe with
silver mounts, 1907.

Mid 19th century American quilted patchwork coverlet, 72 x 90in.

Patchwork quilt with central flower medallion, circa 1820, 108in. square.

American patriotic coverlet in cotton sewn to give the effect of the American flag, 7ft.6in. square, circa 1880.

Late 19th century bedcover made from officer's uniforms, 91½ x 77in.

Late 19th century American Victorian crazy quilt with matching shams, 76in. square.

Early 19th century patchwork quilt in hexagons, square and triangles, 94 x 87in.

Late 19th century embroidered bedspread on a midnight-blue satin ground, 99 x 85in.

Late 19th/early 20th century American patchwork quilt in navy blue and white triangles, 75½in. square.

18th century Portuguese coverlet, couchwork on Chinese silk, 100 x 80in.

Chintz patchwork bedcover with square central medallion and broad border, 65 x 60in.

Early 18th century embroidered bedcover sold with three pillowcases with white cotton ground.

Mid 18th century English 'Italian quilted' bedcover in white cotton, 103 x 93½in.

Herat Beluchistan rug,
circa 1900, 5ft. 11in.
x 4ft. 3in.

Qashqai horse cover,
5ft. 4in. x 4ft. 1in.,
circa 1900.

Beluchistan Bakhtari
prayer rug, circa 1900,
4ft. x 3ft.

Very fine silk Qum rug,
7ft. x 4ft. 8in.

A Yomut Ozmulduk,
2ft. 5in. x 4ft., circa
1850.

Pictorial Kirman rug,
circa 1920, 2ft. 10in.
x 2ft.

Dyrnak Yomut rug,
10ft. 7in. x 6ft. 8in.,
circa 1900.

Beluchistan rug in good
condition, 4ft. 5in. x
3ft. 5in., circa 1880.

Armenian Kelim rug,
circa 1880, 8ft. 10in.
x 5ft. 2in.

Mid 19th century South
Persian antique Quash-
gai bag, 0.61 x 0.61m.

Kashan pictorial
rug, 2ft.7in. x 1ft.
11in.

Attractive Templeton's
carpet, by Charles Rennie
Mackintosh, circa 1910,
455cm. x 358cm.

SAMPLERS

Needlework sampler by Sally Oliver, 1801, of Upper Beverley, America, 19½ x 21in.

Unusual circular map sampler, 1804.

Needlework family record by Martha A. Chamberlain, Westmoreland, New Hampshire, 1833, 17 x 21in.

18th century needlework sampler by Mary Adamson, 1781, 31cm. high.

Sampler worked with a house and a verse by Maria Norman, 1832, 16 x 12in.

Sampler by Elizabeth Brook, 1813, 15 x 11½in.

SEALS

Early 18th century gold combined watch key and seal.

Brass seal from the Hollandia.

Late Victorian silver and agate fob seal.

Faberge gold mounted desk seal with triple head.

Rare English medieval jet seal, 2in. diam., 11th/12th century.

Fine silver and rock crystal swivel seal, 1½in. high, Dutch, circa 1740.

Shibayama box and cover, signed Masasada, 3¼in. wide.

Japanese Shibayama and silver filigree tray, circa 1900, 30cm. wide.

19th century Japanese Shibayama and ivory brush pot, 5in. high.

One of a pair of Japanese Masayasu Shibayama vases, circa 1900.

Fine quality Japanese Shibayama incense burner.

Japanese carved Shibayama and ivory figure, circa 1900, 15.5cm. high.

American kettle advertising sign in metal with iron handle, 22½in. high.

Pub mirror with red and gilt lettering in original molded plaster frame, 26½ x 35in.

19th century Victorian butcher's shop sign of a carved bull's head, 13in. high, made of oak.

Coloured poster for a Chaplin film 'Mademoiselle Charlot.

Late 19th century carved wood tobacco sign, 3ft.8in. high.

Victoria and Albert saxe-Gotha Royal Coat of Arms on wooden shield, 7½in. high.

BASKETS
CAKE

A fine pierced silver cake basket by Paul de Lamerie, 1731.

George III oval shaped cake basket, 14¼in. wide, by Chawner & Emes, London, 1796, 21oz.11dwt.

Regency oblong cake basket by Benjamin and James Smith, 1810, 47oz., 13¼in. long.

SUGAR

Silver sugar basket by Peter and Anne Bateman, 4½oz.

Small George III pierced silver basket by Robt. Hennell, 1787, 4oz.

Early 19th century German oval sugar vase on foot, 7oz.10dwt.

SWEETMEAT

George III silver gilt metal oval sweetmeat basket, 6¾in. wide, by Vere & Lutwyche, London, 1767, 6oz.5dwt.

George III boat-shaped sweetmeat basket, 6in. wide, by Henry Chawner, London, 1791, 8oz.3dwt.

George III octagonal silver footed sweetmeat basket, London, 1794, by Robt. Hennell.

BEAKERS

17th century German silver gilt beaker, 2½in. high, 2oz.18dwt.

Silver gilt and niello beaker, by E. C., Moscow, 1846, 6.7cm. high.

Early 18th century German silver gilt beaker by Esajas Busch, Augsburg, 1705, 3¼in. high, 4oz.12dwt.

BELLS   SILVER

18th century Dutch table
bell, 4¼in. high, by Jan
Bot, Amsterdam, 1748,
8oz.18dwt.

**Table bell by Elkington
& Co. Ltd., Birmingham,
1890, 11.5cm. high.**

George IV coronation bell,
5in. high, by T. Phipps &
E. Robinson, London,
1820, 6oz. 19dwt.

BISCUIT CONTAINERS

Circular biscuit barrel,
5½in. high, London,
1931, 17oz.6dwt.

Art Nouveau lantern style
biscuitiere with glass
liner, 1900.

**George III circular biscuit
barrel, 6¾in. high, by
Solomon Hougham, Lon-
don, 1801, 7oz.14dwt.**

BOWLS

Late 17th century Dutch
brandy bowl, by Thos.
Sibrand Hicht, Dokkum,
1684, 8½in. wide, 5oz.
14dwt.

18th century silver gilt
circular bowl and stand,
63oz.3dwt.

Chinese export silver bowl,
circa 1880.

Jensen silver bowl and
spoon, 10cm. high, circa
1947.

18th century Dutch tub-
shaped covered bowl,
3½in. diam., by Marcelis
de Haan, The Hague, 6oz.
5dwt.

Early Charles II bleeding
bowl, 5½in. diam.,
London, 1664, 7oz.6dwt.

BOWLS
MONTEITH

William III Monteith bowl, by Robert Timbrell, London, 1698, 57oz.4dwt., 11in. diam.

William III Monteith bowl, by Robert Peake, London, 1700, 50oz. 10dwt., 11in. diam.

Large sterling silver Monteith bowl with repousse decoration, with gilded lining, by Charles Harris, London, 1876.

PUNCH

Silver punch bowl by William Davie, Edinburgh, 1785, 64oz.

Large Victorian punch bowl, Birmingham, 1890, 14in. diameter.

Rare early American silver punch bowl, by John Coney.

ROSE

Victorian silver rosebowl, London, 1895, by Child & Child.

Indian silver rosebowl on stand.

Circular silver rosebowl, by Omar Ramsden, 1935, 70oz.18dwt., 11¾in. wide.

SUGAR

Early 19th century Russian sugar bowl, 6½in. wide, 1805, 17oz.17dwt.

Liberty & Co. silver sugar basin and tongs, Birmingham, circa 1903-06, 4cm. high.

George II covered sugar bowl, 4½in. high, by Francis Crump, London, 1750, 9oz.18dwt.

Large George IV brandy saucepan and cover by James Scott, Dublin, 1824, 5½in. high, 21oz. 10dwt.

George III silver saucepan, 4in. high, by F. Knopfell, London, 1768, 19oz.9dwt.

George I brandy saucepan, 2¼in. high, by William Fleming, London, 1720, 5oz.17dwt.

BUCKLES

Silver belt buckle, 1892, 3¼in. long.

A Liberty silver and enamel buckle in the manner of Jessie M. King, Birmingham, 1908.

Art Nouveau belt buckle, 7.75cm. wide, probably American, circa 1900.

CANDELABRA

One of a pair of Sheffield plated three-light candelabra.

One of a pair of 18th century German candelabra, Augsburg, 1793-95, 17in. high, 70oz.12dwt.

One of a pair of George III candelabra, 15¾in. high, by John Winter & Co., Sheffield, 1773.

One of two Victorian seven-light candelabra, 31½in. high, by Messrs. Barnard, 369oz.

Stylish German six-light candelabrum, circa 1910, 57cm. high, in silver colored metal.

One of a pair of silver gilt two-light candelabra, by J. Scofield, 1783, 16½in. high

215

CANDLESTICKS

One of a pair of William and Mary candlesticks, by F.S.S., London, 1690, 4½in. high, 16oz.8dwt.

One of four George II table candlesticks, by Paul de Lamerie, 6½in. high, London, 1731, 65oz.15dwt.

One of a pair of Dutch silver table candlesticks, Delft, 1677, 8½in. high, 29oz.

One of a set of four George III table candlesticks, by T. & J. Settle, Sheffield, 1815, 13½in. high.

One of a set of four George II table candlesticks, by J. Cafe, 1750-52, 226oz., 10½in. high.

One of a pair of James Dixon & Sons large silver candlesticks, Sheffield, 1918, 30.5cm. high.

One of a pair of silver candlesticks, London, 1894.

One of a pair of Wm. Hutton & Sons Ltd. table candlesticks, 28.5cm. high, London, 1910.

CARD CASES

Edwardian engine turned silver card case, Birmingham, 1905, 4in. tall.

Victorian tortoiseshell card case with silver string inlay, 4in. tall.

Victorian parcel gilt woman's visiting card case by Edward Smith, Birmingham, 1850.

CASKETS

German silver rectangular casket, late 19th/early 20th century, 26.6cm. long, 1,116gm.

17th century Dutch marriage casket, 3in. wide, circa 1630, 3oz.17dwt.

An electroplated electrotype jewel casket, 10½in. long, by Alexandre Tahan, circa 1854.

CASTERS

George I octagonal caster, by Glover Johnson, London, 1717. 6oz.13dwt.

Queen Anne cylindrical caster with pierced lid, 6½in. high, 6oz.17dwt.

Silver sugar caster, 7in. high, London, 1934, 7oz. 5dwt.

CENTERPIECES

Large Jensen silver coupe, London, 1922, 19.75cm. high.

WMF Art Nouveau German silver centerpiece, 1925, 30in. high.

Victorian centerpiece by Stephen Smith, 1874, 172oz., 15¼in. high.

CHALICES

18th century Italian chalice and paten, by Giovanni Valadier, Rome, 10¼in. high, circa 1775, 24oz.10dwt.

Rare German gilt metal chalice, by Marcus Purman, 1608, 12.4cm. high.

Elizabeth I chalice and cover, 1570, 7in. high, 8oz. 16dwt.

CHAMBERSTICKS

Victorian taperstick, 4¼in. diam., by Charles Fox, 1838, 4oz.11dwt.

James II chamber candlestick, 3½in. diam., 2oz., maker's mark T.E.

George III chamber candlestick by R. & S. Hennell, London, 1802, 10oz., 5¼in. diameter.

217

CHOCOLATE POTS

Rare George III baluster chocolate pot, by R. Williams, Dublin, circa 1770, 10in. high, 36oz.

18th century German chocolate pot, 7¼in. high, by Johann Heinrich Menzel, Augsburg, circa 1735, 15oz.1dwt.

Short spouted chocolate pot, by David Willaume, Jnr., 1744, 10¼in. high, 45oz.10dwt., with wicker-work handle.

CIGARETTE CASES

Silver and enamel cigarette case, 1925, 8.4cm. high.

Continental rectangular cigarette case, 3½in. high.

Silver Art Nouveau cigarette case, Birmingham, 1905, 9cm. high.

CLARET JUGS

John Foligno claret jug, London, 1806.

Saunders & Shepherd silver mounted glass claret jug, London, 1895, 20.4cm. high.

Late 19th century silver mounted cut glass claret jug.

COASTERS

One of a pair of William IV wine coasters, 5¾in. diam.

One of four Russian shaped circular wine coasters by Nichols & Plinke, 1859.

One of a pair of George IV wine coasters by J. Crouch and W. Reid, London, 1821, 6¼in. diam.

Silver coffee pot by S. Hennell, London, 1841, 34oz.

Silver gilt coffee pot, 1823, on a heater stand, 8in. high, by Wm. Eley.

George III baluster coffee pot, London, 1770, 11¼in. high, 28oz.12dwt.

18th century Swiss coffee pot, 8¼in. high, Geneva, circa 1770, 16oz.

Side-handled coffee pot, by David Tanqueray, 9½in. high, 33oz.10dwt.

A magnificent George II silver coffee pot, by de Lamerie, made in 1738.

CREAM BOATS

George II Scottish creamboat, by John Main, Edinburgh, 1739, 6½in. wide, 7oz.14dwt.

Irish George III silver creamboat, Dublin 1811.

George II creamboat, 5¼in., by William Cripps, London, 1743, 6oz.2dwt.

CRUETS

George III oblong silver gilt egg cruet by John Emes, London, 1806, 37oz.6dwt., 7¼in. wide.

Jensen silver cruet, circa 1950-55.

George III cruet frame, by Paul Storr, 11½in. high, 31oz.1dwt., with six cut glass bottles.

Edwardian silver double-handled prize cup, 5oz. 5dwt.

Commonwealth two-handled cup and cover, marked on base and lid, maker's mark A. F. in a shaped shield, London, 1653.

Coconut cup with 17th century silver mounts, bearing an inscription, 3½in. diam.

Standing cup, by Omar Ramsden, 7¼in. high, London, 1938, 24oz. 15dwt.

Silver loving cup, by Hester Bateman, circa 1789.

Wm. Hutton & Sons Ltd., twin-handled silver cup, 28cm. high, London, 1902.

Charles II caudle cup and cover, by Garthorne, London, 1682, 22oz.6dwt., 6½in. high.

Late 18th century fox mask stirrup cup.

One of a set of three early 18th century parcel gilt tumbler cups, circa 1700, 9oz.2dwt.

Charles S. Harris & Son Ltd., two-handled cup and cover, London, 1904, 30 7cm. high, 1,924gm.

George II silver gilt two-handled cup and cover, by John Le Sage, London, 1736, 24oz.1dwt., 8¼in. high.

Silver Victorian christening cup, by J. Angel, 1851, 4oz.

James I silver gilt wine cup, 8in. high, London, 1610, 10oz.12dwt.

George III wine cup, 6in. high, by Hester Bateman, London, 1787, 5oz. 19dwt.

Unusual Charles II wine cup, circa 1675, 3½in. high, 2oz.6dwt.

DISHES

Silver chafing dish with Belgian hall marks, 1772.

Victorian Irish potato dish, Dublin, 1896, 10in. diam., 24oz.

18th century East European parcel gilt dish and cover, 10¾in. diam. 22oz.5dwt.

One of a pair of George I silver gilt strawberry dishes, 8½in. diam., London, 1719, 24oz.18dwt.

17th century Dutch silver embossed dish, maker's mark H.N., Hague, 1666, 82oz.

Breakfast dish and cover in Sheffield Plate, about 1820.

ENTREE

One of a pair of Victorian, shaped oval entree dishes and covers by R. Garrard, 1848, 13½in. long, 120oz.

George III entree dish and cover, 12¼in. wide, by J. Edwards, London, 41oz. 14dwt.

One of a set of four George IV octagonal entree dishes and covers, 10¾in. wide, by Wm. Eley, London, 1827, 205oz.16dwt.

DISHES
FRUIT

Boat-shaped silver openwork fruit dish by Mappin & Webb, Sheffield, 1913, 752gm.

George IV oval fruit dish, 30in. wide, by Marshall & Sons, Edinburgh, 151oz.

Italian two-handled shaped oval fruit dish, 20th century, 48cm. wide, 1,271gm.

MEAT

One of a pair of George II oval meat dishes, by Simon Jouet, 1759, 18in. long, 124oz.

Kayserzinn meat dish and cover, 55cm. long, circa 1900.   **$340 £150**

George III oval meat dish, 16in. wide, by William Burwash, London, 1817, 49oz.10dwt.

SWEETMEAT

A very fine silver sweetmeat box, maker's mark B.B. with a crescent below, London, 1676, 18.4cm., 21oz.12dwt.

German oval sweetmeat dish, circa 1685, 2oz. 10dwt., 5in. wide.

Charles I circular shaped sweetmeat dish, 6¾in. diam., London, 1638, 4oz.16dwt.

VEGETABLE

One of a pair of George III circular vegetable dishes and covers, 9¼in. diam., by Wakelin & Garrard, London, 1796, 64oz.12dwt.

One of a pair of Victorian silver vegetable dishes on warming stands.

One of a pair of George III plain circular vegetable dishes and covers, 10½in. diam., by Paul Storr, 1808, 116oz.

Silver plated epergne, circa 1825, 15½in. high.

George III epergne, by Emick Romer, London, 1770, 91oz. 19dwt., 17¼in. high.

George III epergne, 15¼in. high, by Thos. Pitts, London, 1774, 129oz.12dwt.

EWERS

17th century Italian ewer, Naples, 24oz.10dwt., 9in. high.

Russian silver ewer and basin, St. Petersburg, 1841.

American silver flask-shaped wine ewer and tray by Gorham Mfg. Co., Providence, R.I. 1882, 1,027gm.

FISH SERVERS

Silver fish trowel by Richard Williams, 1770, 13in. long.

Pair of late 19th century fish servers with bone handles, circa 1880.

FLAGONS

George IV cylindrical flagon by R. Emes and E. Barnard, 1826, 61oz.

Victorian silver flagon, 11in. high, by John Mitchell, Glasgow, 1854, 39oz.16dwt.

Silver replica of a late 17th century flagon, by Lambert & Co., London, 1908, 1,563gm.

FLATWARE

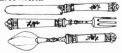

One of ten French dessert services, circa 1825.

Pair of 18th century oyster forks, Old English thread.

Part of a Reed & Barton extensive canteen of 'Francis I' pattern tableware, 301oz., circa 1949.

Part of forty-four pieces of table silver, by Omar Ramsden, London, 1926-38, 54oz.8dwt.

Part of a silver gilt dessert service, 1824-32, 118oz. 15dwt.

Dutch travelling knife, fork and spoon set, circa 1700.

Three pieces of silver, by Charles Rennie Mackintosh.

George III silver caddy spoon by Samuel Pemberton, London 1807.

Charles II silver spoon with rare boar's head finial.

Guild of Handicrafts Ltd. silver butter knife, circa 1900, 13.5cm. long.

Rare early 17th century French two-prong fork.

Part of a George III crested hour glass pattern set of table silver by Wallis & Hayne, London, 116oz.10dwt.

Fine Georg Jensen silver flatware service, circa 1910.

GOBLETS

One of a pair of silver gilt German goblets, 17th century.

Late 19th century Russian cup-shaped goblet, 4¼in. high, 5oz.9dwt.

George IV silver goblet with embossed acorn leaf decoration, London 1823, 12oz.

HONEY POTS

Silver gilt honey pot and matched stand, by Paul Storr, 1798, 4¾in. high, 14oz.

Silver-gilt honey pot by A.P. & C. Houle, London 1860, 11.5cm. high.

Silver plated honey pot with green glass body.

INKSTANDS

George II rectangular inkstand, 9¾in. wide, by William Shaw, London, 1730, 24oz.16dwt.

Early 19th century Portuguese inkstand, circa 1800, 1310gm., 31cm. wide.

George III oblong inkstand, 8in. wide, by Susanna Barker, London, 1770, 20oz. 7dwt.

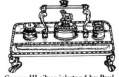

George III silver inkstand by Paul Storr, London 1803, 14¼in. wide.

Harrods Ltd., two-bottle inkstand on molded octagonal base, by R. W. Burbridge, London, 1936, 790gm.

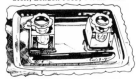

Edwardian silver plated inkwell by Mappin and Webb, about 1910.

225

JUGS

George III baluster silver jug with embossed decoration.

George II silver baluster jug, 12½oz., 11.5cm. high.

Jug with Elizabethan silver mounts, circa 1585, 9½in. high.

Silver jug, by Abraham Pootholt and Jan van Giffen, 6in. high, 1784.

George IV small brandy jug on stand with burner, 7¾in. high, by J. Angell, London 1825, 16oz. 19dwt.

Victorian 'Cellini' jug with hinged lid, 14½in. high, London 1884, 42oz.

BEER

George II baluster beer jug, 8½in. high, by Thos. Coffin, Exeter, 1734, 28oz.7dwt.

George II baluster shaped silver beer jug, by Wm. Darker, London, 1730, 25oz.

George I covered beer jug, by John Edwards, London, 1719, 10in. high, 32oz. 19dwt.

CREAM

Georgian silver cream jug, 3½oz., circa 1820.

George III silver cow creamer, 5¾in. long, by John Schuppe, 1765, 5oz.12dwt.

George II circular cream jug, by Thos. Sutton, Dublin, 1735, 3¼in. high, 4oz.10dwt.

COFFEE

SILVER

18th century baluster
shaped silver coffee jug,
7in. high, 11.9oz.

MILK

George III coffee jug
on stand, 12in. high,
by Paul Storr, London
1807, 54oz. 11dwt.

George III baluster coffee
jug by Wm. Bruce, London,
1814, 21oz.19dwt., 8¾in.
high.

George III helmet-shaped
milk jug, by Robert Sharp,
London, 1793, 5in. high,
7oz.8dwt.

HOT WATER

George III Scottish provincial
covered milk jug, by John
Baillie, Inverness, circa 1780,
4¾in. high, 8oz.4dwt.

George III milk jug, by
Hester Bateman, London,
1777, 6½in. high, 6oz.
12dwt.

A fine Hester Bateman
baluster hot water jug, 1783.

WINE

William IV hot water jug
by J. McKay, Edinburgh,
1834, 9½in. high.

Late Georgian hot water jug,
London, 1831, 27½oz.,
10½in. high.

Queen Anne Irish wine jug,
by Thos. Boulton of Dublin,
1702.

Silver wine jug by John
S. Hunt, London, 1850,
13½in. high.

George II Irish, covered
jug, by Erasmus Cope,
Dublin, 1736, 33oz.8dwt.

227

KOVSCH

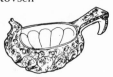

Superb silver Russian kovsch, probably by Maria Somenova.

Enamelled silver gilt kovsch by Carl Faberge, circa 1913, 7in. long.

Enamelled silver kovsch by Carl Faberge, circa 1910, 2½in. long.

LADLES

One of a pair of George II Hanoverian pattern sauce ladles, by Elias Cachart, London, 1744, 5oz.5dwt.

Fluted silver punch ladle, by E. Aldridge, 1742.

Bright cut ladle, by R. Keay, Perth, 1790.

George II toddy ladle with mother-of-pearl handle by John Gamon, London 1731. $210

LEMON STRAINERS

Silver lemon strainer, by H. Northcote, 1799.

Late 18th century, bright cut silver strainer, 10in. across.

George I silver lemon strainer, Francis Nelme, London, 1727.

Early 18th century silver lemon strainer by Thomas Bamford, 6in. long, 2oz. 4dwt. $787

MINIATURE SILVER

Miniature silver slop bowl, 1in. diam., by Hendrik Duller, Amsterdam, 1780.

Miniature tea kettle, 2in. high, by Willem van Strant, Amsterdam, 1734.

Miniature model of a milkmaid, 1½in. high, Amsterdam 1772.

George III silver bosun's call.

Queen Anne parcel gilt stand for a rimmon, by John Ruslen, 1708.

Silver gilt mounted mother-of-pearl scissor case, circa 1700.

Late 16th century silver gilt pomander, European, 2½in. high.

Pair of 17th century Spanish silver gilt altar cruets and a tazza, 4½in. high and 9¾in. diam., 47oz.2dwt.

Enamelled silver flint lighter, 2in. high.

Late 18th century Spanish censer, 8½in. high, 35oz. 15dwt.

Early George III wax jack, 6¼in. high, by Samuel Herbert & Co., London, 1761, 5oz.9dwt.

Georg Jensen silver cocktail shaker, circa 1927, 12¼in. high.

One of twelve silver-gilt menu holders, Birmingham 1905, 25oz.

Silver mounted Meerschaum pipe bowl, circa 1820, 23cm. wide.

One of a rare pair of George III silver spurs, London, 1784, maker

MODELS

Late 19th century silver model of a bull, 72oz. 13dwt., 18¼in. overall.

One of a pair of Portuguese 19th century models of Kylins, 106oz., 14½in. high.

One of a pair of B. Neresheimer & Sohne figures of knights, Hanau, 1911, 2,795gm.

MUGS

George III silver christening mug, London, 1798, by John Emes, 3oz.

George III silver pint baluster mug, by John Deacon, 1769, 5in. high, 10½oz.

A small slightly tapering silver beer mug with scroll handle, London, 1801, 8½oz.

MULLS

Horn snuff mull, probably Tain, circa 1837.

Silver mounted ram's head table snuff mull, about 1880, 13½in. high.

Scottish snuff mull, circa 1800.

MUSTARDS

Italian mustard pot and stand, Naples, 1792, stand 4½in. diam., 7oz.10dwt.

Charles T. and George Fox owl shaped mustard pot, 11.5cm. high, 9.9oz.

Early Victorian mustard pot by Charles Fox, London, 1837, 3in. high, 4oz.12dwt.

NEFS   SILVER

Continental two-masted nef on four wheels, circa 1900, 15¼in. high.

Late 19th century German nef on dolphin stem, with pseudo hallmarks, 732gm.

Continental two-masted nef on four wheels, 17½in. high, dated for 1901.

NUTMEGS

Late 18th century egg-shaped nutmeg grater, by Samuel Meriton.

Silver nutmeg grater by Elkington & Co., Birmingham, 1906, 3in. long.

George III silver nutmeg grater, by Mary Hyde and John Reily, London, 1799, 2in. diam.

PAP BOATS

Georgian silver pap boat, maker's mark TE, 4¾in., 2oz.

George III silver pap boat, by Rebecca Emes and Edward Barnard, 2½oz.

Unmarked silver and coconut shell pap boat, circa 1760, 5in. long.

PEPPERS

George I cylindrical kitchen pepper, by John Hamilton, Dublin, 2½in. high, 2oz.9dwt.

Pair of silver mounted Victorian ivory pepperettes.

One of two Handicrafts Ltd. pepper casters, circa 1900, 6.5cm. high.

PHOTOGRAPH FRAMES

Art Nouveau silver photograph frame, 6in. high.

Liberty & Co. silver and enamel frame, Birmingham, 1910, 27cm. high.

Silver Art Nouveau photograph frame by J. & A. Zimmerman, 29cm. high, Birmingham, 1903.

PLATES

One of twelve George III dinner plates by Paul Storr, London, 1807, 10½in. diam., 271oz.7dwt.

One of twelve George III shaped circular dinner plates, 9¾in. diam., by L. Herne and F. Butty, London, 1762, 212oz.15dwt.

George I Irish circular plate, 9in. diam., Dublin, 1725, 13oz.13dwt.

PORRINGERS

Two-handled George V silver porringer, London, 1915.

Charles II plain two-handled porringer on rim foot, probably West Country, maker's mark IP, circa 1670, 6oz. 3dwt.

Queen Anne porringer on collet foot, 1713, 6oz.

PURSES

Stylish German silver mesh evening purse, circa 1910, 18cm. long.

Art Nouveau silver purse, 1908.

La Minauderie, silver engine turned evening bag by C. van Cleef and Arpels, about 1935.

Queen Anne quaich, by Robt. Ker, Edinburgh, circa 1710.

A typical Stuart quaich, 7¾in. diam, unmarked, Scottish, circa 1675.

One of a small pair of Indian silver quaichs, 7oz.

RATTLES

Victorian silver rattle dated 1886.

Early 18th century child's silver rattle, 5¼in. long, circa 1700.

17th century child's rattle bearing the Edinburgh date letter for 1681.

SALTS

One of a set of four George II capstan salts, London, 1754, by G. Wickes, 32oz.

One of a pair of late 18th century silver gilt salts, complete with spoons, 23oz.

One of a pair of Queen Anne trencher salt cellars, by B. Bentley, 3in. diam., 4oz.2dwt.

One of a set of four George III double salts, 4¼in. wide, by J. Scofield, London, 1784, 28oz.15dwt.

One of a set of four George III oval tub-shaped silver salts, London, 1808, 12½oz.

One of a pair of silver salt cellars by Robert Garrard, 3¼in. high.

SALVERS

George II triangular salver by George Methuen, London, 1752, 16oz.4dwt., 9½in. wide.

George II plain shaped square silver salver, by Robert Abercrombie.

George III shaped circular salver, 11¼in. diam., by J. Carter, London, 1773, 24oz.2dwt.

SAUCEBOATS

One of a pair of Victorian sauceboats, 8¼in. long, by Robert Garrard, London, 1847, 41oz.19dwt.

One of a pair of George III oval sauceboats, by Thos. Evans, London, 1775, 34oz. 7dwt., 7½in. wide.

One of a pair of George II oval sauceboats, by Wm. Cripps, London, 1754, 8in. wide, 28oz.8dwt.

SCISSORS

Ornate Victorian silver scissors and matching thimble, Birmingham 1890.

Gilt and silver metal scissors and paper knife, circa 1935.

Tang silver gilt scissors, 7½in. long.

SCOOPS

Silver marrow scoop, by E. B., London, 1745.

Combined silver marrow scoop and tablespoon, by Elias Cachart, 1750.

Silver cheese scoop by Mary Chawner, 1840.

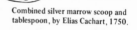

Stilton cheese scoop with ejector slide, Joseph Taylor, Birmingham, 1803.

SKEWERS

Silver skewer, maker's mark rubbed, London, 1779.

Pair of silver meat skewers, by Peter and Ann Bateman, 1798.

SNUFFERS

George III Irish boat-shaped snuffers tray, by James Scott, Dublin, 8oz. 5dwt.

18th century Dutch silver snuffer stand and snuffers, by Jan Pondt of Bremen, Amsterdam, 1756, 9oz. 18dwt.

Charles II snuffer tray with matching snuffers, by W.B., 15oz.12dwt.

Shaped rectangular silver snuff box with gilt interior by Ed. Smith, Birmingham, 1851, 7.2cm. long.

George III Irish silver snuff box, by A. Tuppy, Dublin, 1782, 3¼in. wide.

William IV snuff box by Edward Shaw, Birmingham, 1834, 6oz.3dwt., 3¼in. wide.

William IV silver gilt snuff box by A. J. Strachan, London, 1830, 4¾in. wide.

Rare English double lidded tortoiseshell pique snuff box, 4¼in. long, circa 1780.

George III snuff box with compartment at one end, by John Shaw, Birmingham, 1817, 2½in. wide.

TANKARDS

George II baluster shaped silver tankard, 1732.

Swedish tankard of peg type, repousse decorated with figures and fruits.

Dutch silver mounted horn tankard with silver lining, with portrait of William and Mary on side.

Early George III tankard, 8in. high, by W.F., London, 1767, 15oz.1dwt.

Tankard given to Bismarck by Wilhelm I of Prussia, 24½in. high, 1871.

George III tapering cylindrical tankard, by Peter and Anne Bateman, London, 1797, 7¼in. high, 26oz.6dwt.

TAPERSTICKS

George II taperstick, by
J. Cafe, London, 1743,
4½in. high, 4oz.7dwt.

One of a pair of early
George III tapersticks,
by Ebenezer Coker,
London 1760, 11oz.
13dwt., 5¼in. high.

Silver taperstick, by E.
Barnet, York, 1713,
2¾oz.

TAZZAS

18th century Dutch silver
gilt tazza, by Casparus
Janszonius Haarlem, 4¾in.
diam., 3oz.14dwt.

Early 17th century
Spanish tazza, 10in.
wide, circa 1630,
19oz.

WMF silvered metal tazza,
23.25cm. high, circa 1900.

TEA & COFFEE SETS

Victorian Scottish teaset by Marshall
& Sons, Edinburgh, 1849, 40oz.8dwt.

Juventa Art Nouveau electroplated
metal coffee service, circa 1900.

Four-piece silver tea service by John
Angell, London, 1824.

Late Victorian five-piece tea and coffee
set by Smith, Sissons & Co., London,
61oz.

TEA CADDIES

George III oval tea caddy, 5in. high, by Wm. Vincent, London, 1778, 3oz.10dwt.

Silver tea caddy by Paul de Lamerie, 1724, 13.3cm. high, 15oz.13dwt.

George III silver tea caddy, by Rebecca Emes and Edward Barnard I, London, 1809, 22½oz.

George III oblong tea caddy, by P. Gillois, London, 1763, 11oz. 7dwt., 5½in. high.

George IV tea caddy, by Charles Price, London, 1828, 18oz.4dwt., 6¼in. high.

One of a pair of George II tea caddies, 5¼in. high, by S. Taylor, London, 1756, 16oz.2dwt.

TEA KETTLES

George III tea kettle on stand, 15¾in. high, by John Edwards, London 1792, 69oz. 9dwt.

George II Irish tea kettle on lampstand, by John Taylor, 13in. high, 67oz.14dwt.

George I tea kettle on stand, 14in. high, by John White, London, circa 1720, 73oz. 9dwt.

Bruder Frank kettle and stand, circa 1900, in silver coloured metal.

Silver teapot on spirit stand.

Victorian silver spirit kettle, by Robb & Whittet, Edinburgh, 1837, 74oz.

237

TEAPOTS

George III oval teapot by Hester Bateman, 5in. high, London, 1784, 13oz.6dwt.

Irish George IV silver teapot, Dublin, 1823, by Edward Power, 33oz.

George III shaped oval teapot and stand, 7in. high, by Langlands & Robertson, Newcastle, 1791, 22oz.

Louis XVI cylindrical teapot, 4in. high, by Jacques Antoine Bonhomme, Paris, 1783, 12oz.11dwt.

Swedish teapot, circa 1819, 21oz., 6in. high.

Victorian plated teapot with ivory handle.

TOASTERS

Early Victorian six-section toast rack by Henry Wilkinson & Co., 1839, 8oz.

Heath & Middleton silver toast rack, 1899, 12.5cm. wide.

Victorian toast rack by Robt. Garrard, London, 1869.

TOBACCO BOXES

18th century Dutch oblong tobacco box by Christoffel Woortman, Amsterdam, 1797, 6oz.6dwt., 6¼in. wide.

Dutch silver tobacco box, Leeuwarden, circa 1750, 22oz.10dwt.

17th century oval silver tobacco box, 4¼in. wide, circa 1680.

238

TOILET REQUISITES

Queen Anne toilet service, London, circa 1706, 81oz.12dwt.

Portuguese silver and stained fish-skin necessaire de voyage, circa 1730-40.

TONGS & NIPS

Silver rococo period nips enhanced with gilding, 1745.

Early 18th century silver sugar tongs, by L.E., London, circa 1710.

Chased leaf tongs, by W. & J. Deane, London, circa 1765.

Silver asparagus tongs by G. W. Adams, 1864.

Silver asparagus tongs, by J. Buckett, of London, circa 1770, 23cm. long.

George III bright cut sugar tongs, by G. Smith and T. Hayter, London, 1798.

TRAYS

George III two-handled tray, by J. Wakelin and R. Garrard, 1796, 80oz., 20in. long.

Embossed Indian silver tray, circa 1900, 21in. long.

Two-handled octagonal pierced gallery tea tray by Elkington & Co., London, 1913, 4,700gm.

Large, heavy Walker & Hall two-handled rectangular tray, Sheffield, 1901, 75.2cm. wide, 5,086gm.

TUREENS
SAUCE

One of a pair of George III oval sauce tureens and covers, 9¼in. wide, by D. Smith and R. Sharp, London, 1778, 47oz.7dwt.

One of a pair of George III sauce tureens by Wm. Bennett, London, 1808, 52oz.4dwt.

One of a pair of George III silver sauce tureens, by J. Carter, London, 1776, 45oz.

SOUP

Italian lobed circular two-handled soup tureen and cover, 68.5oz., 31.5cm. wide.

George III oval soup tureen and cover, 15in. wide, by R. Garrard, London, 1814, 121oz.6dwt.

George II two-handled soup tureen and cover, Dublin, 1745, 13¾in. long, 164oz.

URNS

Vase-shaped tea urn, 16¼in. high, by Heath & Middleton, London, 1906, 78oz.4dwt.

Early 18th century Scottish urn, 11½in. high, Edinburgh, circa 1725, 43oz.11dwt.

George III tea urn, by C. Wright, London, 1771, 80oz.

VASES

George III sugar vase, by Robt. Hennell, London, 1784, 5in. high, 7oz.9dwt.

Large WMF electroplated electrotype vase, circa 1900, 49cm. high.

Jensen silver vase, London, 1930, 10.25cm. wide.

VINAIGRETTES

Silver gilt oval vinaigrette by S. Pemberton, Birmingham, 1800.

George IV silver gilt vinaigrette, 1½in. diam., by J. Willmore, Birmingham, 1824.

Silver vinaigrette by J. Butler, Birmingham, 1826.

WINE COOLERS

One of a pair of Catherine the Great wine coolers, by Z. Deichmann, 1766.

One of a pair of George III wine coolers by Paul Storr, London, 1812, 9¾in. high, 242oz.

French vase-shaped wine cooler, 10in. high, circa 1890, 65oz.

WINE FUNNELS

George III wine funnel by George Fenwick, 1817.

George III funnel, by Thos. Graham, London, 1795, 4¼in. high, 1oz.4dwt.

Georgian silver wine funnel, London, 1811, by E. Morley.

WINE LABELS

George III wine label, engraved for claret, by M. Binley, London, circa 1770.

Victorian wine label, pierced 'Brandy' by Edward and John Barnard, London, 1853.

Rare 18th century wine label apparently unmarked, circa 1780.

WINE TASTERS

William III wine taster, London 1695, 3oz.3dwt.

Louis XV wine taster with shell thumbpiece, 3¼in. diam., circa 1740, 4oz.4dwt.

Charles II circular wine taster, 3¼in. diam., London, 1664, 1oz.18dwt.

241

STONE

Central Mexican greenstone mask Teotihuacan III-IV, 18.5cm. high.

Costa Rican volcanic stone metate of concave oval form, 19½in. wide, 1000-1500 A.D.

One of a pair of mid 19th century carved stone vases, 24in. diam.

Large sculpture of a pouter pigeon, 1920's, 34.5cm. high, in composition stone.

Aztec volcanic stone figure, 1300-1500 A.D., 15½in. high.

2nd/3rd century A. D. East Roman basalt head of a horse, 14in. long.

One of a pair of George III ormolu mounted Blue-John solid urns, 10in. high.

11th century Central Indian Matrika group in pink sandstone, 33in. long.

Ming dynasty sandstone head, 11in. high.

Nummulitic limestone head of an Amarna princess, 21cm. high, Egyptian.

10th century black stone stele, 23in. high.

Grey schist stele of Kuan Yin, 26in. high.

Belgian Languillier cast iron and ceramic cooking range, circa 1910.

Pure wood burning stove in cast iron, circa 1880.

Late 19th century English gray enamelled cast iron stove in the Art Nouveau style.

Belgian 'Westminster' freestanding stove, circa 1920, 25½in. high.

French Siberia Niledo cast iron bow fronted stove, circa 1910, 28in. high.

French Poel a Bois 'Le Selecte' wood burning cast iron stove, circa 1910, 22in. high.

TAPESTRIES

Late 17th century Flemish verdure tapestry, 75in. wide.

'Chinoiseries' tapestry by Joshua Morris, circa 1720, 10ft. wide.

Louis XIV Aubusson biblical tapestry, circa 1680, 8 x 6ft.

Late 19th century Chinese wall hanging with purple silk ground, 172in. wide.

19th century Rescht panel with floral decoration on a madder ground, 9ft.2in. long.

Mid 18th century Louis XV Franco-Flemish pastoral tapestry, 8 x 9ft.10in.

Meccano bi-plane construction kit, circa 1933, 1ft.3in. long.

Clockwork 'Wheel of Death', Russian, 1896, 9in. high.

Bing clockwork tinplate two-seater Mercedes, 9½in. long, circa 1912.

German 'Man on a Pig' toy.

Wooden fortress, circa 1950, sold with soldiers and animals.

English clockwork toy 'Home James', circa 1900.

German Arnold tinplate motorcycle, 8in. long, circa 1950.

Wooden doll's house, paper covered to simulate stone.

Edwardian doll's perambulator with folding hood and boat-shaped body.

French 'Jeu de Course' game, circa 1900, 10½ x 10½in.

Mickey Mouse organ grinder, about 1930, possibly by Distler, 6in. long.

Gun mounted on a tank chassis by Britain.

Gunthermann clockwork tram, circa 1920, 9½in. long.

Fine G.G. Kellerman clockwork tinplate frog, German, circa 1930 4¾in. high.

Hess friction drive limousine, 8¼in. long, circa 1920-25.

Hand enamelled clockwork toy, German, 1900, 6in. high.

Mid 19th century Bavarian Noah's Ark, 19in. long, complete with animals.

Marx clockwork walking Popeye, 8in. high.

Clockwork 'Boy on a Swing', English, 1937, 3½in. wide.

Rare Regency painted wooden two-storey doll's house and stand, 3ft.1in. wide.

Early 20th century German clockwork clown toy, 9in. high.

Cast iron model cooking range, American circa 1920 1ft. 1in. wide.

American set of 'Snow White' picture bricks, circa 1946.

Schoenhuts cracker-jack clown with original box and chair.

1930's ice cream tricycle in good condition.

German Lehmann 'anxious bride' clockwork toy, circa 1914, 8½in. long.

German acrobatic clown toy.

Child's pull-along horse covered with pony skin, circa 1850, 11½in. high.

A tinplate clockwork landaulette by Georges Carette, about 1910.

Early 20th century pull along barking dog, English, 1ft. 2in. high.

Distler clockwork organ grinder, circa 1923, German, 7in. high.

Lead set of Snow White and Seven Dwarfs by Britain, 1938.

German Phillip Vielmetter painted tin drawing clown, circa 1900, 5½in. high.

German tinplate clockwork 'Jolly Sambo', 6¾in. high, circa 1920.

Tinplate clockwork horse and cart, by G. and K. Greppert & Keich, Brandenburg, 17cm. long.

Clockwork Steakhouse Joe, made in Japan.

A Victorian uphol-stered bathchair.

Governess cart by Wade of Norwich, circa 1900, 10ft. long overall.

Early 19th century velocipede.

Late 19th century Russian painted wooden sledge.

English ordinary bicycle, circa 1880, 4ft.8in. high.

Wooden Victorian dogcart.

19th century hand milk float of iron and wood, 61in. high.

French pastry cook's van, circa 1900.

Late 18th century hard-topped surrey with iron rimmed wheels.

Beautifully restored Romany Vardo.

Reindeer or horse drawn sleigh, circa 1860, pro-bably Eastern European.

1924 Model T Ford with original engine with bread van body.

TRAYS

Unusual Galle carved and inlaid fruitwood tray, circa 1900.

Rare George I small walnut tray, 1ft.4¾in. wide.

George III mahogany tray inlaid with a conch shell.

Edwardian mahogany tray and stand with painted decoration.

17th century early Lac Burgaute tray, 13in. diam.

Late Victorian mahogany butler's tray with stand.

TSUBAS

Iron tsuba of the Hiragiya school.

Shakudo Nanako tsuba by Yanagawa Naomasa.

Well carved iron tsuba, 8.1cm., signed by Kyokusuiken Okabe Tadamasa.

Iron tsuba pierced and chiselled with cherry blossoms picked out in gold.

Decorative tsuba of red copper and sentoku plate by Ishiguro Masatsune III.

Rare copper tsuba decorated in katakiri with a pair of Sumo wrestlers.

INDEX

The Fires of War, Love and Honor, a Land of Suffering and Hope . . . The Greatest Japanese Epic of All Time!

Takezō: Someday he would be known as Japan's greatest warrior—Musashi. But now he was just an angry young man with dreams of glory, an army straggler on the run from his own villagers, fighting for his future . . .

Matahachi: A strong, affable youth from the Harima mountains, he joined his friend's quest for the honor of battle. When they rose, the sole survivors in a field of dead bodies, their new lives had begun . . .

Akemi: Daughter of a murdered man, she robbed the bodies of dead soldiers to support her lascivious mother—and took the two teenaged soldiers into their home . . .

Otsū: A foundling, delicate and aloof, she waited faithfully for her betrothed, Matahachi, to return. But when months passed and he did not come home, she knew it was Takezō she had secretly longed to hold . . .

Takuan Sōhō: The Zen priest everyone called crazy. But for Otsū and Takezō, he was a man of indescribable power who held the keys to an extraordinary journey . . .

Books in the Musashi Saga by Eiji Yoshikawa

Book I: The Way of the Samurai
Book II: The Art of War

Published by POCKET BOOKS

Book III: The Way of the Sword
Book IV: The Bushido Code
Book V: The Way of Life and Death

Coming Soon from POCKET BOOKS

MUSASHI

BOOK I:
THE WAY
OF THE
SAMURAI

EIJI YOSHIKAWA

Translated from the Japanese by Charles S. Terry
Foreword by Edwin O. Reischauer

POCKET BOOKS

New York   London   Toronto   Sydney   Tokyo

Map design by Ray Lundgren Graphics, Ltd.
Map research by Jim Moser

POCKET BOOKS, a division of Simon & Schuster Inc.
1230 Avenue of the Americas, New York, NY 10020

Published by arrangement with Kodansha International
Library of Congress Catalog Card Number: 80-8791

ISBN: 0-671-64421-1

First Pocket Books printing March 1989

10   9   8   7   6   5   4   3   2   1

CONTENTS

Contents

CHARACTERS AND LOCALES

AGON, the lancer Musashi defeats at the Hōzōin Temple

AKEMI, the daughter of Okō

HIDEYORI, ruler of Osaka Castle and rival of Ieyasu

TOKUGAWA IEYASU, the Shōgun, ruler of Japan

JŌTARŌ, a young follower of Musashi

YOSHIOKA KEMPŌ, father of Yoshioka Seijūrō

SHŌDA KIZAEMON, samurai in the service of the Yagyū family

KYOTO, city in southwestern Japan, rival to Osaka

HON'IDEN MATAHACHI, childhood friend of Musashi

MIMASAKA, home province of Musashi

MIYAMOTO MUSASHI, an apprentice swordsman

SHIMMEN OGIN, the sister of Musashi

OKŌ, a lascivious woman

OSAKA, city in southwestern Japan, rival to Kyoto

HON'IDEN OSUGI, the mother of Matahachi and bitter enemy of Musashi

OTSŪ, former lover of Matahachi

UEDA RYŌHEI, samurai of the Yoshioka school

YOSHIOKA SEIJŪRŌ, Young Master of the Yoshioka school

SEKIGAHARA, battle in which Ieyasu defeated the combined armies of the western daimyō for control of Japan

YAGYŪ SEKISHŪSAI, aging master of the Yagyū style of swordsmanship

Characters and Locales

SHIMMEN TAKEZŌ, former name of Musashi

TAKUAN SŌHŌ, an eccentric monk

TSUJIKAZE TEMMA, bandit slain by Musashi

IKEDA TERUMASA, Lord of the Castle of Himeji, where Musashi studied *The Art of War*

GION TŌJI, samurai of the Yoshioka school and suitor of Okō

HOUSE OF YAGYŪ, a powerful family known for their style of swordsmanship

FOREWORD[1]
by Edwin O. Reischauer[2]

Musashi might well be called the *Gone with the Wind* of Japan. Written by Eiji Yoshikawa (1892–1962), one of Japan's most prolific and best-loved popular writers, it is a long historical novel, which first appeared in serialized form between 1935 and 1939 in the *Asahi Shimbun,* Japan's largest and most prestigious newspaper. It has been published in book form no less than fourteen times, most recently in four volumes of the 53-volume complete works of Yoshikawa issued by Kodansha. It has been produced as a film some seven

---

[1]This Foreword has been taken in its entirety from the original single-volume American hardcover edition of *Musashi: An Epic Novel of the Samurai Era.*

[2]Edwin O. Reischauer was born in Japan in 1910. He has been a professor at Harvard University since 1946, and is now Professor Emeritus. He left the university temporarily to be the United States Ambassador to Japan from 1961 to 1966, and is one of the best-known authorities on the country. Among his numerous works are *Japan: The Story of a Nation* and *The Japanese.*

times, has been repeatedly presented on the stage, and has often been made into television mini-series on at least three nationwide networks.

Miyamoto Musashi was an actual historical person, but through Yoshikawa's novel he and the other main characters of the book have become part of Japan's living folklore. They are so familiar to the public that people will frequently be compared to them as personalities everyone knows. This gives the novel an added interest to the foreign reader. It not only provides a romanticized slice of Japanese history, but gives a view of how the Japanese see their past and themselves. But basically the novel will be enjoyed as a dashing tale of swashbuckling adventure and a subdued story of love, Japanese style.

Comparisons with James Clavell's *Shōgun* seem inevitable, because for most Americans today *Shōgun,* as a book and a television mini-series, vies with samurai movies as their chief source of knowledge about Japan's past. The two novels concern the same period of history. *Shōgun,* which takes place in the year 1600, ends with Lord Toranaga, who is the historical Tokugawa Ieyasu, soon to be the Shōgun, or military dictator of Japan, setting off for the fateful battle of Sekigahara. Yoshikawa's story begins with the youthful Takezō, later to be renamed Miyamoto Musashi, lying wounded among the corpses of the defeated army on that battlefield.

With the exception of Blackthorne, the historical Will Adams, *Shōgun* deals largely with the great lords and ladies of Japan, who appear in thin disguise under names Clavell has devised for them. *Musashi,* while mentioning many great historical figures under their true names, tells about a broader range of Japanese and particularly about the rather extensive group who lived on the ill-defined borderline between the hereditary military aristocracy and the commoners—the peasants, tradesmen and artisans. Clavell freely distorts historical fact to fit his tale and inserts a Western-type love story that not only flagrantly flouts history but is quite unimaginable in the Japan of that time. Yoshikawa remains true to history or at least to historical tradition, and his love story, which runs as a background theme in minor scale throughout the book, is very authentically Japanese.

Yoshikawa, of course, has enriched his account with much imaginative detail. There are enough strange coincidences and deeds of derring-do to delight the heart of any lover of adventure stories. But he sticks faithfully to such facts of history as are known. Not only Musashi himself but many of the other people who figure prominently in the story are real historical individuals. For example, Takuan, who serves as a guiding light and mentor to the youthful Musashi, was a famous Zen monk, calligrapher, painter, poet and tea-master of the time, who became the youngest abbot of the Daitokuji in Kyoto in 1609 and later founded a major monastery in Edo, but is best remembered today for having left his name to a popular Japanese pickle.

The historical Miyamoto Musashi, who may have been born in 1584 and died in 1645, was like his father a master swordsman and became known for his use of two swords. He was an ardent cultivator of self-discipline as the key to martial skills and the author of a famous work on swordsmanship, the *Gorin no sho*. He probably took part as a youth in the battle of Sekigahara, and his clashes with the Yoshioka school of swordsmanship in Kyoto, the warrior monks of the Hōzōin in Nara and the famed swordsman Sasaki Kojirō, all of which figure prominently in this book, actually did take place. Yoshikawa's account of him ends in 1612, when he was still a young man of about 28, but subsequently he may have fought on the losing side at the siege of Osaka castle in 1614 and participated in 1637–38 in the annihilation of the Christian peasantry of Shimabara in the western island of Kyushu, an event which marked the extirpation of that religion from Japan for the next two centuries and helped seal Japan off from the rest of the world.

Ironically, Musashi in 1640 became a retainer of the Hosokawa lords of Kumamoto, who, when they had been the lords of Kumamoto, had been the patrons of his chief rival, Sasaki Kojirō. The Hosokawas bring us back to *Shōgun,* because it was the older Hosokawa, Tadaoki, who figures quite unjustifiably as one of the main villains of that novel, and it was Tadaoki's exemplary Christian wife, Gracia, who is pictured without a shred of plausibility as Blackthorne's great love, Mariko.

The time of Musashi's life was a period of great transition in Japan. After a century of incessant warfare among petty daimyō, or feudal lords, three successive leaders had finally reunified the country through conquest. Oda Nobunaga had started the process but, before completing it, had been killed by a treacherous vassal in 1582. His ablest general, Hideyoshi, risen from the rank of common foot soldier, completed the unification of the nation but died in 1598 before he could consolidate control in behalf of his infant heir. Hideyoshi's strongest vassal, Tokugawa Ieyasu, a great daimyō who ruled much of eastern

Japan from his castle at Edo, the modern Tokyo, then won supremacy by defeating a coalition of western daimyō at Sekigahara in 1600. Three years later he took the traditional title of Shōgun, signifying his military dictatorship over the whole land, theoretically in behalf of the ancient but impotent imperial line in Kyoto. Ieyasu in 1605 transferred the position of Shōgun to his son, Hidetada, but remained in actual control himself until he had destroyed the supporters of Hideyoshi's heir in sieges of Osaka castle in 1614 and 1615.

The first three Tokugawa rulers established such firm control over Japan that their rule was to last more than two and a half centuries, until it finally collapsed in 1868 in the tumultuous aftermath of the reopening of Japan to contact with the West a decade and a half earlier. The Tokugawa ruled through semi-autonomous hereditary daimyō, who numbered around 265 at the end of the period, and the daimyō in turn controlled their fiefs through their hereditary samurai retainers. The transition from constant warfare to a closely regulated peace brought the drawing of sharp class lines between the samurai, who had the privilege of wearing two swords and bearing family names, and the commoners, who though including well-to-do merchants and land owners, were in theory denied all arms and the honor of using family names.

During the years of which Yoshikawa writes, however, these class divisions were not yet sharply defined. All localities had their residue of peasant fighting men, and the country was overrun by rōnin, or masterless samurai, who were largely the remnants of the armies of the daimyō who had lost their domains as the result of the battle of Sekigahara or in earlier wars.

It took a generation or two before society was fully sorted out into the strict class divisions of the Tokugawa system, and in the meantime there was considerable social ferment and mobility.

Another great transition in early seventeenth century Japan was in the nature of leadership. With peace restored and major warfare at an end, the dominant warrior class found that military prowess was less essential to successful rule than administrative talents. The samurai class started a slow transformation from being warriors of the gun and sword to being bureaucrats of the writing brush and paper. Disciplined self-control and education in a society at peace was becoming more important than skill in warfare. The Western reader may be surprised to see how widespread literacy already was at the beginning of the seventeenth century and at the constant references the Japanese made to Chinese history and literature, much as Northern Europeans of the same time continually referred to the traditions of ancient Greece and Rome.

A third major transition in the Japan of Musashi's time was in weaponry. In the second half of the sixteenth century matchlock muskets, recently introduced by the Portuguese, had become the decisive weapons of the battlefield, but in a land at peace the samurai could turn their backs on distasteful firearms and resume their traditional love affair with the sword. Schools of swordsmanship flourished. However, as the chance to use swords in actual combat diminished, martial skills were gradually becoming martial arts, and these increasingly came to emphasize the importance of inner self-control and the character-building qualities of swordsmanship rather than its untested military efficacy. A whole mystique of the sword grew up, which was more akin to philosophy than to warfare.

Yoshikawa's account of Musashi's early life illustrates all these changes going on in Japan. He was himself a typical rōnin from a mountain village and became a settled samurai retainer only late in life. He was the founder of a school of swordsmanship. Most important, he gradually transformed himself from an instinctive fighter into a man who fanatically pursued the goals of Zen-like self-discipline, complete inner mastery over oneself, and a sense of oneness with surrounding nature. Although in his early years lethal contests, reminiscent of the tournaments of medieval Europe, were still possible, Yoshikawa portrays Musashi as consciously turning his martial skills from service in warfare to a means of character building for a time of peace. Martial skills, spiritual self-discipline and aesthetic sensitivity became merged into a single indistinguishable whole. This picture of Musashi may not be far from the historical truth. Musashi is known to have been a skilled painter and an accomplished sculptor as well as a swordsman.

The Japan of the early seventeenth century which Musashi typified has lived on strongly in the Japanese consciousness. The long and relatively static rule of the Tokugawa preserved much of its forms and spirit, though in somewhat ossified form, until the middle of the nineteenth century, not much more than a century ago. Yoshikawa himself was a son of a former samurai who failed like most members of his class to make a successful economic transition to the new age. Though the samurai themselves largely sank into obscurity in the new Japan, most of the new leaders were drawn from this feudal class, and its ethos was popularized through the new compulsory educational system to become the spiritual background and ethics of the whole Japanese nation. Novels like *Musashi* and the films and plays derived from them aided in the process.

The time of Musashi is as close and real to the modern Japanese as is the Civil War to Americans. Thus the comparison to *Gone with the Wind* is by no means far-fetched. The age of the samurai is still very much alive in Japanese minds. Contrary to the picture of the modern Japanese as merely group oriented "economic animals," many Japanese prefer to see themselves as fiercely individualistic, high-principled, self-disciplined and aesthetically sensitive modern-day Musashis. Both pictures have some validity, illustrating the complexity of the Japanese soul behind the seemingly bland and uniform exterior.

Musashi is very different from the highly psychological and often neurotic novels that have been the mainstay of translations of modern Japanese literature into English. But it is nevertheless fully in the mainstream of traditional Japanese fiction and popular Japanese thought. Its episodic presentation is not merely the result of its original appearance as a newspaper serial but is a favorite technique dating back to the beginnings of Japanese storytelling. Its romanticized view of the noble swordsman is a stereotype of the feudal past enshrined in hundreds of other stories and samurai movies. Its emphasis on the cultivation of self-control and inner personal strength through austere Zen-like self-discipline is a major feature of Japanese personality today. So also is the pervading love of nature and sense of closeness to it. *Musashi* is not just a great adventure story. Beyond that, it gives both a glimpse into Japanese history and a view into the idealized self-image of the contemporary Japanese.

January 1981

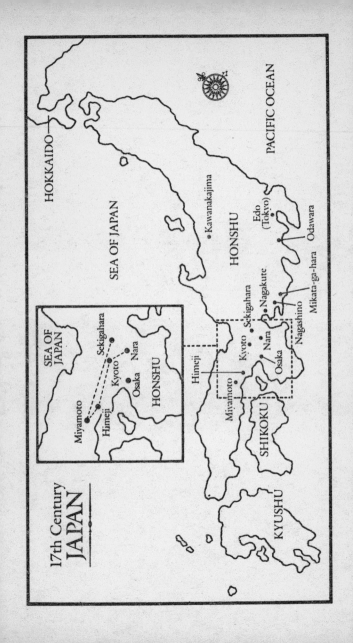

THE WAY
OF THE
SAMURAI

1

The Little Bell

Takezō lay among the corpses. There were thousands of them.

"The whole world's gone crazy," he thought dimly. "A man might as well be a dead leaf, floating in the autumn breeze."

He himself looked like one of the lifeless bodies surrounding him. He tried to raise his head, but could only lift it a few inches from the ground. He couldn't remember ever feeling so weak. "How long have I been here?" he wondered.

Flies came buzzing around his head. He wanted to brush them away, but couldn't even muster the energy to raise his arm. It was stiff, almost brittle, like the rest of his body. "I must've been out for quite a while," he thought, wiggling one finger at a time. Little did he know he was wounded, with two bullets lodged firmly in his thigh.

Low, dark clouds shifted ominously across the sky. The night before, sometime between midnight and dawn, a blinding rain had drenched the plain of

Sekigahara. It was now past noon on the fifteenth of the ninth month of 1600. Though the typhoon had passed, now and then fresh torrents of rain would fall on the corpses and onto Takezō's upturned face. Each time it came, he'd open and close his mouth like a fish, trying to drink in the droplets. "It's like the water they wipe a dying man's lips with," he reflected, savoring each bit of moisture. His head was numb, his thoughts the fleeting shadows of delirium.

His side had lost. He knew that much. Kobayakawa Hideaki, supposedly an ally, had been secretly in league with the Eastern Army, and when he turned on Ishida Mitsunari's troops at twilight, the tide of battle turned too. He then attacked the armies of other commanders—Ukita, Shimazu and Konishi—and the collapse of the Western Army was complete. In only half a day's fighting, the question of who would henceforth rule the country was settled. It was Tokugawa Ieyasu, the powerful Edo daimyō.

Images of his sister and the old villagers floated before his eyes. "I'm dying," he thought without a tinge of sadness. "Is this what it's really like?" He felt drawn to the peace of death, like a child mesmerized by a flame.

Suddenly one of the nearby corpses raised its head. "Takezō."

The images of his mind ceased. As if awakened from the dead, he turned his head toward the sound. The voice, he was sure, was that of his best friend. With all his strength he raised himself slightly, squeezing out a whisper barely audible above the pelting rain. "Matahachi, is that you?" Then he collapsed, lay still and listened.

"Takezō! Are you really alive?"

"Yes, alive!" he shouted in a sudden outburst of bravado. "And you? You'd better not die either. Don't you dare!" His eyes were wide open now, and a smile played faintly about his lips.

"Not me! No, sir." Gasping for breath, crawling on his elbows and dragging his legs stiffly behind him, Matahachi inched his way toward his friend. He made a grab for Takezō's hand but only caught his small finger with his own. As childhood friends they'd often sealed promises with this gesture. He came closer and gripped the whole hand.

"I can't believe you're all right too! We must be the only survivors."

"Don't speak too soon. I haven't tried to get up yet."

"I'll help you. Let's get out of here!"

Suddenly Takezō pulled Matahachi to the ground and growled, "Play dead! More trouble coming!"

The ground began to rumble like a caldron. Peeking through their arms, they watched the approaching whirlwind close in on them. Then they were nearer, lines of jet-black horsemen hurtling directly toward them.

"The bastards! They're back!" exclaimed Matahachi, raising his knee as if preparing for a sprint. Takezō seized his ankle, nearly breaking it, and yanked him to the ground.

In a moment the horses were flying past them—hundreds of muddy lethal hooves galloping in formation, riding roughshod over the fallen samurai. Battle cries on their lips, their armor and weapons clinking and clanking, the riders came on and on.

Matahachi lay on his stomach, eyes closed, hoping against hope they would not be trampled, but

Takezō stared unblinkingly upward. The horses passed so close they could smell their sweat. Then it was over.

Miraculously they were uninjured and undetected, and for several minutes both remained silent in disbelief.

"Saved again!" exclaimed Takezō, reaching his hand out to Matahachi. Still hugging the ground, Matahachi slowly turned his head to show a broad, slightly trembling grin. "Somebody's on our side, that's for sure," he said huskily.

The two friends helped each other, with great difficulty, to their feet. Slowly they made their way across the battlefield to the safety of the wooded hills, hobbling along with arms around each other's shoulders. There they collapsed but after a rest began foraging for food. For two days they subsisted on wild chestnuts and edible leaves in the sodden hollows of Mount Ibuki. This kept them from starving, but Takezō's stomach ached and Matahachi's bowels tormented him. No food could fill him, no drink quench his thirst, but even he felt his strength returning bit by bit.

The storm on the fifteenth marked the end of the fall typhoons. Now, only two nights later, a cold white moon glared grimly down from a cloudless sky.

They both knew how dangerous it was to be on the road in the glaring moonlight, their shadows looming like silhouette targets in clear view of any patrols searching for stragglers. The decision to risk it had been Takezō's. With Matahachi in such misery, saying he'd rather be captured than continue trying to walk, there really didn't seem to be much choice. They had to move on, but it was also clear that they had to find a place to lie low and rest. They made their way slowly in what they thought was the direction of the small town of Tarui.

"Can you make it?" Takezō asked repeatedly. He held his friend's arm around his own shoulder to help him along. "Are you all right?" It was the labored breathing that worried him. "You want to rest?"

"I'm all right." Matahachi tried to sound brave, but his face was paler than the moon above them. Even with his lance for a walking stick, he could barely put one foot in front of the other.

He'd been apologizing abjectly over and over. "I'm sorry, Takezō. I know it's me who's slowing us down. I'm really sorry."

The first few times Takezō had simply brushed this off with "Forget it." Eventually, when they stopped to rest, he turned to his friend and burst out, "Look, I'm the one who should be apologizing. I'm the one who got you into this in the first place, remember? Remember how I told you my plan, how I was finally going to do something that would really have impressed my father? I've never been able to stand the fact that to his dying day he was sure I'd never amount to anything. I was going to show him! Ha!"

Takezō's father, Munisai, had once served under Lord Shimmen of Iga. As soon as Takezō heard that Ishida Mitsunari was raising an army, he was convinced that the chance of a lifetime had finally arrived. His father had been a samurai. Wasn't it only natural that he would be made one too? He ached to enter the fray, to prove his mettle, to have word spread like wildfire through the village that he had decapitated an enemy general. He had wanted desperately to prove he was somebody to be reckoned with, to be respected—not just the village troublemaker.

Takezō reminded Matahachi of all this, and Matahachi nodded. "I know. I know. But I felt the same way. It wasn't just you."

Takezō went on: "I wanted you to come with me because we've always done everything together. But didn't your mother carry on something awful! Yelling and telling everybody I was crazy and no good! And your fiancée Otsū, and my sister and everybody else crying and saying village boys should stay in the village. Oh, maybe they had their reasons. We are both only sons, and if we get ourselves killed there's no one else to carry on the family names. But who cares? Is that any way to live?"

They had slipped out of the village unnoticed and were convinced that no further barrier lay between themselves and the honors of battle. When they reached the Shimmen encampment, however, they came face to face with the realities of war. They were told straightaway they would not be made samurai, not overnight nor even in a few weeks, no matter who their fathers had been. To Ishida and the other generals, Takezō and Matahachi were a pair of country bumpkins, little more than children who happened to have got their hands on a couple of lances. The best they could wangle was to be allowed to stay on as common foot soldiers. Their responsibilities, if they could be called that, consisted of carrying weapons, rice kettles and other utensils, cutting grass, working on the road gangs and occasionally going out as scouts.

"Samurai, ha!" said Takezō. "What a joke. General's head! I didn't even get near an enemy samurai, let alone a general. Well, at least it's all over. Now what are we going to do? I can't leave you here all alone. If I did, I could never face your mother or Otsū again.''

"Takezō, I don't blame you for the mess we're in. It wasn't your fault we lost. If anybody's to blame, it's that two-faced Kobayakawa. I'd really like to get my hands on him. I'd kill the son of a bitch!''

A couple of hours later they were standing on the edge of a small plain, gazing out over a sea of reedlike miscanthus, battered and broken by the storm. No houses. No lights.

There were lots of corpses here too, lying just as they had fallen. The head of one rested in some tall grass. Another was on its back in a small stream. Still another was entangled grotesquely with a dead horse. The rain had washed the blood away, and in the moonlight the dead flesh looked like fish scales. All around them was the lonely autumn litany of bellrings and crickets.

A stream of tears cleared a white path down Matahachi's grimy face. He heaved the sigh of a very sick man.

"Takezō, if I die will you take care of Otsū?"

"What are you talking about?"

"I feel like I'm dying."

Takezō snapped. "Well, if that's the way you feel, you probably will." He was exasperated, wishing his friend were stronger, so he could lean on him once in a while, not physically, but for encouragement. "Come on, Matahachi! Don't be such a crybaby."

"My mother has people to look after her, but Otsū's all alone in the world. Always has been. I feel so sorry for her, Takezō. Promise you'll take care of her if I'm not around."

"Get hold of yourself! People don't die from diarrhea. Sooner or later we're going to find a house, and when we do I'll put you to bed and get some medicine for you. Now stop all this blubbering about dying!"

A little farther on, they came to a place where the piles of lifeless bodies made it look as if a whole division had been wiped out. By this time they were callous to the sight of gore. Their glazed eyes took in the scene with cold indifference and they stopped to rest again.

While they were catching their breath, they heard something move among the corpses. Both of them shrank back in fright, instinctively crouching down with their eyes peeled and senses alerted.

The figure made a quick darting movement, like that of a surprised rabbit. As their eyes focused, they saw that whoever it was was squatting close to the ground. Thinking at first it was a stray samurai, they braced themselves for a dangerous encounter, but to their amazement the fierce warrior turned out to be a young girl. She seemed to be about thirteen or fourteen and wore a kimono with rounded sleeves. The narrow obi around her waist, though patched in places, was of gold brocade; there among the corpses she presented a bizarre sight indeed. She looked over and stared at them suspiciously with shrewd catlike eyes.

Takezō and Matahachi were both wondering the same thing: what on earth could bring a young girl to a ghost-ridden, corpse-strewn field in the dead of night?

For a time they both simply stared back at her. Then Takezō said, "Who are you?"

She blinked a couple of times, got to her feet and sped away.

"Stop!" shouted Takezō. "I just want to ask you a question. Don't go!"

But gone she was, like a flash of lightning in the night. The sound of a small bell receded eerily into the darkness.

"Could it have been a ghost?" Takezō mused aloud as he stared vacantly into the thin mist.

Matahachi shivered and forced a laugh. "If there were any ghosts around here, I think they'd be those of soldiers, don't you?"

"I wish I hadn't scared her away," said Takezō. "There's got to be a village around here somewhere. She could've given us directions."

They went on and climbed the nearer of the two hills ahead of them. In the hollow on the other side was the marsh that stretched south from Mount Fuwa. And a light, only half a mile away.

When they approached the farmhouse, they got the impression that it wasn't of the run-of-the-mill variety. For one thing, it was surrounded by a thick dirt wall. For another, its gate verged on being grandiose. Or at least the remains of the gate, for it was old and badly in need of repair.

Takezō went up to the door and rapped lightly. "Is anybody home?"

Getting no answer, he tried again. "Sorry to bother you at this hour, but my friend here is sick. We don't want to cause any trouble—he just needs some rest."

9

They heard whispering inside and, presently, the sound of someone coming to the door.

"You're stragglers from Sekigahara, aren't you?" The voice belonged to a young girl.

"That's right," said Takezō. "We were under Lord Shimmen of Iga."

"Go away! If you're found around here, we'll be in trouble."

"Look, we're very sorry to bother you like this, but we've been walking a long time. My friend needs some rest, that's all, and—"

"Please go away!"

"All right, if you really want us to, but couldn't you give my friend some medicine? His stomach's in such bad shape it's hard for us to keep moving."

"Well, I don't know. . . ."

After a moment or two, they heard footsteps and a little tinkling sound receding into the house, growing fainter and fainter.

Just then they noticed the face. It was in a side window, a woman's face, and it had been watching them all along.

"Akemi," she called out, "let them in. They're foot soldiers. The Tokugawa patrols aren't going to be wasting time on them. They're nobodies."

Akemi opened the door, and the woman, who introduced herself as Okō, came and listened to Takezō's story.

It was agreed that they could have the woodshed to sleep in. To quiet his bowels, Matahachi was given magnolia charcoal powder and thin rice gruel with scallions in it. Over the next few days, he slept almost without interruption, while Takezō, sitting vigil by his side, used cheap spirits to treat the bullet wounds in his thigh.

One evening about a week later, Takezō and Matahachi sat chatting.

"They must have a trade of some kind," Takezō remarked.

"I couldn't care less what they do. I'm just glad they took us in."

But Takezō's curiosity was aroused. "The mother's not so old," he went on. "It's strange, the two of them living alone here in the mountains."

"Umm. Don't you think the girl looks a little like Otsū?"

"There is something about her that puts me in mind of Otsū, but I don't think they really look alike. They're both nice-looking, that's about it. What do you suppose she was doing the first time we saw her, creeping around all those corpses in the middle of the night? It didn't seem to bother her at all. Ha! I can still see it. Her face was as calm and serene as those dolls they make in Kyoto. What a picture!"

Matahachi motioned for him to be quiet.

"Shh! I hear her bell."

Akemi's light knock on the door sounded like the tapping of a woodpecker. "Matahachi, Takezō," she called softly.

"Yes?"

"It's me."

Takezō got up and undid the lock. She came in carrying a tray of medicine and food and asked them how they were.

"Much better, thanks to you and your mother."

"Mother said that even if you feel better, you shouldn't talk too loud or go outside."

Takezō spoke for the two of them. "We're really sorry to put you to so much trouble."

"Oh, that's okay, you just have to be careful. Ishida Mitsunari and some of the other generals haven't been caught yet. They're keeping a close watch on this area and the roads are crawling with Tokugawa troops."

"They are?"

"So even though you're only foot soldiers, Mother said that if we're caught hiding you, we'll be arrested."

"We won't make a sound," Takezō promised. "I'll even cover Matahachi's face with a rag if he snores too loudly."

Akemi smiled, turned to go and said, "Good night. I'll see you in the morning."

"Wait!" said Matahachi. "Why don't you hang around and talk awhile?"

"I can't."

"Why not?"

"Mother'd be angry."

"Why worry about her? How old are you?"

"Sixteen."

"Small for your age, aren't you?"

"Thanks for telling me."

"Where's your father?"

"I don't have one anymore."

"Sorry. Then how do you live?"

"We make moxa."

"That medicine you burn on your skin to get rid of pain?"

"Yes, the moxa from hereabouts is famous. In spring we cut mugwort on Mount Ibuki. In summer we

12

dry it and in fall and winter make it into moxa. We sell it in Tarui. People come from all over just to buy it."

"I guess you don't need a man around to do that."

"Well, if that's all you wanted to know, I'd better be going."

"Hold on, just another second," said Takezō. "I have one more question."

"Well?"

"The other night, the night we came here, we saw a girl out on the battlefield and she looked just like you. That was you, wasn't it?"

Akemi turned quickly and opened the door.

"What were you doing out there?"

She slammed the door behind her, and as she ran to the house the little bell rang out in a strange, erratic rhythm.

2

The Comb

At five feet eight or nine, Takezō was tall for people of
his time. His body was like a fine steed's: strong and
supple, with long, sinewy limbs. His lips were full and
crimson, and his thick black eyebrows fell short of
being bushy by virtue of their fine shape. Extending
well beyond the outer corners of his eyes, they served
to accentuate his manliness. The villagers called him
"the child of a fat year," an expression used only
about children whose features were larger than aver-
age. Far from an insult, the nickname nonetheless set
him apart from the other youngsters, and for this
reason caused him considerable embarrassment in his
early years.

Although it was never used in reference to Matahachi, the same expression could have been applied to
him as well. Somewhat shorter and stockier than Takezō, he was barrel-chested and round-faced, giving
an impression of joviality if not downright buffoonery.
His prominent, slightly protruding eyes were given to
shifting when he talked, and most jokes made at his

15

expense hinged on his resemblance to the frogs that croaked unceasingly through the summer nights.

Both youths were at the height of their growing years, and thus quick to recover from most ailments. By the time Takezō's wounds had completely healed, Matahachi could no longer stand his incarceration. He took to pacing the woodshed and complaining endlessly about being cooped up. More than once he made the mistake of saying he felt like a cricket in a damp, dark hole, leaving himself wide open to Takezō's retort that frogs and crickets are supposed to like such living arrangements. At some point, Matahachi must have begun peeping into the house, because one day he leaned over to his cellmate as if to impart some earth-shattering news. "Every evening," he whispered gravely, "the widow puts powder on her face and pretties herself up!" Takezō's face became that of a girl-hating twelve-year-old detecting defection, a budding interest in "them," in his closest friend. Matahachi had turned traitor, and the look was one of unmistakable disgust.

Matahachi began going to the house and sitting by the hearth with Akemi and her youthful mother. After three or four days of chatting and joking with them, the convivial guest became one of the family. He stopped going back to the woodshed even at night, and the rare times he did, he had sake on his breath and tried to entice Takezō into the house by singing the praises of the good life just a few feet away.

"You're crazy!" Takezō would reply in exasperation. "You're going to get us killed, or at least picked up. We lost, we're stragglers—can't you get that through your head? We have to be careful and lie low until things cool down."

He soon grew tired of trying to reason with his pleasure-loving friend, however, and started instead to cut him short with curt replies:

"I don't like sake," or sometimes: "I like it out here. It's cozy."

But Takezō was going stir-crazy too. He was bored beyond endurance, and eventually showed signs of weakening. "Is it really safe?" he'd ask. "This neighborhood, I mean? No sign of patrols? You're sure?"

After being entombed for twenty days in the woodshed, he finally emerged like a half-starved prisoner of war. His skin had the translucent, waxen look of death, all the more apparent as he stood beside his sun-and-sake-reddened friend. He squinted up at the clear blue sky, and stretching his arms broadly, yawned extravagantly. When his cavernous mouth finally came closed, one noticed that his brows had been knit all the while. His face wore a troubled air.

"Matahachi," he said seriously, "we're imposing on these people. They're taking a big risk having us around. I think we should start for home."

"I guess you're right," said Matahachi. "But they're not letting anyone through the barriers unchecked. The roads to Ise and Kyoto are both impossible, according to the widow. She says we should stay put until the snow comes. The girl says so too. She's convinced we should stay hidden, and you know she's out and about every day."

"You call sitting by the fire drinking being hidden?"

"Sure. You know what I did? The other day some of Tokugawa's men—they're still looking for General Ukita—came snooping around. I got rid of the bastards just by going out and greeting them." At this point, as Takezō's eyes widened in disbelief, Matahachi let out a rolling belly laugh. When it subsided, he went on. "You're safer out in the open than you are crouching in the woodshed listening for footsteps and going crazy. That's what I've been trying to tell you." Matahachi doubled up with laughter again, and Takezō shrugged.

"Maybe you're right. That could be the best way to handle things."

He still had his reservations, but after this conversation he moved into the house. Okō, who obviously liked having people, more specifically men, around, made them feel completely at home. Occasionally, however, she gave them a jolt by suggesting that one of them marry Akemi. This seemed to fluster Matahachi more than Takezō, who simply ignored the suggestion or countered it with a humorous remark.

It was the season for the succulent, fragrant *matsutake*, which grows at the bases of pine trees, and Takezō relaxed enough to go hunting the large mushrooms on the wooded mountain just behind the house. Akemi, basket in hand, would search from tree to tree. Each time she picked up their scent, her innocent voice reverberated through the woods.

"Takezō, over here! Lots of them!"

Hunting around nearby, he invariably replied, "There are plenty over here too."

Through the pine branches, the autumn sun filtered down on them in thin, slanting shafts. The carpet of pine needles in the cool shelter of the trees was a soft dusty rose. When they tired, Akemi would challenge him, giggling. "Let's see who has the most!"

"I do," he'd always reply smugly, at which point she'd begin inspecting his basket.

This day was no different from the others. "Ha, ha! I knew it!" she cried. Gleefully triumphant, the way only girls that young can be, with no hint of self-consciousness or affected modesty, she bent over his basket. "You've got a bunch of toadstools in your batch!" Then she discarded the poisonous fungi one by one, not actually counting out loud, but with movements so slow and deliberate Takezō could hardly ignore them, even with his eyes closed. She flung each one as far as she could. Her task completed, she looked up, her young face beaming with self-satisfaction.

"Now look how many more I have than you!"

"It's getting late," Takezō muttered. "Let's go home."

"You're cross because you lost, aren't you?"

She started racing down the mountainside like a pheasant, but suddenly stopped dead in her tracks, an expression of alarm clouding her face. Approaching diagonally across the grove, halfway down the slope, was a mountain of a man; his strides were long and languorous, and his glaring eyes were trained directly on the frail young girl before him. He looked frighteningly primitive. Everything about him smacked of the struggle to survive, and he had a distinct air of bellicosity: ferocious bushy eyebrows and a thick, curling upper lip; a heavy sword, a cloak of mail, and an animal skin wrapped around him.

"Akemi!" he roared, as he came closer to her. He grinned broadly, showing a row of yellow, decaying teeth, but Akemi's face continued to register nothing but horror.

"Is that wonderful mama of yours home?" he asked with labored sarcasm.

"Yes," came a peep of a reply.

"Well, when you go home, I want you to tell her something. Would you do that for me?" He spoke mock politely.

"Yes."

His tone became harsh. "You tell her she's not putting anything over on me, trying to make money behind my back. You tell her I'll be around soon for my cut. Have you got that?"

Akemi said nothing.

"She probably thinks I don't know about it, but the guy she sold the goods to came straight to me. I bet you were going to Sekigahara too, weren't you, little one?"

"No, of course not!" she protested weakly.

"Well, never mind. Just tell her what I said. If she pulls any more fast ones, I'll kick her out of the neighborhood." He glared at the girl for a moment, then lumbered off in the direction of the marsh.

Takezō turned his eyes from the departing stranger and looked at Akemi with concern. "Who on earth was that?"

Akemi, her lips still trembling, answered wearily, "His name is Tsujikaze. He comes from the village of Fuwa." Her voice was barely above a whisper.

"He's a freebooter, isn't he?"

"Yes."

"What's he so worked up about?"

She stood there without answering.

"I won't tell anybody," he assured her. "Can't you even tell me?"

Akemi, obviously miserable, seemed to be

searching for words. Suddenly she leaned against Takezō's chest and pleaded, "Promise you won't tell anyone?"

"Who am I going to tell? The Tokugawa samurai?"

"Remember the night you first saw me? At Sekigahara?"

"Of course I remember."

"Well, haven't you figured out yet what I was doing?"

"No. I haven't thought about it," he said with a straight face.

"Well, I was stealing!" She looked at him closely, gauging his reaction.

"Stealing?"

"After a battle, I go to the battlefield and take things off the dead soldiers: swords, scabbard ornaments, incense bags—anything we can sell." She looked at him again for a sign of disapproval, but his face betrayed none. "It scares me," she sighed, then, turning pragmatic, "but we need the money for food and if I say I don't want to go, Mother gets furious."

The sun was still fairly high in the sky. At Akemi's suggestion, Takezō sat down on the grass. Through the pines, they could look down on the house in the marsh.

Takezō nodded to himself, as if figuring something out. A bit later he said, "Then that story about cutting mugwort in the mountains. Making it into moxa. That was all a lie?"

"Oh, no. We do that too! But Mother has such expensive tastes. We'd never be able to make a living on moxa. When my father was alive, we lived in the biggest house in the village—in all seven villages of

Ibuki, as a matter of fact. We had lots of servants, and Mother always had beautiful things.''

"Was your father a merchant?''

"Oh, no. He was the leader of the local freebooters.'' Akemi's eyes shone with pride. It was clear she no longer feared Takezō's reaction and was giving vent to her true feelings, her jaw set, her small hands tightening into fists as she spoke. "This Tsujikaze Temma—the man we just met—killed him. At least, everyone says he did.''

"You mean your father was murdered?''

Nodding silently, she began in spite of herself to weep, and Takezō felt something deep inside himself start to thaw. He hadn't felt much sympathy for the girl at first. Though smaller than most other girls of sixteen, she talked like a grown woman much of the time, and every once in a while made a quick movement that put one on guard. But when the tears began to drop from her long eyelashes, he suddenly melted with pity. He wanted to hug her in his arms, to protect her.

All the same, she was not a girl who'd had anything resembling a proper upbringing. That there was no nobler calling than that of her father seemed to be something she never questioned. Her mother had persuaded her that it was quite all right to strip corpses, not in order to eat, but in order to live nicely. Many out-and-out thieves would have shrunk from the task.

During the long years of feudal strife, it had reached the point where all the shiftless good-for-nothings in the countryside drifted into making their living this way. People had more or less come to expect it of them. When war broke out, the local military rulers even made use of their services, rewarding them generously for setting fire to enemy supplies, spreading false rumors, stealing horses from enemy camps and the like. Most often their services were bought, but even when they were not, a war offered a host of opportunities; besides foraging among corpses for valuables, they could sometimes even wangle rewards for slaying samurai whose heads they'd merely stumbled upon and picked up. One large battle made it possible for these unscrupulous pilferers to live comfortably for six months or a year.

During the most turbulent times, even the ordinary farmer and woodcutter had learned to profit from human misery and bloodshed. The fighting on the outskirts of their village might keep these simple souls from working, but they had ingeniously adapted to the situation and discovered how to pick over the remains of human life like vultures. Partly because of these intrusions, the professional looters maintained strict surveillance over their respective territories. It was an ironclad rule that poachers—namely, brigands who trespassed on the more powerful brigands' turf—could not go unpunished. Those who dared infringe on the assumed rights of these thugs were liable to cruel retribution.

Akemi shivered and said, "What'll we do? Temma's henchmen are on their way here, I just know it."

"Don't worry," Takezō reassured her. "If they do show up, I'll greet them personally."

When they came down from the mountain, twilight had descended on the marsh, and all was still. A smoke trail from the bath fire at the house crept along the top of a row of tall rushes like an airborne undulating snake. Okō, having finished applying her nightly makeup, was standing idly at the back door. When she saw her daughter approaching side by side with Takezō, she shouted, "Akemi, what have you been doing out so late?"

There was sternness in her eyes and voice. The girl, who had been walking along absentmindedly, was brought up short. She was more sensitive to her mother's moods than to anything else in the world. Her mother had both nurtured this sensitivity and learned to exploit it, to manipulate her daughter like a puppet with a mere look or gesture. Akemi quickly fled Takezō's side and, blushing noticeably, ran ahead and into the house.

The next day Akemi told her mother about Tsujikaze Temma. Okō flew into a rage.

"Why didn't you tell me immediately?" she screamed, rushing around like a madwoman, tearing at her hair, taking things out of drawers and closets and piling them all together in the middle of the room.

"Matahachi! Takezō! Give me a hand! We have to hide everything."

Matahachi shifted a board pointed to by Okō and hoisted himself up above the ceiling. There wasn't much space between the ceiling and the rafters. One could barely crawl about, but it served Okō's purpose, and most likely that of her departed husband. Takezō, standing on a stool between mother and daughter, began handing things up to Matahachi one by one. If Takezō hadn't heard Akemi's story the day before, he would've been amazed at the variety of articles he now saw.

Takezō knew the two of them had been at this for a long time, but even so, it was astonishing how much they had accumulated. There was a dagger, a spear tassel, a sleeve from a suit of armor, a helmet without a crown, a miniature, portable shrine, a Buddhist rosary, a banner staff. . . . There was even a lacquered saddle, beautifully carved and ornately decorated with gold, silver and mother-of-pearl inlay.

From the opening in the ceiling Matahachi peered out, a perplexed look on his face. "Is that everything?"

"No, there's one thing more," said Okō, rushing off. In a moment she was back, bearing a four-foot sword of black oak. Takezō started passing it up to Matahachi's outstretched arms, but the weight, the curve, the perfect balance of the weapon impressed him so deeply that he could not let it go.

He turned to Okō, a sheepish look on his face. "Do you think I could have this?" he asked, his eyes showing a new vulnerability. He glanced at his feet, as if to say he knew he'd done nothing to deserve the sword.

"Do you really want it?" she said softly, a motherly tone in her voice.

"Yes . . . Yes . . . I really do!"

Although she didn't actually say he could have it, she smiled, showing a dimple, and Takezō knew the sword was his. Matahachi jumped down from the ceiling, bursting with envy. He fingered the sword covetously, making Okō laugh.

"See how the little man pouts because he didn't get a present!" She tried to placate him by giving him a handsome leather purse beaded with agate. Matahachi didn't look very happy with it. His eyes kept shifting to the black-oak sword. His feelings were hurt and the purse did little to assuage his wounded pride.

When her husband was alive, Okō had apparently acquired the habit of taking a leisurely, steaming hot bath every evening, putting on her makeup, and then drinking a bit of sake. In short, she spent the same amount of time on her toilette as the highest-paid geisha. It was not the sort of luxury that ordinary people could afford, but she insisted on it and had even taught Akemi to follow the same routine, although the girl found it boring and the reasons for it unfathomable. Not only did Okō like to live well; she was determined to remain young forever.

That evening, as they sat around the recessed floor hearth, Okō poured Matahachi's sake and tried to persuade Takezō to have some as well. When he refused, she put the cup in his hand, seized him by the wrist and forced him to raise it to his lips.

"Men are supposed to be able to drink," she chided. "If you can't do it alone, I'll help."

From time to time, Matahachi stared uneasily at her. Okō, conscious of his gaze, became even more familiar with Takezō. Placing her hand playfully on his knee, she began humming a popular love song.

By this time, Matahachi had had enough. Suddenly turning to Takezō, he blurted out, "We ought to be moving on soon!"

This had the desired effect. "But . . . but . . . where would you go?" Okō stammered.

"Back to Miyamoto. My mother's there, and so is my fianceé."

Momentarily taken by surprise, Okō swiftly regained her composure. Her eyes narrowed to slits, her smile froze, her voice turned acid. "Well, please accept my apologies for delaying you, for taking you in and giving you a home. If there's a girl waiting for you, you'd better hurry on back. Far be it from me to keep you!"

* * *

After receiving the black-oak sword, Takezō was never without it. He derived an indescribable pleasure from simply holding it. Often he'd squeeze the handle tightly or run its blunt edge along his palm, just to feel the perfect proportion of the curve to the length. When he slept, he hugged it to his body. The cool touch of the wooden surface against his cheek reminded him of the floor of the dōjō where he'd practiced sword techniques in winter. This nearly perfect instrument of both art and death reawakened in him the fighting spirit he had inherited from his father.

Takezō had loved his mother, but she had left his father and moved away when he was still small, leaving him alone with Munisai, a martinet who wouldn't have known how to spoil a child in the unlikely event that he had wanted to. In his father's presence, the boy had always felt awkward and frightened, never really at ease. When he was nine years old, he'd so craved a kind word from his mother that he had run away from home and gone all the way to Harima Province, where she was living. Takezō never learned why his mother and father had separated, and at that age, an explanation might not have helped much. She had married another samurai, by whom she had one more child.

Once the little runaway had reached Harima, he wasted no time in locating his mother. On that occasion, she took him to a wooded area behind the local shrine, so they wouldn't be seen, and there, with tear-filled eyes, hugged him tightly and tried to explain why he had to go back to his father. Takezō never forgot the scene; every detail of it remained vividly in his mind as long as he lived.

Of course, Munisai, being the samurai he was,

had sent people to retrieve his son the moment he
learned of his disappearance. It was obvious where
the child had gone. Takezō was returned to Miyamoto
like a bundle of firewood, strapped on the back of an
unsaddled horse. Munisai, by way of greeting, had
called him an insolent brat, and in a state of rage
verging on hysteria, caned him until he could cane no
more. Takezō remembered more explicitly than anything else the venom with which his father had spat
out his ultimatum: "If you go to your mother one more
time, I'll disown you."

Not long after this incident, Takezō learned that
his mother had fallen ill and died. Her death had the
effect of transforming him from a quiet, gloomy child
into the village bully. Even Munisai was intimidated
eventually. When he took a truncheon to the boy, the
latter countered with a wooden staff. The only one
who ever stood up to him was Matahachi, also the son
of a samurai; the other children all did Takezō's bid-
ding. By the time he was twelve or thirteen, he was
almost as tall as an adult.

One year, a wandering swordsman named Arima
Kihei put up a gold-emblazoned banner and offered to
take on challengers from the village. Takezō killed him
effortlessly, eliciting praise for his valor from the
villagers. Their high opinion of him, however, was
short-lived, since as he grew older, he became increasingly unmanageable and brutal. Many thought him
sadistic, and soon, whenever he appeared on the
scene, people gave him a very wide berth. His attitude
toward them grew to reflect their coldness.

When his father, as harsh and unrelenting as ever,
finally died, the cruel streak in Takezō widened even
more. If it had not been for his older sister, Ogin,

Takezō would probably have gotten himself into something far over his head and been driven out of the village by an angry mob. Fortunately, he loved his sister and, powerless before her tears, usually did whatever she asked.

Going off to war with Matahachi was a turning point for Takezō. It indicated that somehow he wanted to take his place in society alongside other men. The defeat at Sekigahara had abruptly curtailed such hopes, and he found himself once again plunged into the dark reality from which he thought he had escaped. Still, he was a youth blessed with the sublime light-heartedness that flourishes only in an age of strife. When he slept, his face became as placid as an infant's, completely untroubled by thoughts of the morrow. He had his share of dreams, asleep or awake, but he suffered few real disappointments. Having so little to begin with, he had little to lose, and although he was in a sense uprooted, he was also unfettered by shackles.

Breathing deeply and steadily, holding on to his wooden sword tightly, Takezō at this moment may well have been dreaming, a faint smile on his lips as visions of his gentle sister and his peaceful hometown cascaded like a mountain waterfall before his closed, heavily lashed eyes. Okō, carrying a lamp, slipped into his room. "What a peaceful face," she marveled under her breath; she reached out and lightly touched his lips with her fingers.

Then she blew out the lamp and lay down beside him. Curling up catlike, she inched closer and closer to his body, her whitened face and colorful nightgown, really too youthful for her, hidden by the darkness.

The only sound that could be heard was that of dew-drops dripping onto the windowsill.

"I wonder if he's still a virgin," she mused as she reached out to remove his wooden sword.

The instant she touched it, Takezō was on his feet and shouting, "Thief! Thief!"

Okō was thrown over onto the lamp, which cut into her shoulder and chest. Takezō was wrenching her arm without mercy. She screamed out in pain.

Astonished, he released her. "Oh, it's you. I thought it was a thief."

"Oooh," moaned Okō. "That hurt!"

"I'm sorry. I didn't know it was you."

"You don't know your own strength. You almost tore my arm off."

"I said I was sorry. What are you doing here, anyway?"

Ignoring his innocent query, she quickly recovered from her arm injury and tried to coil the same limb around his neck, cooing, "You don't have to apologize. Takezō . . ." She ran the back of her hand softly against his cheek.

"Hey! What are you doing? Are you crazy?" he shouted, shrinking away from her touch.

"Don't make so much noise, you idiot. You know how I feel about you." She went on trying to fondle him, with him swatting at her like a man attacked by a swarm of bees.

"Yes, and I'm very grateful. Neither of us will ever forget how kind you've been, taking us in and all."

"I don't mean that, Takezō. I'm talking about my woman's feelings—the lovely, warm feeling I have for you."

"Wait a minute," he said, jumping up. "I'll light the lamp!"

"Oh, how can you be so cruel," she whimpered, moving to embrace him again.

"Don't do that!" he cried indignantly. "Stop it—I mean it!"

Something in his voice, something intense and resolute, frightened Okō into halting her attack.

Takezō felt his bones wobbling, his teeth rattling. Never had he encountered such a formidable adversary. Not even when he'd looked up at the horses galloping past him at Sekigahara had his heart palpitated so. He sat cringing in the corner of the room.

"Go away, please," he pleaded. "Go back to your own room. If you don't, I'll call Matahachi. I'll wake the whole house up!"

Okō did not budge. She sat there in the dark, breathing heavily and staring at him with narrowed eyes. She wasn't about to be rebuffed. "Takezō," she cooed again. "Don't you understand how I feel?"

He made no reply.

"Don't you?"

"Yes, but do you understand how I feel, being snuck up on in my sleep, frightened to death and mauled by a tiger in the dark?"

It was her turn to be silent. A low whisper, almost a growl, emerged from a deep part of her throat. She said each syllable with a vengeance. "How can you embarrass me so?"

"*I* embarrass *you?*"

"Yes. This is mortifying."

They were both so tense they hadn't noticed the knocking at the door, which had apparently been going on for some time. Now the pounding was punctuated by shouts. "What's going on in there? Are you deaf? Open the door!"

A light appeared in the crack between the sliding rain shutters. Akemi was already awake. Then Matahachi's footsteps thudded toward them and his voice called, "What's going on?"

From the hallway now, Akemi cried out in alarm, "Mother! Are you in there? Please answer me!"

Blindly Okō scrambled back into her own room, just adjoining Takezō's, and answered from there. The men outside appeared to have pried open the shutters and stormed into the house. When she reached the hearth room she saw six or seven pairs of broad shoulders crowded into the adjacent, dirt-floored kitchen, which was a big step down, since it was set at a lower level than the other rooms.

One of the men shouted, "It's Tsujikaze Temma. Give us some light!"

The men barged rudely into the main part of the house. They didn't even stop to remove their sandals, a sure sign of habitual uncouthness. They began poking around everywhere—in the closets, in the drawers, under the thick straw tatami covering the floor. Temma seated himself royally by the hearth and watched as his henchmen systematically ransacked the rooms. He thoroughly enjoyed being in charge but soon seemed to tire of his own inactivity.

"This is taking too long," he growled, pounding his fist on the tatami. "You must have some of it here. Where is it?"

"I don't know what you're talking about," replied Okō, folding her hands over her stomach forbearingly.

"Don't give me that, woman!" he bellowed. "Where is it? I know it's here!"

"I don't have a thing!"

"Nothing?"

"Nothing."

"Well, then, maybe you don't. Maybe I have the wrong information. . . ." He eyed her warily, tugging and scratching at his beard. "That's enough, men!" he thundered.

Okō had meanwhile sat down in the next room, with the sliding door wide open. She had her back to him, but even so she looked defiant, as though telling him he could go ahead and search wherever he had a mind to.

"Okō," he called gruffly.

"What do you want?" came the icy reply.

"How about a little something to drink?"

"Would you like some water?"

"Don't push me . . ." he warned menacingly.

"The sake's in there. Drink it if you want to."

"Aw, Okō," he said, softening, almost admiring her for her coldhearted stubbornness. "Don't be that way. I haven't been to visit for a long time. Is this any way to treat an old friend?"

"Some visit!"

"Now, take it easy. You're partly to blame, you know. I've been hearing about what the 'moxa man's widow' has been up to from too many different people to think it's all lies. I hear you've been sending your lovely daughter out to rob corpses. Now, why would she be doing a thing like that?"

"Show me your proof!" she shrieked. "Where's the proof!"

"If I'd been planning to dig it out, I wouldn't have given Akemi advance warning. You know the rules of the game. It's my territory, and I've got to go through the motions of searching your house. Otherwise, everybody'd get the idea they could get away with the same thing. Then where'd I be? I've gotta protect myself, you know!"

She stared at him in steely silence, her head half turned toward him, chin and nose proudly raised.

"Well, I'm going to let you off this time. But just remember, I'm being especially nice to you."

"Nice to me? Who, you? That's a laugh!"

"Okō," he coaxed, "come here and pour me a drink."

When she showed no sign of moving, he exploded. "You crazy bitch! Can't you see that if you were nice to me, you wouldn't have to live like this?" He calmed down a bit, then advised her, "Think it over for a while."

"I'm overcome by your kindness, sir," came the venomous reply.

"You don't like me?"

"Just answer me this: Who killed my husband? I suppose you expect me to believe that you don't know?"

"If you want to take revenge on whoever it was, I'll be happy to help. Any way I can."

"Don't play dumb!"

"What do you mean by that?"

"You seem to hear so much from people. Haven't they told you that it was you yourself who killed him? Haven't you heard that Tsujikaze Temma was the murderer? Everyone else knows it. I may be the widow of a freebooter, but I haven't sunk so low that I'd play around with my husband's killer."

"You had to go and say it, didn't you—couldn't leave well enough alone, eh!" With a rueful laugh, he drained the sake cup in one gulp and poured another. "You know, you really shouldn't say things like that. It's not good for your health—or your pretty daughter's!"

"I'll bring Akemi up properly, and after she's married, I'll get back at you. Mark my word!"

Temma laughed until his shoulders, his whole body, shook like a cake of bean curd. After he'd downed all the sake he could find, he motioned to one of his men, who was positioned in a corner of the kitchen, his lance propped vertically against his shoulder. "You there," he boomed, "push aside some of the ceiling boards with the butt of your lance!"

The man did as he was told. As he went around the room, poking at the ceiling, Okō's treasure trove began falling to the floor like hailstones.

"Just as I suspected all along," said Temma, getting clumsily to his feet. "You see it, men. Evidence! She's broken the rules, no question about it. Take her outside and give her her punishment!"

The men converged on the hearth room, but abruptly came to a halt. Okō stood statuesquely in the doorway, as though daring them to lay a hand on her. Temma, who'd stepped down into the kitchen, called back impatiently, "What are you waiting for? Bring her out here!"

Nothing happened. Okō continued to stare the men down, and they remained as if paralyzed. Temma decided to take over. Clicking his tongue, he made for Okō, but he, too, stopped short in front of the doorway. Standing behind Okō, not visible from the kitchen, were two fierce-looking young men. Takezō was holding the wooden sword low, poised to fracture the shins of the first comer and anyone else stupid enough to follow. On the other side was Matahachi, holding a sword high in the air, ready to bring it down on the first neck that ventured through the doorway. Akemi was nowhere to be seen.

"So that's how it is," groaned Temma, suddenly remembering the scene on the mountainside. "I saw that one walking the other day with Akemi—the one with the stick. Who's the other one?"

Neither Matahachi nor Takezō said a word, making it clear that they intended to answer with their weapons. The tension mounted.

"There aren't supposed to be any men in this house," roared Temma. "You two . . . You must be from Sekigahara! You better watch your step—I'm warning you."

Neither of them moved a muscle.

"There isn't anybody in these parts who doesn't know the name of Tsujikaze Temma! I'll show you what we do to stragglers!"

Silence. Temma waved his men out of the way. One of them backed straight into the hearth, in the middle of the floor. He let out a yelp and fell in, sending a shower of sparks from the burning kindling up to the ceiling; in seconds, the room filled completely with smoke.

"Aarrgghh!"

As Temma lunged into the room, Matahachi brought down his sword with both hands, but the older man was too fast for him and the blow glanced off the tip of Temma's scabbard. Okō had taken refuge in the nearest corner while Takezō waited, his black-oak sword horizontally poised. He aimed at Temma's legs and swung with all his strength. The staff whizzed through the darkness, but there was no thud of impact.

36

Somehow this bull of a man had jumped up just in time and on the way down threw himself at Takezō with the force of a boulder.

Takezō felt as though he were tangling with a bear. This was the strongest man he had ever fought. Temma grabbed him by the throat and landed two or three blows that made him think his skull would crack. Then Takezō got his second wind and sent Temma flying through the air. He landed against the wall, rocking the house and everything in it. As Takezō raised the wooden sword to come down on Temma's head, the freebooter rolled over, jumped to his feet, and fled, with Takezō close on his tail.

Takezō was determined to not let Temma escape. That would be dangerous. His mind was made up; when he caught him, he was not going to do a halfway job of killing him. He would make absolutely certain that not a breath of life was left.

That was Takezō's nature; he was a creature of extremes. Even when he was a small child, there had been something primitive in his blood, something harking back to the fierce warriors of ancient Japan, something as wild as it was pure. It knew neither the light of civilization nor the tempering of knowledge. Nor did it know moderation. It was a natural trait, and the one that had always prevented his father from liking the boy. Munisai had tried, in the fashion typical of the military class, to curb his son's ferocity by punishing him severely and often, but the effect of such discipline had been to make the boy wilder, like a wild boar whose true ferocity emerges when it is deprived of food. The more the villagers despised the young roughneck, the more he lorded it over them.

As the child of nature became a man, he grew

bored with swaggering about the village as though he owned it. It was too easy to intimidate the timid villagers. He began to dream of bigger things. Sekigahara had given him his first lesson in what the world was really like. His youthful illusions were shattered—not that he'd really had many to begin with. It would never have occurred to him to brood over having failed in his first "real" venture, or to muse on the grimness of the future. He didn't yet know the meaning of self-discipline, and he'd taken the whole bloody catastrophe in stride.

And now, fortuitously, he'd stumbled onto a really big fish—Tsujikaze Temma, the leader of the freebooters! This was the kind of adversary he had longed to lock horns with at Sekigahara.

"Coward!" he yelled. "Stand and fight!"

Takezō was running like lightning through the pitch-black field, shouting taunts all the while. Ten paces ahead, Temma was fleeing as if on wings. Takezō's hair was literally on end, and the wind made a groaning noise as it swept past his ears. He was happy—happier than he'd ever been in his life. The more he ran, the closer he came to sheer animal ecstasy.

He leapt at Temma's back. Blood spurted out at the end of the wooden sword, and a bloodcurdling scream pierced the silent night. The freebooter's hulking frame fell to the ground with a leaden thud and rolled over. The skull was smashed to bits, the eyes popped out of their sockets. After two or three more heavy blows to the body, broken ribs protruded from the skin.

Takezō raised his arm, wiping rivers of sweat from his brow.

"Satisfied, Captain?" he asked triumphantly.

He started nonchalantly back toward the house. An observer new on the scene might have thought him out for an evening stroll, with not a care in the world. He felt free, no remorse, knowing that if the other man had won, he himself would be lying there, dead and alone.

Out of the darkness came Matahachi's voice. "Takezō, is that you?"

"Yeah," he replied dully. "What's up?"

Matahachi ran up to him and announced breathlessly, "I killed one! How about you?"

"I killed one too."

Matahachi held up his sword, soaked in blood right down to the braiding on the hilt. Squaring his shoulders with pride, he said, "The others ran away. These thieving bastards aren't much as fighters! No guts! Can only stand up to corpses, ha! Real even match, I'd say, ha, ha, ha."

Both of them were stained with gore and as contented as a pair of well-fed kittens. Chattering happily, they headed for the lamp visible in the distance, Takezō with his bloody stick, Matahachi with his bloody sword.

A stray horse stuck his head through the window and looked around the house. His snorting woke the two sleepers. Cursing the animal, Takezō gave him a smart slap on the nose. Matahachi stretched, yawned and remarked on how well he'd slept.

"The sun's pretty high already," said Takezō.

"You suppose it's afternoon?"

"Couldn't be!"

After a sound sleep, the events of the night before

were all but forgotten. For these two, only today and tomorrow existed.

Takezō ran out behind the house and stripped to the waist. Crouching down beside the clean, cool mountain stream, he splashed water on his face, doused his hair and washed his chest and back. Looking up, he inhaled deeply several times, as though trying to drink in the sunlight and all the air in the sky. Matahachi went sleepily into the hearth room, where he bid a cheery good morning to Okō and Akemi.

"Why, what are you two charming ladies wearing sour pusses for?"

"Are we?"

"Yes, most definitely. You look like you're both in mourning. What's there to be gloomy about? We killed your husband's murderer and gave his henchmen a beating they won't soon forget."

Matahachi's dismay was not hard to fathom. He thought the widow and her daughter would be overjoyed at news of Temma's death. Indeed, the night before, Akemi had clapped her hands with glee when she first heard about it. But Okō had looked uneasy from the first, and today, slouching dejectedly by the fire, she looked even worse.

"What's the matter with you?" he asked, thinking she was the most difficult woman in the world to please. "What gratitude!" he said to himself, taking the bitter tea that Akemi had poured for him and squatting down on his haunches.

Okō smiled wanly, envying the young, who know not the ways of the world. "Matahachi," she said wearily, "you don't seem to understand. Temma had hundreds of followers."

"Of course he did. Crooks like him always do. We're not afraid of the kind of people who follow the likes of him. If we could kill him, why should we be afraid of his underlings? If they try to get us, Takezō and I will just—"

"—will just do nothing!" interrupted Okō.

Matahachi pulled back his shoulders and said, "Who says so? Bring on as many of them as you like! They're nothing but a bunch of worms. Or do you think Takezō and I are cowards, that we're just going to slither away on our bellies in retreat? What do you take us for?"

"You're not cowards, but you are childish! Even to me. Temma has a younger brother named Tsujikaze Kōhei, and if *he* comes after you, the two of you rolled into one wouldn't have a chance!"

This was not the kind of talk Matahachi especially liked to hear, but as she went on, he started thinking that maybe she had a point. Tsujikaze Kōhei apparently had a large band of followers around Yasugawa in Kiso, and not only that: he was expert in the martial arts and unusually adept at catching people off their guard. So far, no one Kōhei had publicly announced he would kill had lived out his normal life. To Matahachi's way of thinking, it was one thing if a person attacked you in the open. It was quite another thing if he snuck up on you when you were fast asleep.

"That's a weak point with me," he admitted. "I sleep like a log."

As he sat holding his jaw and thinking, Okō came to the conclusion that there was nothing to do but abandon the house and their present way of life and go somewhere far away. She asked Matahachi what he and Takezō would do.

"I'll talk it over with him," replied Matahachi. "Wonder where he's gone off to?"

He walked outside and looked around, but Takezō was nowhere in sight. After a time he shaded his eyes, looked off into the distance and spotted Takezō riding around in the foothills, bareback on the stray horse that had woken them with his neighing.

"He doesn't have a care in the world," Matahachi said to himself, gruffly envious. Cupping his hands around his mouth, he shouted, "Hey, you! Come home! We've got to talk!"

A little while later they lay in the grass together, chewing on stalks of grass, discussing what they should do next.

Matahachi said, "Then you think we should head home?"

"Yes, I do. We can't stay with these two women forever."

"No, I guess not."

"I don't like women." Takezō was sure of that at least.

"All right. Let's go, then."

Matahachi rolled over and looked up at the sky. "Now that we've made up our minds, I want to get moving. I suddenly realized how much I miss Otsū, how much I want to see her. Look up there! There's a cloud that looks just like her profile. See! That part's just like her hair after she's washed it." Matahachi was kicking his heels into the ground and pointing to the sky.

Takezō's eyes followed the retreating form of the

horse he had just set free. Like many of the vagabonds who live in the fields, stray horses seemed to him to be good-natured things. When you're through with them, they ask for nothing; they just go off quietly somewhere by themselves.

From the house Akemi summoned them to dinner. They stood up.

"Race you!" cried Takezō.

"You're on!" countered Matahachi.

Akemi clapped her hands with delight as the two of them sped neck and neck through the tall grass, leaving a thick trail of dust in their wake.

After dinner, Akemi grew pensive. She had just learned that the two men had decided to go back to their homes. It had been fun having them in the house, and she wanted it to go on forever.

"You silly thing!" chided her mother. "Why are you moping so?" Okō was applying her makeup, as meticulously as ever, and as she scolded the girl, she stared into her mirror at Takezō. He caught her gaze and suddenly recalled the pungent fragrance of her hair the night she invaded his room.

Matahachi, who had taken the big sake jar down from a shelf, plopped down next to Takezō and began filling a small warming bottle, just as though he were master of the house. Since this was to be their last night all together, they planned to drink their fill. Okō seemed to be taking special care with her face.

"Let's not leave a drop undrunk!" she said. "There's no point in leaving it here for the rats."

"Or the worms!" Matahachi chimed in.

They emptied three large jars in no time. Okō

leaned against Matahachi and started fondling him in a way that made Takezō turn his head in embarrassment.

"I . . . I . . . can't walk," mumbled Okō drunkenly.

Matahachi escorted her to her pallet, her head leaning heavily on his shoulder. Once there, she turned to Takezō and said spitefully, "You, Takezō, you sleep over there, by yourself. You like sleeping by yourself. Isn't that right?"

Without a murmur, he lay down where he was. He was very drunk and it was very late.

By the time he woke up, it was broad daylight. The moment he opened his eyes, he sensed it. Something told him the house was empty. The things Okō and Akemi had piled together the day before for the trip were gone. There were no clothes, no sandals—and no Matahachi.

He called out, but there was no reply, nor did he expect one. A vacant house has an aura all its own. There was no one in the yard, no one behind the house, no one in the woodshed. The only trace of his companions was a bright red comb lying beside the open mouth of the water pipe.

"Matahachi's a pig!" he said to himself.

Sniffing the comb, he again recalled how Okō had tried to seduce him that evening not long ago. "This," he thought, "is what defeated Matahachi." The very idea made him boil with anger.

"Fool!" he cried out loud. "What about Otsū? What do you plan to do about her? Hasn't she been deserted too many times already, you pig?"

He stamped the cheap comb under his foot. He

wanted to cry in rage, not for himself, but out of pity for Otsū, whom he could picture so clearly waiting back in the village.

As he sat disconsolately in the kitchen, the stray horse looked in the doorway impassively. Finding that Takezō would not pat his nose, he wandered over to the sink and began lazily to lick some grains of rice that had stuck there.

3

The Flower Festival

In the seventeenth century, the Mimasaka highroad was something of a major thoroughfare. It led up from Tatsuno in Harima Province, winding through a terrain proverbially described as "one mountain after another." Like the stakes marking the Mimasaka-Harima boundary, it followed a seemingly endless series of ridges. Travelers emerging from Nakayama Pass looked down into the valley of the Aida River, where, often to their surprise, they saw a sizable village.

Actually, Miyamoto was more a scattering of hamlets than a real village. One cluster of houses lay along the riverbanks, another huddled farther up in the hills, and a third sat amid level fields that were stony and hence hard to plow. All in all, the number of houses was substantial for a rural settlement of the time.

Until about a year before, Lord Shimmen of Iga had maintained a castle not a mile up the river—a small castle as castles go, but one that nonetheless attracted a steady stream of artisans and tradespeople.

Farther to the north were the Shikozaka silver mines, which were now past their prime but had once lured miners from far and wide.

Travelers going from Tottori to Himeji, or from Tajima through the mountains to Bizen, naturally used the highroad. Just as naturally, they stopped over in Miyamoto. It had the exotic air of a village often visited by the natives of several provinces and boasted of not only an inn, but a clothing store as well. It also harbored a bevy of women of the night, who, throats powdered white as was the fashion, hovered before their business establishments like white bats under the eaves. This was the town Takezō and Matahachi had left to go to war.

Looking down on the rooftops of Miyamoto, Otsū sat and daydreamed. She was a wisp of a girl, with fair complexion and shining black hair. Fine of bone, fragile of limb, she had an ascetic, almost ethereal air. Unlike the robust and ruddy farm girls working in the rice paddies below, Otsū's movements were delicate. She walked gracefully, with her long neck stretched and head held high. Now, perched on the edge of Shippōji temple porch, she was as poised as a porcelain statuette.

A foundling raised in this mountain temple, she had acquired a lovely aloofness rarely found in a girl of sixteen. Her isolation from other girls her age and from the workaday world had given her eyes a contemplative, serious cast which tended to put off men used to frivolous females. Matahachi, her betrothed, was just a year older, and since he'd left Miyamoto with Takezō the previous summer, she'd heard nothing. Even into the first and second months of the new year, she'd yearned for word of him, but now the fourth month was at hand. She no longer dared hope.

Lazily her gaze drifted up to the clouds, and a thought slowly emerged. "Soon it will have been a whole year."

"Takezō's sister hasn't heard from him either. I'd be a fool to think either of them is still alive." Now and then she'd say this to someone, longing, almost pleading with her voice and eyes, for the other person to contradict her, to tell her not to give up. But no one heeded her sighs. To the down-to-earth villagers, who had already gotten used to the Tokugawa troops occupying the modest Shimmen castle, there was no reason in the world to assume they'd survived. Not a single member of Lord Shimmen's family had come back from Sekigahara, but that was only natural. They were samurai; they had lost. They wouldn't want to show their faces among people who knew them. But common foot soldiers? Wasn't it all right for them to come home? Wouldn't they have done so long ago if they had survived?

"Why," wondered Otsū, as she had wondered countless times before, "why do men run off to war?" She had come to enjoy in a melancholy way sitting alone on the temple porch and pondering this imponderable. Lost in wistful reverie, she could have lingered there for hours. Suddenly a male voice calling "Otsū!" invaded her island of peace.

Looking up, Otsū saw a youngish man coming toward her from the well. He was clad in only a loincloth, which barely served its purpose, and his weathered skin glowed like the dull gold of an old Buddhist statue. It was the Zen monk who, three or four years before, had wandered in from Tajima Province. He'd been staying at the temple ever since.

"At last it's spring," he was saying to himself with satisfaction. "Spring—a blessing, but a mixed one. As soon as it gets a little warm, those insidious lice overrun the country. They're trying to take it over, just like Fujiwara no Michinaga, that wily rascal of a regent." After a pause, he went on with his monologue.

"I've just washed my clothes, but where on earth am I going to dry this tattered old robe? I can't hang it on the plum tree. It'd be a sacrilege, an insult to nature to cover those flowers. Here I am, a man of taste, and I can't find a place to hang this robe! Otsū! Lend me a drying pole."

Blushing at the sight of the scantily clad monk, she cried, "Takuan! You can't just walk around half naked till your clothes dry!"

"Then I'll go to sleep. How's that?"

"Oh, you're impossible!"

Raising one arm skyward and pointing the other toward the ground, he assumed the pose of the tiny Buddha statues that worshipers anointed once a year with special tea.

"Actually, I should have just waited till tomorrow. Since it's the eighth, the Buddha's birthday, I could have just stood like this and let the people bow to me. When they ladled the sweet tea over me, I could've shocked everyone by licking my lips." Looking pious, he intoned the first words of the Buddha: "In heaven above and earth below, only I am holy."

Otsū burst out laughing at his irreverent display. "You do look just like him, you know!"

"Of course I do. I am the living incarnation of Prince Siddartha."

"Then stand perfectly still. Don't move! I'll go and get some tea to pour over you."

At this point, a bee began a full-scale assault on the monk's head and his reincarnation pose instantly gave way to a flailing of arms. The bee, noticing a gap in his loosely hung loincloth, darted in, and Otsū doubled up with laughter. Since the arrival of Takuan Sōhō, which was the name he was given on becoming a priest, even the reticent Otsū went few days without being amused by something he'd do or say.

Suddenly, however, she stopped laughing. "I can't waste any more time like this. I have important things to do!"

As she was slipping her small white feet into her sandals, the monk asked innocently, "What things?"

"What things? Have you forgotten too? Your little pantomime just reminded me. I'm supposed to get everything ready for tomorrow. The old priest asked me to pick flowers so we can decorate the flower temple. Then I have to set everything up for the anointing ceremony. And tonight I've got to make the sweet tea."

"Where are you going flower-picking?"

"Down by the river, in the lower part of the field."

"I'll come with you."

"Without any clothes on?"

"You'll never be able to cut enough flowers by yourself. You need help. Besides, man is born unclothed. Nakedness is his natural state."

"That may be, but I don't find it natural. Really, I'd rather go alone."

Hoping to elude him, Otsū hurried around to the rear of the temple. She strapped a basket on her back, picked up a sickle and slipped out the side gate, but only moments later turned to see him close behind her. Takuan was now swathed in a large wrapping cloth, the kind people used to carry their bedding.

"Is this more to your liking?" he called with a grin.

"Of course not. You look ridiculous. People will think you're crazy!"

"Why?"

"Never mind. Just don't walk next to me!"

"You never seemed to mind walking beside a man before."

"Takuan, you're perfectly horrible!" She ran off ahead, with him following in strides that would have befitted the Buddha descending from the Himalayas. His wrapping cloth flapped wildly in the breeze.

"Don't be angry, Otsū! You know I'm teasing. Besides, your boyfriends won't like you if you pout too much."

Eight or nine hundred yards down from the temple, spring flowers were blooming profusely along both banks of the Aida River. Otsū put her basket down and, amid a sea of fluttering butterflies, began swinging her sickle in wide circles, cutting the flowers off near their roots.

After a while, Takuan grew reflective. "How peaceful it is here," he sighed, sounding both religious and childlike. "Why, when we could live out our lives in a flower-filled paradise, do we all prefer to weep, suffer and get lost in a maelstrom of passion and fury, torturing ourselves in the flames of hell? I hope that you, at least, won't have to go through all that."

Otsū, rhythmically filling her basket with yellow rape blossoms, spring chrysanthemums, daisies, poppies and violets, replied, "Takuan, instead of preaching a sermon, you'd better watch out for the bees."

He nodded his head, sighing in despair. "I'm not talking about bees, Otsū. I simply want to pass on to you the Buddha's teaching on the fate of women."

"This woman's fate is none of your business!"

"Oh, but you're wrong! It's my duty as a priest to pry into people's lives. I agree it's a meddlesome trade, but it's no more useless than the business of a merchant, clothier, carpenter or samurai. It exists because it is needed."

Otsū softened. "I suppose you're right."

"It does happen, of course, that the priesthood has been on bad terms with womankind for some three thousand years. You see, Buddhism teaches that women are evil. Fiends. Messengers of hell. I've spent years immersed in the scriptures, so it's no accident that you and I fight all the time."

"And why, according to your scriptures, are women evil?"

"Because they deceive men."

"Don't men deceive women too?"

"Yes, but . . . the Buddha himself was a man."

"Are you saying that if he'd been a woman, things would be the other way around?"

"Of course not! How could a demon ever become a Buddha!"

"Takuan, that doesn't make any sense."

"If religious teachings were just common sense, we wouldn't need prophets to pass them on to us."

"There you go again, twisting everything to your own advantage!"

"A typical female comment. Why attack me personally?"

She stopped swinging her sickle again, a world-weary look on her face.

"Takuan, let's stop it. I'm not in the mood for this today."

"Silence, woman!"

"You're the one who's been doing all the talking."

Takuan closed his eyes as if to summon patience. "Let me try to explain. When the Buddha was young, he sat under the bo tree, where she-demons tempted him night and day. Naturally, he didn't form a high opinion of women. But even so, being all-merciful, he took some female disciples in his old age."

"Because he'd grown wise or senile?"

"Don't be blasphemous!" he warned sharply. "And don't forget the Bodhisattva Nagarjuna, who hated—I mean feared—women as much as the Buddha did. Even he went so far as to praise four female types: obedient sisters, loving companions, good mothers and submissive maidservants. He extolled their virtues again and again, and advised men to take such women as wives."

"Obedient sisters, loving companions, good mothers and submissive maidservants . . . I see you have it all worked out to men's advantage."

"Well, that's natural enough, isn't it? In ancient India, men were honored more and women less than in Japan. Anyway, I'd like you to hear the advice Nagarjuna gave women."

"What advice?"

"He said, 'Woman, marry thyself not to a man—' "

54

"That's ridiculous!"

"Let me finish. He said, 'Woman, marry thyself to the truth.' "

Otsū looked at him blankly.

"Don't you see?" he said, with a wave of his arm. " 'Marry thyself to the truth' means that you shouldn't become infatuated with a mere mortal but should seek the eternal."

"But, Takuan," Otsū asked impatiently, "what is 'the truth'?"

Takuan let both arms fall to his sides and looked at the ground. "Come to think of it," he said thoughtfully, "I'm not really sure myself."

Otsū burst out laughing, but Takuan ignored her. "There is something I know for certain. Applied to your life, wedding honesty means that you shouldn't think of going off to the city and giving birth to weak, namby-pamby children. You should stay in the country, where you belong, and raise a fine, healthy brood instead."

Otsū raised her sickle impatiently. "Takuan," she snapped, exasperated, "did you come out here to help me pick flowers or not?"

"Of course I did. That's why I'm here."

"In that case, stop preaching and grab this sickle."

"All right; if you don't really want my spiritual guidance, I won't impose it on you," he said, pretending hurt.

"While you're busy at work, I'll run over to Ogin's house and see if she's finished the obi I'm supposed to wear tomorrow."

"Ogin? Takezō's sister? I've met her, haven't I?

Didn't she come with you once to the temple?" He dropped the sickle. "I'll come with you."

"In that outfit?"

He pretended not to hear. "She'll probably offer us some tea. I'm dying of thirst."

Totally spent from arguing with the monk, Otsū gave a weak nod and together they set out along the riverbank.

Ogin was a woman of twenty-five, no longer considered in the bloom of youth but by no means bad-looking. Although suitors tended to be put off by her brother's reputation, she suffered no lack of proposals. Her poise and good breeding were immediately evident to everyone. She'd turned down all offers thus far simply on the grounds that she wanted to look after her younger brother a bit longer.

The house she lived in had been built by their father, Munisai, when he was in charge of military training for the Shimmen clan. As a reward for his excellent service, he'd been honored with the privilege of taking the Shimmen name. Overlooking the river, the house was surrounded by a high dirt wall set on a stone foundation and was much too large for the needs of an ordinary country samurai. Although once imposing, it had become run down. Wild irises were sprouting from the roof, and the wall of the dōjō where Munisai once taught martial arts was completely plastered with white swallow droppings.

Munisai had fallen from favor, lost his status, and died a poor man, not an uncommon occurrence in an age of turmoil. Soon after his death, his servants had left, but since they were all natives of Miyamoto, many still dropped in. When they did, they would leave fresh vegetables, clean the unused rooms, fill the water jars, sweep the path, and in countless other ways help keep the old house going. They would also have a pleasant chat with Munisai's daughter.

When Ogin, who was sewing in an inner room, heard the back door open, she naturally assumed it was one of these former servants. Lost in her work, she gave a jump when Otsū greeted her.

"Oh," she said. "It's you. You gave me a fright. I'm just finishing your obi now. You need it for the ceremony tomorrow, don't you?"

"Yes, I do. Ogin, I want to thank you for going to so much trouble. I should have sewn it myself, but there was so much to do at the temple, I never would have had time."

"I'm glad to be of help. I have more time on my hands than is good for me. If I'm not busy, I start to brood."

Otsū, raising her head, caught sight of the household altar. On it, in a small dish, was a flickering candle. By its dim light, she saw two dark inscriptions, carefully brush-painted. They were pasted on boards, an offering of water and flowers before them:

The Departed Spirit of Shimmen Takezō, Aged 17.

The Departed Spirit of Hon'iden Matahachi, Same Age.

"Ogin," Otsū said with alarm. "Have you gotten word they were killed?"

"Well, no . . . But what else can we think? I've accepted it. I'm sure they met their deaths at Sekigahara."

Otsū shook her head violently. "Don't say that! It'll bring bad luck! They aren't dead, they aren't! I know they'll show up one of these days."

Ogin looked at her sewing. "Do you dream about Matahachi?" she asked softly.

"Yes, all the time. Why?"

"That proves he's dead. I dream of nothing but my brother."

"Ogin, don't say that!" Rushing over to the altar, Otsū tore the inscriptions from their boards. "I'm getting rid of these things. They'll just invite the worst."

Tears streamed down her face as she blew out the candle. Not satisfied with that, she seized the flowers and the water bowl and rushed through the next room to the veranda, where she flung the flowers as far as she could and poured the water out over the edge. It landed right on the head of Takuan, who was squatting on the ground below.

"Aaii! That's cold!" he yelped, jumping up, frantically trying to dry his head with an end of the wrapping cloth. "What're you doing? I came here for a cup of tea, not a bath!"

Otsū laughed until fresh tears, tears of mirth, came. "I'm sorry, Takuan. I really am. I didn't see you."

By way of apology, she brought him the tea he'd been waiting for. When she went back inside, Ogin, who was staring fixedly toward the veranda, asked, "Who is that?"

"The itinerant monk who's staying at the temple. You know, the dirty one. You met him one day, with me, remember? He was lying in the sun on his stomach with his head in his hands, staring at the ground. When we asked him what he was doing, he said his lice were having a wrestling match. He said he'd trained them to entertain him.''

"Oh, him!"

"Yes, him. His name's Takuan Sōhō."

"Kind of strange."

"That's putting it mildly."

"What's that thing he's wearing? It doesn't look like a priest's robe."

"It isn't. It's a wrapping cloth."

"A wrapping cloth? He is eccentric. How old is he?"

"He says he's thirty-one, but sometimes I feel like his older sister, he's so silly. One of the priests told me that despite his appearance, he's an excellent monk."

"I suppose that's possible. You can't always judge people by their looks. Where's he from?"

"He was born in Tajima Province and started training for the priesthood when he was ten. Then he entered a temple of the Rinzai Zen sect about four years later. After he left, he became a follower of a scholar-priest from the Daitokuji and traveled with him to Kyoto and Nara. Later on he studied under Gudō of the Myōshinji, Ittō of Sennan and a whole string of other famous holy men. He's spent an awful lot of time studying!"

"Maybe that's why there's something different about him."

Otsū continued her story. "He was made a resident priest at the Nansōji and was appointed abbot of the Daitokuji by imperial edict. I've never learned why from anyone, and he never talks about his past, but for some reason he ran away after only three days."

Ogin shook her head.

Otsū went on. "They say famous generals like Hosokawa and noblemen like Karasumaru have tried again and again to persuade him to settle down. They even offered to build him a temple and donate money for its upkeep, but he's just not interested. He says he prefers to wander about the countryside like a beggar, with only his lice for friends, I think he's probably a little crazy."

"Maybe from his viewpoint we're the ones who are strange."

"That's exactly what he says!"

"How long will he stay here?"

"There's no way of knowing. He has a habit of showing up one day and disappearing the next."

Standing up near the veranda, Takuan called, "I can hear everything you're saying!"

"Well, it's not as though we're saying anything bad," Otsū replied cheerfully.

"I don't care if you do, if you find it amusing, but you could at least give me some sweet cakes to go with my tea."

"That's what I mean," said Otsū. "He's like this all the time."

"What do you mean, I'm 'like this'?" Takuan had a gleam in his eye. "What about you? You sit there looking as though you wouldn't hurt a fly, acting much more cruel and heartless than I ever would."

"Oh, really? And how am I being cruel and heartless?"

"By leaving me out here helpless, with nothing but tea, while you sit around moaning about your lost lover—that's how!"

* * *

The bells were ringing at the Daishōji and the Shippōji. They had started in a measured beat just after dawn and still rang forth now and then long past noon. In the morning a constant procession flowed to the temples: girls in red obis, wives of tradesmen wearing more subdued tones, and here and there an old woman in a dark kimono leading her grandchildren by the hand. At the Shippōji, the small main hall was crowded with worshipers, but the young men among them seemed more interested in stealing a glimpse of Otsū than in taking part in the religious ceremony.

"She's here, all right," whispered one.

"Prettier than ever," added another.

Inside the hall stood a miniature temple. Its roof was thatched with lime leaves and its columns were entwined with wild flowers. Inside this "flower temple," as it was called, stood a two-foot-high black statue of the Buddha, pointing one hand to heaven and the other to earth. The image was placed in a shallow clay basin, and the worshipers, as they passed, poured sweet tea over its head with a bamboo ladle. Takuan stood by with an extra supply of the holy balm, filling bamboo tubes for the worshipers to take home with them for good luck. As he poured, he solicited offerings.

"This temple is poor, so leave as much as you can. Especially you rich folks—I know who you are; you're wearing those fine silks and embroidered obis. You have a lot of money. You must have a lot of troubles too. If you leave a hundredweight of cash for your tea, your worries will be a hundredweight lighter."

On the other side of the flower temple, Otsū was seated at a black-lacquered table. Her face glowed light pink, like the flowers all around her. Wearing her new obi and writing charms on pieces of five-colored paper, she wielded her brush deftly, occasionally dipping it in a gold-lacquered ink box to her right. She wrote:

> Swiftly and keenly,
> On this best of days,
> The eighth of the fourth month,
> Bring judgment to bear on those
> Insects that devour the crops.

From time immemorial it had been thought in these parts that hanging this practical-minded poem on the wall could protect one from not only bugs, but disease and ill fortune as well. Otsū wrote the same verse scores of times—so often, in fact, that her wrist started to throb and her calligraphy began to reflect her fatigue.

Stopping to rest for a moment, she called out to Takuan: "Stop trying to rob these people. You're taking too much."

"I'm talking to those who already have too much. It's become a burden. It's the essence of charity to relieve them of it," he replied.

"By that reasoning, common burglars are all holy men."

Takuan was too busy collecting offerings to reply. "Here, here," he said to the jostling crowd. "Don't push, take your time, just get in line. You'll have your chance to lighten your purses soon enough."

"Hey, priest!" said a young man who'd been admonished for elbowing in.

"You mean me?" Takuan said, pointing to his nose.

"Yeah. You keep telling us to wait our turn, but then you serve the women first."

"I like women as much as the next man."

"You must be one of those lecherous monks we're always hearing stories about."

"That's enough, you tadpole! Do you think I don't know why *you're* here! You didn't come to honor the Buddha, or to take home a charm. You came to get a good look at Otsū! Come on now, own up— isn't that so? You won't get anywhere with women, you know, if you act like a miser."

Otsū's face turned scarlet. "Takuan, stop it! Stop right now, or I'm really going to get mad!"

To rest her eyes, Otsū again looked up from her work and out over the crowd. Suddenly she caught a glimpse of a face and dropped her brush with a clatter. She jumped to her feet, almost toppling the table, but the face had already vanished, like a fish disappearing in the sea. Oblivious of all around her, she dashed to the temple porch, shouting, "Takezō! Takezō!"

4

The Dowager's Wrath

Matahachi's family, the Hon'iden, were the proud members of a group of rural gentry who belonged to the samurai class but who also worked the land. The real head of the family was his mother, an incorrigibly stubborn woman named Osugi. Though nearly sixty, she led her family and tenants out to the fields daily and worked as hard as any of them. At planting time she hoed the fields and after the harvest threshed the barley by trampling it. When dusk forced her to stop working, she always found something to sling on her bent back and haul back to the house. Often it was a load of mulberry leaves so big that her body, almost doubled over, was barely visible beneath it. In the evening, she could usually be found tending her silkworms.

On the afternoon of the flower festival, Osugi looked up from her work in the mulberry patch to see her runny-nosed grandson racing barefoot across the field.

"Where've you been, Heita?" she asked sharply. "At the temple?"

"Uh-huh."

"Was Otsū there?"

"Yes," he answered excitedly, still out of breath. "And she had on a very pretty obi. She was helping with the festival."

"Did you bring back some sweet tea and a spell to keep the bugs away?"

"Unh-unh."

The old woman's eyes, usually hidden amid folds and wrinkles, opened wide in irritation. "And why not?"

"Otsū told me not to worry about them. She said I should run right home and tell you."

"Tell me what?"

"Takezō, from across the river. She said she saw him. At the festival."

Osugi's voice dropped an octave. "Really? Did she really say that, Heita?"

"Yes, Granny."

Her strong body seemed to go limp all at once, and her eyes blurred with tears. Slowly she turned, as though expecting to see her son standing behind her.

Seeing no one, she spun back around. "Heita," she said abruptly, "you take over and pick these mulberry leaves."

"Where're you going?"

"Home. If Takezō's back, Matahachi must be too."

"I'll come too."

"No you won't. Don't be a nuisance, Heita."

The old woman stalked off, leaving the little boy as forlorn as an orphan. The farmhouse, surrounded

66

by old, gnarled oaks, was a large one. Osugi ran past it, heading straight for the barn, where her daughter and some tenant farmers were working. While still a fair distance away, she began calling to them somewhat hysterically.

"Has Matahachi come home? Is he here yet?"

Startled, they stared at her as though she'd lost her wits. Finally one of the men said "no," but the old woman seemed not to hear. It was as though in her overwrought state she refused to take no for an answer. When they continued their noncommittal gaze, she began calling them all dunces and explaining what she'd heard from Heita, how if Takezō was back, then Matahachi must be too. Then, reassuming her role as commander in chief, she sent them off in all directions to find him. She herself stayed behind in the house, and every time she sensed someone approaching, ran out to ask if they had found her son yet.

At sunset, still undaunted, she placed a candle before the memorial tablets of her husband's ancestors. She sat down, seemingly lost in prayer, as immobile as a statue. Since everyone was still out searching, there was no evening meal at the house, and when night fell and there was still no news, Osugi finally moved. As if in a trance, she walked slowly out of the house to the front gate. There she stood and waited, hidden in the darkness. A watery moon shone through the oak tree branches, and the mountains looming before and behind the house were veiled in a white mist. The sweetish scent of pear blossoms floated in the air.

Time, too, floated by unnoticed. Then a figure could be discerned approaching, making its way along the outer edge of the pear orchard. Recognizing the silhouette as Otsū's, Osugi called out and the girl ran forward, her wet sandals clomping heavily on the earth.

"Otsū! They told me you saw Takezō. Is that true?"

"Yes, I'm sure it was him. I spotted him in the crowd outside the temple."

"You didn't see Matahachi?"

"No. I rushed out to ask Takezō about him, but when I called out, Takezō jumped like a scared rabbit. I caught his eye for a second and then he was gone. He's always been strange, but I can't imagine why he ran away like that."

"Ran away?" asked Osugi with a puzzled air. She began to muse, and the longer she did so, the more a terrible suspicion took shape in her mind. It was becoming clear to her that the Shimmen boy, that ruffian Takezō she so hated for luring her precious Matahachi off to war, was once more up to no good.

At length she said ominously, "That wretch! He's probably left poor Matahachi to die somewhere, then sneaked back home safe and sound. Coward, that's what he is!" Osugi began to shake in fury and her voice rose to a shriek. "He can't hide from me!"

Otsū remained composed. "Oh, I don't think he'd do anything like that. Even if he did have to leave Matahachi behind, surely he'd bring us word or at least some keepsake from him." Otsū sounded shocked by the old woman's hasty accusation.

Osugi, however, was by now convinced of Takezō's perfidy. She shook her head decisively and went on. "Oh, no he wouldn't! Not that young demon! He hasn't got that much heart. Matahachi should never have taken up with him."

"Granny . . ." Otsū said soothingly.

"What?" snapped Osugi, not soothed in the least.

"I think that if we go over to Ogin's house, we just might find Takezō there."

The old woman relaxed a bit. "You might be right. She is his sister, and there really isn't anyone else in this village who'd take him in."

"Then let's go and see, just the two of us."

Osugi balked. "I don't see why I should do that. She knew her brother had dragged my son off to war, but she never once came to apologize or to pay her respects. And now that he's back, she hasn't even come to tell me. I don't see why I should go to her. It's demeaning. I'll wait here for her."

"But this isn't an ordinary situation," replied Otsū. "Besides, the main thing at this point is to see Takezō as soon as we can. We've got to find out what happened. Oh, please, Granny, come. You won't have to do anything. I'll take care of all the formalities if you like."

Grudgingly, Osugi allowed herself to be persuaded. She was, of course, as eager as Otsū to find out what was going on, but she'd die before begging for anything from a Shimmen.

The house was about a mile away. Like the Hon'iden family, the Shimmen were country gentry, and both houses were descended from the Akamatsu clan many generations back. Situated across the river from one another, they had always tacitly recognized each other's right to exist, but that was the extent of their intimacy.

When they arrived at the front gate, they found it shut, and the trees were so thick that no light could be seen from the house. Otsū started to walk around to the back entrance, but Osugi stopped mulishly in her tracks.

"I don't think it's right for the head of the Hon'iden family to enter the Shimmen residence by the back door. It's degrading."

Seeing she wasn't going to budge, Otsū proceeded to the rear entrance alone. Presently a light appeared just inside the gate. Ogin herself had come out to greet the older woman, who, suddenly transformed from a crone plowing the fields into a great lady, addressed her hostess in lofty tones.

"Forgive me for disturbing you at this late hour, but my business simply could not wait. How good of you to come and let me in!" Sweeping past Ogin and on into the house, she went immediately, as though she were an envoy from the gods, to the most honored spot in the room, in front of the alcove. Sitting proudly, her figure framed by both a hanging scroll and a flower arrangement, she deigned to accept Ogin's sincerest words of welcome.

The amenities concluded, Osugi went straight to the point. Her false smile disappeared as she glared at the young woman before her. "I have been told that young demon of this house has crawled back home. Please fetch him."

Although Osugi's tongue was notorious for its sharpness, this undisguised maliciousness came as something of a shock to the gentle Ogin.

"Whom do you mean by 'that young demon'"? asked Ogin, with palpable restraint.

Chameleon-like, Osugi changed her tactics. "A slip of the tongue, I assure you," she said with a laugh. "That's what the people in the village call him;

I suppose I picked it up from them. The 'young demon' is Takezō. He is hiding here, isn't he?"

"Why, no," replied Ogin with genuine astonishment. Embarrassed to hear her brother referred to in this way, she bit her lip.

Otsū, taking pity on her, explained that she had spotted Takezō at the festival. Then, in an attempt to smooth over ruffled feelings, she added, "Strange, isn't it, that he didn't come straight here?"

"Well, he didn't," said Ogin. "This is the first I've heard anything about it. But if he is back, as you say, I'm sure he'll be knocking at the door any minute."

Osugi, sitting formally on the floor cushion, legs tucked neatly beneath her, folded her hands in her lap and with the expression of an outraged mother-in-law, launched into a tirade.

"What is all this? Do you expect me to believe you haven't heard from him yet? Don't you understand that I'm the mother whose son your young ne'er-do-well dragged off to war? Don't you know that Matahachi is the heir and the most important member of the Hon'iden family? It was your brother who talked my boy into going off to get himself killed. If my son is dead, it's your brother who killed him, and if he thinks he can just sneak back alone and get away with it . . ."

The old woman stopped just long enough to catch her breath, then her eyes glared in fury once more. "And what about you? Since he's obviously had the indecency to sneak back by himself, why haven't you, his older sister, sent him immediately to me? I'm disgusted with both of you, treating an old woman with such disrespect. Who do you think I am?"

Gulping down another breath, she ranted on. "If your Takezō is back, then bring my Matahachi back to me. If you can't do that, the least you can do is set that young demon down right here and make him explain to my satisfaction what happened to my precious boy and where he is—right now!"

"How can I do that? He isn't here."

"That's a black lie!" she shrieked. "You must know where he is!"

"But I tell you I don't!" Ogin protested. Her voice quivered and her eyes filled with tears. She bent over, wishing with all her might her father were still alive.

Suddenly, from the door opening onto the veranda, came a cracking noise, followed by the sound of running feet.

Osugi's eyes flashed, and Otsū started to stand up, but the next sound was a hair-raising scream—as close to an animal's howl as the human voice is capable of producing.

A man shouted, "Catch him!"

Then came the sound of more feet, several more, running around the house, accompanied by the snapping of twigs and the rustling of bamboo.

"It's Takezō!" cried Osugi. Jumping to her feet, she glared at the kneeling Ogin and spat out her words. "I knew he was here," she said ferociously. "It was as clear to me as the nose on your face. I don't know why you've tried to hide him from me, but bear in mind, I'll never forget this."

She rushed to the door and slid it open with a bang. What she saw outside turned her already pale face even whiter. A young man wearing shin plates was lying face up on the ground, obviously dead but with fresh blood still streaming from his eyes and nose. Judging from the appearance of his shattered skull, someone had killed him with a single blow of a wooden sword.

"There's . . . there's a dead . . . a dead man out there!" she stammered.

Otsū brought the light to the veranda and stood beside Osugi, who was staring terror-stricken at the corpse. It was neither Takezō's nor Matahachi's, but that of a samurai neither of them recognized.

Osugi murmured, "Who could've done this?" Turning swiftly to Otsū, she said, "Let's go home before we get mixed up in something."

Otsū couldn't bring herself to leave. The old woman had said a lot of vicious things. It would be unfair to Ogin to leave before putting salve on the wounds. If Ogin had been lying, Otsū felt she must doubtless have had good reason. Feeling she should stay behind to comfort Ogin, she told Osugi she would be along later.

"Do as you please," snapped Osugi, as she made her departure.

Ogin graciously offered her a lantern, but Osugi was proudly defiant in her refusal. "I'll have you know that the head of the Hon'iden family is not so senile that she needs a light to walk by." She tucked up her kimono hems, left the house and walked resolutely into the thickening mist.

Not far from the house, a man called her to a halt. He had his sword drawn, and his arms and legs were protected by armor. He was obviously a professional samurai of a type not ordinarily encountered in the village.

"Didn't you just come from the Shimmen house?" he asked.

"Yes, but—"

"Are you a member of the Shimmen household?"

"Certainly not!" Osugi snapped, waving her hand in protest. "I am the head of the samurai house across the river."

"Does that mean you are the mother of Hon'iden Matahachi, who went with Shimmen Takezō to the Battle of Sekigahara?"

"Well, yes, but my son didn't go because he wanted to. He was tricked into going by that young demon."

"Demon?"

"That . . . Takezō!"

"I gather this Takezō is not too well thought of in the village."

"Well thought of? That's a laugh. You never saw such a hoodlum! You can't imagine the trouble we've had at my house since my son took up with him."

"Your son seems to have died at Sekigahara. I'm—"

"Matahachi! Dead?"

"Well, actually, I'm not sure, but perhaps it'll be some comfort to you in your grief to know that I'll do everything possible to help you take revenge."

Osugi eyed him skeptically. "Just who are you?"

"I'm with the Tokugawa garrison. We came to Himeji Castle after the battle. On orders from my lord, I've set up a barrier on the Harima Province border to screen everyone who crosses.

"This Takezō, from that house back there," he continued, pointing, "broke through the barrier and fled toward Miyamoto. We chased him all the way here. He's a tough one, all right. We thought that after a few days of walking he'd collapse, but we still haven't caught up with him. He can't go on forever, though. We'll get him.''

Nodding as she listened, Osugi realized now why Takezō hadn't appeared at the Shippōji, and more importantly, that he probably hadn't gone home, since that was the first place the soldiers would search. At the same time, since it seemed he was traveling alone, her fury wasn't diminished in the least. But as for Matahachi being dead, she couldn't believe that either.

"I know Takezō can be as strong and cunning as any wild beast, sir," she said coyly, "But I shouldn't think that samurai of your caliber would have any trouble capturing him."

"Well, frankly, that's what I thought at first. But there aren't many of us and he's just killed one of my men."

"Let an old woman give you a few words of advice." Leaning over, she whispered something in his ear. Her words seemed to please him immensely.

He nodded his approval and enthusiastically exclaimed. "Good idea! Splendid!"

"Be sure to do a thorough job of it," urged Osugi as she took her leave.

Not long afterward, the samurai regrouped his band of fourteen or fifteen men behind Ogin's house. After he briefed them, they piled over the wall, surrounding the house and blocking all exits. Several soldiers then stormed into the house, leaving a trail of mud, and crowded into the inner room where the two young women sat commiserating and dabbing at their tear-stained faces.

Confronted by the soldiers, Otsū gasped and

turned white. Ogin, however, proud to be the daughter of Munisai, was unperturbed. With calm, steely eyes, she stared indignantly at the intruders.

"Which one of you is Takezō's sister?" asked one of them.

"I am," replied Ogin coldly, "and I demand to know why you've entered this house without permission. I will not stand for such brutish behavior in a house occupied only by women." She had turned to face them directly.

The man who had been chatting with Osugi a few minutes earlier pointed to Ogin. "Arrest her!" he ordered.

Barely were the words out of his mouth before violence erupted, the house began to shake and the lights went out. Uttering a cry of terror, Otsū stumbled out into the garden, while at least ten of the soldiers fell upon Ogin and began tying her up with a rope. Despite her heroic resistance, it was all over in a few seconds. They then pushed her down onto the floor and began kicking her as hard as they could.

Otsū couldn't recall afterward which way she had come, but somehow she managed to escape. Barely conscious, she ran barefoot toward the Shippōji in the misty moonlight, relying completely on instinct. She had grown up in peaceful surroundings and now felt as though the world were caving in.

When she reached the foot of the hill where the temple stood, someone called to her. She saw a shape sitting on a rock among the trees. It was Takuan.

"Thank heaven it's you," he said. "I was really starting to worry. You never stay out this late. When I realized the time, I came out looking for you." He looked down toward the ground and asked, "Why are you barefoot?"

He was still gazing at Otsū's bare white feet when she rushed headlong into his arms and began wailing.

"Oh, Takuan! It was awful! What can we do?"

In a calm voice, he tried to soothe her. "There, there. What was awful? There aren't many things in this world that are all that bad. Calm down and tell me what happened."

"They tied Ogin up and took her away! Matahachi didn't come back, and now poor Ogin, who's so sweet and gentle—they were all kicking her. Oh, Takuan, we've got to do something!"

Sobbing and trembling, she clung desperately to the young monk, her head resting on his chest.

It was noon on a still, humid spring day, and a faint mist rose from the young man's sweating face. Takezō was walking alone in the mountains, whither he knew not. He was tired almost beyond endurance, but even at the sound of a bird alighting, his eyes would dart around. Despite the ordeal he'd been through, his mud-spattered body came alive with pent-up violence and the sheer instinct to survive.

"Bastards! Beasts!" he growled. In the absence of the real target of his fury, he swung his black-oak sword screeching through the air, slicing a thick branch off a large tree. The white sap that poured from the wound reminded him of a nursing mother's milk. He stood and stared. With no mother to turn to, there was only loneliness. Instead of offering him comfort, even the running streams and rolling hills of his own home seemed to mock him.

"Why are all the villagers against me?" he wondered. "The minute they see me, they report me to the guards on the mountain. The way they run when they catch sight of me, you'd think I was a madman."

He'd been hiding in the Sanumo mountains for four days. Now, through the veil of the midday mist, he could make out the house of his father, the house where his sister lived alone. Nestled in the foothills just below him was the Shippōji, the temple's roof jutting out from the trees. He knew he could approach neither place. When he'd dared go near the temple on the Buddha's birthday, crowded though it was, he'd risked his life. When he heard his name called, he had no choice but to flee. Aside from wanting to save his own neck, he knew that being discovered there would mean trouble for Otsū.

That night, when he'd gone stealthily to his sister's house, Matahachi's mother—as luck would have it—had been there. For a while he'd just stood outside, trying to come up with an explanation of Matahachi's whereabouts, but as he was watching his sister through a crack in the door, the soldiers had spotted him. Again he had to flee without having the chance to speak to anyone. Since then, it appeared from his refuge in the mountains that the Tokugawa samurai were keeping a very sharp eye out for him. They patrolled every road he might take, while at the same time the villagers had banded together to form search parties and were scouring the mountains.

He wondered what Otsū must think of him and began to suspect that even she had turned against him. Since it appeared that everyone in his own village regarded him as an enemy, he was stymied.

He thought: "It'd be too hard to tell Otsū the real reason her fiancé didn't come back. Maybe I should tell the old woman instead. . . . That's it! If I explain everything to her, she can break it gently to Otsū. Then there won't be any reason for me to hang around here."

His mind made up, Takezō resumed walking, but he knew that it would not do to go near the village before dark. With a large rock he broke another into small pieces and hurled one of them at a bird in flight. After it fell to earth, he barely paused to pluck its feathers before sinking his half-starved teeth into the warm, raw flesh. As he was devouring the bird, he started walking again but suddenly heard a stifled cry. Whoever had caught sight of him was scrambling away frantically through the woods. Angered at the idea of being hated and feared—persecuted—for no reason, he shouted, "Wait!" and began running like a panther after the fleeing form.

The man was no match for Takezō and was easily overtaken. It turned out to be one of the villagers who came to the mountains to make charcoal, and Takezō knew him by sight. Grabbing his collar, he dragged him back to a small clearing.

"Why are you running away? Don't you know me? I'm one of you, Shimmen Takezō of Miyamoto. I'm not going to eat you alive. You know, it's very rude to run away from people without even saying hello!"

"Y-y-y-y-yes, sir!"

"Sit down!"

Takezō released his grip on the man's arm, but the pitiful creature started to flee, forcing Takezō to kick his behind and make as if to strike him with his wooden sword. The man cringed on the ground like a simpering dog, his hands over his head.

"Don't kill me!" he screamed pathetically.

"Just answer my questions, all right?"

"I'll tell you anything—just don't kill me! I have a wife and family."

"Nobody's going to kill you. I suppose the hills are crawling with soldiers, aren't they?"

"Yes."

"Are they keeping close watch on the Shippōji?"

"Yes."

"Are the men from the village hunting for me again today?"

Silence.

"Are you one of them?"

The man jumped to his feet, shaking his head like a deaf-mute.

"No, no, no!"

"That's enough," shouted Takezō. Taking a firm grip on the man's neck, he asked, "What about my sister?"

"What sister?"

"*My* sister, Ogin, of the House of Shimmen. Don't play dumb. You promised to answer my questions. I don't really blame the villagers for trying to capture me, because the samurai are forcing them to do it, but I'm sure they'd never do anything to hurt her. Or would they?"

The man replied, too innocently, "I don't know anything about that. Nothing at all."

Takezō swiftly raised his sword above his head in position to strike. "Watch it! That sounded very suspicious to me. Something has happened, hasn't it? Out with it, or I'll smash your skull!"

"Wait! Don't! I'll talk! I'll tell you everything!"

Hands folded in supplication, the trembling charcoal-maker told how Ogin had been taken away a prisoner, and how an order had been circulated in the village to the effect that anyone providing Takezō with food or shelter would automatically be regarded as an accomplice. Each day, he reported, the soldiers were leading villagers into the mountains, and each family was required to furnish one young man every other day for this purpose.

The information caused Takezō to break out in goose pimples. Not fear. Rage. To make sure he'd heard right, he asked, "What crime has my sister been charged with?" His eyes were glistening with moisture.

"None of us knows anything about it. We're afraid of the district lord. We're just doing what we're told, that's all."

"Where have they taken my sister?"

"Rumor has it that they've got her in Hinagura stockade, but I don't know if that's true."

"Hinagura . . ." repeated Takezō. His eyes turned toward the ridge that marked the provincial border. The backbone of the mountains was already spotted with the shadows of gray evening clouds.

Takezō let the man go. Watching him scramble away, grateful to have his meager life spared, made Takezō's stomach turn at the thought of the cowardice of humanity, the cowardice that forced samurai to pick on a poor helpless woman. He was glad to be alone again. He had to think.

He soon reached a decision. "I have to rescue Ogin, and that's that. My poor sister. I'll kill them all if they've harmed her." Having chosen his course of action, he marched down toward the village with long manly strides.

A couple of hours later, Takezō again furtively approached the Shippōji. The evening bell had just stopped tolling. It was already dark and lights could be seen coming from the temple itself, the kitchen and the priests' quarters, where people seemed to be moving about.

"If only Otsū would come out," he thought.

He crouched motionless under the raised passageway—it was of the sort that had a roof but no walls—which connected the priests' rooms with the main temple. The smell of food being cooked floated in the air, conjuring up visions of rice and steaming soup. For the past few days, Takezō had had nothing in his stomach but raw bird meat and grass shoots, and his stomach now rebelled. His throat burned as he vomited up bitter gastric juices, and in his misery he gasped loudly for breath.

"What was that?" said a voice.

"Probably just a cat," answered Otsū, who came out carrying a dinner tray and started crossing the passageway directly over Takezō's head. He tried to call to her, but was still too nauseated to make an intelligible sound.

This, as it happened, was a stroke of luck, because just then a male voice just behind Otsū inquired, "Which way is the bath?"

The man was wearing a kimono borrowed from the temple, tied with a narrow sash from which dangled a small washcloth. Takezō recognized him as one of the samurai from Himeji. Evidently he was of high rank, high enough to lodge at the temple and pass his evenings eating and drinking his fill while his subordinates and the villages had to scour mountainsides day and night searching for the fugitive.

"The bath?" said Otsū. "Come, I'll show you."

She set her tray down and began leading him along the passageway. Suddenly the samurai rushed forward and hugged her from behind.

"How about joining me in the bath?" he suggested lecherously.

"Stop that! Let go of me!" cried Otsū, but the man, turning her around, held her face in both big hands and brushed his lips against her cheek.

"What's wrong!" he cajoled. "Don't you like men!"

"Stop it! You shouldn't do that!" protested the helpless Otsū. The soldier then clapped his hand over her mouth.

Takezō, oblivious of the danger, leapt up onto the passageway like a cat and thrust his fist at the man's head from behind. The blow was a hard one. Momentarily defenseless, the samurai fell backward, still clinging to Otsū. As she tried to break away from his hold, she let out a shrill scream. The fallen man began shouting, "It's him! It's Takezō! He's here! Come and take him!"

The rumble of feet and the roar of voices thundered from inside the temple. The temple bell began signaling the alarm that Takezō had been discovered, and from the woods throngs of men began converging on the temple grounds. But Takezō was already gone, and before long search parties were once again sent out to scour the hills of Sanumo. Takezō himself hardly knew how he'd slipped through the swiftly tightening net, but by the time the chase was in full swing he found himself standing far away, at the entrance to the large dirt-floored kitchen of the Hon'iden house.

Looking into the dimly lit interior, he called out, "Granny!"

"Who's there!" came the shrill reply. Osugi ambled out from a back room. Lit from below by the paper lantern in her hand, her gnarled face paled at the sight of her visitor.

"You!" she cried.

"I have something important to tell you," Takezō said hurriedly. "Matahachi isn't dead, he's still very much alive and healthy. He's staying with a woman. In another province. That's all I can tell you, because that's all I know. Will you please somehow break the news to Otsū for me? I couldn't do it myself."

Immensely relieved to have unburdened himself of the message, he started to leave, but the old woman called him back.

"Where do you plan to go from here?"

"I have to break into the stockade at Hinagura and rescue Ogin," he replied sadly. "After that, I'll go away somewhere. I just wanted to tell you and your family, as well as Otsū, that I didn't let Matahachi die. Other than that, I have no reason to be here."

"I see." Osugi shifted the lantern from one hand to the other, playing for time. Then she beckoned to him. "I'll bet you're hungry, aren't you?"

"I haven't had a decent meal for days."

"You poor boy! Wait! I'm in the midst of cooking right now, and I can give you a nice warm dinner in no time. As a going-away present. And wouldn't you like to take a bath while I'm getting it ready?"

Takezō was speechless.

"Don't look so shocked. Takezō, your family and ours have been together since the days of the Akamatsu clan. I don't think you should leave here at all, but I certainly won't let you go without giving you a good hearty meal!"

Again Takezō was unable to reply. He raised his arm and wiped his eyes. No one had been this kind to him for a long, long time. Having come to regard everybody with suspicion and distrust, he was suddenly remembering what it was like to be treated as a human being.

"Hurry on round to the bathhouse, now," urged Osugi in grandmotherly tones. "It's too dangerous to stand here—someone might see you. I'll bring you a washcloth, and while you're washing, I'll get out Matahachi's kimono and some underwear for you. Now take your time and have a good soak."

She handed him the lantern and disappeared into the back of the house. Almost immediately, her daughter-in-law left the house, ran through the garden and off into the night.

From the bathhouse, where the lantern swung back and forth, came the sound of splashing water.

"How is it?" Osugi called jovially. "Hot enough?"

"It's just right! I feel like a new man," Takezō called back.

"Take your time and get good and warm. The rice isn't ready yet."

"Thanks. If I'd known it'd be like this, I'd have come sooner. I was sure you'd have it in for me!" He spoke two or three more times, but his voice was drowned out by the sound of the water and Osugi didn't answer.

Before long, the daughter-in-law reappeared at the gate, all out of breath. She was followed by a band of samurai and vigilantes. Osugi came out of the house and addressed them in a whisper.

"Ah, you got him to take a bath. Very clever," said one of the men admiringly. "Yes, that's fine! We've got him for sure this time!"

Splitting into two groups, the men crouched and moved cautiously, like so many toads, toward the fire blazing brightly under the bath.

Something—something indefinable—pricked Takezō's instincts, and he peeped out through a crack in the door. His hair stood on end.

"I've been trapped!" he screamed.

He was stark naked, the bathhouse was tiny, and there was no time to think. Beyond the door he'd spotted what seemed like hordes of men armed with staffs, lances and truncheons.

Still, he wasn't really afraid. Any fear he might have had was blotted out by his anger toward Osugi.

"All right, you bastards, watch this," he growled.

He was well beyond caring how many of them there were. In this situation, as in others, the only thing he knew how to do was to attack rather than be attacked. As his would-be captors made way for each other outside, he abruptly kicked open the door and jumped out and into the air, bellowing a fearsome war whoop. Still naked, his wet hair flying in every direction, he seized and wrenched loose the shaft of the first lance thrust at him, sending its owner flying into the bushes. Taking a firm grip on the weapon, he thrashed about like a whirling dervish, swinging with complete abandon and hitting anyone who came near. He'd learned at Sekigahara that this method was startlingly effective when a man was outnumbered, and that the shaft of a lance could often be used more tellingly than the blade.

The attackers, realizing too late what a blunder they'd made by not sending three or four men charging into the bathhouse in the first place, shouted encouragement to one another. It was clear, however, they'd been outmaneuvered.

About the tenth time Takezō's weapon came in contact with the ground, it broke. He then seized a large rock and threw it at the men, who were already showing signs of backing down.

"Look, he's run inside the house!" shouted one of them, as simultaneously Osugi and her daughter-in-law scrambled out into the back garden.

Making a tremendous clatter as he stormed through the house, Takezō was yelling, "Where are my clothes? Give me back my clothes!"

There were work clothes lying about, not to speak of an elaborate kimono chest, but Takezō paid them no attention. He was straining his eyes in the dim light to find his own ragged garment. Finally spotting it in the corner of the kitchen, he seized it in one hand and finding a foothold atop a large earthenware oven, crawled out of a small high window. While he made his way onto the roof, his pursuers, now totally confused, cursed and made excuses to each other for their failure to ensnare him.

Standing in the middle of the roof, Takezō unhurriedly donned his kimono. With his teeth, he tore off a strip of cloth from his sash, and gathering his damp hair behind, tied it near the roots so tightly that his eyebrows and the corners of his eyes were stretched.

The spring sky was full of stars.

5

The Art of War

The daily search in the mountains continued, and farm work languished; the villagers could neither cultivate their fields nor tend to their silkworms. Large signs posted in front of the village headman's house and at every crossroads announced a substantial reward for anyone who captured or killed Takezō, as well as suitable recompense for any information leading to his arrest. The notices bore the authoritative signature of Ikeda Terumasa, lord of Himeji Castle.

At the Hon'iden residence, panic prevailed. Osugi and her family, trembling in mortal dread lest Takezō come to take his revenge, bolted the main gate and barricaded all entrances. The searchers, under the direction of troops from Himeji, laid fresh plans to trap the fugitive. Thus far all their efforts had proved fruitless.

"He's killed another one!" a villager shouted.

"Where? Who was it this time?"

"Some samurai. No one's identified him yet."

The corpse had been discovered near a path on

the village outskirts, its head in a clump of tall weeds and its legs raised skyward in a bafflingly contorted position. Frightened but incurably nosy, villagers milled about, babbling among themselves. The skull had been smashed, evidently with one of the wooden reward signs, which now lay across the body soaked in blood. Those gawking at the spectacle could not avoid reading the list of promised rewards. Some laughed grimly at the blatant irony.

Otsū's face was drawn and pale as she emerged from the crowd. Wishing she hadn't looked, she hurried toward the temple, trying to somehow blot out the image of the dead man's face lingering before her eyes. At the foot of the hill, she ran into the captain who was lodging at the temple and five or six of his men. They had heard of the gruesome killing and were on their way to investigate. Upon seeing the girl, the captain grinned. "Where've you been, Otsū?" he said with ingratiating familiarity.

"Shopping," she replied curtly. Without bestowing so much as a glance upon him, she hurried up the temple's stone steps. She hadn't liked the man to begin with—he had a stringy mustache which she took particular exception to—but since the night he'd tried to force himself on her, the sight of him filled her with loathing.

Takuan was sitting in front of the main hall, playing with a stray dog. She was hurrying by at some distance to avoid the mangy animal when the monk looked up and called, "Ostū, there's a letter for you."

"For me?" she asked incredulously.

"Yes, you were out when the runner came, so he left it with me." Taking the small scroll out of his

90

kimono sleeve and handing it to her, he said, "You don't look too good. Is something wrong?"

"I feel sick. I saw a dead man lying in the grass. His eyes were still open, and there was blood—"

"You shouldn't look at things like that. But I guess the way things are now, you'd have to walk around with your eyes closed. I'm always tripping over corpses these days. Ha! And I'd heard this village was a little paradise!"

"But why is Takezō killing all these people?"

"To keep them from killing him, of course. They don't have any real reason to kill him, so why should he let them?"

"Takuan, I'm scared!" she said pleadingly. "What would we do if he came here?"

Dark cumulus clouds were drawing their cloak over the mountains. She took her mysterious letter and went to hide in the loom shed. On the loom was an unfinished strip of cloth for a man's kimono, part of the garment which, since the year before, she'd been spending every spare moment spinning silk yarn for. It was for Matahachi, and she was excited by the prospect of sewing all the pieces together into a full kimono. She had woven every strand meticulously, as if the weaving itself were drawing him closer to her. She wanted the garment to last forever.

Seating herself before the loom, she gazed intently at the letter. "Whoever could have sent it?" she whispered to herself, sure that the letter must have really been meant for someone else. She read the address over and over, searching for a flaw.

The letter had obviously made a long journey to reach her. The torn and crumpled wrapper was smudged all over with fingerprints and raindrops. She broke the seal, whereupon not one but two letters fell into her lap. The first was in an unfamiliar woman's hand, a somewhat older woman, she quickly guessed.

> I am writing merely to confirm what is written in the other letter, and will therefore not go into details.
> I am marrying Matahachi and adopting him into my family. However, he still seems concerned about you. I think it would be a mistake to let matters stand as they are. Matahachi is therefore sending you an explanation, the truth of which I hereby witness.
> Please forget Matahachi.
>
> Respectfully, Okō

The other letter was in Matahachi's scrawl and explained at tiresome length all the reasons why it was impossible for him to return home. The gist of it, of course, was that Otsū should forget about her betrothal to him and find another husband. Matahachi added that since it was "difficult" for him to write directly to his mother of these matters, he would appreciate her help. If Otsū happened to see the old woman, she was to tell her Matahachi was alive and well and living in another province.

Otsū felt the marrow of her spine turn to ice. She sat stricken, too shocked to cry or even to blink. The nails of the fingers holding the letter turned the same color as the skin of the dead man she had seen less than an hour before.

The hours passed. Everyone in the kitchen began wondering where she'd gone. The captain in charge of the search was content to let his exhausted men sleep in the woods, but when he himself returned to the temple at dusk, he demanded comforts befitting his status. The bath had to be heated just so; fresh fish from the river had to be prepared to his specifications and someone had to fetch sake of the highest quality from one of the village homes. A great deal of work was entailed in keeping the man happy, and much of it naturally fell to Otsū. Since she was nowhere to be found, the captain's dinner was late.

Takuan went out to search for her. He had no concern whatsoever for the captain, but he was beginning to worry about Otsū herself. It just wasn't like her to go off without a word. Calling her name, the monk crossed the temple grounds, passing by the loom shed several times. Since the door was shut, he didn't bother to look inside.

Several times the temple priest stepped out onto the raised passageway and shouted to Takuan, "Have you found her yet? She's got to be around here somewhere." As time went on, he grew frantic, calling out, "Hurry up and find her! Our guest says he can't drink his sake without her here to pour it for him."

The temple's manservant was dispatched down the hill to search for her, lantern in hand. At almost the same moment he took off, Takuan finally opened the loom shed door.

What he saw inside gave him a start. Otsū was drooped over the loom in a state of obvious desolation. Not wanting to pry, he remained silent, staring at the two twisted and torn letters on the ground. They had been trampled on like a couple of straw effigies.

Takuan picked them up. "Aren't these what the runner brought today?" he asked gently. "Why don't you put them away somewhere?"

Otsū shook her head feebly.

"Everyone's half crazy with worry about you. I've been looking all over. Come, Otsū, let's go back. I know you don't want to, but you really do have work to do. You've got to serve the captain, for one thing. That old priest is nearly beside himself."

"My . . . my head hurts," she whispered. "Takuan, couldn't they let me off tonight—just this once?"

Takuan sighed. "Otsū, I personally think you shouldn't have to serve the captain's sake tonight or any night. The priest, however, is of a different mind. He is a man of this world. He's not the type who can gain the daimyō's respect or support for the temple through high-mindedness alone. He believes he has to wine and dine the captain—keep him happy every minute." He patted Otsū on the back. "And after all, he did take you in and raise you, so you do owe him something. You won't have to stay long."

She consented reluctantly. While Takuan was helping her up, she raised her tear-stained face to him and said, "I'll go, but only if you promise to stay with me."

"I have no objection to that, but old Scraggly Beard doesn't like me, and every time I see that silly mustache I have an irresistible urge to tell him how ridiculous it looks. It's childish, I know, but some people just affect me that way."

"But I don't want to go alone!"

"The priest is there, isn't he?"

"Yes, but he always leaves when I arrive."

"Hmm. That's not so good. All right, I'll go with you. Now stop thinking about it, and go wash your face."

When Otsū finally appeared at the priest's quarters, the captain, already slouching drunkenly, immediately perked up. Straightening his cap, which had been listing noticeably, he became quite jovial and called for refill after refill. Soon his face glowed scarlet and the corners of his bulging eyes began to sag.

He was not enjoying himself to the full, however, and the reason was a singularly unwanted presence in the room. On the other side of the lamp sat Takuan, bent over like a blind beggar, absorbed in reading the book open on his knees.

Mistaking the monk for an acolyte, the captain pointed at him, bellowing, "Hey, you there!"

Takuan continued reading until Otsū gave him a nudge. He raised his eyes absently, and looking all around, said, "You mean me?"

The captain spoke gruffly. "Yes, you! I have no business with you. Leave!"

"Oh, I don't mind staying," Takuan replied innocently.

"Oh, you don't, do you?"

"No, not at all," Takuan said, returning to his book.

"Well, I mind," the captain blustered. "It spoils the taste of good sake to have someone around reading."

"Oh, I'm sorry," responded Takuan with mock solicitude. "How rude of me. I'll just close the book."

"The very sight annoys me."

"All right, then. I'll have Otsū put it away."

"Not the book, you idiot! I'm talking about you! You spoil the setting."

Takuan's expression became grave. "Now, that is a problem, isn't it? It's not as though I were the sacred

Wu-k'ung and could change myself into a puff of smoke, or become an insect and perch on your tray.''

The captain's red neck swelled and his eyes bulged. He looked like a blowfish. "Get out, you fool! Out of my sight!"

"Very well," said Takuan quietly, bowing. Taking Otsū's hand, he addressed her. "The guest says he prefers to be alone. To love solitude is the mark of the sage. We mustn't bother him further. Come."

"Why . . . why, you . . . you . . ."

"Is something wrong?"

"Who said anything about taking Otsū with you, you ugly moron!"

Takuan folded his arms. "I've observed over the years that not many priests or monks are particularly handsome. Not many samurai either, for that matter. Take you, for example."

The captain's eyes nearly leapt from their sockets. "What!"

"Have you considered your mustache? I mean, have you ever really taken the time to look at it, to evaluate it objectively?"

"You crazy bastard," shouted the captain as he reached for his sword, which was leaning against the wall. "Watch yourself!"

As he got to his feet, Takuan, keeping one eye on him, asked placidly. "Hmm. How do I go about watching myself?"

The captain, who was by now screaming, had his sheathed sword in hand. "I've taken all I can take. Now you're going to get what's coming to you!"

Takuan burst out laughing. "Does that mean you plan to cut off my head? If so, forget it. It would be a terrible bore."

"Huh?"

"A bore. I can't think of anything more boring than cutting off a monk's head. It would just fall to the floor and lie there laughing up at you. Not a very grand accomplishment, and what good could it possibly do you?"

"Well," growled the captain, "let's just say I'd have the satisfaction of shutting you up. It'd be pretty hard for you to keep up your insolent chatter!" Filled with the courage such people derive from having a weapon in hand, he laughed a mean belly laugh and moved forward threateningly.

"But, captain!"

Takuan's offhand manner had so enraged him that the hand in which he held his scabbard was shaking violently. Otsū slipped between the two men in an effort to protect Takuan.

"What are you saying, Takuan?" she said, hoping to lighten the mood and slow the action. "People don't talk like that to warriors. Now, just say you're sorry," she entreated. "Come on, apologize to the captain."

Takuan, however, was anything but finished.

"Get out of the way, Otsū. I'm all right. Do you really think I'd let myself be beheaded by a dolt like this, who though commanding scores of able, armed men has wasted twenty days trying to locate one exhausted, half-starved fugitive? If he hasn't enough sense to find Takezō, it would indeed be amazing if he could outwit me!"

"Don't move!" commanded the captain. His bloated face turned purple as he moved to draw his sword. "Stand aside, Otsū! I'm going to cut this big-mouthed acolyte in two!"

Otsū fell at the captain's feet and pleaded, "You

have every reason to be angry, but please be patient. He's not quite right in the head. He talks to everybody this way. He doesn't mean anything by it, really!" Tears began gushing from her eyes.

"What are you saying, Otsū?" objected Takuan. "There's nothing wrong with my mind, and I'm not joking. I'm only telling the truth, which no one seems to like to hear. He's a dolt, so I called him a dolt. You want me to lie?"

"You'd better not say that again," thundered the samurai.

"I'll say it as often as I wish. By the way, I don't suppose it makes any difference to you soldiers how much time you squander looking for Takezō, but it's a terrible burden on the farmers. Do you realize what you're doing to them? They won't be able to eat soon if you keep this up. It probably hasn't even occurred to you that they have to neglect their field work completely to go out on your disorganized wild-goose chases. And with no wages, I might add. It's a disgrace!"

"Hold your tongue, traitor. That's outright slander against the Tokugawa government!"

"It isn't the Tokugawa government I'm criticizing; it's bureaucratic officials like you who stand between the daimyō and the common people, and who might as well be stealing their pay for all they do to earn it. For one thing, exactly why are you lounging around here tonight? What gives you the right to relax in your nice, comfortable kimono all snug and warm, take leisurely baths and have your bedtime sake poured for you by a pretty young girl? You call that serving your lord?"

The captain was speechless.

"Is it not the duty of a samurai to serve his lord faithfully and tirelessly? Isn't it your job to exercise benevolence toward the people who slave on the daimyō's behalf? Look at yourself! You just close your eyes to the fact that you're keeping the farmers from the work which gives them daily sustenance. You don't even have any consideration for your own men. You're supposed to be on an official mission, so what do you do? Every chance you get, you literally stuff yourself with other people's hard-earned food and drink and use your position to get the most comfortable quarters available. I should say you are a classic example of corruption, cloaking yourself with the authority of your superior to do nothing more than dissipate the energies of the common people for your own selfish ends."

The captain was by now too stunned to close his gaping mouth. Takuan pressed on.

"Now just try cutting off my head and sending it to Lord Ikeda Terumasa! That, I can tell you, would surprise him. He'd probably say, 'Why, Takuan! Has only your head come to visit me today? Where in the world is the rest of you?'

"No doubt you'd be interested to learn that Lord Terumasa and I used to partake of the tea ceremony together at the Myōshinji. We've also had several long and pleasant chats at the Daitokuji in Kyoto."

Scraggly Beard's virulence drained from him in an instant. His drunkenness had worn off a bit too, though he still appeared incapable of judging for himself whether Takuan was telling the truth or not. He seemed paralyzed, not knowing how to react.

"First, you'd better sit down," said the monk. "If you think I'm lying, I'll be happy to go with you to the castle and appear before the lord himself. As a gift, I could take him some of the delicious buckwheat flour they make here. He's particularly fond of it.

"However, there's nothing more tedious, nothing I like less, than calling on a daimyō. Moreover, if the subject of your activities in Miyamoto should happen to come up while we were chatting over tea, I couldn't very well lie. It would probably end up with your having to commit suicide for your incompetence. I told you from the beginning to stop threatening me, but you warriors are all the same. You never think about consequences. And that's your greatest failing.

"Now put your sword down and I'll tell you something else."

Deflated, the captain complied.

"Of course, you are familiar with General Sun-tzu's *Art of War*—you know, the classic Chinese work on military strategy? I assume any warrior in your position would be intimately acquainted with such an important book. Anyway, the reason I mention it is that I'd like to give you a lesson illustrating one of the book's main principles. I'd like to show you how to capture Takezō without losing any more of your own men or causing the villagers any more trouble than you have already. Now, this has to do with your official work, so you really should listen carefully." He turned to the girl. "Otsū, pour the captain another cup of sake, will you?"

The captain was a man in his forties, ten years or so older than Takuan, but it was clear from their faces at this moment that strength of character is not a matter of age. Takuan's tongue-lashing had humbled the older man and his bluster had evaporated.

Meekly he said, "No, I don't want any more sake.

I hope you'll forgive me. I had no idea you were a friend of Lord Terumasa. I'm afraid I've been very rude." He was abject to the point of being comical, but Takuan refrained from rubbing it in.

"Let's just forget about that. What I want to discuss is how to capture Takezō. That is what you have to do to carry out your orders and maintain your honor as a samurai, isn't it?"

"Yes."

"Of course, I also know you don't care how long it takes to catch the man. After all, the longer it takes, the longer you can stay on at the temple, eating, drinking and ogling Otsū."

"Please, don't bring that up anymore. Particularly before his lordship." The soldier looked like a child ready to burst into tears.

"I'm prepared to consider the whole incident a secret. But if this running around in the mountains all day long keeps up, the farmers will be in serious trouble. Not only the farmers but all the rest of the people as well. Everyone in this village is too upset and frightened to settle down and get on with their normal work. Now, as I see it, your trouble is that you have not employed the proper strategy. Actually, I don't think you've employed any strategy at all. I take it that you do not know *The Art of War?*"

"I'm ashamed to admit it, but I don't."

"Well, you should be ashamed! And you shouldn't be surprised when I call you a dolt. You may be an official, but you are sadly uneducated and totally ineffectual. There's no use in my beating you over the head with the obvious, however. I'll simply make you a proposition. I personally offer to capture Takezō for you in three days."

"*You* capture him?"

"Do you think I'm joking?"

"No, but . . ."

"But what?"

"But counting the reinforcements from Himeji and all the farmers and foot soldiers, we've had more than two hundred men combing the mountains for nearly three weeks."

"I'm well aware of that fact."

"And since it's spring, Takezō has the advantage. There's plenty to eat up there this time of year."

"Are you planning on waiting till it snows, then? Another eight months or so?"

"No, uh, I don't think we can afford to do that."

"You certainly can't. That's precisely why I'm offering to catch him for you. I don't need any help; I can do it alone. On second thoughts, though, maybe I should take Otsū along with me. Yes, the two of us would be enough."

"You aren't serious, are you?"

"Would you please be quiet! Are you implying that Takuan Sōhō spends all his time making up jokes?"

"Sorry."

"As I said, you don't know *The Art of War*, and as I see it, that is the most important reason for your abominable failure. I, on the other hand, may be a simple priest, but I believe I understand Sun-tzu. There's only one stipulation, and if you won't agree to it, I'll just have to sit back and watch you bumble about until the snow falls, and maybe your head as well."

"What's the condition?" said the captain warily.

"If I bring back the fugitive, you'll let me decide his fate."

"What do you mean by that?" The captain pulled at his mustache, a string of thoughts racing through his mind. How could he be sure that this strange monk wasn't deceiving him completely? Although he spoke eloquently, it could be that he was completely insane. Could he be a friend of Takezō's, an accomplice? Might he know where the man was hiding? Even if he didn't, which was likely at this stage, there was no harm in leading him on, just to see whether he'd go through with this crazy scheme. He'd probably worm out of it at the last minute anyway. With this in mind, the captain nodded his assent. "All right, then. If you catch him, you can decide what to do with him. Now, what happens if you *don't* find him in three days?"

"I'll hang myself from the big cryptomeria tree in the garden."

Early the next day, the temple's manservant, looking extremely worried, came rushing into the kitchen, out of breath and half shouting: "Has Takuan lost his mind? I heard he promised to find Takezō himself!"

Eyes rounded.

"No!"

"Not really!"

"Just how does he plan to do it?"

Wisecracks and mocking laughter followed, but there was also an undercurrent of worried whispering.

When word reached the temple priest, he nodded sagely and remarked that the human mouth is the gateway to catastrophe.

But the person most genuinely disturbed was

Otsū. Only the day before, the farewell note from Matahachi had hurt her more than news of his death could ever have. She had trusted her fiancé and had even been willing to suffer the formidable Osugi as a slave-driving mother-in-law for his sake. Who was there to turn to now?

For Otsū, plunged into darkness and despair, Takuan was life's one bright spot, her last ray of hope. The day before, weeping alone in the loom shed, she'd seized a sharp knife and cut to shreds the kimono cloth into which she'd literally woven her soul. She'd also considered plunging the fine blade into her own throat. Though she was sorely tempted to do so, Takuan's appearance had finally driven that thought from her mind. After soothing her and getting her to agree to pour the captain's sake, he'd patted her on the back. She could still feel the warmth of his strong hand as he led her out of the loom shed.

And now he'd made this insane agreement.

Otsū wasn't nearly as concerned over her own safety as she was over the possibility that her only friend in the world might be lost to her because of his silly proposal. She felt lost and utterly depressed. Her common sense alone told her it was ridiculous to think that she and Takuan could locate Takezō in so short a time.

Takuan even had the audacity to exchange vows with Scraggly Beard before the shrine of Hachiman, the god of war. After he returned, she took him severely to task for his rashness, but he insisted there was nothing to worry about. His intention, he said, was to relieve the village of its burden, to make travel on the highways safe once more and to prevent any further waste of human life. In view of the number of lives that could be saved by quickly apprehending Takezō, his own seemed unimportant, she must see that. He also told her to get as much rest as she could before the evening of the following day, when they would depart. She was to come along without complaint, trusting in his judgment completely. Otsū was too distraught to resist, and the alternative of staying behind and worrying was even worse than the thought of going.

Late the following afternoon, Takuan was still napping with the cat in the corner of the main temple building. Otsū's face was hollow. The priest, the manservant, the acolyte—everybody had tried to persuade her not to go. "Go and hide" was their practical advice, but Otsū, for reasons she herself could hardly fathom, didn't feel the least inclined to do so.

The sun was sinking fast, and the dense shadows of evening had begun to envelop the crevices in the mountain range that marked the course of the Aida River. The cat sprang down from the temple porch, and presently Takuan himself stepped onto the veranda. Like the cat before him, he stretched his limbs, with a great yawn.

"Otsū," he called, "we'd better get going."

"I've already packed everything—straw sandals, walking sticks, leggings, medicine, paulownia-oil paper."

"You forgot something."

"What? A weapon? Should we take a sword or a lance or something?"

"Certainly not! I want to take along a supply of food."

"Oh, you mean some box lunches?"

"No, good food. I want some rice, some salty

bean paste and—oh, yes—a little sake. Anything tasty will do. I also need a pot. Go to the kitchen and make up a big bundle. And get a pole to carry it with.''

The nearby mountains were now blacker than the best black lacquer, those in the distance paler than mica. It was late spring, and the breeze was perfumed and warm. Striped bamboo and wisteria vines entrapped the mist, and the farther Takuan and Otsū went from the village, the more the mountains, where every leaf shone faintly in the dim light, seemed to have been bathed by an evening shower. They walked through the darkness in single file, each shouldering an end of the bamboo pole from which swung their well-packed bundle.

"It's a nice evening for a walk, isn't it, Otsū?" Takuan said, glancing over his shoulder.

"I don't think it's so wonderful," she muttered. "Where are we going, anyway?"

"I'm not quite sure yet," he replied with a slightly pensive air, "but let's go on a bit farther."

"Well, I don't mind walking."

"Aren't you tired?"

"No," replied the girl, but the pole obviously hurt her, for every once in a while she shifted it from one shoulder to the other.

"Where is everyone? We haven't seen a soul."

"The captain didn't show his face at the temple all day today. I bet he called the searchers back to the village so we can have three days all to ourselves. Takuan, just how do you propose to catch Takezō?"

"Oh, don't worry. He'll turn up sooner or later."

"Well, he hasn't turned up for anyone else. But even if he does, what are we going to do? With all those men pursuing him for so long, he must be desperate by now. He'll be fighting for his life, and he's very strong to begin with. My legs start shaking just thinking about it."

"Careful! Watch your step!" Takuan shouted suddenly.

"Oh!" Otsū cried in terror, stopping dead in her tracks. "What's the matter? Why did you scare me like that?"

"Don't worry, it's not Takezō. I just want you to watch where you walk. There are wisteria-vine and bramble traps all along the side of the road here."

"The searchers set them there to catch Takezō?"

"Uh-huh. But if we're not careful, we'll fall into one ourselves."

"Takuan, if you keep saying things like that I'll be so nervous I won't be able to put one foot in front of the other!"

"What are you worried about? If we do walk into one, I'll fall in first. No need for you to follow me." He grinned back at her. "I must say, they went to an awful lot of trouble for nothing." After a moment's silence, he added, "Otsū, doesn't the ravine seem to be getting narrower?"

"I don't know, but we passed the back side of Sanumo some time ago. This should be Tsujinohara."

"If that's the case, we may have to walk all night."

"Well, I don't even know where we're going. Why talk to me about it?"

"Let's put this down for a minute." After they'd lowered the bundle to the ground, Takuan started toward a nearby cliff.

"Where are you going?"

"To relieve myself."

A hundred feet below him, the waters that joined to form the Aida River were crashing thunderously from boulder to boulder. The sound roared up to him, filling his ears and penetrating his whole being. As he urinated, he gazed at the sky as if counting the stars. "Oh, this feels good!" he exulted. "Am I one with the universe, or is the universe one with me?"

"Takuan," called Otsū, "aren't you finished yet? You certainly do take your time!"

Finally he reappeared and explained himself. "While I was about it, I consulted the Book of Changes, and now I know exactly what course of action we have to take. It's all clear to me now."

"The Book of Changes? You aren't carrying a book."

"Not the written one, silly, the one inside me. My very own original Book of Changes. It's in my heart or belly or somewhere. While I was standing there, I was considering the lay of the land, the look of the water and the condition of the sky. Then I shut my eyes, and when I opened them, something said, 'Go to that mountain over there.' " He pointed to a nearby peak.

"Are you talking about Takateru Mountain?"

"I have no idea what it's called. It's that one, with the level clearing about halfway up."

"People call that Itadori Pasture."

"Oh, it has a name, does it?"

When they reached it, the pasture proved to be a small plain, sloping to the southeast and affording a splendid view of the surroundings. Farmers usually turned horses and cows loose here to graze, but that night not an animal could be seen or heard. The stillness was broken only by the warm spring breeze caressing the grass.

"We'll camp here," announced Takuan. "The enemy, Takezō, will fall into my hands just as General Ts'ao Ts'ao of Wei fell into the hands of Ch'u-ko K'ung-ming."

As they laid down their load, Otsū inquired, "What are we going to do here?"

"We are going to sit," replied Takuan firmly.

"How can we catch Takezō by just sitting here?"

"If you set up nets, you can catch birds on the wing without having to fly around yourself."

"We haven't set up any nets. Are you sure you haven't become possessed by a fox or something?"

"Let's build a fire, then. Foxes are afraid of fire, so if I am I'll soon be exorcised."

They gathered some dry wood, and Takuan built a fire. It seemed to lift Otsū's spirits.

"A good fire cheers a person up, doesn't it?"

"It warms a person up, that's for sure. Anyway, were you unhappy?"

"Oh, Takuan, you can see the mood I've been in! And I don't think anyone really likes to spend a night in the mountains like this. What would we do if it rained right now?"

"On the way up I saw a cave near the road. We could take shelter there till it stopped."

"That's what Takezō probably does at night in bad weather, don't you think? There must be places like that all over the mountain. That's probably where he hides most of the time, too."

"Probably. He doesn't really have much sense, but he must have enough to get in out of the rain."

She grew pensive. "Takuan, why do the people in the village hate him so much?"

"The authorities make them hate him. Otsū, these people are simple. They're afraid of the government, so afraid that if it so decrees, they'll drive away their fellow villagers, even their own kin."

"You mean they only worry about protecting their own skins."

"Well, it's not really their fault. They're completely powerless. You have to forgive them for putting their own interests first, since it's a case of self-defense. What they really want is just to be left alone."

"But what about the samurai? Why are they making such a fuss about an insignificant person like Takezō?"

"Because he's a symbol of chaos, an outlaw. They have to preserve the peace. After Sekigahara, Takezō was obsessed with the idea that the enemy was chasing him. He made his first big mistake by breaking through the barrier at the border. He should've used his wits somehow, snuck through at night or gone through in disguise. Anything. But not Takezō! He had to go and kill a guard and then kill other people later on. After that it just snowballed. He thinks he has to keep on killing to protect his own life. But he's the one who started it. The whole unfortunate situation was brought about by one thing: Takezō's complete lack of common sense."

"Do you hate him too?"

"I loathe him! I abhor his stupidity! If I were lord of the province, I'd have him suffer the worst punishment I could devise. In fact, as an object lesson to the people, I'd have him torn limb from limb. After all, he's no better than a wild beast, is he? A provincial lord cannot afford to be generous with the likes of Takezō, even if he does seem to some to be no more than a young ruffian. It would be detrimental to law and order, and that's not good, particularly in these unsettled times.''

"I always thought you were kind, Takuan, but deep down you're quite hard, aren't you? I didn't think you cared about the daimyō's laws.''

"Well, I do. I think that good should be rewarded and evil punished, and I came here with the authority to do just that.''

"Oh, what was that?" cried Otsū, jumping up from her place by the fire. "Didn't you hear it? It was a rustling sound, like footsteps, in those trees over there!''

"Footsteps?" Takuan, too, became alert, but after listening closely for a few moments he burst into laughter. "Ha, ha. It's only some monkeys. Look!" They could see the silhouettes of a big monkey and a little one, swinging through the trees.

Otsū, visibly relieved, sat down again. "Whew, that scared me half to death!''

For the next couple of hours, the two sat silently, staring at the fire. Whenever it would dwindle, Takuan would break some dry branches and throw them on.

"Otsū, what are you thinking about?''

"Me?''

"Yes, you. Although I do it all the time, I really hate holding conversations with myself.''

Otsū's eyes were puffy from the smoke. Looking up at the starry sky, she spoke softly. "I was thinking of how strange the world is. All those stars way up there in the empty blackness— No, I don't mean that.

"The night is full. It seems to embrace everything. If you stare at the stars a long time, you can see them moving. Slowly, slowly moving. I can't help thinking the whole world is moving. I feel it. And I'm just a little speck in it all—a speck controlled by some awesome power I can't even see. Even while I sit here thinking, my fate is changing bit by bit. My thoughts seem to go round and round in circles."

"You're not telling the truth!" said Takuan sternly. "Of course those ideas entered your head, but you really had something much more specific on your mind."

Otsū was silent.

"I apologize if I violated your privacy, Otsū, but I read those letters you received."

"You did? But the seal wasn't broken!"

"I read them after finding you in the loom shed. When you said you didn't want them, I stuck them in my sleeve. I guess it was wrong of me, but later, when I was in the privy, I took them out and read them just to pass the time."

"You're awful! How could you do such a thing! And just to pass the time!"

"Well, for whatever reason. Anyway, now I understand what started that flood of tears. Why you looked half dead when I found you. But listen, Otsū, I think you were lucky. In the long run, I think it's better that things turned out the way they did. You think I'm awful? Look at him!"

"What do you mean?"

"Matahachi was and still is irresponsible. If you married him, and then one day he surprised you with a letter like that, what would you do then? Don't tell me, I know you. You'd dive into the sea from a rocky cliff. I'm glad it's all over before it could come to that.''

"Women don't think that way."

"Oh, really? How do they think?"

"I'm so angry I could scream!" She tugged angrily at the sleeve of her kimono with her teeth. "Someday I'll find him! I swear I will! I won't rest until I've told him, to his face, exactly what I think of him. And the same goes for that Okō woman."

She broke into tears of rage. As Takuan stared at her, he mumbled cryptically, "It's started, hasn't it?"

She looked at him dumbfounded. "What?"

He stared at the ground, seemingly composing his thoughts. Then he began. "Otsū, I'd really hoped that you, of all people, would be spared the evils and duplicities of this world. That your sweet, innocent self would go through all the stages of life unsullied and unharmed. But it looks like the rough winds of fate have begun to buffet you, as they buffet everyone else."

"Oh, Takuan! What should I do? I'm so . . . so . . . angry!" Her shoulders shook with her sobbing as she buried her face in her lap.

By dawn, she'd cried herself out, and the two of them hid in the cave to sleep. That night they kept watch by the fire and slept through the next day in the cave again. They had plenty of food, but Otsū was baffled. She kept saying she couldn't see how they'd ever capture Takezō at this rate. Takuan, on the other hand, remained sublimely unperturbed. Otsū hadn't a clue to what he was thinking. He made no move to search anywhere, nor was he the slightest bit disconcerted by Takezō's failure to appear.

On the evening of the third day, as on the previous nights, they kept vigil by the fireside.

"Takuan," Otsū finally blurted, "this is our last night, you know. Our time is up tomorrow."

"Hmm. That's true, isn't it?"

"Well, what do you plan to do?"

"Do about what?"

"Oh, don't be so difficult! You do remember, don't you, the promise you made to the captain?"

"Why, yes, of course!"

"Well, if we don't bring Takezō back—"

He interrupted her. "I know, I know. I'll have to hang myself from the old cryptomeria tree. But don't worry. I'm not ready to die just yet."

"Then why don't you go and look for him?"

"If I did, do you really think I'd find him? In these mountains?"

"Oh, I don't understand you at all! And yet somehow, just sitting here, I feel like I'm getting braver, mustering up the nerve to let things turn out whatever way they will." She laughed. "Or maybe I'm just going crazy, like you."

"I'm not crazy. I just have nerve. That's what it takes."

"Tell me, Takuan, was it nerve and nothing else that made you take this on?"

"Yes."

"Nothing but nerve! That's not very encouraging. I thought you must have some foolproof scheme up your sleeve."

Otsū had been on her way toward sharing her companion's confidence, but his disclosure that he was operating on sheer audacity sent her into a fit of despondency. Was he totally insane? Sometimes people who are not quite right in the mind are taken by others to be geniuses. Takuan might be one of those. Otsū was beginning to think this was a distinct possibility.

The monk, serene as ever, continued to gaze absently into the fire. Presently he mumbled, as though he'd just noticed. "It's very late, isn't it?"

"It certainly is! It'll be dawn soon," snapped Otsū with deliberate tartness. Why had she trusted this suicidal lunatic?

Paying no attention to the sharpness of her response, he muttered, "Funny, isn't it?"

"What *are* you muttering about, Takuan?"

"It just occurred to me that Takezō has to show up pretty soon."

"Yes, but maybe he doesn't realize you two have an appointment." Looking at the monk's unsmiling face, she softened. "Do you really think he will?"

"Of course I do!"

"But why would he just walk right into a trap?"

"It's not exactly that. It has to do with human nature, that's all. People aren't strong at heart, they're weak. And solitude is not their natural state, particularly when it involves being surrounded by enemies and chased with swords. You may think it's natural, but I'd be very much surprised if Takezō manages to resist the temptation to pay us a call and warm himself by the fire."

"Isn't that just wishful thinking? He may be nowhere near here."

Takuan shook his head and said, "No, it is not just wishful thinking. It isn't even my own theory, it's that of a master of strategy." He spoke so confidently that Otsū found herself relieved that his disagreement was so definite.

"I suspect that Shimmen Takezō is somewhere very close by, but hasn't yet decided whether we're friends or enemies. He's probably plagued, poor boy, by a multitude of doubts, struggling with them, unable to advance or retreat. It'd be my guess he's hiding in the shadows right now, looking out at us furtively, wondering desperately what to do. Ah, I know. Let me have the flute you carry in your obi!"

"My bamboo flute?"

"Yes, let me play it for a while."

"No. Impossible. I never let anyone touch it."

"Why?" Takuan insisted.

"Never mind why!" she cried with a shake of her head.

"What harm would it do to let me use it? Flutes improve the more they're played. I won't hurt it."

"But . . ." Otsū clasped her right hand firmly on the flute in her obi.

She always carried it next to her body, and Takuan knew how much she treasured the instrument. He had never imagined, however, she would refuse to let him play it.

"I really won't break it, Otsū. I've handled dozens of flutes. Oh, come now, at least let me hold it."

"No."

"Whatever happens?"

"Whatever happens."

"You're stubborn!"

"Okay, I'm stubborn."

Takuan gave up. "Well, I'd just as soon listen to you play it. Will you play me just one little piece?"

"I don't want to do that either."

"Why not?"

"Because I'd start to cry, and I can't play the flute when I'm crying."

"Hmm," mused Takuan. While he felt pity for this obstinate tenacity, so characteristic of orphans, he was aware of a void deep within their stubborn hearts. They seemed to him doomed to yearn desperately for that which they could not have, for the parental love with which they were never blessed.

Otsū was constantly calling out to the parents she'd never known, and they to her, but she had no firsthand knowledge of parental love. The flute was the only thing her parents had left her, the only image of them she'd ever had. When, barely old enough to see the light of day, she'd been left like an abandoned kitten on the porch of the Shippōji, the flute had been tucked in her tiny obi. It was the one and only link that might in the future enable her to seek out people of her own blood. Not only was it the image, it was the voice of the mother and father she'd never seen.

"So she cries when she plays it!" thought Takuan. "No wonder she's so reluctant to let anyone handle it, or even to play it herself." He felt sorry for her.

On this third night, for the first time, a pearly moon shimmered in the sky, now and then dissolving behind misty clouds. The wild geese that always migrate to Japan in fall and go home in spring were apparently on their way back north; occasionally their quacking reached them from among the clouds.

Rousing himself from his reverie, Takuan said, "The fire's gone down, Otsū. Would you put some more wood on it? . . . Why, what's the matter? Is something wrong?"

Otsū didn't answer.

"Are you crying?"

Still she said nothing.

"I'm sorry I reminded you of the past. I didn't mean to upset you."

"It's nothing," she whispered. "I shouldn't have been so stubborn. Please take the flute and play it." She brought the instrument out from her obi and offered it to him across the fire. It was in a wrapper of old, faded brocade; the cloth was worn, the cords tattered, but there still remained a certain antique elegance.

"May I look at it?" asked Takuan.

"Yes, please do. It doesn't matter anymore."

"But why don't you play it instead of me? I think I really would rather listen. I'll just sit here like this." He turned sideways and clasped his arms around his knees.

"All right. I'm not very good," she said modestly, "but I'll try."

She knelt in formal fashion on the grass, straightened her kimono collar and bowed to the flute laying before her. Takuan said no more. He seemed no longer to even be there; there was only the great lonely universe enveloped in night. The monk's shadowy form might well have been a rock that had rolled down from the hillside and settled on the plain.

Otsū, her white face turned slightly to one side, put the cherished heirloom to her lips. As she wetted the mouthpiece and prepared herself inwardly to play, she seemed a different Otsū altogether, an Otsū embodying the strength and dignity of art. Turning to Takuan, she once again, in proper fashion, disavowed any claim to skill. He nodded perfunctorily.

The liquid sound of the flute began. As the girl's

thin fingers moved over the seven holes of the instrument, her knuckles looked like tiny gnomes absorbed in a slow dance. It was a low sound, like the gurgling of a brook. Takuan felt that he himself had turned into flowing water, splashing through a ravine, playing in the shallows. When the high notes sounded, he felt his spirit wafted into the sky to gambol with the clouds. The sound of earth and the reverberations of heaven mingled and were transformed into the wistful sighs of the breeze blowing through the pines, lamenting the impermanence of this world.

As he listened raptly, his eyes closed, Takuan could not help but recall the legend of Prince Hiromasa, who, while strolling on a moonlit night at Suzaku Gate in Kyoto and playing his flute as he walked, heard another flute harmonizing with his. The prince searched out the player and found him in the upper story of the gate. Having exchanged flutes, the two played music together throughout the night. Only later did the prince discover that his companion had been a devil in human form.

"Even a devil," thought Takuan, "is moved by music. How much more deeply must a human being, subject to the five passions, be affected by the sound of the flute in the hands of this beautiful girl!" He wanted to weep but shed no tears. His face sank deeper between his knees, which he unconsciously hugged more tightly.

As the light from the fire gradually faded, Otsū's cheeks turned a deeper red. She was so absorbed in her music that it was difficult to distinguish her from the instrument she was playing.

Was she calling to her mother and father? Were these sounds ascending into the sky really asking,

"Where are you?" And was there not mingled with this plea the bitter resentment of a maiden who'd been deserted and betrayed by a faithless man?

She seemed intoxicated by the music, overwhelmed by her own emotions. Her breathing began to show signs of fatigue; tiny beads of sweat appeared around the edges of her hair. Tears flowed down her face. Though the melody was broken by stifled sobs, it seemed to go on and on forever.

And then suddenly there was a movement in the grass. It was no more than fifteen or twenty feet from the fire and sounded like a creeping animal. Takuan's head shot up. Looking straight at the black object, he quietly raised his hand and waved a greeting.

"You over there! It must be chilly in the dew. Come over here by the fire and warm yourself. Come and talk with us, please."

Startled, Otsū stopped playing and said, "Takuan, are you talking to yourself again?"

"Didn't you notice?" he asked, pointing. "Takezō has been over there for some time, listening to you play the flute."

She turned to look, and then, with a shriek, threw her flute at the black form. It was indeed Takezō. He jumped like a startled deer and started to flee.

Takuan, as astonished as Takezō by Otsū's scream, felt as though the net he was so carefully hauling in had broken and the fish escaped. Jumping to his feet, he called out at the top of his lungs, "Takezō! Stop!"

There was overpowering strength in his voice, a commanding force that could not easily be ignored. The fugitive stopped as though nailed to the ground and looked back, a little stupefied. He stared at Takezō with suspicious eyes.

The monk said no more. Slowly crossing his arms on his chest, he stared back at Takezō as steadily as Takezō was staring at him. The two seemed even to be breathing in unison.

Gradually there appeared at the corners of Takuan's eyes the wrinkles that mark the beginning of a friendly smile. Unfolding his arms, he beckoned to Takezō and said, "Now, come here."

At the sound of the words, Takezō blinked; a strange expression came over his dark face.

"Come on over here," Takuan urged, "and we can all talk to each other."

There followed a puzzled silence.

"There's lots to eat and we even have some sake. We're not your enemies, you know. Come over by the fire. Let's talk."

More silence.

"Takezō, aren't you making a big mistake? There's a world outside where there are fires and food and drink and even human sympathy. You persist in driving yourself about in your own private hell. You're taking a pretty warped view of the world, you know.

"But I'll stop trying to argue with you. In your condition, you could hardly have much of an ear for reason. Just come over here by the fire. Otsū, warm up the potato stew you made a while ago. I'm hungry too."

Otsū put the pot on the fire, and Takuan placed a jar of sake near the flames to heat it. This peaceful scene allayed Takezō's fears, and he inched nearer. When he was almost on top of them, he stopped and stood still, apparently held back by some inner embarrassment.

Takuan rolled a rock up near the fire and patted Takezō on the back. "You sit here," he said.

Abruptly, Takezō sat down. Otsū, for her part, couldn't even look her ex-fiance's friend in the face. She felt as though she were in the presence of an unchained beast.

Takuan, lifting the lid of the pot, said, "It seems to be ready." He stuck the tips of his chopsticks into a potato, drew it out, and popped it into his mouth. Chewing heartily, he proclaimed, "Very nice and tender. Won't you have some, Takezō?"

Takezō nodded and for the first time grinned, showing a set of perfect white teeth. Otsū filled a bowl and gave it to him, whereupon he began alternately to blow on the hot stew and slurp it up in big mouthfuls. His hands trembled and his teeth clattered against the edge of the bowl. Pitifully hungry as he was, the trembling was uncontrollable. Frighteningly so.

"Good, isn't it?" asked the monk, putting down his chopsticks. "How about some sake?"

"I don't want any sake."

"Don't you like it?"

"I don't want any now." After all that time in the mountains, he was afraid it might make him sick.

Presently he said, politely enough. "Thank you for the food. I'm warmed up now."

"Have you had enough?"

"Plenty, thank you." As he handed his bowl back to Otsū, he asked, "Why did you come up here? I saw your fire last night too."

The question startled Otsū and she had no answer ready, but Takuan came to the rescue by saying forthrightly, "To tell the truth, we came here to capture you."

Takezō showed no particular surprise, though he seemed hesitant to take what Takuan had said at face value. He hung his head in silence, then looked from one to the other of them.

Takuan saw that the time had come to act. Turning to face Takezō directly, he said, "How about it? If you're going to be captured anyway, wouldn't it be better to be tied up with the bonds of the Buddha's Law? The daimyō's regulations are law, and the Buddha's Law is law, but of the two, the bonds of the Buddha are the more gentle and humane."

"No, no!" said Takezō, shaking his head angrily.

Takuan continued mildly. "Just listen for a minute. I understand that you are determined to hold out to the death, but in the long run, can you really win?"

"What do you mean, can I win?"

"I mean, can you successfully hold out against the people who hate you, against the laws of the province and against your own worst enemy, yourself?"

"Oh, I know I've already lost," groaned Takezō. His face was sadly contorted and his eyes brimmed with tears. "I'll be cut down in the end, but before I am I'll kill the old Hon'iden woman and the soldiers from Himeji and all the other people I hate! I'll kill as many as I can!"

"What will you do about your sister?"

"Huh?"

"Ogin. What are you going to do about her? She's locked up in the stockade at Hinagura, you know!"

Despite his earlier resolve to rescue her, Takezō could not answer.

"Don't you think you should start considering the well-being of that good woman? She's done so much for you. And what about your duty to carry on the name of your father, Shimmen Munisai? Have you forgotten that it goes back through the Hirata family to the famous Akamatsu clan of Harima?"

Takezō covered his face with his blackened, now nearly clawed hands, his sharp shoulders piercing upward as they shook in his haggard, trembling body. He broke into bitter sobs. "I . . . I . . . don't know. What . . . what difference does it make now?"

At that, Takuan suddenly clenched his fist and let go with a solid punch to Takezō's jaw.

"Fool!" the monk's voice thundered.

Taken by surprise, Takezō reeled from the blow and before he could recover took another punch on the other side.

"You irresponsible oaf! You stupid ingrate! Since your father and mother and ancestors are not here to punish you, I'll do it for them. Take that!" The monk struck him again, this time knocking him all the way to the ground. "Does it hurt yet?" he asked belligerently.

"Yes, it hurts," the fugitive whined.

"Good. If it hurts, you may still have a little human blood coursing through your veins. Otsū, hand me that rope, please. . . . Well, what are you waiting for? Bring me the rope! Takezō already knows I'm going to tie him up. He's prepared for it. It's not the rope of authority, it's the rope of compassion. There's no reason for you to either fear or pity him. Quick, girl, the rope!"

Takezō lay still on his stomach, making no effort

to move. Takuan easily straddled his back. If Takezō had wanted to resist, he could have kicked Takuan in the air like a little paper ball. They both knew that. Yet he lay passively, arms and legs outstretched, as though he'd finally surrendered to some invisible law of nature.

6

The Old Cryptomeria Tree

Although it was not the time of the morning when the
temple bell was usually rung, its heavy, regular gong-
ing resounded through the village and echoed far into
the mountains. This was the day of reckoning, when
Takuan's time limit was up, and the villagers raced up
the hill to find out whether he'd done the impossible.
The news that he had spread like wildfire.

"Takezō's been captured!"

"Really! Who got him?"

"Takuan!"

"I can't believe it! Without a weapon?"

"It can't be true!"

The crowd surged up to the Shippōji to gawk at
the collared outlaw, who was tied like an animal to the
stair railing in front of the main sanctuary. Some
gulped and gasped at the sight, as though they were
beholding the countenance of the dreaded demon of
Mount Ōe. As if to deflate their exaggerated reaction,
Takuan sat a bit farther up the stairs, leaning back on
his elbows and grinning amiably.

"People of Miyamoto," he shouted, "now you can go back to your fields in peace. The soldiers will be gone soon!"

To the intimidated villagers, Takuan had become a hero overnight, their savior and protector from evil. Some bowed deeply to him, their heads nearly touching the ground of the temple courtyard; others pushed their way forward to touch his hand or robe. Others knelt at his feet. Takuan, appalled at this display of idolatry, pulled away from the mob and held up his hand for silence.

"Listen, men and women of Miyamoto. I have something to say, something important." The hue and cry died down. "It is not I who deserve the credit for capturing Takezō. It was not I who accomplished it, but the law of nature. Those who break it always lose in the end. It is the law that you should respect."

"Don't be ridiculous! You caught him, not nature!"

"Don't be so modest, monk!"

"We give credit where it's due!"

"Forget the law. We have you to thank!"

"Well, then thank me," continued Takuan. "I don't mind that. But you should pay homage to the law. Anyway, what's done is done, and right now there's something very important I'd like to ask you about. I need your help."

"What is it?" came the question from the curious crowd.

"Just this: what shall we do with Takezō now that we've got him? My agreement with the House of Ikeda's representative, who I'm sure you all know by sight, was that if I didn't bring the fugitive back in three days' time, I'd hang myself from that big cryptomeria. If I did succeed, I was promised, I could decide his fate."

People started to murmur.

"We heard about that!"

He assumed a judicial pose. "Well, then, what shall we do with him? As you see, the dreaded monster is here in the flesh. Not very fearsome, really, is he? In fact, he came along without a fight, the weakling. Shall we kill him, or let him go?"

There was a rumble of objections at the idea of setting Takezō free. One man shouted, "We've got to kill him! He's no good, he's a criminal! If we let him live, he'll be the curse of the village."

While Takuan paused, seeming to consider the possibilities, angry, impatient voices from the rear shouted, "Kill him! Kill him!"

At that point, an old woman pushed her way to the front, shoving aside men twice her size with sharp jabs of her elbows. It was, of course, the irate Osugi. When she reached the steps, she glared at Takezō for a moment, then turned and faced the villagers. Waving a mulberry branch in the air, she cried, "I won't be satisfied with just killing him! Make him suffer first! Just look at that hideous face!" Turning back to the prisoner, she raised her switch, screaming, "You degenerate, loathsome creature!" and brought it down on him several times, until she ran out of breath and her arm dropped to her side. Takezō cringed in pain as Osugi turned to Takuan with a menacing look.

"What do you want from me?" the monk asked.

"It was because of this murderer that my son's life has been ruined." Shaking violently, she screeched, "And without Matahachi there is no one to carry on our family name."

"Well," countered Takuan, "Matahachi, if you don't mind my saying so, never amounted to much anyway. Won't you be better off in the long run taking your son-in-law as heir? Giving him the honored Hon'iden name?"

"How dare you say such a thing!" Suddenly the proud dowager burst into sobs. "I don't care about what you think. Nobody understood him. He wasn't really bad; he was my baby." Her fury rose again and she pointed at Takezō. "He led him astray, he made him a good-for-nothing like himself. I have the right to take my revenge." Addressing the crowd, she beseeched them, "Let me decide. Leave it to me. I know what to do with him!"

Just then a loud and angry shout from the back cut the old woman off. The crowd parted like rent cloth, and the latecomer marched quickly to the front. It was Scraggly Beard himself, in a towering rage.

"What's going on here? This isn't a sideshow! All of you, get out of here. Go back to work. Go home. Immediately!" There was shuffling, but no one turned to go. "You heard what I said! Get a move on! What are you waiting for?" He stepped threateningly toward them, his hand poised above his sword. Those in the front shrank back wide-eyed.

"No!" interrupted Takuan. "There's no reason for these good people to go. I called them here for the express purpose of discussing what's to be done with Takezō."

"You be quiet!" commanded the captain. "You have nothing to say in this matter." Drawing himself up and glaring first at Takuan, then at Osugi, and finally at the crowd, he boomed, "This Shimmen Takezō has not only committed grave and serious

130

crimes against the laws of this province; he is also a fugitive from Sekigahara. His punishment cannot be decided by the people. He must be turned over to the government!"

Takuan shook his head. "Nonsense!" Seeing that Scraggly Beard was ready to respond, he raised a silencing finger. "That's not what you agreed to!"

The captain, his dignity seriously threatened, started to argue. "Takuan, you will no doubt receive the money the government has offered as a reward. But as an official representative of Lord Terumasa, it is my duty to take charge of the prisoner at this point. His fate need no longer be of any concern to you. Don't trouble yourself even thinking about it."

Takuan, making no effort to answer, broke into peals of laughter. Every time it seemed to subside, it would come rolling up again.

"Watch your manners, monk!" warned the captain. He started to spit and sputter. "What's so funny? Huh? You think this is all a joke?"

"My manners?" repeated Takuan, cracking up in laughter again. "My manners? Look, Scraggly Beard, are you thinking of breaking our agreement, going back on your sacred word? If you are, I warn you, I'll turn Takezō loose here and now!"

With a unanimous gasp, the villagers began edging away.

"Ready?" asked Takuan, reaching toward the rope that bound Takezō.

The captain was speechless.

"And when I unleash him, I'm going to sic him on you first. You can fight it out between yourselves. Then arrest him, if you can!"

"Now, hold on—just a minute!"

"I kept my part of the bargain." Takuan continued to make as if he were about to remove the prisoner's fetters.

"Stop, I say," The samurai's forehead beaded with sweat.

"Why?"

"Well, because—because—" He was almost stuttering. "Now that he's tied up, there's no point in letting him go, just to cause more trouble—now, is there? I'll tell you what! You can kill Takezō yourself. Here—here's my sword. Just let me have his head to take back with me. That's fair, isn't it?"

"Give you his head! Not on your life! It's the business of the clergy to conduct funerals, but giving away the corpses, or parts of them . . . Well, that'd give us priests a bad name, wouldn't it? No one would trust us with their dead, and anyway, if we started to just give them away, the temples would go broke in no time." Even with the samurai's hand resting on his sword handle, Takuan couldn't resist baiting him.

Turning to the mob, the monk became serious again. "I ask you to talk it over among yourselves and give me an answer. What shall we do? The old woman says it's not enough to kill him outright, we should torture him first. What do you think of lashing him to a branch of the cryptomeria tree for a few days? We could bind him hand and foot, and he would be exposed to the elements day and night. The crows will probably gouge out his eyeballs. How does that sound?"

His proposal struck his listeners as so inhumanly cruel that at first no one could answer.

Except Osugi, who said, "Takuan, this idea of yours shows what a wise man you really are, but I think we should string him up for a week—no, more! Let him hang there ten or twenty days. Then I myself will come and strike the fatal blow.''

Without further ado, Takuan nodded. ''All right. So be it!''

He took hold of the rope after freeing it from the railing and dragged Takezō, like a dog on a leash, to the tree. The prisoner went meekly, head bowed, uttering not a sound. He seemed so repentant that some of the softer-hearted members of the crowd felt a bit sorry for him. The excitement of capturing the ''wild beast'' had hardly worn off, however, and with great gusto everyone joined in the fun. Having tied several lengths of rope together, they hoisted him up to a branch about thirty feet from the ground and lashed him tightly. So bound, he looked less like a living man than a big straw doll.

After Otsū came back to the temple from the mountains, she began feeling a strange and intense melancholy whenever she was alone in her room. She wondered why, since being alone was nothing new to her. And there were always some people around the temple. She had all the comforts of home, yet felt lonelier now than she had at any time during those three long days on the desolate hillside with only Takuan as a companion. Sitting at the low table by her window, her chin resting on her palms, she reflected on her feelings for half a day before coming to a conclusion.

She felt that this experience had given her an insight into her own heart. Loneliness, she mused, is like hunger; it isn't outside but inside oneself. To be lonely, she thought, is to sense that one lacks something, something vitally necessary, but what she knew not.

Neither the people around her nor the amenities of life at the temple could assuage the feeling of isolation she now felt. In the mountains there had only been the silence, the trees and the mist, but there had also been Takuan. It came to her like a revelation that he was not entirely outside herself. His words had gone straight to her heart, had warmed and lighted it as no fire or lamp could. She then came to the innocent realization that she was lonely because Takuan was not around.

Having made this discovery, she stood up, but her mind still grappled with the problem at hand. After deciding Takezō's punishment, Takuan had been closeted in the guest room with the samurai from Himeji a good deal of the time. What with having to go back and forth to the village on this errand and that, he'd had no time to sit down and talk with her as he had in the mountains. Otsū sat down again.

If only she had a friend! She didn't need many; just one who knew her well, someone she could lean on, someone strong and completely trustworthy. That was what she longed for, craved so badly that she was nearly at her wit's end.

There was always, of course, her flute, but by the time a girl is sixteen, there are questions and uncertainties inside her that can't be answered by a piece of bamboo. She needed intimacy and a sense of partaking in, not just observing, real life.

"It's all so disgusting!" she said out loud, but voicing her feeling in no way mitigated her hatred for Matahachi. Tears spilled onto the little lacquered table; the angry blood coursing through her veins turned her temples blue. Her head throbbed.

Silently the door behind her slid open. In the temple kitchen, the fire for the evening meal burned brightly.

"Ah ha! So this is where you've been hiding! Sitting here letting the whole day slip through your fingers!"

The figure of Osugi appeared at the door. Startled out of her abstraction, Otsū hesitated a moment before welcoming the old woman and putting a cushion down for her to sit on. Without so much as a by-your-leave, Osugi seated herself.

"My good daughter-in-law . . ." she began in grandiose tones.

"Yes, ma'am," answered Otsū, cowed into bowing deeply before the old harridan.

"Now that you have acknowledged the relationship, there's a little something I want to talk to you about. But first bring me some tea. I've been talking till now with Takuan and the samurai from Himeji, and the acolyte here didn't even serve us refreshments. I'm parched!"

Otsū obeyed and brought her some tea.

"I want to talk about Matahachi," the old woman said without prelude. "Of course, I'd be a fool to believe anything that lying Takezō says, but it seems Matahachi is alive and staying in a different province."

"Is that so?" said Otsū coldly.

"I can't be sure, but the fact remains that the priest here, acting as your guardian, agreed to your marriage to my son, and the Hon'iden family has already accepted you as his bride. Whatever happens in the future, I trust you don't have any ideas about going back on your word."

"Well . . ."

"You'd never do such a thing, would you?"

Otsū let out a soft sigh.

"All right then, I'm glad of that!" She spoke as though adjourning a meeting. "You know how people talk, and there's no telling when Matahachi will be back, so I want you to leave this temple and come live with me. I've more work than I can handle, and since my daughter-in-law's got so much on her hands with her own family, I can't drive her too hard. So I need your help."

"But I—"

"Who else but Matahachi's bride could come into the Hon'iden house?"

"I don't know, but—"

"Are you trying to say you don't want to come? Don't you like the idea of living under my roof? Most girls would jump at the chance!"

"No, it's not that. It's—"

"Well, then, stop dawdling! Get your things together!"

"Right now? Wouldn't it be better to wait?"

"Wait for what?"

"Until . . . until Matahachi comes back."

"Absolutely not!" Her tone was final. "You just might start getting ideas in your head about other men before that. It's my duty to see that you don't misbehave. In the meantime, I'll also see that you learn how to do field work, care for the silkworms, sew a straight seam and act like a lady."

"Oh. I . . . see." Otsū had no strength to protest. Her head still pounded and with all this talk of Matahachi, her chest tightened. She feared saying another word lest she release a torrent of tears.

"And there's one other thing," said Osugi. Heedless of the girl's distress, she raised her head imperiously. "I'm still not quite sure what that unpredictable monk plans to do with Takezō. It worries me. I want you to keep a sharp eye on the two of them until we're sure Takezō is dead. At night as well as in the daytime. If you don't take special care at night, there's no telling what Takuan might do. They may be in cahoots!"

"So you don't mind if I stay here?"

"For the time being, no, since you can't be in two places at once, can you? You will come with your belongings to the Hon'iden house the day that Takezō's head is separated from his body. Understand?"

"Yes, I understand."

"Make sure you don't forget!" Osugi barked as she whooshed out of the room.

Thereupon, as though waiting for the chance, a shadow appeared on the paper-covered window and a male voice called softly, "Otsū! Otsū!"

Hoping it was Takuan, she hardly looked at the shape of the shadow before rushing to open the window. When she did, she jerked back in surprise, for the eyes meeting hers were the captain's. He reached through, grabbing her hand and squeezing it hard.

"You've been kind to me," he said, "but I've just received orders from Himeji to go back."

"Why, that's too bad." She tried to pull her hand from his, but the grip was too firm.

"They seem to be conducting an investigation into the incident here," he explained. "If only I had Takezō's head, I could say I had discharged my duty with honor. I'd be vindicated. That crazy, stubborn Takuan won't let me take it. He won't listen to anything I say. But I think you're on my side; that's why I've come here. Take this letter, will you, and read it later, somewhere where no one will see you?''

He pressed the letter into her hand and was off in a shot. She could hear him hurriedly walking down the steps to the road.

It was more than a letter, for a large gold piece was enclosed. But the message itself was straightforward enough: it asked Otsū to cut off Takezō's head within the next few days and bring it to Himeji, where the writer would make her his wife, and she would live amid wealth and glory for the rest of her days. The missive was signed "Aoki Tanzaemon," a name that, according to the writer's own testimony, belonged to one of the most celebrated warriors of the region. She wanted to burst out laughing, but was too indignant.

As she finished reading, Takuan called, "Otsū, have you eaten yet?"

Slipping her feet into her sandals, she went out to talk with him.

"I don't feel like eating. I have a headache."

"What's that in your hand?"

"A letter."

"Another one?"

"Yes."

"From whom?"

"Takuan, you're so nosy!"

"Curious, my girl, inquisitive. Not nosy!"

"Would you like to have a look at it?"

"If you don't mind."

"Just to pass the time?"

"That's as good a reason as any."

"Here. I don't mind at all."

Otsū handed him the letter, and after reading it, Takuan laughed heartily. She couldn't help but let the corners of her mouth turn up too.

"That poor man! He's so desperate he's trying to bribe you with both love and money. This letter is hilarious! I must say, our world is fortunate indeed to be blessed with such outstanding, upright samurai! He's so brave he asks a mere girl to do his beheading for him. And so stupid as to put it in writing."

"The letter doesn't bother me," said Otsū, "but what am I going to do with the money?" She handed Takuan the gold piece.

"This is worth quite a lot," he said, weighing it in his hand.

"That's what bothers me."

"Don't worry. I never have any trouble disposing of money."

Takuan walked around to the front of the temple, where there was an alms box. Preparing to toss the coin in, he touched it to his forehead in deference to the Buddha. Then he changed his mind. "On second thought, you keep it. I daresay it won't be in the way."

"I don't want it. It'll just cause trouble. I might be questioned about it later. I'd rather just pretend I never saw it."

"This gold, Otsū, no longer belongs to Aoki Tanzaemon. It has become an offering to the Buddha, and the Buddha has bestowed it on you. Keep it for good luck."

Without further protest, Otsū tucked the coin into her obi; then, looking up at the sky, she remarked,

"Windy, isn't it? I wonder if it'll rain tonight. It hasn't rained for ages."

"Spring's almost over, so we're due for a good downpour. We need it to wash away all the dead flowers, not to mention relieving the people's boredom."

"But if it's a heavy rain, what'll happen to Takezō?"

"Hmm. Takezō . . ." the monk mused.

Just as the two of them turned toward the cryptomeria, a call came from its upper branches.

"Takuan! Takuan!"

"What? Is that you, Takezō?"

As Takuan squinted to look up into the tree, Takezō hurled down a stream of imprecations. "You swine of a monk! You filthy impostor! Come and stand under here! I have something to say to you!"

The wind was beating at the tree's branches violently, and the voice came through broken and disjointed. Leaves swirled around the tree and onto Takuan's upturned face.

The monk laughed. "I see you're still full of life. That's okay; that suits me fine. I hope it's not just the false vitality that comes from the knowledge that you're soon going to die."

"Shut up!" cried Takezō, who was not so much full of life as full of anger. "If I were afraid to die, why would I have just kept still while you tied me up?"

"You did that because I am strong and you are weak!"

"That's a lie, and you know it!"

"Then I'll put it another way. I'm clever, and you are unspeakably stupid!"

"You might be right. It was certainly stupid of me to let you catch me."

"Don't squirm so much, monkey in the tree! It won't do you any good, it'll make you bleed if you've any blood left, and frankly, it's quite unbecoming."

"Listen, Takuan!"

"I'm listening."

"If I had wanted to fight you on the mountain, I could've easily squashed you under one foot like a cucumber."

"That's not a very flattering analogy. In any case you didn't, so you'd be better off leaving that line of thought. Forget about what happened. It's too late for regrets."

"You tricked me with your high-sounding priest talk. That was pretty mean, you bastard. You got me to trust you and you betrayed me. I let you capture me, yes, but only because I thought you were different from the others. I never thought I'd be humiliated like this."

"Get to the point, Takezō," Takuan said impatiently.

"Why are you doing this to me?" the straw bundle shrieked. "Why don't you just cut off my head and get it over with! I thought that if I had to die, it'd be better to let you choose how to execute me than let that bloodthirsty mob do it. Although you are a monk, you also claim to understand the Way of the Samurai."

"Oh, I do, you poor misguided boy. Much better than you!"

"I would've been better off letting the villagers catch up with me. At least they're human."

"Was that your only mistake, Takezō? Hasn't just about everything you've ever done been some kind of mistake? While you're resting up there, why don't you try thinking about the past a little."

"Oh, shut up, you hypocrite! I'm not ashamed! Matahachi's mother can call me anything she wants, but he is my friend, my best friend. I considered it my responsibility to come and tell the old hag what happened to him and what does she do? She tries to incite that mob to torture me! Bringing her news of her precious son was the only reason I broke through the barrier and came here. Is that a violation of the warrior's code?"

"That's not the point, you imbecile! The trouble with you is that you don't even know how to think. You seem to be under the misconception that if you perform one brave deed, that alone makes you a samurai. Well, it doesn't! You let that one act of loyalty convince you of your righteousness. The more convinced you became, the more harm you caused yourself and everyone else. And now where are you? Caught in a trap you set for yourself, that's where!" He paused. "By the way, how's the view from up there, Takezō?"

"You pig! I won't forget this!"

"You'll forget everything soon. Before you turn into dried meat, Takezō, take a good look at the wide world around you. Gaze out onto the world of human beings, and change your selfish way of thinking. And then, when you arrive in that other world beyond and are reunited with your ancestors, tell them that just before you died a man named Takuan Sōhō told you this. They'll be overjoyed to learn you had such excellent guidance, even if you did learn what life was all about too late to bring anything but shame to your family name."

Otsū, who had been standing transfixed some distance away, came running forward and attacked Takuan in shrill tones.

"You're carrying this too far, Takuan! I've been listening. I heard everything. How can you be so cruel to someone who can't even defend himself? You're a religious man, or you're supposed to be! Takezō's telling the truth when he says he trusted you and let you take him without a struggle."

"Now what's all this? Is my comrade in arms turning against me?"

"Have a heart, Takuan! When I hear you talk like that, I hate you, I really do. If you intend to kill him, then kill him and be done with it! Takezō is resigned to dying. Let him die in peace!" She was so outraged she grabbed frantically at Takuan's chest.

"Be quiet!" he said with uncharacteristic brutality. "Women know nothing of these matters. Hold your tongue, or I'll hang you up there with him."

"No, I won't, I won't!" she screamed. "I should have a chance to speak too. Didn't I go to the mountains with you and stay there three days and three nights?"

"That has nothing to do with it. Takuan Sōhō will punish Takezō as he sees fit."

"So punish him! Kill him! Now. It's not right for you to ridicule his misery while he's lying up there half dead."

"That happens to be my only weakness, ridiculing fools like him."

"It's inhuman!"

"Get out of here, now! Go away, Otsū; leave me alone."

"I will not!"

"Stop being so stubborn," Takuan shouted, giving Otsū a hard shove with his elbow.

When she recovered, she was slumped against the tree. She pressed her face and chest to its trunk and began wailing. She had never dreamed Takuan could be so cruel. The people in the village believed that even if the monk had Takezō tied up for a while, eventually he'd soften and lighten the punishment. Now Takuan had admitted that it was his "weakness" to enjoy seeing Takezō suffer! Otsū shuddered at the savagery of men.

If even Takuan, whom she'd trusted so deeply, could become heartless, then the whole world must indeed be evil beyond comprehension. And if there was no one at all whom she could trust . . .

She felt a curious warmth in this tree, felt somehow that through its great, ancient trunk, so thick that ten men with arms outstretched could not encompass it, there coursed the blood of Takezō, flowing down into it from his precarious prison in the upper branches.

How like a samurai's son he was! How courageous! When Takuan had first tied him up, and again just now, she had seen Takezō's weaker side. He, too, was able to weep. Until now, she'd gone along with the opinion of the crowd, been swayed by it, without having any real idea of the man himself. What was there about him that made people hate him like a demon and hunt him down like a beast?

Her back and shoulders heaved with her sobs. Clinging tightly to the tree trunk, she rubbed her tear-stained cheeks against the bark. The wind whistled loudly through the upper branches, which were waving broadly to and fro. Large raindrops fell on her kimono neck and flowed down her back, chilling her spine.

"Come on, Otsū," Takuan shouted, covering his head with his hands. "We'll get soaked."

She didn't even answer.

"It's all your fault, Otsū! You're a crybaby! You start weeping, the heavens weep too." Then, the teasing tone gone from his voice: "The wind's getting stronger, and it looks like we're in for a big storm, so let's get inside. Don't waste your tears on a man who's going to die anyway! Come on!" Takuan, sweeping the skirt of his kimono up over his head, ran toward the shelter of the temple.

Within seconds it was pouring, the raindrops making little white spots as they pummeled the ground. Though the water was streaming down her back, Otsū didn't budge. She couldn't tear herself away, even after her drenched kimono was clinging to her skin and she was chilled to the marrow. When her thoughts turned to Takezō, the rain ceased to matter. It didn't occur to her to wonder why she should suffer simply because he was suffering; her mind was consumed by a newly formed image of what a man should be. She silently prayed his life would be spared.

She wandered in circles round the foot of the tree, looking up to Takezō often, but unable to see him because of the storm. Without thinking, she called his name, but there was no answer. A suspicion arose in her mind that he might regard her as a member of the Hon'iden family, or as just another hostile villager.

"If he stays out in this rain," she thought in despair, "he's sure to die before morning. Oh, isn't there anyone in the world who can save him?"

She started running at full speed, partially propelled by the raging wind. Behind the main temple, the kitchen building and the priests' quarters were tightly shuttered. Water overflowing from the roof gutters slashed deep gullies in the ground as it rushed downhill.

"Takuan!" she screamed. She'd reached the door of his room, and began banging on it with all her strength.

"Who is it?" came his voice from within.

"It's me—Otsū!"

"What are you doing still out there?" He quickly opened the door and looked at her in astonishment. Despite the building's long eaves, rain showered in on him. "Come inside quick!" he exclaimed, making a grab for her arm, but she pulled back.

"No. I came to ask a favor, not to dry off. I beg you, Takuan, take him down from that tree!"

"What? I'll do no such thing!" he said adamantly.

"Oh, please, Takuan, you must. I'd be grateful to you forever." She fell on her knees in the mud and lifted her hands in supplication. "It doesn't matter about me, but you must help him! Please! You can't just let him die—you can't!"

The sound of the torrent nearly blotted out her tearful voice. With her hands still raised before her, she looked like a Buddhist practicing austerities by standing under a freezing waterfall.

"I bow before you, Takuan. I beg you. I'll do anything you ask, but please save him!"

Takuan was silent. His eyes were tightly closed, like the doors to the shrine where a secret Buddha is kept. Heaving a deep sigh, he opened them and breathed fire.

146

"Go to bed! This minute! You're weak to begin with, and being out in this weather is suicidal."

"Oh, please, please," she pleaded, reaching for the door.

"I'm going to bed. I advise you to do the same." His voice was like ice. The door slammed shut.

Still, she would not give up. She crawled under the house till she reached the spot she guessed was beneath where he slept. She called up to him: "Please! Takuan, it's the most important thing in the world to me! Takuan, can you hear me? Answer me, please! You're a monster! A heartless, cold-blooded fiend!"

For a while, the monk listened patiently without replying, but she was making it impossible for him to sleep. Finally, in a fit of temper, he jumped out of bed, shouting, "Help! Thief! There's a thief under my floor. Catch him!"

Otsū scrambled out into the storm again and retired in defeat. But she was not finished yet.

7

The Rock and the Tree

By early morning, wind and rain had washed spring away without a trace. A throbbing sun beat down furiously and few villagers walked around without a wide-brimmed hat for protection.

Osugi made her way uphill to the temple, arriving at Takuan's door thirsty and breathless. Beads of sweat emerged from her hairline, converged in rivulets and coursed straight down her righteous nose. She took no notice of this, for she was brimming over with curiosity about her victim's fate.

"Takuan," she called, "did Takezō survive the storm?"

The monk appeared on his veranda. "Oh, it's you. Terrific downpour, wasn't it?"

"Yes." She smiled crookedly. "It was murderous."

"I'm sure you know, however, that it wasn't very difficult to live through a night or two of even the heaviest rain. The human body can take a lot of buffeting. It's the sun that's really deadly."

"You don't mean he's still alive?" said Osugi in disbelief, at once turning her wrinkled face toward the old cryptomeria. Her needlelike eyes squinted in the glare. She raised a hand to shield them and in a moment relaxed a bit. "He's just drooping up there like a wet rag," she said with renewed hope. "He can't have any life left in him, he can't."

"I don't see any crows picking at his face yet." Takuan smiled. "I think that means he's still breathing."

"Thank you for telling me. A man of learning like you must surely know more than I do about such matters." She craned her neck and peered around him into the building. "I don't see my daughter-in-law anywhere. Would you please call her for me?"

"Your daughter-in-law? I don't believe I've ever met her. In any case, I don't know her name. How can I call her?"

"Call her, I say!" Osugi repeated impatiently.

"Who on earth are you talking about?"

"Why, Otsū, of course!"

"Otsū! Why do you call her your daughter-in-law? She hasn't entered the Hon'iden family, has she?"

"No, not yet, but I plan to take her in very soon as Matahachi's bride."

"That's hard to imagine. How can she marry someone when he's not around?"

Osugi became more indignant. "Look, you vagabond! This has nothing to do with you! Just tell me where Otsū is!"

"I imagine she's still in bed."

"Oh, yes, I should've thought of that," the old woman muttered, half to herself. "I did tell her to watch Takezō nights, so she must become pretty tired by daybreak. Incidentally,'' she said accusingly, "aren't you supposed to be watching him during the day?"

Without waiting for an answer, she did an about-face and marched under the tree. There she stared upward for a long time, as if in a trance. When it finally broke, she plodded off toward the village, mulberry stick in hand.

Takuan returned to his room, where he stayed until evening.

Otsū's room was not far from his, in the same building. Her door was also closed all day except when opened by the acolyte, who several times brought her medicine or an earthenware pot full of thick rice gruel. When they had found her half dead in the rain the night before, they'd had to drag her in kicking and screaming and force her to swallow some tea. The priest had then given her a severe scolding while she sat mutely propped against a wall. By morning she had a high fever and was hardly able to lift her head to drink the gruel.

Night fell, and in sharp contrast to the previous evening, a bright moon shone like a clearly cut hole in the sky. When everyone else was sound asleep, Takuan put down the book he was reading, slipped into his wooden clogs and went out into the yard.

"Takezō!" he called.

High above him a branch shook and glistening dewdrops fell.

"Poor boy, I guess he doesn't have the strength to reply," Takuan said to himself. "Takezō! Takezō!"

"What do you want, you bastard of a monk?" came the ferocious response.

Takuan was seldom taken off guard, but he could not conceal his surprise. "You certainly howl loudly for a man at death's door. Sure you're not really a fish or some kind of sea monster? At this rate you ought to last another five or six days. By the way, how's your stomach? Empty enough for you?"

"Forget the small talk, Takuan. Just cut my head off and get it over with."

"Oh, no! Not so fast! One has to be careful about things like that. If I cut your head off right now, it'd probably fly down and try to bite me." Takuan's voice trailed off and he stared at the sky. "What a beautiful moon! You're lucky to be able to view it from such an excellent vantage point."

"Okay, just watch me, you filthy mongrel of a monk! I'll show you what I can do if I put my mind to it!" With every ounce of strength of him, Takezō then began to shake himself violently, flinging his weight up and down and nearly breaking off the branch he was bound to. Bark and leaves rained down on the man below, who remained unruffled but perhaps a bit affectedly nonchalant.

The monk calmly brushed his shoulders clean, and when he was finished he looked up again. "That's the spirit, Takezō! It's good to get as angry as you are now. Go ahead! Feel your strength to the fullest, show you're a real man, show us what you're made of! People these days think it's a sign of wisdom and character to be able to control their anger, but I say they're foolish. I hate seeing the young being so restrained, so proper. They have more spirit than their elders and they should show it. Don't hold back, Takezō! The madder you get, the better!"

"Just wait, Takuan, just wait! If I have to chew

through this rope with my bare teeth, I will, just to get my hands on you and tear you limb from limb!"

"Is that a promise or a threat? If you really think you can do it, I'll stay down here and wait. Are you sure you can keep it up without killing yourself before the rope breaks?"

"Shut up!" Takezō screamed hoarsely.

"Say, Takezō, you really are strong! The whole tree is swaying. But I don't notice the earth shaking, sorry to say. You know, the trouble with you is that, in reality, you're weak. Your kind of anger is nothing more than personal malice. A real man's anger is an expression of moral indignation. Anger over petty emotional trifles is for women, not men."

"It won't be long now," he threatened. "I'll go straight for the neck!"

Takezō struggled on, but the thick rope showed no sign of weakening. Takuan looked on for a time, then offered some friendly advice. "Why don't you cut that out, Takezō—you're getting nowhere. You'll just wear yourself out, and what good is that going to do you? Squirm and wriggle all you like, you couldn't break a single branch of this tree, much less make a dent in the universe."

Takezō gave out a mighty groan. His tantrum was over. He realized the monk was right.

"I daresay all that strength would be put to better use working for the good of the country. You really should try doing something for others, Takezō, although it is a little late to start now. If you'd just tried, you'd have had a chance at moving the gods or even the universe, not to mention plain, everyday people." Takuan's voice took on a slightly pontifical tone. "It's a pity, a great pity! Though you were born human,

153

you're more like an animal, no better than a boar or wolf. How sad it is that a handsome young man like you has to meet his end here, without ever having become truly human! What a waste!"

"You call yourself human?" Takezō spat.

"Listen, you barbarian! All along you've had too much confidence in your own brute strength, thinking you didn't have a match in the world. But look where you are now!"

"I've got nothing to be ashamed of. It wasn't a fair fight."

"In the long run, Takezō, it doesn't make any difference. You were outwitted and outtalked instead of being outpummeled. When you've lost, you've lost. And whether you like it or not, I'm sitting on this rock and you're lying up there helpless. Can't you see the difference between you and me!"

"Yeah. You fight dirty. You're a liar and a coward!"

"It would have been crazy of me to try to take you by force. You're too strong physically. A human being doesn't have much chance wrestling a tiger. Luckily, he rarely has to, being the more intelligent of the two. Not many people would argue with the fact that tigers are inferior to humans."

Takezō gave no indication that he was still listening.

"It's the same with your so-called courage. Your conduct up till now gives no evidence that it's anything more than animal courage, the kind that has no respect for human values and life. That's not the kind of courage that makes a samurai. True courage knows fear. It knows how to fear that which should be feared. Honest people value life passionately, they hang on to

154

it like a precious jewel. And they pick the right time and place to surrender it, to die with dignity."

Still no answer.

"That's what I meant when I said it's a pity about you. You were born with physical strength and fortitude, but you lack both knowledge and wisdom. While you managed to master a few of the more unfortunate features of the Way of the Samurai, you made no effort to acquire learning or virtue. People talk about combining the Way of Learning with the Way of the Samurai, but when properly combined, they aren't two—they're one. Only one Way, Takezō."

The tree was as silent as the rock on which Takuan sat. The darkness, too, was still. After several moments, Takuan rose slowly and deliberately. "Think about it one more night, Takezō. After you do, I'll cut off your head for you." He started walking away, taking long, thoughtful strides, his head bowed. He hadn't gone more than twenty paces when Takezō's voice rang out urgently.

"Wait!"

Takuan turned and called back, "What do you want now?"

"Come back."

"Mm. Don't tell me you want to hear more? Could it be that at last you're beginning to think?"

"Takuan! Save me!" Takezō's cry for help was loud and plaintive. The branch began to tremble, as though it, as though the whole tree, were weeping.

"I want to be a better man. I realize now how important it is, what a privilege it is to be born human. I'm almost dead, but I understand what it means to be alive. And now that I know, my whole life will consist of being tied to this tree! I can't undo what I've done."

"You're finally coming to your senses. For the first time in your life, you're talking like a human being."

"I don't want to die," Takezō cried. "I want to live. I want to go out, try again, do everything right this time." His body convulsed with his sobbing. "Takuan . . . please! Help me . . . help me!"

The monk shook his head. "Sorry, Takezō. It's out of my hands. It's the law of nature. You can't do things over again. That's life. Everything in it is for keeps. Everything! You can't put your head back on after the enemy's cut it off. That's the way it is. Of course, I feel sorry for you, but I can't undo that rope, because it wasn't me who tied it. It was you. All I can do is give you some advice. Face death bravely and quietly. Say a prayer and hope someone bothers to listen. And for the sake of your ancestors, Takezō, have the decency to die with a peaceful look on your face!"

The clatter of Takuan's sandals faded into the distance. He was gone, and Takezō cried out no more. Following the spirit of the monk's advice, he shut the eyes that had just experienced a great awakening and forgot everything. He forgot about living and about dying, and under the myriad tiny stars lay perfectly still as the night breeze sighed through the tree. He was cold, very cold.

After a while, he sensed that someone was at the base of the tree. Whoever it was was clutching the broad trunk and trying frantically but not very adroitly to climb up to the lowest branch. Takezō could hear the climber slipping downward after almost every upward advance. He could also hear chips of bark falling to the ground and was sure that the hands were being skinned much worse than the tree was. But the climber kept at it doggedly, digging into the tree again and again until finally the first branch was within reach. Then the form rose with relative ease to where Takezō, barely distinguishable from the branch he was stretched on, lay depleted of every ounce of strength. A panting voice whispered his name.

With great difficulty he opened his eyes and found himself face to face with a veritable skeleton; only the eyes were alive and vibrant. The face spoke. "It's me!" it said with childlike simplicity.

"Otsū?"

"Yes, me. Oh, Takezō, let's run away! I heard you scream out that you wanted with all your heart to live."

"Run away? You'll untie me, set me free?"

"Yes. I can't stand this village anymore either. If I stay here—oh, I don't even want to think about it. I have my reasons. I just want to get out of this stupid, cruel place. I'll help you, Takezō! We can help each other." Otsū was already wearing traveling clothes, and all her worldly possessions hung from her shoulder in a small fabric bag.

"Quick, cut the rope! What are you waiting for? Cut it!"

"It won't take a minute."

She unsheathed a small dagger and in no time severed the captive's bonds. Several minutes passed before the tingling in his limbs eased and he could flex his muscles. She tried to support his entire weight, with the result that when he slipped, she went down with him. The two bodies clung to each other, bounced off a limb, twisted in the air and crashed to the ground.

Takezō stood up. Dazed from the thirty-foot fall

and numbingly weak, he nevertheless planted his feet firmly on the earth. Otsū writhed in pain on her hands and knees.

"O-o-h-h," she moaned.

Putting his arms around her, he helped her up.

"Do you think you broke something?"

"I have no idea, but I think I can walk."

"We had all those branches to break the fall, so you're probably not too badly hurt."

"What about you? You okay?"

"Yes . . . I'm . . . I'm okay. I'm . . ." He paused a second or two, then blurted out, "I'm alive! I'm really alive!"

"Of course you are!"

"It's not 'of course.' "

"Let's get out of here fast. If anybody finds us here, we'll be in real trouble."

Otsū started limping away and Takezō followed . . . slowly, silently, like two frail wounded insects walking on the autumn frost.

They proceeded as best they could, hobbling along in silence, a silence broken only much later, when Otsū cried, "Look! It's getting light over toward Harima."

"Where are we?"

"At the top of Nakayama Pass."

"Have we really come that far?"

"Yes." Otsū smiled weakly. "Surprising what you can do when you're determined. But, Takezō . . ." Otsū looked alarmed. "You must be famished. You haven't eaten anything for days."

At the mention of food, Takezō suddenly realized his shrunken stomach was cramped with pain. Now that he was aware of it, it was excruciating, and it seemed like hours before Otsū managed to undo her bag and take out the food. Her gift of life took the form of rice cakes, stuffed generously with sweet bean paste. As their sweetness slid smoothly down his throat, Takezō grew giddy. The fingers holding the cake shook. "I'm alive," he thought over and over, vowing that from that moment on he'd live a very different sort of life.

The reddish clouds of morning turned their cheeks rosy. As he began to see Otsū's face more clearly and hunger gave way to a sated calm, it seemed like a dream that he was sitting here safe and sound with her.

"When it gets light, we'll have to be very careful. We're almost at the provincial border," said Otsū.

Takezō's eyes widened. "The border! That's right, I forgot. I have to go to Hinagura."

"Hinagura? Why?"

"That's where they've got my sister locked up. I have to get her out of there. Guess I'll have to say good-bye."

Otsū peered into his face in stunned silence. "If that's the way you feel about it, go! But if I'd thought you were going to desert me, I wouldn't have left Miyamoto."

"What else can I do? Just leave her there in the stockade?"

With a look that pressed in on him, she took his hand in hers. Her face, her whole body, was aflame with passion. "Takezō," she pleaded, "I'll tell you how I feel about this later, when there's time, but please, don't leave me alone here! Take me with you, wherever you go!"

"But I can't!"

"Remember"—she gripped his hand tight—"whether you like it or not, I'm staying with you. If you think I'll be in the way when you're trying to rescue Ogin, then I'll go to Himeji and wait."

"All right, do that," he agreed instantly.

"You'll definitely come, won't you?"

"Of course."

"I'll be waiting at Hanada Bridge, just outside Himeji. I'll wait for you there, whether it takes a hundred days or a thousand."

Answering with a slight nod, Takezō was off without further ado, racing along the ridge leading from the pass into the far-distant mountains. Otsū raised her head to watch him till his body melted into the scenery.

Back in the village, Osugi's grandson came charging up to the Hon'iden manor house, shouting, "Grandma! Grandma!"

Wiping his nose with the back of his hand, he peered into the kitchen and said excitedly, "Grandma, have you heard? Something awful's happened!"

Osugi, who was standing before the stove, coaxing a fire with a bamboo fan, barely looked his way. "What's all the fuss about?"

"Grandma, don't you know? Takezō's escaped!"

"Escaped?" She dropped the fan in the flames. "What are you talking about?"

"This morning he wasn't in the tree. The rope was cut."

"Heita, you know what I said about telling tales!"

"It's the truth, Grandma, honest. Everybody's talking about it."

"Are you absolutely sure?"

"Yes, ma'am. And up at the temple, they're searching for Otsū. She's gone too. Everybody's running around shouting."

The visible effect of the news was colorful. Osugi's face whitened shade by shade as the flames of her burning fan turned from red to blue to violet. Her face soon seemed drained of all blood, so much so that Heita shrank in fear.

"Heita!"

"Yes?"

"Run as fast as your legs can carry you. Fetch your daddy right away. Then go down to the riverbank and get Uncle Gon! And hurry!" Osugi's voice quivered.

Before Heita even reached the gate, a crowd of muttering villagers had arrived. Among them were Osugi's son-in-law, Uncle Gon, other relatives and a number of tenants.

"That girl Otsū's run away too, hasn't she?"

"And Takuan's not around either!"

"Looks pretty funny if you ask me!"

"They were in it together, that's for sure."

"Wonder what the old woman'll do? Her family honor's at stake!"

The son-in-law and Uncle Gon, carrying lances passed down to them from their ancestors, stared blankly toward the house. Before they could do anything, they needed guidance, so they stood there restlessly waiting for Osugi to appear and issue orders.

"Granny," someone finally shouted, "haven't you heard the news?"

"I'll be there in a minute," came the reply. "All of you, just be quiet and wait."

Osugi quickly rose to the occasion. When she'd realized the awful news had to be true, her blood boiled, but she managed to control herself enough to kneel before the family altar. After silently saying a prayer of supplication, she raised her head, opened her eyes and turned around. Calmly she opened the doors of the sword chest, pulled out a drawer and withdrew a treasured weapon. Having already donned attire suitable for a manhunt, she slipped the short sword in her obi and went to the entranceway, where she tied her sandal thongs securely round her ankles.

The awed hush that greeted her as she approached the gate made clear they knew what she was dressed for. The stubborn old woman meant business and was more than ready to avenge the insult to her house.

"Everything's going to be all right," she announced in clipped tones. "I'm going to chase down that shameless hussy myself and see to it she receives her proper punishment." Her jaw clamped shut.

She was already walking briskly down the road before someone in the crowd spoke up. "If the old woman is going, we should go too." All the relatives and tenants stood up, and fell in behind their doughty matriarch. Arming themselves as they went with sticks, fashioning bamboo lances hastily as they walked, they marched directly to Nakayama Pass, not even pausing to rest on the way. They reached it just before noon, only to find that they were too late.

"We've let them get away!" one man shouted. The crowd seethed with anger. To add to their frustration, a border official approached to inform them such a large group could not pass through.

Uncle Gon came forward and pleaded earnestly with the official, describing Takezō as a "criminal,"

162

Otsū as "evil" and Takuan as "crazy." "If we drop this matter now," he explained, "it will sully the name of our ancestors. We'll never be able to hold up our heads. We'll be the laughingstock of the village. The Hon'iden family might even have to abandon its land."

The official said he understood their predicament but could do nothing to help. The law's the law. He could perhaps send an inquiry on to Himeji and get them special permission to cross the border, but that would take time.

Osugi, after conferring with her relatives and tenants, stepped in front of the official and asked, "In that case, is there any reason why two of us, myself and Uncle Gon, can't go through?"

"Up to five people are permitted."

Osugi nodded her acquiescence. Then, although it looked as if she was about to deliver a moving farewell, she instead called her followers together in a very matter-of-fact way. They lined up before her, staring attentively at her thin-lipped mouth and large protruding teeth.

When they were all quiet, she said, "There's no reason for you to be upset. I anticipated something like this happening before we even set out. When I put on this short sword, one of the most prized Hon'iden heirlooms, I knelt before our ancestors' memorial tablets and bade them a formal farewell. I also made two vows.

"One was that I would overtake and punish the brazen female who has smeared our name with mud. The other was that I'd find out for sure, even if I died trying, whether my son Matahachi is alive. And if he is, I'll bring him home to carry on the family name. I swore to do this, and I will do it, even if it means tying a rope around his neck and dragging him all the way back. He has an obligation not only to me and to those departed, but to you as well. He will then find a wife a hundred times better than Otsū and blot out this disgrace for all time, so that the villagers will once again recognize our house as a noble and honorable one."

As they were applauding and cheering, one man uttered something sounding like a groan. Osugi stared fixedly at her son-in-law.

"Now Uncle Gon and I," she went on, "are both old enough to retire. We are both in agreement on everything I've vowed to do, and he, too, is resolved to accomplish them, even if it means spending two or three years doing nothing else, even if it means walking the length and breadth of the country. While I'm gone, my son-in-law will take my place as head of the house. During that time, you must promise to work as hard as ever. I don't want to hear of any of you neglecting the silkworms or letting weeds grow wild in the fields. Do you understand?"

Unce Gon was nearly fifty, Osugi ten years older. The crowd seemed hesitant to let them go it alone, since they were obviously no match for Takezō in the event that they should ever find him. They all imagined him to be a madman who would attack and kill for the smell of blood alone.

"Wouldn't it be better," someone suggested, "if you took three young men along with you? The man said that five can pass through."

The old woman shook her head with vehemence. "I don't need any help. I never have, and never will. Ha! Everyone thinks Takezō is so strong, but he doesn't scare me! He's only a brat, with not much more hair on him than when I knew him as a baby. I'm not his equal in physical strength, of course, but I haven't lost my wits. I can still outsmart an enemy or two. Uncle Gon's not senile yet either.

"Now I've told you what I'm going to do," she said, pointing her index finger at her nose. "And I'm going to do it. There's nothing left for you to do but go home, so go and take care of everything till we return."

She shooed them away and walked up to the barrier. No one tried to stop her again. They called their good-byes and watched as the old couple started their journey eastward down the mountainside.

"The old lady really has guts, doesn't she?" someone remarked.

Another man cupped his hands and shouted, "If you get sick, send a messenger back to the village."

A third called solicitously, "Take care of yourselves!"

When she could no longer hear their voices, Osugi turned to Uncle Gon. "We don't have a thing to worry about," she assured him. "We're going to die before those young people anyway."

"You're absolutely right," he replied with conviction. Uncle Gon made his living hunting, but in his younger days he had been a samurai involved, to hear him tell it, in many a gory battle. Even now his skin was healthily ruddy and his hair as black as ever. His surname was Fuchikawa; Gon stood for Gonroku, his given name. As Matahachi's uncle, he was naturally quite concerned and upset about the recent goings-on.

"Granny," he said.

"What?"

"You had the foresight to dress for the road, but

I'm just wearing my everyday clothes. I'll have to stop somewhere for sandals and a hat."

"There's a teahouse about halfway down this hill."

"So there is! Yes, I remember. It's called the Mikazuki Teahouse, isn't it? I'm sure they'll have what I need."

By the time they reached the teahouse they were surprised to see that the sun was beginning to set. They had thought they had more daylight hours ahead of them, since the days were growing longer with the approach of summer—more time to search on this, their first day in pursuit of their lost family honor.

They had some tea and rested for a while. Then, as Osugi laid down the money for the bill, she said, "Takano's too far to reach by nightfall. We'll have to make do with sleeping on those smelly mats at the packhorse driver's inn in Shingū, although not sleeping at all might be better than that."

"We need our sleep now more than ever. Let's get going," said Gonroku, rising to his feet and clutching the new straw hat he had just bought. "But wait just a minute."

"Why?"

"I want to fill this bamboo tube with drinking water."

Going around behind the building, he submerged his tube in a clear running brook till the bubbles stopped rising to the surface. Walking back toward the road in front, he glanced through a side window into the dim interior of the teahouse. Suddenly he came to a halt, surprised to see a figure lying on the floor, covered with straw matting. The smell of medicine permeated the air. Gonroku couldn't see the face, but he could discern long black hair strewn every which way on the pillow.

"Uncle Gon, hurry up!" Osugi cried impatiently.

"Coming."

"What kept you?"

"There seems to be a sick person inside," he said, walking behind her like a chastened dog.

"What's so unusual about that? You're as easy to distract as a child."

"Sorry, sorry," he apologized hastily. He was as intimidated by Osugi as anyone else but knew better than most how to manage her.

They set off down the fairly steep hill leading to the Harima road. The road, used daily by packhorses from the silver mines, was pitted with potholes.

"Don't fall down, Granny," Gon advised.

"How dare you patronize me! I can walk on this road with my eyes closed. Be careful yourself, you old fool."

Just then a voice greeted them from behind. "You two are pretty spry, aren't you?"

They turned to see the owner of the teahouse on horseback.

"Oh, yes; we just had a rest at your place, thank you. And where are you off to?"

"Tatsuno."

"At this hour?"

"There's no doctor between here and there. Even on horseback, it'll take me at least till midnight."

"Is it your wife who's sick?"

"Oh, no." His brows knitted. "If it were my wife, or one of the children, I wouldn't mind. But it's a lot of trouble to go to for a stranger, someone who just stopped in to take a rest."

"Oh," said Uncle Gon, "is it the girl in your back room? I happened to glance in and see her."

Osugi's brows now knitted as well.

"Yes," the shopkeeper said. "While she was resting, she started shivering, so I offered her the back room to lie down in. I felt I had to do something. Well, she didn't get any better. In fact, she seems much worse. She's burning up with fever. Looks pretty bad."

Osugi stopped in her tracks. "Is the girl about sixteen and very slender?"

"Yes, about sixteen, I'd say. Says she comes from Miyamoto."

Osugi, winking at Gonroku, began poking around in her obi. A look of distress came over her face as she exclaimed, "Oh, I've left them back at the teahouse!"

"Left what?"

"My prayer beads. I remember now—I put them down on a stool."

"Oh, that's too bad," said the shopkeeper, turning his horse around. "I'll go back for them."

"Oh, no! You've got to fetch the doctor. That sick girl's more important than my beads. We'll just go back and pick them up ourselves."

Uncle Gon was already on his way, striding rapidly back up the hill. As soon as Osugi disposed of the solicitous teahouse owner, she hurried to catch up. Before long they were both puffing and panting. Neither spoke.

It had to be Otsū!

Otsū had never really shaken off the fever she caught the night they dragged her in out of the storm.

Somehow she forgot about feeling sick during the few hours she was with Takezō, but after he left her she'd walked only a short way before beginning to give in to pain and fatigue. By the time she got to the teahouse, she felt miserable.

She did not know how long she had been lying in the back room, deliriously begging for water time and time again. Before leaving, the shopkeeper had looked in on her and urged her to try to stick it out. Moments later she had forgotten he'd ever spoken to her.

Her mouth was parched. She felt as if she had a mouthful of thorns. "Master, water, please," she called out feebly. Hearing no reply, she raised herself on her elbows and craned her neck toward the water basin just outside the door. Slowly she managed to crawl to it, but as she put her hand on the bamboo dipper at the side, she heard a rain shutter fall to the ground somewhere behind her. The teahouse was little more than a mountain hut to begin with, and there was nothing to prevent anyone from simply lifting out any or all of the loosely fitted shutters.

Osugi and Uncle Gon stumbled in through the opening.

"I can't see a thing," complained the old woman in what she thought was a whisper.

"Wait a minute," Gon replied, heading toward the hearth room, where he stirred up the embers and threw on some wood to get a bit of light.

"She's not in here, Granny!"

"She must be! She can't have gotten away!" Almost immediately, Osugi noticed that the door in the back room was ajar.

"Look, out there!" she shouted.

Otsū, who was standing just outside, threw the

dipperful of water through the narrow opening into the old woman's face and sped downhill like a bird in the wind, sleeves and skirt trailing behind her.

Osugi ran outside and spat out an imprecation.

"Gon, Gon. Do something, do something!"

"Did she get away?"

"Of course she did! We certainly gave her enough warning, making all that noise. You would have to drop the shutter!" The old woman's face contorted with rage. "Can't you do something?"

Uncle Gon directed his attention to the deerlike form flying in the distance. He raised his arm and pointed. "That's her, right? Don't worry, she doesn't have much of a head start. She's sick and anyway she only has the legs of a girl. I'll catch up with her in no time." He tucked his chin in and broke into a run. Osugi followed close behind.

"Uncle Gon," she cried, "you can use your sword on her, but don't cut off her head until after I've had a chance to give her a piece of my mind."

Uncle Gon suddenly let out a scream of dismay and fell to his hands and knees.

"What's the matter?" cried Osugi, coming up behind him.

"Look down." Osugi did. Directly in front of them was a steep drop into a bamboo-covered ravine.

"She dived into that?"

"Yes. I don't think it's very deep, but it's too dark to tell. I'll have to go back to the teahouse and get a torch."

As he knelt staring into the ravine, Osugi cried, "What are you waiting for, you dolt?" and gave him a violent shove. There was the sound of feet trying to gain a footing, scrambling desperately before coming to a stop at the bottom of the ravine.

"You old witch!" shouted Uncle Gon angrily. "Now just get on down here yourself! See how you like it!"

Takezō, arms folded, sat atop a large boulder and stared across the valley at the Hinagura stockade. Under one of those roofs, he reflected, his sister was imprisoned. But he'd sat there from dawn to dusk the previous day and all day today, unable to devise a plan to get her out. He intended to sit until he did.

His thinking had progressed to the point where he was confident he could outmaneuver the fifty or a hundred soldiers guarding the stockade, but he continued to ponder the lay of the land. He had to get not only in but out. It was not encouraging: behind the stockade was a deep gorge, and at the front the road into the stockade was well protected by a double gate. To make matters worse, the two of them would be forced to flee across a flat plateau, which offered not a single tree to hide behind; on a cloudless day such as this, a better target would be hard to find.

The situation thus called for a night assault; but he'd observed that the gates were closed and locked before sunset. Any attempt to jimmy them open would doubtless set off a cacophonous alarm of wooden clappers. There seemed no foolproof way to approach the fortress.

"There's no way," Takezō thought sadly. "Even if I just took a long shot, risked my life and hers, it wouldn't work." He felt humiliated and helpless. "How," he asked himself, "did I get to be such a coward? A week ago I wouldn't have even thought about the chances of getting out alive.''

For another half day his arms remained folded over his breast as if locked. He feared something he couldn't define and hesitated getting any closer to the stockade. Time and time again he upbraided himself. ''I've lost my nerve. I never used to be this way. Maybe staring death in the face makes cowards out of everyone.''

He shook his head. No, it wasn't that, not cowardice.

He had simply learned his lesson, the one Takuan had taken so much trouble to teach, and could now see things more clearly. He felt a new calm, a sense of peace. It seemed to flow in his breast like a gentle river. Being brave was very different from being ferocious; he saw that now. He didn't feel like an animal, he felt like a man, a courageous man who's outgrown his adolescent recklessness. The life that had been given to him was something to be treasured and cherished, polished and perfected.

He stared at the lovely clear sky, whose color alone seemed a miracle. Still, he could not leave his sister stranded, even if it meant violating, one last time, the precious self-knowledge he'd so recently and painfully acquired.

A plan began to take shape. ''After nightfall, I'll cross the valley and climb the cliff on the other side. The natural barrier may be a blessing in disguise; there's no gate at the back, and it doesn't seem heavily guarded.''

He had hardly arrived at this decision when an arrow whizzed toward him and thudded into the ground inches from his toes. Across the valley, he saw a crowd of people milling about just inside the stockade. Obviously they'd spotted him. Almost immediately they dispersed. He surmised it had been a test shot, to see how he'd react, and deliberately remained motionless upon his perch.

Before long, the light of the evening sun began to fade behind the peaks of the western mountains. Just before darkness dropped, he arose and picked up a rock. He had spotted his dinner flying in the air over his head. He downed the bird on the first try, tore it apart and sank his teeth into the warm flesh.

While he ate, twenty-odd soldiers moved noisily into position and surrounded him. Once in place, they let out a battle cry, one man shouting, "It's Takezō! Takezō from Miyamoto!"

"He's dangerous! Don't underestimate him!" someone else warned.

Looking up from his feast of raw fowl, Takezō trained a murderous eye on his would-be captors. It was the same look animals flash when disturbed in the midst of a meal.

"Y-a-a-h-h!" he yelled, seizing a huge rock and hurling it at the perimeter of this human wall. The rock turned red with blood, and in no time he was over it and away, running straight toward the stockade gate.

The men were agape.

"What's he doing?"

"Where's the fool going?"

"He's out of his mind!"

He flew like a crazed dragonfly, with the war-whooping soldiers in full chase. By the time they reached the outer gate, however, he'd already leapt over it. But now he was between the gates, in what was in fact a cage. Takezō's eyes took in none of this.

He could see neither the pursuing soldiers nor the fence, nor the guards inside the second gate. He wasn't even conscious of knocking out, with a single blow, the sentinel who tried to jump him. With almost superhuman strength, he wrenched at a post of the inner gate, shaking it furiously till he was able to pull it out of the ground. Then he turned on his pursuers. He didn't know their number; all he knew was that something big and black was attacking him. Taking aim as best he could, he struck at the amorphous mass with the gatepost. A good number of lances and swords broke, flew into the air and fell useless to the ground.

"Ogin!" cried Takezō, running toward the rear of the stockade. "Ogin, it's me—Takezō!"

He glared at the buildings with fiery eyes, calling out repeatedly to his sister. "Has it all been a trick?" he wondered in panic. One by one he began battering down doors with the gatepost. The guards' chickens, squawking for dear life, flew in every direction.

"Ogin!"

When he failed to locate her, his hoarse cries became nearly unintelligible.

In the shadows of one of the small, dirty cells he saw a man trying to sneak away.

"Halt!" he shouted, throwing the bloodstained gatepost at the weasel-like creature's feet. When Takezō leaped at him, he began to cry shamelessly. Takezō slapped him sharply on the cheek. "Where's my sister?" he roared. "What have they done to her? Tell me where she is or I'll beat you to death!"

"She . . . she's not here. Day before yesterday they took her away. Orders from the castle."

"Where, you stupid bastard, where?"

"Himeji."

"Himeji?"

"Y-y-yes."

"If you're lying, I'll . . ." Takezō grabbed the sniveling mass by its hair.

"It's true—true. I swear!"

"It better be, or I'll come back just for you!"

The soldiers were closing in again, and Takezō lifted the man and hurled him at them. Then he disappeared into the shadows of the dingy cells. Half a dozen arrows flew by him, one sticking like a giant sewing needle in the skirt of his kimono. Takezō bit his thumbnail and watched the arrows speed by, then suddenly dashed for the fence and was over it in a flash.

Behind him there was a loud explosion. The echo of the gunshot roared across the valley.

Takezō sped down the gorge, and as he ran, fragments of Takuan's teachings were racing through his head: "Learn to fear that which is fearsome. . . . Brute strength is child's play, the mindless strength of beasts. . . . Have the strength of the true warrior . . . real courage. . . . Life is precious."

8

The Birth of Musashi

Takezō waited on the outskirts of the castle town of Himeji, sometimes keeping out of sight under Hanada Bridge but more often standing on the bridge unobtrusively surveying the passersby. When not in the immediate vicinity of the bridge, he would make short excursions around town, careful to keep his hat low and his face concealed, like a beggar's, behind a piece of straw matting.

It baffled him that Otsū had not yet appeared; only a week had gone by since she swore to wait there—not a hundred but a thousand days. Once Takezō had made a promise, he was loath to break it. But with every passing moment he grew more and more tempted to be on the move, though his promise to Otsū was not the only reason he made his way to Himeji. He also had to find out where they were keeping Ogin.

He was near the center of town one day when he heard a voice shouting his name. Footsteps came running after him. He looked up sharply, to see Takuan approaching, calling, "Takezō! Wait!"

Takezō was startled, and as usual in the presence of this monk, felt slightly humiliated. He had thought his disguise was foolproof and had been sure that no one, not even Takuan, would recognize him.

The monk grabbed him by the wrist. "Come with me," he commanded. The urgency in his voice was impossible to ignore. "And don't make any trouble. I've spent a lot of time looking for you."

Takezō followed meekly. He had no idea where they were going, but he once again found himself powerless to resist this particular man. He wondered why. He was free now, and for all he knew they were headed straight back to the dreaded tree in Miyamoto. Or perhaps into a castle dungeon. He had suspected they had his sister locked up somewhere in the castle's confines, but he hadn't a shred of evidence to back this up. He hoped he was right: if he, too, was taken there, at least they could die together. If they had to die, he could think of no one else he loved enough to share the final moments of precious life with.

Himeji Castle loomed before his eyes. He could see now why it was called the "White Crane Castle": the stately edifice stood upon huge stone ramparts, like a great and proud bird descended from the heavens. Takuan preceded him across the wide arcing bridge spanning the outer moat. A row of guards stood at attention before the riveted iron gate. The sunlight glancing off their drawn lances made Takezō, for a split second, hesitant to pass. Takuan, without even turning, sensed this and with a slightly impatient gesture urged him to keep moving. Passing under the gate turret, they approached the second gate, where the soldiers looked even more tense and alert, ready to fight at a moment's notice. This was the castle of a daimyō. It would take its inhabitants a while to relax and accept the fact that the country was successfully unified. Like many other castles of the time, it was far from accustomed to the luxury of peace.

Takuan summoned the captain of the guard. "I've brought him," he announced. Handing Takezō over, the monk advised the man to take good care of him as previously instructed, but added, "Be careful. He's a lion cub with fangs. He's far from tamed. If you tease him, he bites."

Takuan went through the second gate to the central compound, where the daimyō's mansion was located. Apparently he knew the way well; he needed neither a guide nor directions. He barely raised his head as he walked and not a soul interrupted his progress.

Heeding Takuan's instructions, the captain didn't lay a finger on his charge. He simply asked Takezō to follow him. Takezō silently obeyed. They soon arrived at a bathhouse, and the captain instructed him to go in and get cleaned up. At this point Takezō's spine stiffened, for he remembered all too well his last bath, at Osugi's house, and the trap from which he had narrowly escaped. He folded his arms and tried to think, stalling for time and inspecting the surroundings. It was all so peaceful—an island of tranquillity where a daimyō could, when not plotting strategies, enjoy the luxuries of life. Soon a servant bearing a black cotton kimono and *hakama* arrived, bowing and saying politely, "I'll lay these here. You can put them on when you come out."

Takezō nearly wept. The outfit included not only

a folding fan and some tissue paper, but a pair of long and short samurai swords. Everything was simple and inexpensive, but nothing was lacking. He was being treated like a human being again and wanted to lift the clean cotton to his face, rub it to his cheek and inhale its freshness. He turned and entered the bathhouse.

Ikeda Terumasa, lord of the castle, leaned on an armrest and gazed out into the garden. He was a short man, with a cleanly shaven head, and dark pockmarks lining his face. Although not dressed in formal attire, his countenance was stern and dignified.

"Is that him?" he asked Takuan, pointing his folding fan.

"Yes, that's him," answered the monk with a deferential bow.

"He has a good face. You did well to save him."

"He owes his life to you, your lordship. Not me."

"That's not so, Takuan, and you know it. If I just had a handful of men like you under my command, no doubt a lot of useful people would be saved, and the world would be the better for it." The daimyō sighed. "My trouble is that all my men think their sole duty is to tie people up or behead them."

An hour later, Takezō was seated in the garden beyond the veranda, his head bowed and his hands resting flat on his knees in an attitude of respectful attentiveness.

"Your name is Shimmen Takezō, isn't it?" Lord Ikeda asked.

Takezō glanced up quickly to see the face of the famous man, then respectfully cast his eyes downward again.

"Yes, sir," he answered clearly.

"The House of Shimmen is a branch of the Akamatsu family, and Akamatsu Masanori, as you well know, was once lord of this castle.''

Takezō's throat went dry. He was, for once, at a loss for words. Having always thought of himself as the black sheep of the Shimmen family, with no particular feelings of respect or awe for the daimyō, he was nonetheless filled with shame at having brought such complete dishonor on his ancestors and his family name. His face burned.

"What you have done is inexcusable," continued Terumasa in a sterner tone.

"Yes, sir."

"And I am going to have to punish you for it." Turning to Takuan, he asked, "Is it true that my retainer, Aoki Tanzaemon, without my leave, promised you that if you captured this man, you could decide and mete out his punishment?"

"I think you can best find that out by asking Tanzaemon directly."

"I've already questioned him."

"Then did you think I would lie to you?"

"Of course not. Tanzaemon has confessed, but I wanted your confirmation. Since he is my direct vassal, his oath to you constitutes one from me. Therefore, even though I am lord of this fief, I have lost my right to penalize Takezō as I see fit. Of course, I will not permit him to go unpunished, but it is up to you what form the punishment is to take."

"Good. That is exactly what I had in mind."

"Then I assume you have given it some thought. Well, what shall we do with him?"

"I think it would be best to place the prisoner in—what shall we say?—'straitened circumstances' for a while."

"And how do you propose to do that?"

"I believe you have somewhere in this castle a closed room, one long rumored to be haunted?"

"Yes, I do. The servants refused to enter it, and my retainers avoided it consistently, so it went unused. I now leave it as it is, since there is no reason to open it again."

"But don't you think it's beneath the dignity of one of the strongest warriors in the Tokugawa realm, you, Ikeda Terumasa, to have a room in your castle where a light never shines?"

"I never thought of it that way."

"Well, people think of things like that. It's a reflection on your authority and prestige. I say we should put a light there."

"Hmm."

"If you'll let me make use of that chamber, I'll keep Takezō there until I'm ready to pardon him. He's had enough of living in total darkness. You hear that, don't you, Takezō?"

There was not a peep from Takezō, but Terumasa began laughing and said, "Fine!"

It was obvious from their excellent rapport that Takuan had been telling Aoki Tanzaemon the truth that night at the temple. He and Terumasa, both followers of Zen, seemed to be on friendly, almost brotherly, terms.

"After you've taken him to his new quarters, why don't you join me in the teahouse?" Terumasa asked the monk as he rose to leave.

"Oh, are you planning to demonstrate once again how inept you are at the tea ceremony?"

"That's not even fair, Takuan. These days I've really started to get the knack of it. Come along later and I'll prove to you I'm no longer simply an uncouth soldier. I'll be waiting." With that, Terumasa retired to the inner part of the mansion. Despite his short stature—he was barely five feet tall—his presence seemed to fill the many-storied castle.

It was always pitch dark high in the donjon, where the haunted room was located. There was no calendar here: no spring, no fall, no sounds of everyday life. There was only one small lamp, lighting a pale and sallow-cheeked Takezō.

The topography section of Sun-tzu's *Art of War* lay open on the low table before him.

Sun-tzu said: "Among topographical features,
　　　　　There are those that are passable.
　　　　　There are those that suspend.
　　　　　There are those that confine.
　　　　　There are those that are steep.
　　　　　There are those that are distant."

Whenever he came to a passage that particularly appealed to him, like this one, he would read it aloud over and over, like a chant.

He who knows the art of the warrior is not
　　confused in his movements. He acts and is
　　not confined.
Therefore Sun-tzu said, "He who knows
　　himself and knows his enemy wins without
　　danger. He who knows the heavens and the
　　earth wins out over all."

When his eyes blurred from fatigue, he rinsed them with cool water from a small bowl he kept beside him. If the oil ran low and the lamp wick sputtered, he simply put it out. Around the table was a mountain of books, some in Japanese, some in Chinese. Books on Zen, volumes on the history of Japan. Takezō was virtually buried in these scholarly tomes. They had all been borrowed from Lord Ikeda's collection.

When Takuan had sentenced him to confinement, he had said, "You may read as much as you want. A famous priest of ancient times once said, 'I become immersed in the sacred scriptures and read thousands of volumes. When I come away, I find that my heart sees more than before.'

"Think of this room as your mother's womb and prepare to be born anew. If you look at it only with your eyes, you will see nothing more than an unlit, closed cell. But look again, more closely. Look with your mind and think. This room can be the wellspring of enlightenment, the same fountain of knowledge found and enriched by sages in the past. It is up to you to decide whether this is to be a chamber of darkness or one of light."

Takezō had long since stopped counting the days. When it was cold, it was winter; when hot, summer. He knew little more than that. The air remained the same, dank and musty, and the seasons had no bearing on his life. He was almost positive, however, that the next time the swallows came to nest in the donjon's boarded-over gun slots, it would be the spring of his third year in the womb.

"I'll be twenty-one years old," he said to himself. Seized by remorse, he groaned as if in mourning. "And what have I done in those twenty-one years?"

Sometimes the memory of his early years pressed in on him unrelentingly, engulfing him in grief. He would wail and moan, flail and kick, and sometimes sob like a baby. Whole days were swallowed up in agony, which, once it subsided, left him spent and lifeless, hair disheveled and heart torn apart.

Finally, one day, he heard the swallows returning to the donjon eaves. Once again, spring had flown from across the seas.

Not long after its arrival, a voice, now sounding strange, almost painful to the ears, inquired, "Takezō, are you well?"

The familiar head of Takuan appeared at the top of the stairs. Startled and much too deeply moved to utter a sound, Takezō grabbed hold of the monk's kimono sleeve and pulled him into the room. The servants who brought his food had never once spoken a word. He was overjoyed to hear another human voice, especially this one.

"I've just returned from a journey," said Takuan. "You're in your third year here now, and I've decided that after gestating this long, you must be pretty well formed."

"I am grateful for your goodness, Takuan. I understand now what you've done. How can I ever thank you?"

"Thank me?" Takuan said incredulously. Then he laughed. "Even though you've had no one to converse with but yourself, you've actually learned to speak like a human being! Good! Today you will leave this place. And as you do so, hug your hard-earned enlightenment to your bosom. You're going to need it when you go forth into the world to join your fellow men."

Takuan took Takezō just as he was to see Lord Ikeda. Although he had been relegated to the garden in the previous audience, a place was now made for him on the veranda. After the salutations and some perfunctory small talk, Terumasa lost no time in asking Takezō to serve as his vassal.

Takezō declined. He was greatly honored, he explained, but he did not feel the time was yet right to go into a daimyō's service. "And if I did so in this castle," he said, "ghosts would probably start appearing in the closed room every night, just as everyone says they do."

"Why do you say that? Did they come to keep you company?"

"If you take a lamp and inspect the room closely, you'll see black spots spattering the doors and beams. It looks like lacquer, but it's not. It's human blood, mostly likely blood spilled by the Akamatsus, my forebears, when they went down to defeat in this castle."

"Hmm. You may very well be right."

"Seeing those stains infuriated me. My blood boiled to think that my ancestors, who once ruled over this whole region, ended up being annihilated, their souls just blow about in the autumn winds. They died violently, but it was a powerful clan and they can be roused.

"That same blood flows in my veins," he went on, an intense look in his eyes. "Unworthy though I am, I am a member of the same clan, and if I stay in this castle, the ghosts may rouse themselves and try to reach me. In a sense, they already have, by making it clear to me in that room just who I am. But they could cause chaos, perhaps rebel and even set off another bloodbath. We are not in an era of peace. I owe it to the people of this whole region not to tempt the vengeance of my ancestors."

Terumasa nodded. "I see what you mean. It's better if you leave this castle, but where will you go? Do you plan to return to Miyamoto? Live out your life there?"

Takezō smiled silently. "I want to wander about on my own for a while."

"I see," the lord replied, turning to Takuan. "See that he receives money and suitable clothing," he commanded.

Takuan bowed. "Let me thank you for your kindness to the boy."

"Takuan!" Ikeda laughed. "This is the first time you've ever thanked me twice for anything!"

"I suppose that's true." Takuan grinned. "It won't happen again."

"It's all right for him to roam about while he's still young," said Terumasa. "But now that he's going out on his own—reborn, as you put it—he should have a new name. Let it be Miyamoto, so that he never forgets his birthplace. From now on, Takezō, call yourself Miyamoto."

Takezō's hands went automatically to the floor. Palms down, he bowed deep and long. "Yes, sir, I will do that."

"You should change your first name too," Takuan interjected. "Why not read the Chinese characters of your name as 'Musashi' instead of 'Takezō'? You can keep writing your name the same as before. It's only fitting that everything should begin anew on this day of your rebirth."

Terumasa, who was by this time in a very good

mood, nodded his approval enthusiastically. "Miya-moto Musashi! It's a good name, a very good name. We should drink to it."

They moved into another room, sake was served, and Takezō and Takuan kept his lordship company far into the night. They were joined by several of Teru-masa's retainers, and eventually Takuan got to his feet and performed an ancient dance. He was expert, his vivid movements creating an imaginary world of delight. Takezō, now Musashi, watched with admira-tion, respect and enjoyment as the drinking went on and on.

The following day they both left the castle. Mu-sashi was taking his first steps into a new life, a life of discipline and training in the martial arts. During his three-year incarceration, he had resolved to master the Art of War.

Takuan had his own plans. He had decided to travel about the countryside, and the time had come, he said, to part again.

When they reached the town outside the castle walls, Musashi made as if to take his leave, but the monk grabbed his sleeve and said, "Isn't there some-one you'd like to see?"

"Who?"

"Ogin?"

"Is she still alive?" he asked in bewilderment. Even in his sleep, he'd never forgotten the gentle sister who'd been a mother to him so long.

Takuan told him that when he'd attacked the stockade at Hinagura three years earlier, Ogin had indeed already been taken away. Although no charges were pressed against her, she had been reluctant to return home and so went instead to stay with a relative in a village in the Sayo district. She was now living comfortably there.

"Wouldn't you like to see her?" asked Takuan. "She's very eager to see you. I told her three years ago that she should consider you dead, since in one sense, you were. I also told her, however, that after three years I'd bring her a new brother, different from the old Takezō."

Musashi pressed his palms together and raised them in front of his head, as he would have done in prayer before a statue of the Buddha. "Not only have you taken care of me," he said with deep emotion, "but you've seen to Ogin's well-being too. Takuan, you are truly a compassionate man. I don't think I'll ever be able to thank you for what you've done."

"One way to thank me would be to let me take you to your sister."

"No . . . No, I don't think I should go. Hearing about her from you has been as good as meeting her."

"Surely you want to see her yourself, if only for a few minutes."

"No, I don't think so. I did die, Takuan, and I do feel reborn. I don't think that now is the time to return to the past. What I have to do is take a resolute step forward, into the future. I've barely found the way along which I'll have to travel. When I've made some progress toward the knowledge and self-perfection I'm seeking, perhaps I'll take the time to relax and look back. Not now."

"I see."

"I find it hard to put into words, but I hope you'll understand anyway."

"I do. I'm glad to see you're as serious about

your goal as you are. Keep following your own judgment."

"I'll say good-bye now, but someday, if I don't get myself killed along the way, we'll meet again."

"Yes, yes. If we have a chance to meet, let's by all means do so." Takuan turned, took a step, and then halted. "Oh, yes. I suppose I should warn you that Osugi and Uncle Gon left Miyamoto in search of you and Otsū three years ago. They resolved never to return until they've taken their revenge, and old as they are, they're still trying to track you down. They may cause you some inconvenience, but I don't think they can make any real trouble. Don't take them too seriously.

"Oh, yes, and then there's Aoki Tanzaemon. I don't suppose you ever knew his name, but he was in charge of the search for you. Perhaps it had nothing to do with anything you or I said or did, but that splendid samurai managed to disgrace himself, with the result that he's been dismissed permanently from Lord Ikeda's service. He's no doubt wandering about too." Takuan grew grave. "Musashi, your path won't be an easy one. Be careful as you make your way along it."

"I'll do my best." Musashi smiled.

"Well, I guess that's everything. I'll be on my way." Takuan turned and walked westward. He didn't look back.

"Keep well," Musashi called after him. He stood at the crossroads watching the monk's form recede until it was out of sight. Then, once again alone, he started to walk toward the east.

"Now there's only this sword," he thought. "The only thing in the world I have to rely on." He rested his hand on the weapon's handle and vowed to himself,

"I will live by its rule. I will regard it as my soul, and by learning to master it, strive to improve myself, to become a better and wiser human being. Takuan follows the Way of Zen, I will follow the Way of the Sword. I must make of myself an even better man than he is."

After all, he reflected, he was still young. It was not too late.

His footsteps were steady and strong, his eyes full of youth and hope. From time to time he raised the brim of his basket hat, and stared down the long road into the future, the unknown path all humans must tread.

He hadn't gone far—in fact, he was just on the outskirts of Himeji—when a woman came running toward him from the other side of Hanada Bridge. He squinted into the sunlight.

"It's you!" Otsū cried, clutching his sleeve.

Musashi gasped in surprise.

Otsū's tone was reproachful. "Takezō, surely you haven't forgotten? Don't you remember the name of this bridge? Did it slip your mind that I promised to wait here for you, no matter how long it took?"

"You've been waiting here for the last three years?" He was astounded.

"Yes. Osugi and Uncle Gon caught up with me right after I left you. I was sick and had to take a rest. And I almost got myself killed. But I got away. I've been waiting here since about twenty days after we said good-bye at Nakayama Pass."

Pointing to a basket-weaving shop at the end of the bridge, a typical little highroad stall selling souvenirs to travelers, she continued: "I told the people there my story, and they were kind enough to take me on as a sort of helper. So I could stay and wait for you. Today is the nine hundred and seventieth day, and I've kept my promise faithfully." She peered into his face, trying to fathom his thoughts. "You will take me with you, won't you?"

The truth, of course, was that Musashi had no intention of taking her or anyone else with him. At this very moment, he was hurrying away to avoid thinking about his sister, whom he wanted to see so badly and felt so strongly drawn toward.

The questions raced through his agitated mind: "What can I do? How can I embark on my quest for truth and knowledge with a woman, with anyone, interfering all the time? And this particular girl is, after all, still betrothed to Matahachi." Musashi couldn't keep his thoughts from showing on his face.

"Take you with me? Take you where?" he demanded bluntly.

"Wherever you go."

"I'm setting out on a long, hard journey, not a sightseeing trip!"

"I won't get in your way. And I'm prepared to endure some hardships."

"Some? Only some?"

"As many as I have to."

"That's not the point. Otsū, how can a man master the Way of the Samurai with a woman tagging along? Wouldn't that be funny. People'd say, 'Look at Musashi, he needs a wet nurse to take care of him.' " She pulled harder at his kimono, clinging like a child. "Let go of my sleeve," he ordered.

"No, I won't! You lied to me, didn't you?"

"When did I lie to you?"

"At the pass. You promised to take me with you."

"That was ages ago. I wasn't really thinking then either, and I didn't have time to explain. What's more, it wasn't my idea, it was yours. I was in a hurry to get moving, and you wouldn't let me go until I promised. I went along with what you said because I had no choice."

"No, no, no! You can't mean what you're saying, you can't," she cried, pinning him against the bridge railing.

"Let go of me! People are watching."

"Let them! When you were tied up in the tree, I asked you if you wanted my help. You were so happy you told me twice to cut the rope. You don't deny that, do you?"

She was trying to be logical in her argument, but her tears betrayed her. First abandoned as an infant, then jilted by her betrothed and now this. Musashi, knowing how alone she was in the world and caring for her deeply, was tongue-tied, though outwardly more composed.

"Let go!" he said with finality. "It's broad daylight and people are staring at us. Do you want us to be a sideshow for these busybodies?"

She released his sleeve and fell sobbing against the railing, her shiny hair falling over her face.

"I'm sorry," she mumbled. "I shouldn't have said all that. Please forget it. You don't owe me anything."

Leaning over and pushing her hair from her face with both hands, he looked into her eyes. "Otsū," he said tenderly. "During all that time you were waiting,

193

until this very day, I've been shut up in the castle donjon. For three years I haven't even seen the sun.''

"Yes, I heard."

"You knew?"

"Takuan told me."

"Takuan? He told you everything?"

"I guess so. I fainted at the bottom of a ravine near the Mikazuki Teahouse. I was running away from Osugi and Uncle Gon. Takuan rescued me. He also helped me make arrangements to work here, at the souvenir shop. That was three years ago. And he's stopped several times. Only yesterday he came and had some tea. I wasn't sure what he meant, but he said, 'It's got to do with a man and a woman, so who can say how it'll turn out?' ''

Musashi dropped his hands and looked down the road leading west. He wondered if he'd ever again meet the man who'd saved his life. And again he was struck by Takuan's concern for his fellow man, which seemed all-encompassing and completely devoid of selfishness. Musashi realized how narrowminded he himself had been, how petty, to suppose that the monk felt a special compassion for him alone; his generosity encompassed Ogin, Otsū, anyone in need whom he thought he could help.

"It has to do with a man and a woman. . . ." Takuan's words to Otsū sat heavily on Musashi's mind. It was a burden for which he was ill prepared, since in all the mountains of books he'd pored over those three years, there wasn't one word about the situation he was in now. Even Takuan had shrunk from becoming involved in this matter between him and Otsū. Had Takuan meant that relationships between men and women had to be worked out alone by the people involved? Did he mean that no rules applied, as they did in the Art of War? That there was no foolproof strategy, no way to win? Or was this meant as a test for Musashi, a problem only Musashi would be able to solve for himself?

Lost in thought, he stared down at the water flowing under the bridge.

Otsū gazed up into his face, now distant and calm. "I can come, can't I?" she pleaded. "The shopkeeper's promised to let me quit whenever I wish. I'll just go and explain everything and then pack my things. I'll be back in a minute."

Musashi covered her small white hand, which was resting on the railing, with his own. "Listen," he said plaintively. "I beg of you, just stop and think."

"What's there to think about?"

"I told you. I've just become a new man. I stayed in that musty hole for three years. I read books. I thought. I screamed and cried. Then suddenly the light dawned. I understood what it means to be human. I have a new name, Miyamoto Musashi. I want to dedicate myself to training and discipline. I want to spend every moment of every day working to improve myself. I know now how far I have to go. If you chose to bind your life to mine, you'd never be happy. There will be nothing but hardship, and it won't get easier as it goes along. It'll get more and more difficult."

"When you talk like that, I feel closer to you than ever. Now I'm convinced I was right. I've found the best man I could ever find, even if I searched for the rest of my life."

He saw he was just making things worse. "I'm sorry, I can't take you with me."

"Well, then, I'll just follow along. As long as I don't interfere with your training, what harm would it do? You won't even know I'm around."

Musashi could find no answer.

"I won't bother you. I promise."

He remained silent.

"It's all right then, isn't it? Just wait here; I'll be back in a second. And I'll be furious if you try to sneak away." Otsū ran off toward the basket-weaving shop.

Musashi thought of ignoring everything and running too, in the opposite direction. Though the will was there, his feet wouldn't move.

Otsū looked back and called. "Remember, don't try to sneak off!" She smiled, showing her dimples, and Musashi inadvertently nodded. Satisfied by this gesture, she disappeared into the shop.

If he was going to escape, this was the time. His heart told him so, but his body was still shackled by Otsū's pretty dimples and pleading eyes. How sweet she was! It was certain no one in the world save his sister loved him so much. And it wasn't as though he disliked her.

He looked at the sky, he looked into the water, desperately gripped the railing, troubled and confused. Soon tiny bits of wood began floating from the bridge into the flowing stream.

Otsū reappeared on the bridge in new straw sandals, light yellow leggings and a large traveling hat tied under the chin with a crimson ribbon. She'd never looked more beautiful.

But Musashi was nowhere to be seen.

With a cry of shock, she burst into tears. Then her eyes fell upon the spot on the railing from which the chips of wood had fallen. There, carved with the point of a dagger, was the clearly inscribed message. "Forgive me. Forgive me."

9

The Yoshioka School

The life of today, which cannot know the morrow . . .

In the Japan of the early seventeenth century, an awareness of the fleeting nature of life was as common among the masses as it was among the elite. The famous general Oda Nobunaga, who laid the foundations for Toyotomi Hideyoshi's unification of Japan, summed up this view in a short poem:

> Man's fifty years
> Are but a phantom dream
> In his journey through
> The eternal transmigrations.

Defeated in a skirmish with one of his own generals, who attacked him in a sudden fit of revenge, Nobunaga committed suicide in Kyoto at the age of forty-eight.

By 1605, some two decades later, the incessant warring among the daimyō was essentially over, and Tokugawa Ieyasu had ruled as shōgun for two years. The lanterns on the streets of Kyoto and Osaka glowed brightly, as they had in the best days of the Ashikaga shogunate, and the prevailing mood was lighthearted and festive.

But few were certain the peace would last. More than a hundred years of civil strife had so colored people's view of life that they could only regard the present tranquillity as fragile and ephemeral. The capital was thriving, but the tension of not knowing how long this would last whetted the people's appetite for merrymaking.

Though still in control, Ieyasu had officially retired from the position of shōgun. While still strong enough to control the other daimyō and defend the family's claim to power, he had passed on his title to his third son, Hidetada. It was rumored that the new shōgun would visit Kyoto soon to pay his respects to the emperor, but it was common knowledge that his trip west meant more than a courtesy call. His greatest potential rival, Toyotomi Hideyori, was the son of Hideyoshi, Nobunaga's able successor. Hideyoshi had done his best to ensure that power remain with the Toyotomis until Hideyori was old enough to exercise it, but the victor at Sekigahara was Ieyasu.

Hideyori still resided at Osaka Castle, and although Ieyasu, rather than have him done away with, permitted him to enjoy a substantial annual income, he was aware that Osaka was a major threat as a possible rallying point of resistance. Many feudal lords knew this too, and hedging their bets, paid equal court to both Hideyori and the shōgun. It was often remarked that the former had enough castles and gold to hire every masterless samurai, or rōnin, in the country, if he wanted to.

Idle speculation on the country's political future formed the bulk of gossip in the Kyoto air.

"War's bound to break out sooner or later."

"It's just a matter of time."

"These street lanterns could be snuffed out tomorrow."

"Why worry about it? What happens happens."

"Let's enjoy ourselves while we can!"

The bustling nightlife and booming pleasure quarters were tangible evidence that much of the populace were doing just that.

Among those so inclined was a group of samurai now turning a corner into Shijō Avenue. Beside them ran a long wall of white plaster, leading to an impressive gate with an imposing roof. A wooden plaque, blackened with age, announced in barely legible writing: "Yoshioka Kempō of Kyoto. Military Instructor to the Ashikaga Shōguns."

The eight young samurai gave the impression of having practiced sword fighting all day without respite. Some bore wooden swords in addition to the two customary steel ones, and others were carrying lances. They looked tough, the kind of men who'd be the first to see bloodshed the moment a clash of arms erupted. Their faces were as hard as stone and their eyes threatening, as if always on the brink of exploding in a rage.

"Young Master, where are we headed tonight?" they clamored, surrounding their teacher.

"Anywhere but where we were last night," he replied gravely.

"Why? Those women were falling all over you! They barely looked at the rest of us."

"Maybe he's right," another man put in. "Why

don't we try someplace new, where no one knows the Young Master or any of the rest of us." Shouting and carrying on among themselves, they seemed totally consumed by the question of where to go drinking and whoring.

They moved on to a well-lit area along the banks of the Kamo River. For years the land had been vacant and weed-filled, a veritable symbol of wartime desolation, but with the coming of peace, its value had shot up. Scattered here and there were flimsy houses, red and pale yellow curtains hanging crookedly in their doorways, where prostitutes plied their trade. Girls from Tamba Province, white powder smeared carelessly on their faces, whistled to prospective customers; unfortunate women who had been purchased in droves plunked on their shamisens, a newly popular instrument, as they sang bawdy songs and laughed among themselves.

The Young Master's name was Yoshioka Seijūrō, and a tasteful dark brown kimono draped his tall frame. Not long after they'd entered the brothel district, he looked back and said to one of his group, "Tōji, buy me a basket hat."

"The kind that hides your face, I suppose?"

"Yes."

"You don't need one here, do you?" Gion Tōji replied.

"I wouldn't have asked for one if I didn't!" Seijūrō snapped impatiently. "I don't care to have people see the son of Yoshioka Kempō walking about in a place like this."

Tōji laughed. "But it just attracts attention. All the women around here know that if you hide your face under a hat, you must be from a good family and probably a rich one. Of course, there are other reasons why they won't leave you alone, but that's one of them."

Tōji was, as usual, both teasing and flattering his master. He turned and ordered one of the men to get the hat and stood waiting for him to thread his way through the lanterns and merrymakers. The errand accomplished, Seijūrō donned the hat and began to feel more relaxed.

"In that hat," commented Tōji, "you look more than ever like the fashionable man about town." Turning to the others, he continued his flattery indirectly. "See, the women are all leaning out their doors to get a good look at him."

Tōji's sycophancy aside, Seijūrō did cut a fine figure. With two highly polished scabbards hanging from his side, he exuded the dignity and class one would expect from the son of a well-to-do family. No straw hat could stop the women from calling out to him as he walked.

"Hey there, handsome! Why hide your face under that silly hat?"

"Come on, over here! I want to see what's under there."

"Come on, don't be shy. Give us a peek."

Seijūrō reacted to these teasing come-ons by trying to look even taller and more dignified. It had only been a short time since Tōji had first persuaded him to set foot in the district, and it still embarrassed him to be seen there. Born the eldest son of the famous swordsman Yoshioka Kempō, he had never lacked money, but he had remained until recently unacquainted with the seamier side of life. The attention he was getting made his pulse race. He still felt enough shame to hide, though as a rich man's spoiled son he'd always been something of a show-off. The flattery of his entourage, no less than the flirting of the women, bolstered his ego like sweet poison.

"Why, it's the master from Shijō Avenue!" one of the women exclaimed. "Why are you hiding your face? You're not fooling anybody."

"How does that woman know who I am?" Seijūrō growled at Tōji, pretending to be offended.

"That's easy," the woman said before Tōji could open his mouth. "Everybody knows that the people at the Yoshioka School like to wear that dark brown color. It is called 'Yoshioka dye,' you know, and it's very popular around here."

"That's true, but as you say, a lot of people wear it."

"Yes, but they don't have the three-circle crest on their kimonos."

Seijūrō looked down at his sleeve. "I must be more careful," he said as a hand from behind the lattice reached out and latched onto the garment.

"My, my," said Tōji. "He hid his face but not his crest. He must have wanted to be recognized. I don't think we can really avoid going in here now."

"Do whatever you want," said Seijūrō, looking uncomfortable, "but make her let go of my sleeve."

"Let go, woman," Tōji roared. "He says we're coming in!"

The students crowded in under the shop curtain. The room they entered was so tastelessly decorated with vulgar pictures and messily arranged flowers that it was difficult for Seijūrō to feel at ease. The others, however, took no notice of the shabbiness of their surroundings.

"Bring on the sake!" Tōji demanded, also ordering assorted tidbits.

After the food arrived, Ueda Ryōhei, who was Tōji's match with a sword, cried, "Bring on the women!" The order was given in exactly the same surly tone Tōji had used to order their food and drink.

"Hey, old Ueda says bring the women!" the others chorused, mimicking Ryōhei's voice.

"I don't like being called old," Ryōhei said, scowling. "It's true I've been at the school longer than any of you, but you won't find a gray hair on my head."

"You probably dye it."

"Whoever said that come forward and drink a cup as punishment!"

"Too much trouble. Throw it here!"

The sake cup sailed through the air.

"Here's the repayment!" And another cup flew through the air.

"Hey, somebody dance!"

Seijūrō called out, "You dance, Ryōhei! Dance, and show us how young you are!"

"I am prepared, sir. Watch!" Going to the corner of the veranda, he tied a maid's red apron around the back of his head, stuck a plum blossom in the knot and seized a broom.

"Why, look! He's going to do the Dance of the Hida Maiden! Let's hear the song too, Tōji!"

He invited them all to join in, and they began rapping rhythmically on the dishes with their chopsticks, while one man clanged the fire tongs against the edge of the brazier.

> Across the bamboo fence, the bamboo
>   fence, the bamboo fence,
> I caught sight of a long-sleeved kimono,
> A long-sleeved kimono in the snow. . . .

Drowned in applause after the first verse, Tōji bowed out, and the women took up where he had left off, accompanying themselves on shamisen.

> The girl I saw yesterday
> Is not here today.
> The girl I see today,
> She'll not be here tomorrow.
> I know not what the morrow will bring,
> I want to love her today.

In one corner, a student held up a huge bowl of sake to a comrade and said, "Say, why don't you down this in one gulp?"

"No, thanks."

"No, thanks? You call yourself a samurai, and you can't even put this away?"

"Sure I can. But if I do, you have to too!"

"Fair enough!"

The contest began, with them gulping like horses at the trough and dribbling sake out of the corners of their mouths. An hour or so later a couple of them started vomiting, while others were reduced to immobility and blankly staring bloodshot eyes.

One, whose customary bluster became more strident the more he drank, declaimed, "Does anyone in this country besides the Young Master truly understand the techniques of the Kyōhachi Style? If there is—*hic*—I want to meet him. . . . Oops!"

Another stalwart, seated near Seijūrō, laughed and stammered through his hiccups. "He's piling on the flattery because the Young Master's here. There are other schools of martial arts besides the eight here in Kyoto, and the Yoshioka School's not necessarily the greatest anymore. In Kyoto alone, there's the school of Toda Seigen in Kurotani, and there's Ogasawara Genshinsai in Kitano. And let's not forget Itō Ittōsai in Shirakawa, even though he doesn't take students."

"And what's so wonderful about them?"

"I mean, we shouldn't get the idea we're the only swordsmen in the world."

"You simple-minded bastard!" shouted a man whose pride had been offended. "Come forward!"

"Like this?" retorted the critic, standing up.

"You're a member of this school, and you're belittling Yoshioka Kempō's style?"

"I'm not belittling it! It's just that things aren't what they used to be in the old days when the master taught the shōguns and was considered the greatest of swordsmen. There are far more people practicing the Way of the Sword these days, not only in Kyoto but in Edo, Hitachi, Echizen, the home provinces, the western provinces, Kyushu—all over the country. Just because Yoshioka Kempō was famous doesn't mean the Young Master and all of us are the greatest swordsmen alive. It's just not true, so why kid ourselves?"

"Coward! You pretend to be a samurai, but you're afraid of other schools!"

"Who's afraid of them? I just think we should guard ourselves against becoming complacent."

"And who are you to be giving warnings?" With

this the offended student punched the other in the chest, knocking him down.

"You want to fight?" growled the fallen man.

"Yeah, I'm ready."

The seniors, Gion Tōji and Ueda Ryōhei, intervened. "Stop it, you two!" Jumping to their feet, they pulled the two men apart and tried to smooth their ruffled feathers.

"Quiet down now!"

"We all understand how you feel."

A few more cups of sake were poured into the combatants, and presently things were back to normal. The firebrand was once again eulogizing himself and the others, while the critic, his arm draped around Ryōhei, pleaded his case tearfully. "I only spoke up for the sake of the school," he sobbed. "If people keep spouting flattery, Yoshioka Kempō's reputation will eventually be ruined. Ruined, I tell you!"

Seijūrō alone remained relatively sober. Noticing this, Tōji said, "You're not enjoying the party, are you?"

"Unh. Do you think they really enjoy it? I wonder."

"Sure; this is their idea of a good time."

"I don't see how, when they carry on like that."

"Look, why don't we go someplace quieter? I've had enough of this too."

Seijūrō, looking much relieved, quickly assented. "I'd like to go to the place we were last night."

"You mean the Yomogi?"

"Yes."

"That's much nicer. I thought all along you wanted to go there, but it would've been a waste of money to take along this bunch of oafs. That's why I steered them here—it's cheap."

"Let's sneak out, then. Ryōhei can take care of the rest."

"Just pretend you're going to the toilet. I'll come along in a few minutes."

Seijurō skillfully disappeared. No one noticed.

Outside a house not far away, a woman stood on tiptoe, trying to hang a lantern back on its nail. The wind had blown out the candle, and she had taken it down to relight it. Her back was stretched out under the eaves, and her recently washed hair fell loosely around her face. Strands of hair and the shadows from the lantern made lightly shifting patterns on her outstretched arms. A hint of plum blossoms floated on the evening breeze.

"Okō! Shall I hang it for you?"

"Oh, it's the Young Master," she said with surprise.

"Wait a minute." When the man came forward, she saw that it was not Seijurō but Tōji.

"Will that do?" he asked.

"Yes, that's fine. Thank you."

But Tōji squinted at the lantern, decided it was crooked, and rehung it. It was amazing to Okō how some men, who would flatly refuse to lend a hand in their own homes, could be so helpful and considerate when visiting a place like hers. Often they would open or close the windows for themselves, get out their own cushions, and do a dozen other little chores they'd never dream of doing under their own roofs.

Tōji, pretending not to have heard, showed his master indoors.

Seijūrō, as soon as he was seated, said, "It's awfully quiet."

"I'll open the door to the veranda," said Tōji.

Below the narrow veranda rippled the waters of the Takase River. To the south, beyond the small bridge at Sanjō Avenue, lay the broad compound of the Zuisenin, the dark expanse of Teramachi—the "Town of Temples"—and a field of miscanthus. This was near Kayahara, where Toyotomi Hideyoshi's troops had slain the wife, concubines and children of his nephew, the murderous regent Hidetsugu, an event still fresh in many people's memory.

Tōji was getting nervous. "It's still too quiet. Where are the women hiding? They don't seem to have any other customers tonight." He fidgeted a bit. "I wonder what's taking Okō so long. She hasn't even brought us our tea." When his impatience made him so jumpy he could no longer sit still, he got up to go see why the tea hadn't been served.

As he stepped out onto the veranda, he nearly collided with Akemi, who was carrying a gold-lacquered tray. The little bell in her obi tinkled as she exclaimed, "Be careful! You'll make me spill the tea!"

"Why are you so late with it? The Young Master's here; I thought you liked him."

"See, I've spilled some. It's your fault. Go fetch me a rag."

"Ha! Pretty sassy, aren't you? Where's Okō?"

"Putting on her makeup, of course."

"You mean she's not finished yet?"

"Well, we were busy during the daytime."

"Daytime? Who came during the daytime?"

"That's none of your business. Please let me by."

He stepped aside and Akemi entered the room

and greeted the guest. "Good evening. It was good of you to come."

Seijūrō, feigning nonchalance, looked aside and said, "Oh, it's you, Akemi. Thanks for last night." He was embarrassed.

From the tray she took a jar that looked like an incense burner and placed on it a pipe with a ceramic mouthpiece and bowl.

"Would you like a smoke?" she asked politely.

"I thought tobacco was recently banned."

"It was, but everybody still smokes anyway."

"All right, I'll have some."

"I'll light it for you."

She took a pinch of tobacco from a pretty little mother-of-pearl box and stuffed it into the tiny bowl with her dainty fingers. Then she put the pipe to his mouth. Seijūrō, not being in the habit of smoking, handled it rather awkwardly.

"Hmm, bitter, isn't it?" he said. Akemi giggled. "Where did Tōji go?"

"He's probably in Mother's room."

"He seems fond of Okō. At least, it looks that way to me. I suspect he comes here without me sometimes. Does he?" Akemi laughed but did not answer. "What's funny about that? I think your mother rather likes him too."

"I really wouldn't know!"

"Oh, I'm sure of it! Absolutely sure! It's a cozy arrangement, isn't it? Two happy couples—your mother and Tōji, you and me."

Looking as innocent as he could, he put his hand on top of Akemi's, which was resting on her knee. Primly, she brushed it away, but this only made Seijūrō bolder. As she started to rise, he put his arm around her thin waist and drew her to him.

"You don't have to run away," he said. "I'm not going to hurt you."

"Let go of me!" she protested.

"All right, but only if you sit down again."

"The sake . . . I'll just go and get some."

"I don't want any."

"But if I don't bring it, Mother'll get angry."

"Your mother's in the other room, having a nice chat with Tōji."

He tried to rub his cheek against her lowered face, but she turned her head away and called frantically for help. "Mother! *Mother!*" He released her and she flew toward the back of the house.

Seijūrō was becoming frustrated. He was lonely but didn't really want to force himself on the girl. Not knowing what to do with himself, he grunted out loud, "I'm going home," and started tramping down the outer corridor, his face growing more crimson with each step.

"Young Master, where are you going? You're not leaving, are you?" Seemingly from out of nowhere, Okō appeared behind him and rushed down the hall. As she put her arm about him, he noticed that her hair was in place and her makeup was in order. She summoned Tōji to the rescue, and together they persuaded Seijūrō to go back and sit down. Okō brought sake and tried to cheer him up, then Tōji led Akemi back into the room. When the girl saw how crestfallen Seijūrō was, she flashed a smile at him.

"Akemi, pour the Young Master some sake."

"Yes, Mother," she said obediently.

"You see how she is, don't you?" said Okō. "Why does she always want to act like a child?"

"That's her charm—she's young," said Tōji, sliding his cushion up closer to the table.

"But she's already twenty-one."

"Twenty-one? I didn't think she was that old. She's so small she looks about sixteen or seventeen!"

Akemi, suddenly as full of life as a minnow, said, "Really? That makes me happy, because I'd like to be sixteen all my life. Something wonderful happened to me when I was sixteen."

"What?"

"Oh," she said, clasping her hands to her breast. "I can't tell anybody about it, but it happened. When I was sixteen. Do you know what province I was in then? That was the year of the Battle of Sekigahara."

With a menacing look, Okō said, "Chatterbox! Stop boring us with your talk. Go and get your shamisen."

Pouting slightly, Akemi stood up and went for her instrument. When she returned, she started playing and singing a song, more intent, it seemed, upon amusing herself than upon pleasing the guests.

> Tonight then,
> If it's to be cloudy,
> Let it be cloudy,
> Hiding the moon
> I can see only through my tears

Breaking off, she said, "Do you understand, Tōji?"

"I'm not sure. Sing some more."

Even in the darkest night
I do not lose my way
But oh! How you fascinate me!

"She is twenty-one, after all," said Tōji.

Seijūrō, who had been sitting silently with his forehead resting on his hand, came to life and said, "Akemi, let's have a cup of sake together."

He handed her the cup and filled it from the sake warmer. She drank it down without flinching and briskly handed him back the cup to drink from.

Somewhat surprised, Seijūrō said, "You know how to drink, don't you."

Finishing off his draft, he offered her another, which she accepted and downed with alacrity. Apparently dissatisfied with the cup's size, she took out a larger one and for the next half hour matched him drink for drink.

Seijūrō marveled. There she was, looking like a sixteen-year-old girl, with lips that had never been kissed and an eye that shrank with shyness, and yet she was putting away her sake like a man. In that tiny body, where did it all go?

"You may as well give up now," Okō said to Seijūrō. "For some reason the child can drink all night without getting drunk. The best thing to do is to let her play the shamisen."

"But this is fun!" said Seijūrō, now thoroughly enjoying himself.

Sensing something strange in his voice, Tōji asked, "Are you all right? Sure you haven't had too much?"

"It doesn't matter. Say, Tōji, I may not go home tonight!"

"That's all right too," replied Tōji. "You can stay as many nights as you wish—can't he, Akemi?"

Tōji winked at Okō, then led her off to another room, where he began whispering rapidly. He told Okō that with the Young Master in such high spirits, he would certainly want to sleep with Akemi, and that there would be trouble if Akemi refused; but that, of course, a mother's feelings were the most important thing of all in cases like this—or in other words, how much?

"Well?" Tōji demanded abruptly.

Okō put her finger to her thickly powdered cheek and thought.

"Make up your mind!" urged Tōji. Drawing closer to her, he said, "It's not a bad match, you know. He's a famous teacher of the martial arts, and his family has lots of money. His father had more disciples than anybody else in the country. What's more, he's not married yet. Any way you look at it, it's an attractive offer."

"Well, I think so too, but—"

"But nothing. It's settled! We'll both spend the night."

There was no light in the room and Tōji casually rested his hand on Okō's shoulder. At just that moment, there was a loud noise in the next room back.

"What was that?" asked Tōji. "Do you have other customers?"

Okō nodded silently, then put her moist lips to his ear and whispered, "Later." Trying to appear casual, the two went back to Seijūrō's room, only to find him alone and sound asleep.

Tōji, taking the adjacent room, stretched out on the pallet. He lay there, drumming his fingers on the tatami, waiting for Okō. She failed to appear. Eventually his eyelids grew heavy and he drifted off to sleep. He woke up quite late the next morning with a resentful look on his face.

Seijūrō had already arisen and was again drinking in the room overlooking the river. Both Okō and Akemi looked bright and cheerful, as though they'd forgotten about the night before. They were coaxing Seijūrō into some sort of promise.

"Then you'll take us?"

"All right, we'll go. Put together some box lunches and bring some sake."

They were talking about the Okuni Kabuki, which was being performed on the riverbank at Shijō Avenue. This was a new kind of dance with words and music, the current rage in the capital. It had been invented by a shrine maiden named Okuni at the Izumo Shrine, and its popularity had already inspired many imitations. In the busy area along the river, there were rows of stages where troupes of women performers competed to attract audiences, each trying to achieve a degree of individuality by adding special provincial dances and songs to their repertoire. The actresses, for the most part, had started out as women of the night; now that they had taken to the stage, however, they were summoned to perform in some of the greatest mansions in the capital. Many of them took masculine names, dressed in men's clothing, and put on stirring performances as valiant warriors.

Seijūrō sat staring out the door. Beneath the small bridge at Sanjō Avenue, women were bleaching cloth in the river; men on horseback were passing back and forth over the bridge.

"Aren't those two ready yet?" he asked irritably.

It was already past noon. Sluggish from drink and tired of waiting, he was no longer in the mood for Kabuki.

Tōji, still smarting from the night before, was not his usual ebullient self. "It's fun to take women out," he grumbled, "but why is it that just when you're ready to leave, they suddenly start worrying about whether their hair is just right or their obi straight? What a nuisance!"

Seijūrō's thoughts turned to his school. He seemed to hear the sound of wooden swords and the clack of lance handles. What were his students saying about his absence? No doubt his younger brother, Denshichirō, was clicking his tongue in disapproval.

"Tōji," he said, "I don't really want to take them to see Kabuki. Let's go home."

"After you've already promised?"

"Well . . ."

"They were so thrilled! They'll be furious if we back out. I'll go and hurry them up."

On his way down the hallway, Tōji glanced into a room where the women's clothes were strewn about. He was surprised to see neither of them. "Where can they have got to?" he wondered aloud.

They weren't in the adjoining room either. Beyond that was another gloomy little room, sunless and musty with the odor of bedclothes. Tōji opened the door and was greeted with an angry roar: "Who's there?"

Jumping back a step, Tōji peered into the dark cubbyhole; it was floored with old tattered mats and was as different from the pleasant front rooms as night is from day. Sprawled on the floor, a sword handle lying carelessly across his belly, was an unkempt samurai whose clothing and general appearance left no doubt that he was one of the rōnin often seen roaming the streets and byways with nothing to do. The soles of his dirty feet stared Tōji in the face. Making no effort to get up, he lay there in a stupor.

Tōji said, "Oh, I'm sorry. I didn't know there was a guest in here."

"I'm not a guest!" the man shouted toward the ceiling. He reeked of sake, and though Tōji had no idea who he was, he was sure he wanted nothing more to do with him.

"Sorry to bother you," he said quickly, and turned to leave.

"Hold on there!" the man said roughly, raising himself up slightly. "Close the door behind you!"

Startled by his rudeness, Tōji did as he was told and left.

Almost immediately Tōji was replaced by Okō. Dressed to kill, she was obviously trying to look the great lady. As though tut-tutting a child, she said to Matahachi, "Now what are you so angry about?"

Akemi, who was just behind her mother, asked, "Why don't you come with us?"

"Where?"

"To see the Okuni Kabuki."

Matahachi's mouth twisted with repugnance. "What husband would be seen in the company of a man who's chasing after his wife?" he asked bitterly.

Okō had the feeling that cold water had been thrown in her face. Her eyes lighting up with anger, she said, "What are you talking about? Are you implying that there's something going on between Tōji and me?"

"Who said anything was going on?"

"You just said as much."

Matahachi made no reply.

"And you're supposed to be a man!" Though she hurled the words at him contemptuously, Matahachi maintained his sullen silence. "You make me sick!" she snapped. "You're always getting jealous over nothing! Come, Akemi. Let's not waste our time on this madman."

Matahachi reached out and caught her skirt. "Who're you calling a madman? What do you mean, talking to your husband that way?"

Okō pulled free of him. "And why not?" she said viciously. "If you're a husband, why don't you act like one? Who do you think's keeping you in food, you worthless layabout!"

"Heh!"

"You've hardly earned anything since we left Ōmi Province. You've just been living off me, drinking your sake and loafing. What've you got to complain about?"

"I told you I'd go out and work! I told you I'd even haul stones for the castle wall. But that wasn't good enough for you. You say you can't eat this, you can't wear that, you can't live in a dirty little house—there's no end to what you can't put up with. So instead of letting me do honest labor, you start this rotten teahouse. Well, stop it, I tell you, stop it!" he shouted. He began to shake.

"Stop what?"

"Stop running this place."

"And if I did, what would we eat tomorrow?"

"I can make enough for us to live on, even hauling rocks. I could manage for the three of us."

"If you're so eager to carry rocks or saw wood, why don't you just go away? Go on, be a laborer, anything, but if you do, you can live by yourself! The trouble with you is that you were born a clod, and you'll always be a clod. You should have stayed in Mimasaka! Believe me, I'm not begging you to stay. Feel free to leave anytime you want!"

While Matahachi made an effort to hold back his angry tears, Okō and Akemi turned their backs on him. But even after they were out of sight, he stood staring at the doorway. When Okō had hidden him at her house near Mount Ibuki, he'd thought he was lucky to have found someone who would love and take care of him. Now, however, he felt that he might as well have been captured by the enemy. Which was better, after all? To be a prisoner, or to become the pet of a fickle widow and cease to be a real man? Was it worse to languish in prison than to suffer here in the dark, a constant object of a shrew's scorn? He had had great hopes for the future, and he had let this slut, with her powdered face and her lascivious sex, pull him down to her level.

"The bitch!" Matahachi trembled with anger. "The rotten bitch!"

Tears welled up from the bottom of his heart. Why, oh, why, hadn't he returned to Miyamoto? Why hadn't he gone back to Otsū? His mother was in Miyamoto. His sister too, and his sister's husband, and Uncle Gon. They'd all been so good to him.

The bell at the Shippōji would be ringing today, wouldn't it? Just as it rang every day. And the Aida River would be flowing along its course as usual, flowers would be blooming on the riverbank, and the birds would be heralding the arrival of spring.

"What a fool I am! What a crazy, stupid fool!" Matahachi pounded his head with his fists.

Outside, mother, daughter and the two overnight guests strolled along the street, chatting merrily.

"It's just like spring."

"It ought to be. It's almost the third month."

"They say the shōgun will come to the capital soon. If he does, you two ladies should take in a lot of money, eh?"

"Oh, no, I'm sure we won't."

"Why? Don't the samurai from Edo like to play?"

"They're much too uncouth—"

"Mother, isn't that the music for the Kabuki? I hear bells. And a flute too."

"Listen to the child! She's always like this. She thinks she's already at the theater!"

"But, Mother, I can hear it."

"Never mind that. Carry the Young Master's hat for him."

The footsteps and voices drifted into the Yomogi. Matahachi, with eyes still red with fury, stole a look out the window at the happy foursome. He found the sight so humiliating he once again plopped down on the tatami in the dark room, cursing himself.

"What are you doing here? Have you no pride left? How can you let things go on this way? Idiot! *Do* something!" The speech was addressed to himself, his anger at Okō eclipsed by his indignation at his own craven weakness.

"She said get out. Well, get out!" he argued. "There's no reason to sit here gnashing your teeth. You're only twenty-two. You're still young. Get out and do something on your own."

He felt he couldn't abide staying in the empty, silent house another minute, yet for some reason, he couldn't leave. His head ached with confusion. He realized that living the way he had been for the past few years, he had lost the ability to think clearly. How had he stood it? His woman was spending her evenings entertaining other men, selling them the charms she had once lavished on him. He couldn't sleep nights, and in the daytime he was too dispirited to go out. Brooding here in this dark room, there was nothing to do but drink.

And all, he thought, for that aging whore!

He was disgusted with himself. He knew that the only way out of his agony was to kick the whole ugly business sky high and return to the aspirations of his younger days. He must find the way he had lost.

And yet . . . and yet . . .

Some mysterious attraction bound him. What sort of evil spell was it that held him here? Was the woman a demon in disguise? She would curse him, tell him to go away, swear he was nothing but trouble to her, and then in the middle of the night she would melt like honey and say it had all been a joke, she really hadn't meant any of it. And even if she was nearly forty, there were those lips—those bright red lips that were as appealing as her daughter's.

This, however, was not the whole story. In the final analysis, Matahachi did not have the courage to let Okō and Akemi see him working as a day laborer. He had grown lazy and soft; the young man who dressed in silk and could distinguish Nada sake from the local brew by its taste was a far cry from the simple, rugged Matahachi who had been at Sekigahara. The worst aspect was that living this strange life with an older woman had robbed him of his youthfulness. In years he was still young, but in spirit he was dissolute and spiteful, lazy and resentful.

"But I'll do it!" he vowed. "I'll get out now!" Giving himself a final angry blow on the head, he jumped to his feet, shouting, "I'll get out of here this very day!"

As he listened to his own voice, it suddenly sank in that there was no one around to hold him back, nothing that actually bound him to this house. The only thing he really owned and could not leave behind was his sword, and this he quickly slipped into his obi. Biting his lips, he said determinedly, "After all, I am a man."

He could have marched out the front door waving his sword like a victorious general, but by force of habit he jumped into his dirty sandals and left by the kitchen door.

So far, so good. He was out of doors! But now what? His feet came to a halt. He stood motionless in the refreshing breeze of early spring. It was not the light dazzling his eyes that kept him from moving. The question was, where was he headed?

At that moment it seemed to Matahachi that the world was a vast, turbulent sea on which there was nothing to cling to. Aside from Kyoto, his experience encompassed only his village life and one battle. As he puzzled over his situation, a sudden thought sent him scurrying like a puppy back through the kitchen door.

"I need money," he said to himself. "I'll certainly have to have some money."

Going straight to Okō's room, he rummaged through her toilet boxes, her mirror stand, her chest of drawers, and everywhere else he could think of. He ransacked the place but found no money at all. Of course, he should have realized Okō wasn't the type of woman who would fail to take precautions against something like this.

Frustrated, Matahachi flopped down on the clothes that still lay on the floor. The scent of Okō lingered like a thick mist about her red silk underrobe, her Nishijin obi and her Momoyama-dyed kimono. By now, he reflected, she would be at the open-air theater by the river, watching the Kabuki dances with Tōji at her side. He formed an image of her white skin and that provoking, coquettish face.

"The evil slut!" he cried. Bitter and murderous thoughts arose from his very bowels.

Then, unexpectedly, he had a painful recollection of Otsū. As the days and months of their separation added up, he had grown at last to understand the purity and devotion of this girl who had promised to wait for him. He would gladly have bowed down and lifted his hands in supplication to her, if he'd thought she would ever forgive him. But he had broken with Otsū, abandoned her in such a way that it would be impossible to face her again.

"All for the sake of that woman," he thought ruefully. Now that it was too late, everything was clear to him; he should never have let Okō know that Otsū existed. When Okō had first heard of the girl, she had smiled a little smile and pretended not to mind in the slightest, but in fact, she was consumed with jealousy. Afterward, whenever they quarreled, she would raise the subject and insist that he write a letter breaking his engagement. And when he finally gave in and did so, she had brazenly enclosed a note in her own obviously feminine hand, and callously had the missive delivered by an impersonal runner.

"What must Otsū think of me?" groaned Matahachi sorrowfully. The image of her innocent girlish face came to his mind—a face full of reproach. Once again he saw the mountains and the river in Mimasaka. He wanted to call out to his mother, to his relatives. They had been so good. Even the soil now seemed to have been warm and comforting.

"I can never go home again!" he thought. "I threw all of it away for . . . for . . ." Enraged afresh, he dumped Okō's clothes out of the clothes chests and ripped them apart, strewing strips and pieces all over the house.

Slowly he became aware of someone calling from the front door.

"Pardon me," said the voice. "I'm from the Yoshioka School. Are the Young Master and Tōji here?"

"How should I know?" replied Matahachi gruffly.

"They must be here! I know it's rude to disturb them when they've gone off to have some fun, but something terribly important has happened. It involves the good name of the Yoshioka family."

"Go away! Don't bother me!"

"Please, can't you at least give them a message? Tell them that a swordsman named Miyamoto Musashi has appeared at the school, and that, well, none of our people can get the better of him. He's waiting for the Young Master to return—refuses to budge until he's had a chance to face him. Please tell them to hurry home!"

"Miyamoto? Miyamoto?"

10

The Wheel of Fortune

It was a day of unforgettable shame for the Yoshioka
School. Never before had this prestigious center of the
martial arts suffered such total humiliation.

Ardent disciples sat around in abject despair, long
faces and whitened knuckles mirroring their distress
and frustration. One large group was in the wood-
floored anteroom, smaller groups in the side rooms. It
was already twilight, when ordinarily they would have
been heading home, or out to drink. No one made a
move to leave. The funereal silence was broken only
by the occasional clatter of the front gate.

"Is that him?"

"Is the Young Master back?"

"No, not yet." This from a man who had spent
half the afternoon leaning disconsolately against a
column at the entranceway.

Each time this happened, the men sank deeper
into their morass of gloom. Tongues clicked in dismay
and eyes shone with pathetic tears.

The doctor, coming out of a back room, said to

the man at the entranceway, "I understand Seijūrō isn't here. Don't you know where he is?"

"No. Men are out looking for him. He'll probably be back soon."

The doctor harrumphed and departed.

In front of the school, the candle on the altar of the Hachiman Shrine was surrounded by a sinister corona.

No one would have denied that the founder and first master, Yoshioka Kempō, was a far greater man than Seijūrō or his younger brother. Kempō had started life as a mere tradesman, a dyer of cloth, but in the course of endlessly repeating the rhythms and movements of paste-resist dyeing, he had conceived of a new way of handling the short sword. After learning the use of the halberd from one of the most skillful of the warrior-priests at Kurama and then studying the Kyōhachi style of swordsmanship, he had then created a style completely his own. His short-sword technique had subsequently been adopted by the Ashikaga shōguns, who summoned him to be an official tutor. Kempō had been a great master, a man whose wisdom was equal to his skill.

Although his sons, Seijūrō and Denshichirō, had received training as rigorous as their father's, they had fallen heir to his considerable wealth and fame, and that, in the opinion of some, was the cause of their weakness. Seijūrō was customarily addressed as "Young Master," but he had not really attained the level of skill that would attract a large following. Students came to the school because under Kempō the Yoshioka style of fighting had become so famous that just gaining entrance meant being recognized by society as a skilled warrior.

After the fall of the Ashikaga shogunate three decades earlier, the House of Yoshioka had ceased to receive an official allowance, but during the lifetime of the frugal Kempō, it had gradually accumulated a great deal of wealth. In addition, it had this large establishment on Shijō Avenue, with more students than any other school in Kyoto, which was by far the largest city in the country. But in truth, the school's position at the top level in the world of swordsmanship was a matter of appearances only.

The world outside these great white walls had changed more than most of the people inside realized. For years they had boasted, loafed, and played around, and time had, as it will, passed them by. Today their eyes had been opened by their disgraceful loss to an unknown country swordsman.

A little before noon, one of the servants came to the dōjō and reported that a man who called himself Musashi was at the door, requesting admittance. Asked what sort of a fellow he was, the servant replied that he was a rōnin, that he hailed from Miyamoto in Mimasaka, was twenty-one or twenty-two years old, about six feet tall, and seemed rather dull. His hair, uncombed for at least a year, was carelessly tied up behind in a reddish mop, and his clothing was too filthy to tell whether it was black or brown, plain or figured. The servant, while admitting that he might be mistaken, thought he detected an odor about the man. He did have on his back one of the webbed leather sacks people called warriors' study bags, and this did probably mean he was a *shugyōsha,* one of those samurai, so numerous these days, who wandered about devoting their every waking hour to the study of swordsmanship. Nevertheless, the servant's overall impression was that this Musashi was distinctly out of place at the Yoshioka School.

If the man had simply been asking for a meal, there would have been no problem. But when the group heard that the rustic intruder had come to the great gate to challenge the famous Yoshioka Seijūrō to a bout, they burst into uproarious laughter. Some argued for turning him away without further ado, while others said they should first find out what style he employed and the name of his teacher.

The servant, as amused as anyone else, left and came back to report that the visitor had, as a boy, learned the use of the truncheon from his father and had later on picked up what he could from warriors passing through the village. He left home when he was seventeen and "for reasons of his own" spent his eighteenth, nineteenth and twentieth years immersed in scholarly studies. All the previous year he had been alone in the mountains, with the trees and the mountain spirits as his only teachers. Consequently, he couldn't lay claim to any particular style or teacher. But in the future he hoped to learn the teachings of Kiichi Hōgen, master the essence of the Kyōhachi Style; and emulate the great Yoshioka Kempō by creating a style of his own, which he had already decided to call the Miyamoto Style. Despite his many flaws, this was the goal toward which he proposed to work with all his heart and soul.

It was an honest and unaffected answer, the servant conceded, but the man had a country accent and stammered at almost every word. The servant obligingly provided his listeners with an imitation, again throwing them into gales of laughter.

The man must be out of his senses. To proclaim

that his goal was to create a style of his own was sheer madness. By way of enlightening the lout, the students sent the servant out again, this time to ask whether the visitor had appointed anyone to take his corpse away after the bout.

To this Musashi replied, "If by any chance I should be killed, it makes no difference whether you discard my body on Toribe Mountain or throw it into the Kamo River with the garbage. Either way, I promise not to hold it against you."

His way of answering this time, said the servant, was very clear, with nothing of the clumsiness of his earlier replies.

After a moment's hesitation, someone said, "Let him in!"

That was how it started, with the disciples thinking they would cut the newcomer up a bit, then throw him out. In the very first bout, however, it was the school's champion who came away the loser. His arm was broken clean through. Only a bit of skin kept his wrist attached to his forearm.

One by one others accepted the stranger's challenge, and one by one they went down in ignominious defeat. Several were wounded seriously, and Musashi's wooden sword dripped with blood. After about the third loss, the disciples' mood turned murderous; if it took every last one of them, they would not let this barbaric madman get away alive, taking the honor of the Yoshioka School with him.

Musashi himself ended the bloodshed. Since his challenge had been accepted, he had no qualms about the casualties, but he announced, "There's no point in continuing until Seijūrō returns," and refused to fight anymore. There being no alternative, he was shown, at his own request, to a room where he could wait. Only then did one man come to his senses and call for the doctor.

It was soon after the doctor left that voices screaming out the names of two of the wounded brought a dozen men to the back room. They clustered around the two samurai in stunned disbelief, their faces ashen and their breathing uneven. Both were dead.

Footsteps hurried through the dōjō and into the death room. The students made way for Seijūrō and Tōji. Both were as pale as though they'd just emerged from an icy waterfall.

"What's going on here?" demanded Tōji. "What's the meaning of all this?" His tone was surly, as usual.

A samurai kneeling grim-faced by the pillow of one of his dead companions fixed accusing eyes on Tōji and said, "You should explain what's going on. You're the one who takes the Young Master out carousing. Well, this time you've gone too far!"

"Watch your tongue, or I'll cut it out!"

"When Master Kempō was alive, a day never passed when he wasn't in the dōjō!"

"What of it? The Young Master wanted a little cheering up, so we went to the Kabuki. What do you mean, talking that way in front of him? Just who do you think you are?"

"Does he have to stay out all night to see the Kabuki? Master Kempō must be turning in his grave."

"That's enough!" cried Tōji, lunging toward the man.

As others moved in and tried to separate and calm down the two, a voice heavy with pain rose slightly

232

above the sound of the scuffle. "If the Young Master's back, it's time to stop squabbling. It's up to him to retrieve the honor of the school. That rōnin can't leave here alive."

Several of the wounded screamed and pounded on the floor. Their agitation was an eloquent rebuke to those who had not faced Musashi's sword.

To the samurai of this age, the most important thing in the world was honor. As a class, they virtually competed with each other to see who would be the first to die for it. The government had until recently been too busy with its wars to work out an adequate administrative system for a country at peace, and even Kyoto was governed only by a set of loose, makeshift regulations. Still, the emphasis of the warrior class on personal honor was respected by farmers and townsmen alike, and it played a role in preserving peace. A general consensus regarding what constituted honorable behavior, and what did not, made it possible for the people to govern themselves even with inadequate laws.

The men of the Yoshioka School, though uncultured, were by no means shameless degenerates. When after the initial shock of defeat they returned to their normal selves, the first thing they thought of was honor. The honor of their school, the honor of the master, their own personal honor.

Putting aside individual animosities, a large group gathered around Seijūrō to discuss what was to be done. Unfortunately, on this of all days, Seijūrō felt bereft of fighting spirit. At the moment when he should have been at his best, he was hung over, weak and exhausted.

"Where is the man?" he asked, as he hitched up his kimono sleeves with a leather thong.

"He's in the small room next to the reception room," said one student, pointing across the garden.

"Call him!" Seijūrō commanded. His mouth was dry from tension. He sat down in the master's place, a small raised platform, and prepared himself to receive Musashi's greeting. Choosing one of the wooden swords proffered by his disciples, he held it upright beside him.

Three or four men acknowledged the command and started to leave, but Tōji and Ryōhei told them to wait.

There ensued a good deal of whispering, just out of Seijūrō's earshot. The muted consultations centered around Tōji and other of the school's senior disciples. Before long family members and a few retainers joined in, and there were so many heads present that the gathering split into groups. Though heated, the controversy was settled in a relatively short time.

The majority, not only concerned about the school's fate but uncomfortably aware of Seijūrō's shortcomings as a fighter, concluded that it would be unwise to let him face Musashi man to man, then and there. With two dead and several wounded, if Seijūrō were to lose, the crisis facing the school would become extraordinarily grave. It was too great a risk to take.

The unspoken opinion of most of the men was that if Denshichirō were present, there would be little cause for alarm. In general, it was thought that he would have been better suited than Seijūrō to carry on his father's work, but being the second son and having no serious responsibilities, he was an exceedingly easygoing type. That morning he had left the house with friends to go to Ise and hadn't even bothered to say when he'd return.

Tōji approached Seijūrō and said, "We've reached a conclusion."

As Seijūrō listened to the whispered report, his face grew more and more indignant, until finally he gasped with barely controlled fury, "Trick him?"

Tōji tried to silence him with his eyes, but Seijūrō was not to be silenced. "I can't agree to anything like that! It's cowardly. What if word got out that the Yoshioka School was so afraid of an unknown warrior that it hid and ambushed him?"

"Calm down," Tōji pleaded, but Seijūrō continued to protest. Drowning him out, Tōji said loudly, "Leave it to us. We'll take care of it."

But Seijūrō would have none of it. "Do you think that I, Yoshioka Seijūrō, would lose to this Musashi, or whatever his name is?"

"Oh, no, it's not that at all," lied Tōji. "It's just that we don't see how you would gain any honor by defeating him. You're of much too high a status to take on a brazen vagabond like that. Anyway, there's no reason why anybody outside this house should know anything about it, is there? Only one thing is important—not to let him get away alive."

Even while they argued, the number of men in the hall shrank by more than half. As quietly as cats, they were disappearing into the garden, toward the back door and into the inner rooms, fading almost imperceptibly into the darkness.

"Young Master, we can't put it off any longer," Tōji said firmly, and blew out the lamp. He loosened his sword in its scabbard and raised his kimono sleeves.

Seijūrō remained seated. Though to some extent relieved at not having to fight the stranger, he was by no means happy. The implication, as he saw it, was that his disciples had a low opinion of his ability. He thought back on how he had neglected practice since his father's death, and the thought made him despondent.

The house grew as cold and quiet as the bottom of a well. Unable to sit still, Seijūrō got up and stood by the window. Through the paper-covered doors of the room given Musashi, he could see the softly flickering light of the lamp. That was the only light anywhere.

Quite a number of other eyes were peering in the same direction. The attackers, their swords on the ground in front of them, held their breath and listened intently for any sound that might tell them what Musashi was up to.

Tōji, whatever his shortcomings, had experienced the training of a samurai. He was trying desperately to figure out what Musashi might do. "He's completely unknown in the capital, but he's a great fighter. Could he just be sitting silently in that room? Our approach has been quiet enough, but with this many people pressing in on him, he must have noticed. Anyone trying to make it through life as a warrior would notice; otherwise he'd be dead by now.

"Mm, maybe he's dozed off. It rather looks that way. After all, he's been waiting a long time.

"On the other hand, he's already proved he's clever. He's probably standing there fully prepared for battle, leaving the lamp lit to put us off guard, just waiting for the first man to attack.

"That must be it. That *is* it!"

The men were edgily cautious, for the target of their murderous intent would be just as eager to slay them. They exchanged glances, silently asking who would be the first to run forward and risk his life.

Finally the wily Tōji, who was just outside Musashi's room, called out, "Musashi! Sorry to have kept you waiting! Could I see you for a moment?"

There being no answer, Tōji concluded that Musashi was indeed ready and waiting for the attack. Vowing not to let him escape, Tōji signaled to right and left, then aimed a kick at the shoji. Dislodged from its groove by the blow, the bottom of the door slid about two feet into the room. At the sound, the men who were supposed to storm into the room unintentionally fell back a pace. But in a matter of seconds, someone shouted for the attack, and all the other doors of the room clattered open.

"He's not here!"

"The room's empty!"

Voices full of restored courage muttered disbelievingly. Musashi had been sitting there just a short while ago, when someone had brought him the lamp. The lamp still burned, the cushion he had been sitting on was still there, the brazier still had a good fire in it, and there was a cup of untouched tea. But no Musashi!

One man ran out on the veranda and let the others know that he had gotten away. From under the veranda and from dark spots in the garden, students and retainers assembled, stamping the ground angrily and cursing the men who had been standing guard on the small room. The guards, however, insisted that Musashi could not have gotten away. He had walked down to the toilet less than an hour earlier but had returned to the room immediately. There was no way he could have gotten out without being seen.

"Are you saying he's invisible, like the wind?" one man asked scornfully.

Just then a man who had been poking around in a closet shouted, "Here's how he got away! See, these floorboards have been ripped up."

"It hasn't been very long since the lamp was trimmed. He can't have gone far!"

"After him!"

If Musashi had indeed fled, he must at heart be a coward! The thought fired his pursuers with the fighting spirit that had been so notably lacking a bit earlier. They were streaming out the front, back and side gates when someone yelled, "There he is!"

Near the back gate, a figure shot out of the shadows, crossed the street and entered a dark alley on the other side. Running like a hare, it swerved off to one side when it reached the wall at the end of the alley. Two or three of the students caught up with the man on the road between the Kūyadō and the burned ruins of the Honnōji.

"Coward!"

"Run away, will you?"

"After what you did today?"

There was the sound of heavy scuffling and kicking, and a defiant howl. The captured man had regained his strength and was turning on his captors. In an instant, the three men who had been dragging him by the back of his neck plummeted to the ground. The man's sword was about to descend on them when a fourth man ran up and shouted, "Wait! It's a mistake! He's not the one we're after."

Matahachi lowered his sword and the men got to their feet.

"Hey, you're right! That's not Musashi."

As they were standing there looking perplexed, Tōji arrived on the scene. "Did you catch him?" he asked.

"Uh, wrong man—not the one who caused all the trouble."

Tōji took a closer look at the captive and said with astonishment, "Is that the man you were chasing?"

"Yes. You know him?"

"I saw him just today at the Yomogi Teahouse."

While they eyed Matahachi silently and suspiciously, he calmly straightened his tousled hair and brushed off his kimono.

"Is he the master of the Yomogi?"

"No, the mistress of the place told me he wasn't. He seems to be just a hanger-on of some sort."

"He looks shady, all right. What was he doing around the gate? Spying?"

But Tōji had already started to move on. "If we waste time with him, we'll lose Musashi. Split up and get moving. If nothing else, we can at least find out where he's staying."

There was a murmur of assent and they were off.

Matahachi, facing the moat of the Honnōji, stood silently with his head bowed while the men ran by. As the last one passed, he called out to him.

The man stopped. "What do you want?" he asked.

Going toward him, Matahachi asked, "How old was this man called Musashi?"

"How would I know?"

"Would you say he was about my age?"

"I guess that's about right. Yes."

"Is he from the village of Miyamoto in Mimasaka Province?"

"Yes."

"I guess 'Musashi' is another way of reading the two characters used to write 'Takezō,' isn't it?"

"Why are you asking all these questions? Is he a friend of yours?"

"Oh, no. I was just wondering."

"Well, in the future, why don't you just stay away from places where you don't belong? Otherwise you might find yourself in some real trouble one of these days." With that warning, the man ran off.

Matahachi started walking slowly beside the dark moat, stopping occasionally to look up at the stars. He didn't seem to have any particular destination.

"It is him after all!" he decided. "He must have changed his name to Musashi and become a swordsman. I guess he must be pretty different from the way he used to be." He slid his hands into his obi and began kicking a stone along with the toe of his sandal. Every time he kicked, he seemed to see Takezō's face before him.

"It's not the right time," he mumbled. "I'd be ashamed for him to see me the way I am now. I've got enough pride not to want him to look down on me. . . . If that Yoshioka bunch catches up with him, though, they're likely to kill him. Wonder where he is. I'd like to at least warn him."

11

Encounter and Retreat

Along the stony path leading up to the Kiyomizudera
Temple stood a row of shabby houses, their planked
roofs lined up like rotten teeth and so old that moss
covered their eaves. Under the hot noonday sun, the
street reeked of salted fish broiling over charcoal.

A dish flew through the door of one of the ram-
shackle hovels and broke into smithereens on the
street. A man of about fifty, apparently an artisan of
sorts, came tumbling out after it. Close on his heels
was his barefooted wife, her hair a tangled mess and
her tits hanging down like a cow's.

"What're you saying, you lout?" she screamed
shrilly. "You go off, leave your wife and children to
starve, then come crawling back like a worm!"

From inside the house came the sound of children
crying and nearby a dog howled. She caught up with
the man, seized him by his topknot and began beating
him.

"Now where do you think you're going, you old
fool?"

Neighbors rushed up, trying to restore order.

Musashi smiled ironically and turned back toward the ceramics shop. For some time before the domestic battle erupted, he had been standing just outside it, watching the potters with childlike fascination. The two men inside were unaware of his presence. Eyes riveted on their work, they seemed to have entered into the clay, become a part of it. Their concentration was complete.

Musashi would have liked to have a try at working with the clay. Since boyhood he had enjoyed doing things with his hands, and he thought he might at least be able to make a simple tea bowl. Just then, however, one of the potters, an old man of nearly sixty, started fashioning a tea bowl. Musashi, observing how deftly he moved his fingers and handled his spatula, realized he'd overestimated his own abilities. "It takes so much technique just to make a simple piece like that," he marveled.

These days he often felt deep admiration for other people's work. He found he respected technique, art, even the ability to do a simple task well, particularly if it was a skill he himself had not mastered.

In one corner of the shop, on a makeshift counter made of an old door panel, stood rows of plates, jars, sake cups, and pitchers. They were sold as souvenirs, for the paltry sum of twenty or thirty pieces of cash, to people on their way to and from the temple. In stark contrast to the earnestness the potters devoted to their work was the humbleness of their boarded shack. Musashi wondered whether they always had enough to eat. Life, it appeared, wasn't as easy as it sometimes seemed.

Contemplating the skill, concentration and devotion put into making wares, even as cheap as these, made Musashi feel he still had a long way to go if he was ever to reach the level of perfection in swordsmanship that he aspired to. The thought was a sobering one, for in the past three weeks he'd visited other well-known training centers in Kyoto besides the Yoshioka School and had begun to wonder whether he had not been too critical of himself since his confinement at Himeji. His expectation had been to find Kyoto full of men who had mastered the martial arts. It was, after all, the imperial capital, as well as the former seat of the Ashikaga shogunate, and it had long been a gathering place for famous generals and legendary warriors. During his stay, however, he had not found a single training center that had taught him anything to be genuinely grateful for. Instead, at each school he had experienced disappointment. Though he always won his bouts, he was unable to decide whether this was because he was good or his opponents were bad. In either case, if the samurai he had met were typical, the country was in sorry shape.

Encouraged by his success, he had reached the point of taking a certain pride in his expertise. But now, reminded of the danger of vanity, he felt chastened. He mentally bowed in deep respect to the clay-smudged old men at the wheel and started up the steep slope to Kiyomizudera.

He had not gone far when a voice called to him from below. "You there, sir. The rōnin!"

"Do you mean me?" asked Musashi, turning around.

Judging from the man's padded cotton garment, his bare legs, and the pole he carried, he was a palanquin bearer by trade. From behind his beard, he said, politely enough for one of his lowly status, "Sir, is your name Miyamoto?"

"Yes."

"Thank you." The man turned and went down toward Chawan Hill.

Musashi watched him enter what appeared to be a teahouse. Passing through the area a while earlier, he had noticed a large crowd of porters and palanquin bearers standing about in a sunny spot. He couldn't imagine who had sent one of them to ask his name but supposed that whoever it was would soon come to meet him. He stood there awhile, but when no one appeared, resumed his climb.

He stopped along the way to look at several well-known temples, and at each of them he bowed and said two prayers. One was: "Please protect my sister from harm." The other was: "Please test the lowly Musashi with hardship. Let him become the greatest swordsman in the land, or let him die."

Arriving at the edge of a cliff, he dropped his basket hat on the ground and sat down. From there he could look out over the whole city of Kyoto. As he sat clasping his knees, a simple, but powerful, ambition welled up in his young breast.

"I want to lead an important life. I want to do it because I was born a human being."

He had once read that in the tenth century two rebels named Taira no Masakado and Fujiwara no Sumitomo, both wildly ambitious, had gotten together and decided that if they emerged from the wars victorious, they would divide Japan up between them. The story was probably apocryphal to begin with, but Musashi remembered thinking at the time how stupid and unrealistic it would have been for them to believe they could carry out so grandiose a scheme. Now, however, he no longer felt it laughable. While his own dream was of a different sort, there were certain similarities. If the young cannot harbor great dreams in their souls, who can? At the moment Musashi was imagining how he could create a place of his own in the world.

He thought of Oda Nobunaga and Toyotomi Hideyoshi, of their visions of unifying Japan and of the many battles they had fought to that end. But it was clear that the path to greatness no longer lay in winning battles. Today the people wanted only the peace for which they'd thirsted so long. And as Musashi considered the long, long struggle Tokugawa Ieyasu had had to endure to make this desire a reality, he realized once again how hard it was to hold fast to one's ideal.

"This is a new age," he thought. "I have the rest of my life before me. I came along too late to follow in the footsteps of Nobunaga or Hideyoshi, but I can still dream of my own world to conquer. No one can stop me from doing that. Even that palanquin bearer must have a dream of some sort."

For a moment he put these ideas out of his mind and tried to view his situation objectively. He had his sword, and the Way of the Sword was the way he had chosen. It might be fine to be a Hideyoshi or an Ieyasu, but the times no longer had use for people of their particular talents. Ieyasu had everything neatly tied up; there was no more need for bloody wars. In Kyoto, stretched out below him, life was no longer a touch-and-go affair.

For Musashi, the important thing from now on would be his sword and the society around him, his swordsmanship as it related to existing as a human being. In a moment of insight, he was satisfied that he had found the link between the martial arts and his own visions of greatness.

As he sat lost in thought, the palanquin bearer's face came into view beneath the cliff. He pointed his bamboo pole at Musashi and shouted, "There he is, up there!"

Musashi looked down to where the porters were milling about and shouting. They began climbing the hill toward him. He got to his feet and, trying to ignore them, walked farther up the hill, but soon discovered that his path was blocked. Locking arms and thrusting out their poles, a sizable group of men had encircled him at a distance. Looking over his shoulder, he saw that the men behind him had come to a halt. One of them grinned, showing his teeth, and informed the others that Musashi seemed to be "staring at a plaque or something."

Musashi, now before the steps of the Hongandō, was indeed gazing up at a weatherbeaten plaque hanging from the crossbeam of the temple entrance. He felt ill at ease and wondered if he should try frightening them away with a battle cry. Even though he knew he could make quick work of them, there was no point in brawling with a bunch of lowly laborers. It was probably all a mistake anyway. If so, they would disperse sooner or later. He stood there patiently, reading and rereading the words on the plaque: "Original Vow."

"Here she comes!" one of the porters cried.

They began talking among themselves in hushed tones. Musashi's impression was that they were working themselves into a frenzy. The compound within the western gate of the temple had quickly filled with people, and now priests, pilgrims and vendors were straining their eyes to see what was going on. Their faces brimming with curiosity, they formed circles outside the ring of porters surrounding Musashi.

From the direction of Sannen Hill came the rhythmical, pace-setting chants of men carrying a load. The voices came closer and closer until two men entered the temple grounds bearing on their backs an old woman and a rather tired-looking country samurai.

From her porter's back, Osugi waved her hand briskly and said, "This will do." The bearer bent his legs, and as she jumped spryly to the ground, she thanked him. Turning to Uncle Gon, she said, "We won't let him get away this time, will we?" The two were clothed and shod as though they expected to spend the rest of their lives traveling.

"Where is he?" called Osugi.

One of the bearers said, "Over there," and pointed proudly toward the temple.

Uncle Gon moistened the handle of his sword with spittle, and the two pushed through the circle of people.

"Take your time," cautioned one of the porters.

"He looks pretty tough," said another.

"Just make sure you're well prepared," advised still another.

While the laborers offered words of encouragement and support to Osugi, the spectators looked on in dismay.

"Is the old woman actually planning to challenge that rōnin to a duel?"

"Looks that way."

"But she's so old! Even her second is shaky on

his legs! They must have good reason to try taking on a man so much younger.''

"Must be a family feud of some kind!"

"Look at that now, will you! She's lighting into the old man. Some of these old grannies really have guts, don't they!"

A porter ran up with a dipper of water for Osugi. After drinking a mouthful she handed it to Uncle Gon and addressed him sternly. "Now see that you don't get flustered, because there's nothing to be flustered about. Takezō's a man of straw. Oh, he may have learned a little about using a sword, but he couldn't have learned all that much. Just stay calm!"

Taking the lead, she went straight to the front staircase of the Hongandō and sat down on the steps, not ten paces from Musashi. Paying no attention whatever either to him or to the crowd watching her, she took out her prayer beads, and closing her eyes, began moving her lips. Inspired by her religious fervor, Uncle Gon put his hands together and did likewise.

The sight proved to be a little too melodramatic, and one of the spectators started snickering. Immediately, one of the porters spun around and said challengingly, "Who thinks this is funny? This is no laughing matter, you imbecile! The old woman's come all the way from Mimasaka to find the good-for-nothing who ran off with her son's bride. She's been praying at the temple here every day for almost two months and today he finally showed up."

"These samurai are different from the rest of us," was the opinion of another porter. "At that age, the old woman could be living comfortably at home, playing with her grandchildren, but no, here she is, in place of her son, seeking to avenge an insult to her family. If nothing else, she deserves our respect."

A third one said, "We're not supporting her just because she's been giving us tips. She's got spirit, she has! Old as she is, she's not afraid to fight. I say we should give her all the help we can. It's only right to help the underdog! If she should lose, let's take care of the rōnin ourselves."

"You're right! But let's do it now! We can't stand here and let her get herself killed."

As the crowd learned of the reasons for Osugi's being there, the excitement mounted. Some of the spectators began goading the porters on.

Osugi put her prayer beads back into her kimono, and a hush fell over the temple grounds. "Takezō!" she called loudly, putting her left hand on the short sword at her waist.

Musashi had all the while been standing by in silence. Even when Osugi called out his name, he acted as if he hadn't heard. Unnerved by this, Uncle Gon, at Osugi's side, chose this moment to assume an attacking stance, and thrusting his head forward, uttered a cry of challenge.

Musashi again failed to respond. He couldn't. He simply did not know how to. He recalled Takuan's having warned him in Himeji that he might run into Osugi. He was prepared to ignore her completely, but he was very upset by the talk the porters had been spreading among the mob. Furthermore, it was difficult for him to restrain his resentment at the hatred the Hon'idens had harbored against him all this time. The whole affair amounted to nothing more than a petty matter of face and feelings in the little village of

Miyamoto, a misunderstanding that could be easily cleared up if only Matahachi were present.

Nevertheless, he was at a loss as to what to do here and now. How was one to respond to a challenge from a doddering old woman and a shrunken-faced samurai? Musashi stared on in silence, his mind in a quandary.

"Look at the bastard! He's afraid!" a porter shouted.

"Be a man! Let the old woman kill you!" taunted another.

There was not a soul who was not on Osugi's side.

The old woman blinked her eyes and shook her head. Then she looked at the bearers and snapped angrily, "Shut up! I just want you as witnesses. If the two of us should happen to be killed, I want you to send our bodies back to Miyamoto. Otherwise I don't need your talk, and I don't want your help!" Pulling her short sword partway out of its scabbard, she took a couple of steps in Musashi's direction.

"Takezō!" she said again. "Takezō was always your name in the village, so why don't you answer to it? I've heard you've taken a fine new name—Miyamoto Musashi, is it?—but you'll always be Takezō to me! Ha, ha, ha!" Her wrinkled neck quivered as she laughed. Evidently she hoped to kill Musashi with words before swords were drawn.

"Did you think you could keep me from tracking you down just by changing your name? How stupid! The gods in heaven have guided me to you, as I knew they would. Now fight! We'll see whether I take your head home with me, or you manage somehow to stay alive!"

250

Uncle Gon, in his withered voice, issued his own challenge. "It's been four long years since you gave us the slip, and we've been searching for you all this time. Now our prayers here at the Kiyomizudera have brought you into our grasp. Old I may be, but I'm not going to lose to the likes of you! Prepare to die!" Whipping out his sword, he cried to Osugi, "Get out of the way!"

She turned on him furiously. "What do you mean, you old fool? You're the one who's shaking."

"Never mind! The bodhisattvas of this temple will protect us!"

"You're right, Uncle Gon. And the ancestors of the Hon'idens are with us too! There's nothing to fear."

"Takezō! Come forward and fight!"

"What are you waiting for?"

Musashi did not move. He stood there like a deaf-mute, staring at the two old people and their drawn swords.

Osugi cried, "What's the matter, Takezō! Are you scared?"

She edged sideways, preparing to attack, but suddenly tripped on a rock and pitched forward, landing on her hands and knees almost at Musashi's feet.

The crowd gasped, and someone screamed, "She'll be killed!"

"Quick, save her!"

But Uncle Gon only stared at Musashi's face, too stunned to move.

The old woman then startled one and all by snatching up her sword and walking back to Uncle Gon's side, where she again took a challenging stance. "What's wrong, you lout?" Osugi cried. "Is that sword in your hand just an ornament? Don't you know how to use it?''

Musashi's face was like a mask, but he spoke at last, in a thunderous voice. "I can't do it!"

He started walking toward them, and Uncle Gon and Osugi instantly fell back to either side.

"Wh-where are you going, Takezō?"

"I can't use my sword!"

"Stop! Why don't you stop and fight?"

"I told you! I can't use it!"

He walked straight ahead, looking neither right nor left. He marched directly through the crowd, without once swerving.

Recovering her senses, Osugi cried, "He's running away! Don't let him escape!"

The crowd now moved in on Musashi, but when they thought they had him hemmed in, they discovered he was no longer there. Their bewilderment was acute. Eyes flared in surprise, then became dull patches in blank faces.

Breaking up into smaller groups, they continued until sunset to run about, searching frantically under the floors of the temple buildings and in the woods for their vanished prey.

Still later, as people were going back down the darkened slopes of Sannen and Chawan hills, one man swore that he had seen Musashi jump with the effortlessness of a cat to the top of the six-foot wall by the western gate and disappear.

Nobody believed this, least of all Osugi and Uncle Gon.

12

The Water Sprite

In a hamlet northwest of Kyoto, the heavy thuds of a mallet pounding rice straw shook the ground. Unseasonal torrents of rain soaked into the brooding thatched roofs. This was a sort of no-man's-land, between the city and the farming district, and the poverty was so extreme that at twilight the smoke of kitchen fires billowed from only a handful of houses.

A basket hat suspended under the eaves of one small house proclaimed in bold, rough characters that this was an inn, albeit one of the cheapest variety. The travelers who stopped here were impecunious and rented only floor space. For pallets they paid extra, but few could afford such luxury.

In the dirt-floored kitchen beside the entranceway, a boy leaned with his hands on the raised tatami of the adjoining room, in the center of which was a sunken hearth.

"Hello! . . . Good evening! . . . Anybody here?" It was the errand boy from the drinking shop, another shabby affair just down the road.

The boy's voice was too loud for his size. He could not have been more than ten or eleven years old, and with his hair wet from the rain and hanging down over his ears, he looked no more substantial than a water sprite in a whimsical painting. He was dressed for the part too: thigh-length kimono with tubular sleeves, a thick cord for an obi, and mud splattered clear up his back from running in his wooden clogs.

"That you, Jō?" called the old innkeeper from a back room.

"Yes. Would you like me to bring you some sake?"

"No, not today. The lodger isn't back yet. I don't need any."

"Well, he'll want some when he does come back, won't he? I'll bring the usual amount."

"If he does, I'll come get it myself."

Reluctant to leave without an order, the boy asked, "What are you doing in there?"

"I'm writing a letter, going to send it by the packhorse up to Kurama tomorrow. But it's a bit difficult. And my back's getting sore. Be quiet, don't bother me."

"That's pretty funny, isn't it? You're so old you're beginning to stoop, and you still don't know how to write properly!"

"That's enough out of you. If I hear any more sass, I'll take a stick of firewood to you."

"Want me to write it for you?"

"Ha, as if you could."

"Oh, I can," the boy asserted as he came into the room. He looked over the old man's shoulder at the letter and burst into laughter. "Are you trying to write 'potatoes'? The character you've written means 'pole.' "

"Quiet!"

"I won't say a word, if you insist. But your writing's terrible. Are you planning to send your friends some potatoes, or some poles?"

"Potatoes."

The boy read a moment longer, then announced, "It's no good. Nobody but you could guess what this letter's supposed to mean!"

"Well, if you're so smart, see what you can do with it then."

"All right. Just tell me what you want to say." Jōtarō sat down and took up the brush.

"You clumsy ass!" the old man exclaimed.

"Why call me clumsy? You're the one who can't write!"

"Your nose is dripping on the paper."

"Oh, sorry. You can give me this piece for my pay." He proceeded to blow his nose on the soiled sheet. "Now, what is it you want to say?" Holding the brush firmly, he wrote with ease as the old man dictated.

Just as the letter was finished, the lodger returned, casually throwing aside a charcoal sack he had picked up somewhere to put over his head.

Musashi, stopping by the door, wrung the water out of his sleeves and grumbled, "I guess this'll be the end of the plum blossoms." In the twenty-odd days Musashi had been there, the inn had come to seem like home. He was gazing out at the tree by the front gate, where pink blossoms had greeted his eye every morning since his arrival. The fallen petals lay scattered about in the mud.

Entering the kitchen, he was surprised to catch a glimpse of the boy from the sake shop, head to head with the innkeeper. Curious as to what they were doing, he stole up behind the old man and peered over his shoulder.

Jōtarō looked up into Musashi's face, then hastily hid the brush and paper behind him. "You shouldn't sneak up on people like that," he complained.

"Let me see," said Musashi teasingly.

"No," said Jōtarō with a defiant shake of his head.

"Come on, show me," said Musashi.

"Only if you buy some sake."

"Oh, so that's your game, is it? All right, I'll buy some."

"Five gills?"

"I don't need that much."

"Three gills?"

"Still too much."

"Well, how much? Don't be such a tightwad!"

"Tightwad? Now, you know I'm only a poor swordsman. Do you think I have money to throw away?"

"All right. I'll measure it out myself, give you your money's worth. But if I do, you have to promise to tell me some stories."

The bargaining concluded, Jōtarō splashed cheerfully off into the rain.

Musashi picked up the letter and read it. After a moment or two, he turned to the innkeeper and asked, "Did he really write this?"

"Yes. Amazing, isn't it? He seems very bright."

While Musashi went to the well, poured some cold water over himself and put on dry clothes, the old man hung a pot over the fire and set out some pickled vegetables and a rice bowl. Musashi came back and sat down by the hearth.

"What's that rascal up to?" muttered the innkeeper. "He's taking a long time with the sake."

"How old is he?"

"Eleven, I think he said."

"Mature for his age, don't you think?"

"Mm. I suppose it's because he's been working at the sake shop since he was seven. He runs up against all kinds there—wagon drivers, the papermaker down the way, travelers, and what have you."

"I wonder how he learned to write so well."

"Is he really that good?"

"Well, his writing has a certain childish quality, but there's an appealing—what can I say?—directness about it. If I had a swordsman in mind, I would say it shows spiritual breadth. The boy may eventually be somebody."

"What do you mean?"

"I mean become a real human being."

"Oh?" The old man frowned, took the lid off the pot and resumed his grumbling. "Still not back. I'll bet he's dawdling somewhere."

He was about to put on his sandals and go for the sake himself when Jōtarō returned. "What have you been up to?" he asked the boy. "You've been keeping my guest waiting."

"I couldn't help it. There was a customer in the shop, very drunk, and he grabbed hold of me and started asking a lot of questions."

"What kind of questions?"

"He was asking about Miyamoto Musashi."

"And I suppose you did a lot of blabbering."

257

"It wouldn't matter if I did. Everybody around here knows what happened at Kiyomizudera the other day. The woman next door, the daughter of the lacquer man—both of them were at the temple that day. They saw what happened."

"Stop talking about that, won't you?" Musashi said, almost in a pleading tone.

The sharp-eyed boy sized up Musashi's mood and asked, "Can I stay here for a while and talk with you?" He started washing off his feet, preparing to come into the hearth room.

"It's all right with me, if your master won't mind."

"Oh, he doesn't need me right now."

"All right."

"I'll warm up your sake for you. I'm good at that." He settled a sake jar into the warm ashes around the fire and soon announced it was ready.

"Fast, aren't you?" said Musashi appreciatively.

"Do you like sake?"

"Yes."

"But being so poor, I guess you don't drink very much, do you?"

"That's right."

"I thought men who were good at the martial arts served under great lords and got big allowances. A customer at the shop told me once that Tsukahara Bokuden always used to go around with seventy or eighty retainers, a change of horses and a falcon."

"That's true."

"And I heard that a famous warrior named Yagyū, who serves the House of Tokugawa, has an income of fifty thousand bushels of rice."

"That's true too."

"Then why are you so poor?"

"I'm still studying."

"How old will you have to be before you have lots of followers?"

"I don't know if I ever will."

"What's the matter? Aren't you any good?"

"You heard what the people who saw me at the temple said. Any way you look at it, I ran away."

"That's what everybody's saying: that *shugyōsha* at the inn—that's you—is a weakling. But it makes me mad to listen to them." Jōtarō's lips tightened in a straight line.

"Ha, ha! Why should you mind? They're not talking about you."

"Well, I feel sorry for you. Look, the papermaker's son and the cooper's son and some of the rest of the young men all get together sometimes behind the lacquer shop for sword practice. Why don't you fight one of them and beat him?"

"All right. If that's what you want, I will."

Musashi was finding it difficult to refuse anything the boy asked, partly because he himself was in many ways still a boy at heart and was able to sympathize with Jōtarō. He was always looking, mostly unconsciously, for something to take the place of the family affection lacking from his own boyhood.

"Let's talk about something else," he said. "I'll ask you a question for a change. Where were you born?"

"In Himeji."

"Oh, so you're from Harima."

"Yes, and you're from Mimasaka, aren't you? Somebody said you were."

"That's right. What does your father do?"

"He used to be a samurai. A real honest-to-goodness samurai!"

At first Musashi looked astonished, but actually the answer explained several things, not the least of which was how the boy had learned to write so well. He asked the father's name.

"His name is Aoki Tanzaemon. He used to have an allowance of twenty-five hundred bushels of rice, but when I was seven he left his lord's service and came to Kyoto as a rōnin. After all his money was gone, he left me at the sake shop and went to a temple to become a monk. But I don't want to stay at the shop. I want to become a samurai like my father was, and I want to learn swordsmanship like you. Isn't that the best way to become a samurai?"

The boy paused, then continued earnestly: "I want to become your follower—go around the country studying with you. Won't you take me on as your pupil?"

Having blurted out his purpose, Jōtarō put on a stubborn face reflecting clearly his determination not to take no for an answer. He could not know, of course, that he was pleading with a man who had caused his father no end of trouble. Musashi, for his part, could not bring himself to refuse out of hand. Yet what he was really thinking of was not whether to say yes or no but of Aoki Tanzaemon and his unfortunate fate. He could not help sympathizing with the man. The Way of the Samurai was a constant gamble, and a samurai had to be ready at all times to kill or be killed. Mulling over this example of life's vicissitudes, Musashi was saddened, and the effect of the sake wore off quite suddenly. He felt lonely.

Jōtarō was insistent. When the innkeeper tried to

get him to leave Musashi alone, he replied insolently and redoubled his efforts. He caught hold of Musashi's wrist, then hugged his arm, finally broke into tears.

Musashi, seeing no way out, said, "All right, all right, that's enough. You can be my follower, but only after you go and talk it over with your master."

Jōtarō, satisfied at last, trotted off to the sake shop.

The next morning, Musashi rose early, dressed, and called to the innkeeper, "Would you please fix me a lunch box? It's been nice staying here these few weeks, but I think I'll go on to Nara now."

"Leaving so soon?" asked the innkeeper, not expecting the sudden departure. "It's because that boy was pestering you, isn't it?"

"Oh, no, it's not his fault. I've been thinking about going to Nara for some time—to see the famous lance fighters at the Hōzōin. I hope he doesn't give you too much trouble when he finds out I'm gone."

"Don't worry about it. He's only a child. He'll scream and yell for a while, then forget all about it."

"I can't imagine that the sake man would let him leave anyway," said Musashi as he stepped out onto the road.

The storm had passed, as if wiped away, and the breeze brushed gently against Musashi's skin, quite unlike the fierce wind of the day before.

The Kamo River was up, the water muddy. At one end of the wooden bridge at Sanjō Avenue, samurai were examining all the people who came and went. Asking the reason for the inspection, Musashi was told it was because of the new shōgun's impending visit. A vanguard of influential and minor feudal lords had already arrived, and steps were being taken to keep dangerous unattached samurai out of the city. Musashi, himself a rōnin, gave ready answers to the questions asked and was allowed to pass.

The experience set him to thinking about his own status as a wandering masterless warrior pledged neither to the Tokugawas nor to their rivals in Osaka. Running off to Sekigahara and taking sides with the Osaka forces against the Tokugawas was a matter of inheritance. That had been his father's allegiance, unchanged from the days when he served under Lord Shimmen of Iga. Toyotomi Hideyoshi had died two years before the battle; his supporters, loyal to his son, made up the Osaka faction. In Miyamoto, Hideyoshi was considered the greatest of heroes, and Musashi remembered how as a child he had sat at the hearth and listened to tales of the great warrior's prowess. These ideas formed in his youth lingered with him, and even now, if pressed to say which side he favored, he'd probably have said Osaka.

Musashi had since learned a few things and now recognized that his actions at the age of seventeen had been both mindless and devoid of accomplishment. For a man to serve his lord faithfully, it was not enough to jump blindly into the fray and brandish a lance. He must go all the way, to the brink of death.

"If a samurai dies with a prayer for his lord's victory on his lips, he has done something fine and meaningful," was the way Musashi would have put it now. But at the time neither he nor Matahachi had had any sense of loyalty. What they had been thirsting for was fame and glory, and more to the point, a means of gaining a livelihood without giving up anything of their own.

It was odd that they should have thought of it that way. Having since learned from Takuan that life is a jewel to be treasured, Musashi knew that far from giving up nothing, he and Matahachi had unwittingly been offering their most precious possession. Each had literally wagered everything he had on the hope of receiving a paltry stipend as a samurai. In retrospect, he wondered how they could have been so foolish.

He noticed that he was approaching Daigo, south of the city, and since he'd worked up quite a sweat, decided to stop for a rest.

From a distance, he heard a voice shouting, "Wait! Wait!" Gazing far down the steep mountain road, he made out the form of the little water sprite Jōtarō, running for all he was worth. Presently the boy's angry eyes were glaring into his.

"You lied to me!" Jōtarō shouted. "Why did you do that!" Breathless from running, face flushed, he spoke with belligerence, though it was clear he was on the verge of tears.

Musashi had to laugh at his getup. He had discarded the work clothes of the day before in favor of an ordinary kimono, but it was only half big enough for him, the skirt barely reaching his knees and the arms stopping at the elbows. At his side hung a wooden sword that was longer than the boy was tall, on his back a basket hat that looked as big as an umbrella.

Even as he shouted at Musashi for having left him behind, he burst into tears. Musashi hugged and tried to comfort him, but the boy wailed on, apparently feeling that in the mountains, with no one around, he could let himself go.

Finally Musashi said, "Does it make you feel good, acting like a crybaby?"

"I don't care!" Jōtarō sobbed. "You're a grownup, and yet you lied to me. You said you'd let me be your follower—then went off and left me. Are grownups supposed to act like that?"

"I'm sorry," said Musashi.

This simple apology turned the boy's crying into a pleading whine.

"Stop it now," said Musashi. "I didn't mean to lie to you, but you have a father and you have a master. I couldn't bring you with me unless your master consented. I told you to go and talk with him, didn't I? It didn't seem likely to me that he'd agree."

"Why didn't you at least wait until you heard the answer?"

"That's why I'm apologizing to you now. Did you really discuss this with him?"

"Yes." He got his sniffling under control and pulled two leaves from a tree, on which he blew his nose.

"And what did he say?"

"He told me to go ahead."

"Did he now?"

"He said no self-respecting warrior or training school would take on a boy like me, but since the samurai at the inn was a weakling, he ought to be just the right person. He said maybe you could use me to carry your luggage, and he gave me this wooden sword as a going-away present."

Musashi smiled at the man's line of reasoning.

"After that," continued the boy. "I went to the inn. The old man wasn't there, so I just borrowed this hat from off the hook under the eaves."

"But that's the inn's signboard; it has 'Lodgings' written on it."

"Oh, I don't mind. I need a hat in case it rains."

It was clear from Jōtarō's attitude that as far as he was concerned, all necessary promises and vows had been exchanged, and he was now Musashi's disciple. Sensing this, Musashi resigned himself to being more or less stuck with the child, but it also occurred to him that maybe it was all for the best. Indeed, when he considered his own part in Tanzaemon's loss of status, he concluded that perhaps he should be grateful for the opportunity to see to the boy's future. It seemed the right thing to do.

Jōtarō, now calm and reassured, suddenly remembered something and reached inside his kimono. "I almost forgot. I have something for you. Here it is." He pulled out a letter.

Eyeing it curiously, Musashi asked, "Where did you get that?"

"Remember last night I said there was a rōnin drinking at the shop, asking a lot of questions?"

"Yes."

"Well, when I went home, he was still there. He kept on asking about you. He's some drinker, too— drank a whole bottle of sake by himself! Then he wrote this letter and asked me to give it to you."

Musashi cocked his head to one side in puzzlement and broke the seal. Looking first at the bottom, he saw it was from Matahachi, who must have been drunk indeed. Even the characters looked tipsy. As Musashi read the scroll, he was seized with mixed feelings of nostalgia and sadness. Not only was the writing chaotic; the message itself was rambling and imprecise.

Since I left you at Mount Ibuki, I haven't forgotten the village. And I haven't forgotten my old friend. By accident I heard your name at the Yoshioka School. At the time, I got confused and couldn't decide whether to try to see you. Now I'm in a sake shop. I've had a lot to drink.

Thus far the meaning was clear enough, but from this point on the letter was difficult to follow.

Ever since I parted from you, I've been kept in a cage of lust, and idleness has eaten into my bones. For five years I've spent my days in a stupor, doing nothing. In the capital, you are now famous as a swordsman. I drink to you! Some people say Musashi is a coward, good only at running away. Some say you're an incomparable swordsman. I don't care which is true, I'm just happy that your sword has the people in the capital talking.

You're smart. You should be able to make your way with the sword. But as I look back, I wonder about me, the way I am now. I'm a fool! How can a stupid wretch like me face a wise friend like you without dying of shame?

But wait! Life is long, and it's too early to say what the future will bring. I don't want to see you now, but there will come a day when I will.

I pray for your health.

Then came a rapidly scrawled postscript informing him, at some length, that the Yoshioka School took a serious view of the recent incident, that they were looking everywhere for him, and that he should be careful about his movements. It ended: "You mustn't die now that you're just beginning to make a name for yourself. When I, too, have made something of myself, I want to see you and talk over old times. Take care of yourself, stay alive, so you can be an inspiration to me."

Matahachi had no doubt meant well, but there was something twisted about his attitude. Why must he praise Musashi so and in the next breath carry on so about his own failings? "Why," wondered Musashi, "couldn't he just write and say that it's been a long time, and why don't we get together and have a long talk?"

"Jō, did you ask this man for his address?"

"No."

"Did the people at the shop know him?"

"I don't think so."

"Did he come there often?"

"No, this was the first time."

Musashi was thinking that if he knew where Matahachi lived, he would go back to Kyoto right now to see him. He wanted to talk to his childhood comrade, try to bring him to his senses, reawaken in him the spirit he had once had. Since he still considered Matahachi to be his friend, he would have liked to pull him out of his present mood, with its apparently self-destructive tendencies. And of course, he would also have liked to have Matahachi explain to his mother what a mistake she was making.

The two walked on silently. They were on their

way down the mountain at Daigo, and the Rokujizō crossing was visible below them.

Abruptly Musashi turned to the boy and said, "Jō, there's something I want you to do for me."

"What is it?"

"I want you to go on an errand."

"Where to?"

"Kyoto."

"That means turning around and going back where I just came from."

"That's right. I want you to take a letter from me to the Yoshioka School on Shijō Avenue."

Jōtarō, crestfallen, kicked a rock with his toe.

"Don't you want to go?" asked Musashi, looking him in the face.

Jōtarō shook his head uncertainly. "I don't mind going, but aren't you just doing this to get rid of me?"

His suspicion made Musashi feel guilty, for wasn't he the one who had broken the child's faith in adults?

"No!" he said vigorously. "A samurai does not lie. Forgive me for what happened this morning. It was just a mistake."

"All right, I'll go."

Entering a teahouse at the crossroads known as Rokuamida, they ordered tea and ate lunch.

Musashi then wrote a letter, which he addressed to Yoshioka Seijūrō:

> I am told that you and your disciples are searching for me. As it happens, I am now on the Yamato highroad, my intention being to travel around in the general area of Iga and Ise for about a year to continue my study of swordsmanship. I do not wish to change my

plans at this time, but since I regret as much as you do that I was unable to meet you during my previous visit to your school, I should like to inform you that I shall certainly be back in the capital by the first or the second month of next year. Between now and then, I expect to improve my technique considerably. I trust that you yourself will not neglect your practice. It would be a great shame if Yoshioka Kempō's flourishing school were to suffer a second defeat like the one it sustained the last time I was there. In closing, I send my respectful wishes for your continued good health.

Shimmen Miyamoto Musashi Masana

Though the letter was polite, it left little doubt as to Musashi's confidence in himself. Having amended the address to include not only Seijūrō but all the disciples in the school, he laid down his brush and gave the letter to Jōtarō.

"Can I just throw it in at the school and come back?" the boy asked.

"No. You must call at the front entrance and hand it personally to the servant there."

"I understand."

"There's something else I want you to do, but it may be a little difficult."

"What is it?"

"I want you to see if you can find the man who gave you the letter. His name is Hon'iden Matahachi. He's an old friend of mine."

"That should be no trouble at all."

"You think not? Just how do you propose to do it?"

"Oh, I'll ask around at all the drinking shops."

Musashi laughed. "That's not a bad idea. I gather from Matahachi's letter, however, that he knows somebody at the Yoshioka School. I think it would be quicker to ask about him there."

"What do I do when I find him?"

"I want you to deliver a message. Tell him that from the first to the seventh day of the new year, I'll go every morning to the great bridge at Gojō Avenue and wait for him. Ask him to come on one of those days to meet me."

"Is that all?"

"Yes, but also tell him that I want very badly to see him."

"All right, I think I have it. Where will you be when I come back?"

"I'll tell you what. When I get to Nara, I'll arrange it so that you can find out where I am by asking at the Hōzōin. That's the temple that's famous for its lance technique."

"You'll really do that?"

"Ha, ha! You're still suspicious, aren't you? Don't worry. If I don't keep my promise this time, you can cut off my head."

Musashi was still laughing as he left the teahouse. Outside, he turned toward Nara, and Jōtarō set off in the opposite direction, toward Kyoto.

The crossroads was a jumble of people under basket hats, of swallows and of neighing horses. As the boy made his way through the throng, he looked back and saw Musashi standing where he had been, watching him. They smiled a distant farewell, and each went on his way.

13

A Spring Breeze

On the bank of the Takase River, Akemi was rinsing a strip of cloth and singing a song she had learned at the Okuni Kabuki. Each time she pulled at the flower-patterned cloth, it created an illusion of swirling cherry blossoms.

> The breeze of love
> Tugs at the sleeve of my kimono.
> Oh, the sleeve weighs heavy!
> Is the breeze of love heavy?

Jōtarō stood on top of the dike. His lively eyes surveyed the scene and he smiled amicably. "You sing well, Auntie," he called out.

"What's that?" asked Akemi. She looked up at the gnomelike child with his long wooden sword and his enormous basket hat. "Who are you?" she asked. "And what do you mean, calling me Auntie? I'm still young!"

"Okay—Sweet Young Girl. How's that?"

"Stop it," she said with a laugh. "You're much too little to be flirting. Why don't you blow your nose instead?"

"I only wanted to ask a question."

"Oh, my!" she cried in consternation. "There goes my cloth!"

"I'll get it for you."

Jōtarō chased down the riverbank after the cloth, then fished it out of the water with his sword. At least, he reflected, it comes in handy in a situation like this one. Akemi thanked him and asked what he wanted to know.

"Is there a teahouse around here called the Yomogi?"

"Why, yes, it's my house, right over there."

"Am I glad to hear that! I've spent a long time looking for it."

"Why? Where do you come from?"

"Over that way," he replied, pointing vaguely.

"And just where might that be?"

He hesitated. "I'm not really sure."

Akemi giggled. "Never mind. But why are you interested in our teahouse?"

"I'm looking for a man named Hon'iden Matahachi. They told me at the Yoshioka School that if I went to the Yomogi, I'd find him."

"He's not there."

"You're lying!"

"Oh, no; it's true. He used to stay with us, but he went off some time ago."

"Where to?"

"I don't know."

"But someone at your house must know!"

"No. My mother doesn't know either. He just ran away."

"Oh, no." The boy crouched down and stared worriedly into the river. "Now what am I supposed to do?" he sighed.

"Who sent you here?"

"My teacher."

"Who's your teacher?"

"His name is Miyamoto Musashi."

"Did you bring a letter?"

"No," said Jōtarō, shaking his head.

"A fine messenger you are! You don't know where you came from, and you don't have a letter with you."

"I have a message to deliver."

"What is it? He may never come back, but if he does, I'll tell him for you."

"I don't think I should do that, do you?"

"Don't ask me. Make up your own mind."

"Maybe I should, then. He said he wanted to see Matahachi very much. He said to tell Matahachi that he'd wait on the great bridge at Gojō Avenue every morning from the first day to the seventh day of the new year. Matahachi should meet him there on one of those days."

Akemi broke into uncontrollable laughter. "I never heard of such a thing! You mean he's sending a message *now* telling Matahachi to meet him next year? Your teacher must be as strange as you are! Ha, ha!"

A scowl came over Jōtarō's face, and his shoulders tensed with anger. "What's so funny?"

Akemi finally managed to stop laughing. "Now you're angry, aren't you?"

"Of course I am. I just asked you politely to do me a favor, and you start laughing like a lunatic."

"I'm sorry, I really am. I won't laugh anymore. And if Matahachi comes back, I'll give him your message."

"Is that a promise?"

"Yes, I swear." Biting her lips to avoid smiling, Akemi asked, "What was his name again? The man who sent you with the message."

"Your memory's not too good, is it? His name is Miyamoto Musashi."

"How do you write Musashi?"

Picking up a bamboo stick, Jōtarō scratched the two characters in the sand.

"Why, those are the characters for Takezō!" exclaimed Akemi.

"His name isn't Takezō. It's Musashi."

"Yes, but they can also be read Takezō."

"Stubborn, aren't you?" snapped Jōtarō, tossing the bamboo stick into the river.

Akemi stared fixedly at the characters in the sand, lost in thought. Finally she lifted her gaze from the ground to Jōtarō, reexamined him from head to toe, and in a soft voice asked, "I wonder if Musashi is from the Yoshino area in Mimasaka."

"Yes. I'm from Harima; he's from the village of Miyamoto in the neighboring province of Mimasaka."

"Is he tall and manly? And does he leave the top of his head unshaved?"

"Yes. How did you know?"

"I remember him telling me once that when he was a child he had a carbuncle on the top of his head. If he shaved it the way samurai usually do, you would see an ugly scar."

"Told you? When?"

"Oh, it's been five years now."

"Have you known my teacher that long?"

Akemi did not answer. The memory of those days evoked stirrings in her heart that made even speaking difficult. Convinced from the little the boy had said that Musashi was Takezō, she was gripped by a yearning to see him again. She had seen her mother's way of doing things, and she had watched Matahachi go from bad to worse. From the first, she had preferred Takezō and had since grown more and more confident in the rightness of his choice. She was glad to be still single. Takezō—he was so different from Matahachi.

Many were the times she had resolved to never let herself wind up with the likes of the men who always drank at the teahouse. She scorned them, holding on firmly to the image of Takezō. Deep within her heart, she nourished the dream of finding him again; he, only he, was the lover in her mind when she sang love songs to herself.

His mission fulfilled, Jōtarō said, "Well, I'd better be going now. If you find Matahachi, be sure to tell him what I told you." He hurried off, trotting along the narrow top of the dike.

The oxcart was loaded with a mountain of sacks, containing rice perhaps, or lentil beans, or some other local product. On top of the pile, a plaque proclaimed that this was a contribution being sent by faithful Buddhists to the great Kōfukuji in Nara. Even Jōtarō knew of this temple, for its name was virtually synonymous with Nara.

Jōtarō's face lit up with childish joy. Chasing after the vehicle, he climbed up on back. If he faced backward, there was just enough room to sit down. As an added luxury, he had the sacks to lean against.

On either side of the road, the rolling hills were covered with neat rows of tea bushes. The cherry trees had begun to bloom, and farmers were plowing their barley—praying, no doubt, that this year it would once again be safe from the trampling feet of soldiers and horses. Women knelt by the streams washing their vegetables. The Yamato highroad was at peace.

"What luck!" thought Jōtarō, as he settled back and relaxed. Comfortable on his perch, he was tempted to go to sleep but thought better of it. Fearing they might reach Nara before he awoke, he was thankful every time the wheels struck a rock and the wagon shook, since it helped him keep his eyes open. Nothing could have given him more pleasure than to be not only moving along like this but actually heading toward his destination.

Outside one village, Jōtarō lazily reached out and plucked a leaf from a camellia tree. Putting it to his tongue, he began to whistle a tune.

The wagon driver looked back, but could see nothing. Since the whistling went on and on, he looked over his left shoulder, then his right shoulder, several more times. Finally he stopped the wagon and walked around to the back. The sight of Jōtarō threw him into a rage, and the blow from his fist was so sharp the boy cried out in pain.

"What're you doing up there?" he snarled.

"It's all right, isn't it?"

"It is not all right!"

"Why not? You're not pulling it yourself!"

"You impudent little bastard!" shouted the driver, tossing Jōtarō onto the ground like a ball. He bounced and rolled against the foot of a tree. Starting off with a rumble, the wheels of the wagon seemed to be laughing at him.

Jōtarō picked himself up and began to search carefully around on the ground. He'd just noticed he no longer had the bamboo tube containing the reply from the Yoshioka School to Musashi. He had hung it from his neck with a cord, but now it was gone.

As the totally distraught boy gradually widened the area of his search, a young woman in traveling clothes, who had stopped to watch him, asked, "Did you lose something?"

He glanced at her face, which was partially hidden by a broad-brimmed hat, nodded and resumed his search.

"Was it money?"

Jōtarō, thoroughly absorbed, paid little attention to the question, but managed a negative grunt.

"Well, was it a bamboo tube about a foot long with a cord attached?"

Jōtarō jumped up. "Yes! How did you know?"

"So it was you the drivers near the Mampukuji were yelling at for teasing their horse!"

"Ah-h-h . . . well . . ."

"When you got scared and ran, the cord must've broken. The tube fell on the road, and the samurai who'd been talking to the drivers picked it up. Why don't you go back and ask him about it?"

"Are you sure?"

"Yes, of course."

"Thanks."

Just as he started to run off, the young woman called after him. "Wait! There's no need to go back. I can see the samurai coming this way. The one in the field *hakama*." She pointed toward the man.

Jōtarō stopped and waited, eyes wide.

The samurai was an impressive man of about forty. Everything about him was a little bigger than life—his height, his jet-black beard, his broad shoulders, his massive chest. He wore leather socks and straw sandals, and when he walked, his firm footsteps seemed to compact the earth. Jōtarō, certain at a glance that this was a great warrior in the service of one of the more prominent daimyō, felt too frightened to address him.

Fortunately, the samurai spoke first, summoning the boy. "Weren't you the imp who dropped this bamboo tube in front of the Mampukuji?" he asked.

"Oh, that's it! You found it!"

"Don't you know how to say thank you?"

"I'm sorry. Thank you, sir."

"I daresay there's an important letter inside. When your master sends you on a mission, you shouldn't be stopping along the way to tease horses, hitching rides on wagons, or loafing by the wayside."

"Yes, sir. Did you look inside, sir?"

"It's only natural when you've found something to examine it and return it to its owner, but I did not break the seal on the letter. Now that you have it back, you should check and see that it's in good order."

Jōtarō took the cap from the tube and peered inside. Satisfied that the letter was still there, he hung the tube from his neck and swore not to lose it a second time.

The young woman looked as pleased as Jōtarō. "It was very kind of you, sir," she said to the samurai, in an attempt to make up for Jōtarō's inability to express himself properly.

The bearded samurai started walking along with the two of them. "Is the boy with you?" he asked her.

"Oh, no. I've never seen him before."

The samurai laughed. "I thought you made a rather strange pair. He's a funny-looking little devil, isn't he—'Lodgings' written on his hat and all?"

"Perhaps it's his youthful innocence that's so appealing. I like him too." Turning to Jōtarō, she asked, "Where are you going?"

Walking along between them, Jōtarō was once again in high spirits. "Me? I'm going to Nara, to the Hōzōin." A long, narrow object wrapped in gold brocade and nestled in the girl's obi caught his eye. Staring at it, he said, "I see you have a letter tube too. Be careful you don't lose it."

"Letter tube? What do you mean?"

"There, in your obi."

She laughed. "This isn't a letter tube, silly! It's a flute."

"A flute?" Eyes burning with curiosity, Jōtarō unabashedly moved his head close to her waist to inspect the object. Suddenly, a strange feeling came over him. He pulled back and seemed to be examining the girl.

Even children have a sense of feminine beauty, or at least they understand instinctively whether a woman is pure or not. Jōtarō was impressed with the girl's loveliness and respected it. It seemed to him an unimaginable stroke of good luck that he should be walking along with one so pretty. His heart throbbed and he felt giddy.

"I see. A flute . . . Do you play the flute, Auntie?"

he asked. Then, obviously remembering Akemi's reaction to the word, he abruptly changed his question.
"What's your name?"

The girl laughed and cast an amused glance over
the boy's head at the samurai. The bearlike warrior
joined in the laughter, displaying a row of strong white
teeth behind his beard.

"You're a fine one, you are! When you ask
someone's name, it's only good manners to state your
own first."

"My name's Jōtarō."

This brought forth more laughter.

"That's not fair!" cried Jōtarō. "You made me
tell my name, but I still don't know yours. What's
your name, sir?"

"My name's Shōda," said the samurai.

"That must be your family name. What's your
other name?"

"I'll have to ask you to let me off on that one."

Undaunted, Jōtarō turned to the girl and said,
"Now it's your turn. We told you our names. It
wouldn't be polite for you not to tell us yours."

"Mine is Otsū."

"Otsū?" Jōtarō repeated. He seemed satisfied for
a moment, but then chattered on. "Why do you go
around with a flute in your obi?"

"Oh, I need this to make my living."

"Are you a flute player by profession?"

"Well, I'm not sure there's any such thing as a
professional flute player, but the money I get for
playing makes it possible for me to take long trips like
this one. I suppose you could call it my profession."

"Is the music you play like the music I've heard

at Gion and the Kamo Shrine? The music for the sacred dances?''

''No.''

''Is it like the music for other kinds of dancing— Kabuki maybe?''

''No.''

''Then what kind do you play?''

''Oh, just ordinary melodies.''

The samurai had meanwhile been wondering about Jōtarō's long wooden sword. ''What's that you've got stuck in your waist?'' he asked.

''Don't you know a wooden sword when you see one? I thought you were a samurai.''

''Yes, I am. I'm just surprised to see one on you. Why are you carrying it?''

''I'm going to study swordsmanship.''

''Oh, are you now? Do you have a teacher yet?''

''I do.''

''And is he the person to whom the letter is addressed?''

''Yes.''

''If he's your teacher, he must be a *real* expert.''

''He's not all that good.''

''What do you mean?''

''Everybody says he's weak.''

''Doesn't it bother you to have a weak man for a teacher?''

''No. I'm no good with the sword either, so it doesn't make any difference.''

The samurai could hardly contain his amusement. His mouth quivered as if to break into a smile, but his eyes remained grave. ''Have you learned any techniques?''

"Well, not exactly. I haven't learned anything at all yet."

The samurai's laughter finally burst forth. "Walking with you makes the road seem shorter! . . . And you, young lady, where are you going?"

"Nara, but exactly where in Nara I don't know. There's a rōnin I've been trying to locate for a year or so, and since I've heard that a lot of them have gathered in Nara recently, I'm planning to go there, though I admit the rumor's not much to go on."

The bridge at Uji came into view. Under the eaves of a teahouse, a very proper old man with a large teakettle was purveying his stock-in-trade to his customers, who were seated around him on stools. Catching sight of Shōda, he greeted him warmly. "How nice to see someone from the House of Yagyū!" he called. "Come in, come in!"

"We'd just like to take a short rest. Could you bring the boy here some sweet cakes?"

Jōtarō remained on his feet while his companions sat. To him, the idea of sitting down and resting was a bore; once the cakes arrived, he grabbed them and ran up the low hill behind the teahouse.

Otsū, sipping her tea, inquired of the old man, "Is it still a long way to Nara?"

"Yes. Even a fast walker'd probably get no farther than Kizu before sunset. A girl like you should plan to spend the night at Taga or Ide."

Shōda spoke up immediately. "This young lady has been searching for someone for months. But I wonder, do you think it's safe these days for a young woman to travel to Nara alone, with no place to stay in mind?"

The old man grew wide-eyed at the question.

"She shouldn't even consider it!" he said decisively. Turning to Otsū, he waved his hand back and forth before his face and said, "Give the idea up entirely. If you were sure you had someone to stay with, it'd be a different matter. If you don't, Nara can be a very dangerous place."

The proprietor poured a cup of tea for himself and told them what he knew of the situation in Nara. Most people, it seemed, had the impression that the old capital was a quiet, peaceful place where there were lots of colorful temples and tame deer—a place undisturbed by war or famine—but in fact the town was no longer like that at all. After the Battle of Sekigahara, nobody knew how many rōnin from the losing side had come to hide there. Most of them were Osaka partisans from the Western Army, samurai who now had no income and little hope of finding another profession. With the Tokugawa shogunate growing in power year by year, it was doubtful whether these fugitives would ever again be able to make a living out in the open with their swords.

According to most estimates, 120,000 to 130,000 samurai had lost their positions. Being the victors, the Tokugawas had confiscated estates representing an annual income of 33 million bushels of rice. Even if the feudal lords who had since been allowed to reestablish themselves on a more modest scale were taken into consideration, at least eighty daimyō, with incomes thought to total 20 million bushels, had been dispossessed. On the basis that for every 500 bushels, three samurai had been cut loose from their moorings and forced into hiding in various provinces—and including their families and retainers—the total number could not be less than 100,000.

The area around Nara and Mount Kōya was full of temples and therefore difficult for the Tokugawa forces to patrol. By the same token, it was an ideal hiding place, and the fugitives moved there in droves.

"Why," said the old man, "the famous Sanada Yukimura is in hiding at Mount Kudo, and Sengoku Sōya is said to be in the vicinity of the Hōryūji, and Ban Dan'emon at the Kōfukuji. I could name many more." All these were marked men, who would be killed instantly if they showed themselves; their one hope for the future was for war to break out again.

The old man's opinion was that it wouldn't be so bad if it were only these famous rōnin hiding out, since they all had a degree of prestige and could make a living for themselves and their families. Complicating the picture, however, were the indigent samurai who prowled the city's back streets in such straits that they'd sell their swords if they could. Half of them had taken to picking fights, gambling and otherwise disturbing the peace, in the hope that the havoc they caused would make the Osaka forces rise up and take arms. The once tranquil city of Nara had turned into a nest of desperadoes. For a nice girl like Otsū to go there would be tantamount to her pouring oil on her kimono and jumping into a fire. The teahouse proprietor, stirred by his own recitation, concluded by strongly begging Otsū to change her mind.

Now doubtful, Otsū sat silently for a while. If she had had the slightest indication that Musashi might be in Nara, she would not have given danger a second thought. But she really had nothing to go on. She had merely wandered toward Nara—just as she had wandered around to various other places in the year since Musashi had left her stranded at the bridge in Himeji.

Shōda, seeing the perplexity on her face, said, "You said your name is Otsū, didn't you?"

"Yes."

"Well, Otsū, I hesitate to say this, but why don't you give up the idea of going to Nara and come with me to the Koyagyū fief instead?" Feeling obliged to tell her more about himself and assure her that his intentions were honorable, he continued, "My full name is Shōda Kizaemon, and I'm in the service of the Yagyū family. It happens that my lord, who's now eighty, is no longer active. He suffers terribly from boredom. When you said you make your living by playing the flute, it occurred to me that it might be a great comfort to him if you were around to play for him from time to time. Do you think you'd like that?"

The old man immediately chimed in with enthusiastic approval. "You should definitely go with him," he urged. "As you probably know, the old lord of Koyagyū is the great Yagyū Muneyoshi. Now that he's retired, he's taken the name Sekishūsai. As soon as his heir, Munenori, lord of Tajima, returned from Sekigahara, he was summoned to Edo and appointed an instructor in the shōgun's household. Why, there's no greater family in Japan than the Yagyūs. To be invited to Koyagyū is an honor in itself. Please, by all means, accept!"

On hearing that Kizaemon was an official in the famous House of Yagyū, Otsū congratulated herself for having guessed that he was no ordinary samurai. Still, she found it difficult to reply to his proposal.

Faced with her silence, Kizaemon asked, "Don't you want to come?"

"It's not that. I couldn't wish for a better offer.

I'm simply afraid my playing isn't good enough for a great man like Yagyū Muneyoshi.''

"Oh, don't give it a second thought. The Yagyūs are very different from the other daimyō. Sekishūsai in particular has the simple, quiet tastes of a teamaster. He would be more upset, I think, by your diffidence than by what you fancy to be your lack of skill.''

Otsū realized that going to Koyagyū, rather than wandering aimlessly to Nara, offered some hope, however slight. Since the death of Yoshioka Kempō, the Yagyūs had been considered by many to be the greatest exponents of the martial arts in the country. It was only to be expected that swordsmen from all over the country would call at their gate, and there might even be a registry of visitors. How happy she would be if on that list she found the name of Miyamoto Musashi!

With that possibility foremost in mind, she said brightly, "If you really think it's all right, I'll go.''

"You will? Wonderful! I'm very grateful. . . . Hmm, I doubt that a woman could walk all the way there before nightfall. Can you ride a horse?''

"Yes.''

Kizaemon ducked under the eaves of the shop and raised his hand toward the bridge. The groom waiting there came running forward with a horse, which Kizaemon let Otsū ride, while he himself walked along beside her.

Jōtarō spotted them from the hill behind the teahouse and called, "Are you leaving already?''

"Yes, we're off.''

"Wait for me!''

They were halfway across Uji Bridge when Jōtarō caught up with them. Kizaemon asked him what he had been up to, and he answered that a lot of men in a grove on the hill were playing some kind of game. He didn't know what game it was, but it looked interesting.

The groom laughed. "That would be the rōnin riffraff having a gambling session. They don't have enough money to eat, so they lure travelers into their games and take them for everything they're worth. It's disgraceful!"

"Oh, so they gamble for a living?" asked Kizaemon.

"The gamblers are among the better ones," replied the groom. "Many others have become kidnappers and blackmailers. They're such a rough lot nobody can do anything to stop them."

"Why doesn't the lord of the district arrest them or drive them away?"

"There are too many of them—far more than he can cope with. If all the rōnin from Kawachi, Yamato and Kii joined together, they'd be stronger than his own troops."

"I hear Kōga's swarming with them too."

"Yes. The ones from Tsutsui fled there. They're determined to hang on until the next war."

"You keep talking that way about the rōnin," Jōtarō broke in, "but some of them must be good men."

"That's true," agreed Kizaemon.

"My teacher's a rōnin!"

Kizaemon laughed and said, "So that's why you spoke up in their defense. You're loyal enough. . . . You did say you were on your way to the Hōzōin, didn't you? Is that where your teacher is?"

"I don't know for sure, but he said if I went there, they'd tell me where he is."

"What style does he use?"

"I don't know."

"You're his disciple, and you don't know his style?"

"Sir," the groom put in, "swordsmanship is a fad these days; everybody and his brother's going around studying it. You can meet five or ten wandering on this road alone any day of the week. It's all because there are so many more rōnin around to give lessons than there used to be."

"I suppose that's part of it."

"They're attracted to it because they hear somewhere that if a fellow's good with a sword, the daimyō will fall all over each other trying to hire him for four or five thousand bushels a year."

"A quick way to get rich, uh?"

"Exactly. When you think about it, it's frightening. Why, even this boy here has a wooden sword. He probably thinks he just has to learn how to hit people with it to become a real man. We get a lot like that, and the sad part is, in the end, most of them will go hungry."

Jōtarō's anger rose in a flash. "What's that? I dare you to say that again!"

"Listen to him! He looks like a flea carrying a toothpick, but he already fancies himself a great warrior."

Kizaemon laughed. "Now, Jōtarō, don't get mad, or you'll lose your bamboo tube again."

"No I won't! Don't worry about me!"

They walked on, Jōtarō sulking silently, the others looking at the sun as it slowly set. Presently they arrived at the Kizu River ferry landing.

"This is where we leave you, my boy. It'll be dark soon, so you'd better hurry. And don't waste time along the way."

"Otsū?" said Jōtarō, thinking she would come with him.

"Oh, I forgot to tell you," she said. "I've decided to go along with this gentleman to the castle at Koyagyū." Jōtarō looked crushed. "Take good care of yourself," Otsū said, smiling.

"I should've known I'd wind up alone again." He picked up a stone and sent it skimming across the water.

"Oh, we'll see each other again one of these days. Your home seems to be the road, and I do a bit of traveling myself."

Jōtarō didn't seem to want to move. "Just who are you looking for?" he asked. "What sort of person?"

Without answering, Otsū waved farewell.

Jōtarō ran along the bank and jumped into the very middle of the small ferryboat. When the boat, red in the evening sun, was halfway across the river, he looked back. He could just make out Otsū's horse and Kizaemon on the Kasagi Temple road. They were in the valley, beyond the point where the river suddenly grows narrower, slowly being swallowed up by the early shadows of the mountain.

14

The Hōzōin

Students of the martial arts invariably knew of the Hōzōin. For a man who claimed to be a serious student to refer to it as just another temple was sufficient reason for him to be regarded as an imposter. It was well known among the local populace too, though, oddly enough, few were familiar with the much more important Shōsōin Repository and its priceless collection of ancient art objects.

The temple was located on Abura Hill in a large, dense forest of cryptomeria trees. It was just the kind of place goblins might inhabit. Here, too, were reminders of the glories of the Nara period—the ruins of a temple, the Ganrin'in, and of the huge public bathhouse built by the Empress Kōmyō for the poor—but today all that was left was a scattering of foundation stones peeking out through the moss and weeds.

Musashi had no difficulty getting directions to Abura Hill, but once there he stood looking all around in bewilderment, for there were quite a few other temples nestled in the forest. The cryptomerias had weathered the winter and been bathed in the early spring rains, and their leaves were now at their darkest. Above them one could make out in the approaching twilight the soft feminine curves of Mount Kasuga. The distant mountains still lay in bright sunlight.

Although none of the temples looked like the right one, Musashi went from gate to gate inspecting the plaques on which their names were inscribed. His mind was so preoccupied with the Hōzōin that when he saw the plaque of the Ōzōin, he at first misread it, since only the first character, that for Ō, was different. Although he immediately realized his mistake, he took a look inside anyway. The Ōzōin appeared to belong to the Nichiren sect; as far as he knew, the Hōzōin was a Zen temple having no connection with Nichiren.

As he stood there, a young monk returning to the Ōzōin passed by him, staring suspiciously.

Musashi removed his hat and said, "Could I trouble you for some information?"

"What would you like to know?"

"This temple is called the Ōzōin?"

"Yes. That's what it says on the plaque."

"I was told that the Hōzōin is on Abura Hill. Isn't it?"

"It's just in back of this temple. Are you going there for a fencing bout?"

"Yes."

"Then let me give you some advice. Forget it."

"Why?"

"It's dangerous. I can understand someone born crippled going there to get his legs straightened out, but I see no reason why anyone with good straight limbs should go there and be maimed."

The monk was well built and somehow different from the ordinary Nichiren monk. According to him, the number of would-be warriors had reached the point where even the Hōzōin had come to regard them as a nuisance. The temple was, after all, a holy sanctuary for the light of the Buddha's Law, as its name indicated. Its real concern was religion. The martial arts were only a sideline, so to speak.

Kakuzenbō In'ei, the former abbot, had often called on Yagyū Muneyoshi. Through his association with Muneyoshi and with Lord Kōizumi of Ise, Muneyoshi's friend, he had developed an interest in the martial arts and eventually taken up swordsmanship as a pastime. From that he had gone on to devise new ways of using the lance, and this, as Musashi already knew, was the origin of the highly regarded Hōzōin Style.

In'ei was now eighty-four years old and completely senile. He saw almost no one. Even when he did receive a caller, he was unable to carry on a conversation; he could only sit and make unintelligible movements with his toothless mouth. He didn't seem to comprehend anything said to him. As for the lance, he had forgotten about it completely.

"And so you see," concluded the monk after explaining all this, "it wouldn't do you much good to go there. You probably couldn't meet the master, and even if you did, you wouldn't learn anything." His brusque manner made it clear that he was eager to be rid of Musashi.

Though aware he was being made light of, Musashi persisted. "I've heard about In'ei, and I know what you've said about him is true. But I've also heard that a priest named Inshun has taken over as his successor. They say he's still studying but already knows all the secrets of the Hōzōin Style. According to what I've heard, although he already has many students, he never refuses to give guidance to anyone who calls on him.''

"Oh, Inshun," said the monk disdainfully. "There's nothing in those rumors. Inshun is actually a student of the abbot of the Ōzōin. After In'ei began to show his age, our abbot felt it would be a shame for the reputation of the Hōzōin to go to waste, so he taught Inshun the secrets of lance fighting—what he himself had learned from In'ei—and then saw to it that Inshun became abbot.''

"I see," said Musashi.

"But you still want to go over there?''

"Well, I've come all this distance. . . .''

"Yes, of course.''

"You said it's behind here. Is it better to go around to the left or to the right?''

"You don't have to go around. It's much quicker just to walk straight through our temple. You can't miss it.''

Thanking him, Musashi walked past the temple kitchen to the back of the compound, which with its woodshed, a storehouse for bean paste and a vegetable garden of an acre or so, very much resembled the area around the house of a well-to-do farmer. Beyond the garden he saw the Hōzōin.

Walking on the soft ground between rows of rape, radishes and scallions, he noticed, off to one side, an old man hoeing vegetables. Hunched over his hoe, he was looking intently at the blade. All Musashi could see of his face was a pair of snow-white eyebrows, and save for the clank of the hoe against the rocks, it was perfectly quiet.

Musashi assumed that the old man must be a monk from the Ōzōin. He started to speak, but the man was so absorbed in his work that it seemed rude to disturb him.

As he walked silently by, however, he suddenly became aware that the old man was staring out of the corner of his eye at Musashi's feet. Although the other man neither moved nor spoke, Musashi felt a terrifying force attack him—a force like lightning splitting the clouds. This was no daydream. He actually felt the mysterious power pierce his body and, terrified, he leaped into the air. He felt hot all over, as if he'd just narrowly avoided a death blow from a sword or lance.

Looking over his shoulder, he saw that the hunched back was still turned toward him, the hoe continuing its unbroken rhythm. "What on earth was that all about?" he wondered, dumbfounded by the power he'd been hit with.

He found himself in front of the Hōzōin, his curiosity unabated. While waiting for a servant to appear, he thought: "Inshun should still be a young man. The young monk said In'ei was senile and had forgotten all about the lance, but I wonder. . . ." The incident in the garden lingered in the back of his mind.

He called out loudly two more times, but the only reply was an echo from the surrounding trees. Noticing a large gong beside the entrance, he struck it. Almost immediately an answering call came from deep inside the temple.

A priest came to the door. He was big and brawny; had he been one of the warrior-priests of Mount Hiei, he might well have been the commander of a battalion. Accustomed as he was to receiving visits from people like Musashi day in and day out, he gave him a brief glance and said, "You're a *shu-gyōsha?*"

"Yes."

"What are you here for?"

"I'd like to meet the master."

The priest said, "Come in," and gestured to the right of the entrance, suggesting obliquely that Musashi should wash his feet first. There was a barrel overflowing with water supplied by a bamboo pipe and, pointing this way and that, about ten pairs of worn and dirty sandals.

Musashi followed the priest down a wide dark corridor and was shown into an anteroom. There he was told to wait. The smell of incense was in the air, and through the window he could see the broad leaves of a plantain tree. Aside from the offhand manner of the giant who'd let him in, nothing he saw indicated there was anything unusual about this particular temple.

When he reappeared, the priest handed him a registry and ink box, saying, "Write down your name, where you studied, and what style you use." He spoke as though instructing a child.

The title on the registry was: "List of Persons Visiting This Temple to Study. Steward of the Hō-zōin." Musashi opened the book and glanced over the names, each listed under the date on which the samurai or student had called. Following the style of the last entry, he wrote down the required information, omitting the name of his teacher.

The priest, of course, was especially interested in that.

Musashi's answer was essentially the one he'd given at the Yoshioka School. He had practiced the use of the truncheon under his father, "without working very hard at it." Since making up his mind to study in earnest, he had taken as his teacher everything in the universe, as well as the examples set by his predecessors throughout the country. He ended up by saying, "I'm still in the process of learning."

"Mm. You probably know this already, but since the time of our first master, the Hōzōin has been celebrated everywhere for its lance techniques. The fighting that goes on here is rough, and there are no exceptions. Before you go on, perhaps you'd better read what's written at the beginning of the registry."

Musashi picked up the book, opened it and read the stipulation, which he had skipped over before. It said: "Having come here for the purpose of study, I absolve the temple of all responsibility in the event that I suffer bodily injury or am killed."

"I agree to that," said Musashi with a slight grin—it amounted to no more than common sense for anyone committed to becoming a warrior.

"All right. This way."

The dōjō was immense. The monks must have sacrificed a lecture hall or some other large temple building in favor of having it. Musashi had never before seen a hall with columns of such girth, and he also observed traces of paint, gold foil and Chinese-white primer on the frame of the transom—things not to be found in ordinary practice halls.

He was by no means the only visitor. More than ten student-warriors were seated in the waiting area, with a similar number of student-priests. In addition, there were quite a few samurai who seemed to be merely observers. All were tensely watching two lancers fighting a practice bout. No one even glanced Musashi's way as he sat down in a corner.

According to a sign on the wall, if anyone wanted to fight with real lances, the challenge would be accepted, but the combatants now on the floor were using long oak practice poles. A strike could, nevertheless, be extremely painful, even fatal.

One of the fighters was eventually thrown in the air, and as he limped back to his seat in defeat, Musashi could see that his thigh had already swollen to the size of a tree trunk. Unable to sit down, he dropped awkwardly to one knee and extended the wounded leg out before him.

"Next!" came the summons from the man on the floor, a priest of singularly arrogant manner. The sleeves of his robe were tied up behind him, and his whole body—legs, arms, shoulders, even his forehead—seemed to consist of bulging muscles. The oak pole he held vertically was at least ten feet in length.

A man who seemed to be one of those who'd arrived that day spoke up. He fastened up his sleeves with a leather thong and strode into the practice area. The priest stood motionless as the challenger went to the wall, chose a halberd, and came to face him. They bowed, as was customary, but no sooner had they done this than the priest let out a howl like that of a wild hound, simultaneously bringing his pole down forcefully on the challenger's skull.

"Next," he called, reverting to his original position.

That was all: the challenger was finished. While he did not appear to be dead yet, the simple act of lifting his head from the floor was more than he could manage. A couple of the student-priests went out and dragged him back by the sleeves and waist of his kimono. On the floor behind him stretched a thread of saliva mixed with blood.

"Next!" shouted the priest again, as surly as ever.

At first Musashi thought he was the second-generation master Inshun, but the men sitting around him said no, he was Agon, one of the senior disciples who were known as the "Seven Pillars of the Hōzōin." Inshun himself, they said, never had to engage in a bout, because challengers were always put down by one of these.

"Is there no one else?" bellowed Agon, now holding his practice lance horizontally.

The brawny steward was comparing his registry with the faces of the waiting men. He pointed at one.

"No, not today. . . . I'll come again some other time."

"How about you?"

"No. I don't feel quite up to it today."

One by one they backed out, until Musashi saw the finger pointing at him.

"How about you?"

"If you please."

" 'If you please'? What's that supposed to mean?"

"It means I'd like to fight."

All eyes focused on Musashi as he rose. The haughty Agon had retired from the floor and was talking and laughing animatedly with a group of priests, but when it appeared that another challenger had been found, a bored look came over his face, and he said lazily, "Somebody take over for me."

"Go ahead," they urged. "There's only one more."

Giving in, Agon walked nonchalantly back to the center of the floor. He took a fresh grip on the shiny black wooden pole, with which he seemed totally familiar. In quick order, he assumed an attacking stance, turned his back on Musashi, and charged off in the other direction.

"Yah-h-h-h!" Screaming like an enraged roc, he hurtled toward the back wall and thrust his lance viciously into a section used for practice purposes. The boards had been recently replaced, but despite the resilience of the new wood, Agon's bladeless lance plowed straight through.

"Yow-w-w!" His grotesque scream of triumph reverberated through the hall as he disengaged the lance and started to dance, rather than walk, back toward Musashi, steam rising from his muscle-bound body. Taking a stance some distance away, he glared at his latest challenger ferociously. Musashi had come forward with only his wooden sword and now stood quite still, looking a little surprised.

"Ready!" cried Agon.

A dry laugh was heard outside the window, and a voice said, "Agon, don't be a fool! Look, you stupid oaf, look! That's not a board you're about to take on."

Without relaxing his stance, Agon looked toward the window. "Who's there?" he bellowed.

The laughter continued, and then there came into view above the windowsill, as though it had been hung there by an antique dealer, a shinny pate and a pair of snow-white eyebrows.

"It won't do you any good, Agon. Not this time.

Let the man wait until the day after tomorrow, when Inshun returns."

Musashi, who had also turned his head toward the window, saw that the face belonged to the old man he had seen on his way to the Hōzōin, but no sooner had he realized this than the head disappeared.

Agon heeded the old man's warning to the extent of relaxing his hold on his weapon, but the minute his eyes met Musashi's again, he swore in the direction of the now empty window—and ignored the advice he had received.

As Agon tightened his grip on his lance, Musashi asked, for the sake of form, "Are you ready now?"

This solicitude drove Agon wild. His muscles were like steel, and when he jumped, he did so with awesome lightness. His feet seemed to be on the floor and in the air at the same time, quivering like moonlight on ocean waves.

Musashi stood perfectly still, or so it seemed. There was nothing unusual about his stance; he held his sword straight out with both hands, but being slightly smaller than his opponent and not so conspicuously muscular, he looked almost casual. The greatest difference was in the eyes. Musashi's were as sharp as a bird's, their pupils a clear coral tinted with blood.

Agon shook his head, perhaps to shake off the streams of sweat pouring down from his forehead, perhaps to shake off the old man's warning words. Had they lingered on? Was he attempting to cast them out of his mind? Whatever the reason, he was extremely agitated. He repeatedly shifted his position, trying to draw out Musashi, but Musashi remained motionless.

Agon's lunge was accompanied by a piercing

scream. In the split second that decided the encounter, Musashi parried and counterattacked.

"What happened?"

Agon's fellow priests hastily ran forward and crowded around him in a black circle. In the general confusion, some tripped over his practice lance and went sprawling.

A priest stood up, his hands and chest smeared with blood, shouting, "Medicine! Bring the medicine. Quick!"

"You won't need any medicine." It was the old man, who had come in the front entrance and quickly assessed the situation. His face turned sour. "If I'd thought medicine would save him, I wouldn't have tried to stop him in the first place. The idiot!"

No one paid any attention to Musashi. For lack of anything better to do, he walked to the front door and began putting his sandals on.

The old man followed him. "You!" he said.

Over his shoulder, Musashi replied, "Yes?"

"I'd like to have a few words with you. Come back inside."

He led Musashi to a room behind the practice hall—a simple, square cell, the only opening in the four walls being the door.

After they were seated, the old man said, "It would be more proper for the abbot to come and greet you, but he's on a trip and won't be back for two or three days. So I'll act on his behalf."

"This is very kind of you," said Musashi, bowing his head. "I'm grateful for the good training I received today, but I feel I should apologize for the unfortunate way it turned out—"

"Why? Things like that happen. You have to be

ready to accept it before you start fighting. Don't let it worry you."

"How are Agon's injuries?"

"He was killed instantly," said the old man. The breath with which he spoke felt like a cold wind on Musashi's face.

"He's dead?" To himself, he said: "So, it's happened again." Another life cut short by his wooden sword. He closed his eyes and in his heart called on the name of the Buddha, as he had on similar occasions in the past.

"Young man!"

"Yes sir."

"Is your name Miyamoto Musashi?"

"That's correct."

"Under whom did you study the martial arts?"

"I've had no teacher in the ordinary sense. My father taught me how to use the truncheon when I was young. Since then, I've picked up a number of points from older samurai in various provinces. I've also spent some time traveling about the countryside, learning from the mountains and the rivers. I regard them, too, as teachers."

"You seem to have the right attitude. But you're so strong! Much too strong!"

Believing he was being praised, Musashi blushed and said, "Oh, no! I'm still immature. I'm always making blunders."

"That's not what I mean. Your strength is your problem. You must learn to control it, become weaker."

"What?" Musashi asked perplexedly.

"You will recall that a short while ago you passed through the vegetable garden where I was at work."

"Yes."

"When you saw me, you jumped away, didn't you?"

"Yes."

"Why did you do that?"

"Well, somehow I imagined that you might use your hoe as a weapon and strike my legs with it. Then, too, though your attention seemed to be focused on the ground, my whole body felt transfixed by your eyes. I felt something murderous in that look, as though you were searching for my weak spot—so as to attack it."

The old man laughed. "It was the other way around. When you were still fifty feet from me, I perceived what you call 'something murderous' in the air. I sensed it in the tip of my hoe—that's how strongly your fighting spirit and ambition manifest themselves in every step you take. I knew I had to be prepared to defend myself.

"If it had been one of the local farmers passing by, I myself would have been no more than an old man tending vegetables. True, you sensed belligerence in me, but it was only a reflection of your own."

So Musashi had been right in thinking, even before they first exchanged words, that here was no ordinary man. Now he keenly felt that the priest was the master, and he the pupil. His attitude toward the old man with the bent back became appropriately deferential.

"I thank you for the lesson you have given me. May I ask your name and your position in this temple?"

"Oh, I don't belong to the Hōzōin. I'm the abbot of the Ōzōin. My name is Nikkan."

"I see."

"I'm an old friend of In'ei, and since he was studying the use of the lance, I decided to study along with him. Later, I had an afterthought or two. Now I never touch the weapon."

"I guess that means that Inshun, the present abbot here, is your disciple."

"Yes, it could be put that way. But priests shouldn't have any use for weapons, and I consider it unfortunate that the Hōzōin has become famous for a martial art, rather than for its religious fervor. Still, there were people who felt that it would be a pity to let the Hōzōin Style die out, so I taught it to Inshun. And to no one else."

"I wonder if you'd let me stay in your temple until Inshun returns."

"Do you propose to challenge him?"

"Well, as long as I'm here, I'd like to see how the foremost master uses his lance."

Nikkan shook his head reproachfully. "It's a waste of time. There's nothing to be learned here."

"Is that so?"

"You've already seen the Hōzōin lancemanship, just now, when you fought Agon. What more do you need to see? If you want to learn more, watch me. Look into my eyes."

Nikkan drew up his shoulders, put his head slightly forward, and stared at Musashi. His eyes seemed about to jump from their sockets. As Musashi stared back, Nikkan's pupils shone first with a coral flame, then gradually took on an azure profundity. The glow burned and numbed Musashi's mind. He looked away. Nikkan's crackling laugh was like the clatter of bone-dry boards.

He relaxed his stare only when a younger priest came in and whispered to him. "Bring it in," he commanded.

Presently the young priest returned with a tray and a round wooden rice container, from which Nikkan scooped rice into a bowl. He gave it to Musashi.

"I recommend the tea gruel and pickles. It's the practice of the Hōzōin to serve them to all those who come here to study, so don't feel they're going to any special trouble for you. They make their own pickles—called Hōzōin pickles, in fact—cucumbers stuffed with basil and red pepper. I think you'll find they taste rather good."

As Musashi picked up his chopsticks, he felt Nikkan's keen eyes on him again. He could not tell at this point whether their piercing quality originated within the priest or was a response to something he himself emitted. As he bit into a pickle, the feeling swept over him that Takuan's fist was about to smite him again, or perhaps the lance near the threshold was about to fly at him.

After he had finished a bowl of rice mixed with tea and two pickles, Nikkan asked, "Would you care for another helping?"

"No, thank you. I've had plenty."

"What do you think of the pickles?"

"Very good, thank you."

Even after he'd left, the sting of the red pepper on Musashi's tongue was all he could recall of the pickles' flavor. Nor was that the only sting he felt, for he came away convinced that somehow he'd suffered a defeat. "I lost," he grumbled to himself, walking slowly through a grove of cryptomerias. "I've been outclassed!'' In the dim light, fleeting shadows ran across his path, a small herd of deer, frightened by his footsteps.

"When it was only a matter of physical strength, I won, but I left there feeling defeated. Why? Did I win outwardly only to lose inwardly?"

Suddenly remembering Jōtarō, he retraced his steps to the Hōzōin, where the lights were still burning. When he announced himself, the priest standing watch at the door poked his head out and said casually, "What is it? Did you forget something?"

"Yes. Tomorrow, or the next day, I expect someone to come here looking for me. When he does, will you tell him I'll be staying in the neighborhood of Sarusawa Pond? He should ask for me at the inns there."

"All right."

Since the reply was so casual, Musashi felt constrained to add, "It'll be a boy. His name is Jōtarō. He's very young, so please be sure you make the message clear to him."

Once again striding down the path he had taken earlier, Musashi muttered to himself, "That proves I lost. I even forgot to leave a message for Jōtarō. I was beaten by the old abbot!" Musashi's dejection persisted. Although he had won against Agon, the only thing that stuck in his mind was the immaturity he had felt in Nikkan's presence. How could he ever become a great swordsman, the greatest of them all? This was the question that obsessed him night and day, and today's encounter had left him utterly depressed.

During the past twenty years or so, the area between Sarusawa Pond and the lower reaches of the Sai River had been built up steadily, and there was a jumble of new houses, inns and shops. Only recently, Ōkubo Nagayasu had come to govern the city for the Tokugawas and had set up his administrative offices nearby. In the middle of the town was the establishment of a Chinese who was said to be a descendant of Lin Ho-ching; he had done so well with his stuffed dumplings that an expansion of his shop in the direction of the pond was under way.

Musashi stopped amid the lights of the busiest district and wondered where he should stay. There were plenty of inns, but he had to be careful about his expenses; at the same time, he wanted to choose a place not too far off the beaten track, so Jōtarō could find him easily.

He had just eaten at the temple, but when he caught a whiff of the stuffed dumplings, he felt hungry again. Entering the shop, he sat down and ordered a whole plateful. When they arrived, Musashi noted that the name Lin was burned into the bottom of the dumplings. Unlike the hot pickles at the Hōzōin, the dumplings had a flavor he could savor with pleasure.

The young girl who poured his tea asked politely, "Where are you planning to stay tonight?"

Musashi, unfamiliar with the district, welcomed the opportunity to explain his situation and ask her advice. She told him one of the proprietor's relatives had a private boardinghouse where he would be welcome, and without waiting for his answer, trotted off. She returned with a youngish woman, whose shaved eyebrows indicated she was married—presumably the proprietor's wife.

The boardinghouse was on a quiet alley not far from the restaurant, apparently an ordinary residence that sometimes took in guests. The eyebrowless mistress of the shop, who had shown him the way, tapped lightly on the door, then turned to Musashi and said quietly, "It's my elder sister's house, so don't worry about tipping or anything."

The maid came out of the house and the two of them exchanged whispers for a moment or two. Apparently satisfied, she led Musashi to the second floor.

The room and its furnishings were too good for an ordinary inn, making Musashi feel a bit ill at ease. He wondered why a house as well-off as this one would take in boarders and asked the maid about it, but she just smiled and said nothing. Having already eaten, he had his bath and went to bed, but the question was still on his mind when he went off to sleep.

Next morning, he said to the maid, "Someone is supposed to come looking for me. Will it be all right if I stay over a day or two until he arrives?"

"By all means," she replied, without even asking the lady of the house, who soon came herself to pay her respects.

She was a good-looking woman of about thirty, with fine smooth skin. When Musashi tried to satisfy his curiosity about why she was accepting roomers, she laughingly replied, "To tell the truth, I'm a widow—my husband was a Nō actor by the name of Kanze—and I'm afraid to be without a man in the house, what with all these ill-bred rōnin in the vicinity." She went on to explain that while the streets were full of drinking shops and prostitutes, many of the indigent samurai were not satisfied with these diversions. They would pump information from the local youths and attack houses where there were no men about. They spoke of this as "calling on the widows."

"In other words," said Musashi, "you take in people like me to act as your bodyguard, right?"

"Well," she said, smiling, "as I said, there are no men in the household. Please feel free to stay as long as you like."

"I understand perfectly. I hope you'll feel safe as long as I'm here. There's only one request I'd like to make. I'm expecting a visitor, so I wonder if you'd mind putting a marker with my name on it outside the gate."

The widow, not at all unhappy to let it be known that she had a man in the house, obligingly wrote "Miyamoto Musashi" on a strip of paper and pasted it on the gatepost.

Jōtarō did not show up that day, but on the next, Musashi received a visit from a group of three samurai. Pushing their way past the protesting maid, they came straight upstairs to his room. Musashi saw immediately that they were among those who had been present at the Hōzōin when he had killed Agon. Sitting down around him as though they'd known him all their lives, they started pouring on the flattery.

"I never saw anything like it in my life," said one. "I'm sure nothing of the kind ever happened at the Hōzōin before. Just think! An unknown visitor arrives and, just like that, downs one of the Seven Pillars. And not just anyone—the terrifying Agon himself. One grunt and he was spitting blood. You don't often see sights like that!"

Another went on in the same vein. "Everyone we know is talking about it. All the rōnin are asking each other just who this Miyamoto Musashi is. That was a bad day for the Hōzōin's reputation."

"Why, you must be the greatest swordsman in the country!"

"And so young, too!"

"No doubt about it. And you'll get even better with time."

"If you don't mind my asking, how does it happen that with your ability you're only a rōnin? It's a waste of your talents not to be in the service of a daimyō!"

They paused only long enough to slurp some tea and devour the tea cakes with gusto, spilling crumbs all over their laps and on the floor.

Musashi, embarrassed by the extravagance of their praise, shifted his eyes from right to left and back again. For a time, he listened with an impassive face, thinking that sooner or later their momentum would run down. When they showed no signs of changing the subject, he took the initiative by asking their names.

"Oh, I'm sorry. I'm Yamazoe Dampachi. I used to be in the service of Lord Gamō," said the first.

The man next to him said, "I'm Ōtomo Banryū. I've mastered the Bokuden Style, and I have a lot of plans for the future."

"I'm Yasukawa Yasubei," said the third with a chuckle, "and I've never been anything but a rōnin, like my father before me."

Musashi wondered why they were taking up their time and his with their small talk. It became apparent that he would not find out unless he asked, so the next time there was a break in the conversation, he said, "Presumably you came because you had some business with me."

They feigned surprise at the very idea but soon admitted they had come on what they regarded as a very important mission. Moving quickly forward, Yasubei said, "As a matter of fact, we do have some business with you. You see, we're planning to put on a public 'entertainment' at the foot of Mount Kasuga, and we wanted to talk to you about it. Not a play or anything like that. What we have in mind is a series of matches that would teach the people about the martial arts, and at the same time give them something to lay bets on."

He went on to say that the stands were already being put up, and that the prospects looked excellent. They felt, however, that they needed another man, because with just the three of them, some really strong samurai might show up and beat them all, which would mean that their hard-earned money would go down the drain. They had decided that Musashi was just the right person for them. If he would join in with them, they would not only split the profits but pay for his food and lodging while the matches were in progress. That way he could easily earn some fast money for his future travels.

Musashi listened with some amusement to their blandishments, but by and by he grew tired and broke in. "If that's all you want, there's no point in discussing it. I'm not interested."

"But why?" asked Dampachi. "Why aren't you interested?"

Musashi's youthful temper erupted. "I'm not a gambler!" he stated indignantly. "And I eat with chopsticks, not with my sword!"

"What's that?" protested the three, insulted by his implication. "What do you mean by that?"

"Don't you understand, you fools? I am a samurai, and I intend to remain a samurai. Even if I starve in the process. Now clear out of here!"

One man's mouth twisted into a nasty snarl, and another, red with anger, shouted, "You'll regret this!"

They well knew that the three of them together were no match for Musashi, but to save face, they stamped out noisily, scowling and doing their best to give the impression they weren't through with him yet.

That night, as on other recent nights, there was a milky, slightly overcast moon. The young mistress of the house, free from worry as long as Musashi was in residence, was careful to provide him with delicious food and sake of good quality. He ate downstairs with the family and in the process drank himself into a mellow mood.

Returning to his room, he sprawled on the floor. His thoughts soon came to rest on Nikkan.

"It's humiliating," he said to himself.

The adversaries he had defeated, even the ones he had killed or half killed, always disappeared from his mind like so much froth, but he couldn't forget anyone who got the better of him in any way or, for that matter, anyone in whom he sensed an overpowering presence. Men like that dwelt in his mind like living spirits, and he thought constantly of how one day he might be able to overshadow them.

"Humiliating!" he repeated.

He clutched at his hair and pondered how he could get the better of Nikkan, how he could face that unearthly stare without flinching. For two days this question had gnawed at him. It wasn't that he wished Nikkan any harm, but he was sorely disappointed with himself.

"Is it that I'm no good?" he asked himself ruefully. Having learned swordsmanship on his own, and thus lacking an objective appraisal of his own strength, he couldn't help but doubt his own ability to ever achieve power such as the old priest exuded.

Nikkan had told him he was too strong, that he had to learn to become weaker. This was the point that sent his mind off on tangent after tangent, for he couldn't fathom the meaning. Wasn't strength a warrior's most important quality? Was that not what made one warrior superior to others? How could Nikkan speak of it as a flaw?

"Maybe," thought Musashi, "the old rascal was toying with me. Maybe he considered my youth and decided to talk in riddles just to confuse me and amuse himself. Then after I left, he had a good laugh. It's possible."

At times like this, Musashi wondered whether it had been wise to read all those books at Himeji Castle. Until then, he had never bothered much about figuring things out, but now, whenever something happened, he couldn't rest until he'd found an explanation satisfying to his intellect. Previously he'd acted on instinct; now he had to understand each small thing before he could accept it. And this applied not only to swordsmanship but to the way he viewed humanity and society.

It was true that the daredevil in him had been tamed. Yet Nikkan said he was "too strong." Musashi assumed that Nikkan was referring not to physical strength but to the savage fighting spirit with which he had been born. Could the priest really have perceived it, or was he guessing?

"The knowledge that comes from books is of no use to the warrior," he reassured himself. "If a man worries too much about what others think or do, he's apt to be slow to act. Why, if Nikkan himself closed his eyes for a moment and made one misstep, he'd crumble and fall to pieces!''

The sound of footsteps on the stairs intruded upon his musings. The maid appeared, and after her Jōtarō, his dark skin further blackened by the grime acquired on his journey, but his spritelike hair white with dust. Musashi, truly happy to have the diversion of his little friend, welcomed him with open arms.

The boy plopped down on the floor and stretched his dirty legs out straight. "Am I tired!" he sighed.

"Did you have trouble finding me?"

"Trouble! I almost gave up. I've been searching all over!"

"Didn't you ask at the Hōzōin?"

"Yes, but they said they didn't know anything about you."

"Oh, they did, did they?" Musashi's eyes narrowed. "And after I said specifically that you'd find me near Sarusawa Pond. Oh, well, I'm glad you made it."

"Here's the answer from the Yoshioka School." He handed Musashi the bamboo tube. "I couldn't find Hon'iden Matahachi, so I asked the people at his house to give him the message."

"Fine. Now run along and have a bath. They'll give you some dinner downstairs."

Musashi took the letter from its container and read it. It said that Seijūrō looked forward to a "second bout"; if Musashi didn't show up as promised the following year, it would be assumed that he'd lost his nerve. Should that happen, Seijūrō would make sure that Musashi became the laughingstock of Kyoto. This braggadocio was set down in clumsy handwriting, presumably by someone other than Seijūrō.

As Musashi tore the letter to bits and burned it, the charred pieces fluttered up into the air like so many black butterflies.

Seijūrō had spoken of a "bout," but it was clear that it was going to be more than that. It would be a battle to the death. Next year, as a result of this insulting note, which one of the combatants would end up in ashes?

Musashi took it for granted that a warrior must be content to live from day to day, never knowing each morning if he'd live to see nightfall. Nevertheless, the thought that he might really die in the coming year worried him somewhat. There were so many things he still wanted to do. For one thing, there was his burning desire to become a great swordsman. But that wasn't all. So far, he reflected, he hadn't done any of the things people ordinarily do in the course of a lifetime.

At this stage of his life, he was still vain enough to think he'd like to have retainers—a lot of them— leading his horses and carrying his falcons, just like Bokuden and Lord Kōizumi of Ise. He would like, too, to have a proper house, with a good wife and loyal servants. He wanted to be a good master and to enjoy the warmth and comfort of home life. And of course, before he settled down, he had a secret longing to have a passionate love affair. During all these years of thinking solely about the Way of the Samurai he had, not unnaturally, remained chaste. Still, he was struck by some of the women he saw on the streets of Kyoto and Nara, and it was not their aesthetic qualities alone that pleased him; they aroused him physically.

His thoughts turned to Otsū. Though she was now a creature of the distant past, he felt closely bound to her. How many times, when he was lonely or melancholy, had the vague recollection of her alone cheered him up.

Presently he came out of his reverie. Jōtarō had rejoined him, bathed, satiated and proud to have carried out his mission successfully. Sitting with his short legs crossed and his hands between his knees, he didn't take long to succumb to fatigue. He was soon snoozing blissfully, his mouth open. Musashi put him to bed.

When morning came, the boy was up with the sparrows. Musashi also arose early, since he intended to resume his travels.

As he was dressing, the widow appeared and said in a regretful tone, "You seem in a hurry to leave." In her arms she was carrying some clothing, which she offered him. "I've sewn these things together for you as a parting gift—a kimono with a short cloak. I'm not sure you'll like them, but I hope you'll wear them."

Musashi looked at her in astonishment. The garments were much too expensive for him to accept after having stayed there only two days. He tried to refuse, but the widow insisted. "No, you must take them. They aren't anything very special anyway. I have a lot of old kimono and Nō costumes left by my husband. I have no use for them. I thought it would be nice for you to have some. I do hope you won't refuse. Now that I've altered them to fit you, if you don't take them, they'll just go to waste."

She went behind Musashi and held up the kimono for him to slip his arms into. As he put it on, he realized that the silk was of very good quality and felt more embarrassed than ever. The sleeveless cloak was particularly fine; it must have been imported from China. The hem was gold brocade, the lining silk crepe, and the leather fastening straps had been dyed purple.

"It looks perfect on you!" exclaimed the widow.

Jōtarō, looking on enviously, suddenly said to her, "What're you going to give me?"

The widow laughed. "You should be happy for the chance to accompany your fine master."

"Aw," grumbled Jōtarō, "who wants an old kimono anyway?"

"Is there anything you do want?"

Running to the wall in the anteroom and taking a Nō mask down from its hook, the boy said, "Yes, this!" He'd coveted it since first spying it the night before, and now he rubbed it tenderly against his cheek.

Musashi was surprised at the boy's good taste. He himself had found it admirably executed. There was no way of knowing who had made it, but it was certainly two or three centuries old and had evidently been used in actual Nō performances. The face, carved with exquisite care, was that of a female demon, but whereas the usual mask of this type was grotesquely painted with blue spots, this was the face of a beautiful and elegant young girl. It was peculiar only in that one side of her mouth curved sharply upward in the eeriest fashion imaginable. Obviously not a fictitious face conjured up by the artist, it was the portrait of a real, living madwoman, beautiful yet bewitched.

"That you cannot have," said the widow firmly, trying to take the mask away from the boy.

Evading her reach, Jōtarō put the mask on the top of his head and danced about the room, shouting defiantly, "What do you need it for? It's mine now; I'm going to keep it!"

Musashi, surprised and embarrassed by his ward's conduct, made an attempt to catch him, but Jōtarō stuffed the mask into his kimono and fled down the stairs, the widow giving chase. Although she was laughing, not angry at all, she clearly didn't intend to part with the mask.

Presently Jōtarō climbed slowly back up the stairs. Musashi, ready to scold him severely, was seated with his face toward the door. But as the boy entered, he cried, "Boo!" and held the mask out before him. Musashi was startled; his muscles tensed and his knees shifted inadvertently.

He wondered why Jōtarō's prank had such an effect on him, but as he stared at the mask in the dim light, he began to understand. The carver had put something diabolical into his creation. That crescent smile, curving up on the left side of the white face, was haunted, possessed of a devil.

"If we're going, let's go," said Jōtarō.

Musashi, without rising, said, "Why haven't you given the mask back yet? What do you want with a thing like that?"

"But she said I could keep it! She gave it to me."

"She did not! Go downstairs and give it back to her."

"But she gave it to me! When I offered to return it, she said that if I wanted it so badly, I could keep it. She just wanted to make sure I'd take good care of it, so I promised her I would."

"What am I going to do with you!" Musashi felt ashamed about accepting, first, the beautiful kimono and then this mask that the widow seemed to treasure.

He would have liked to do something in return, but she was obviously not in need of money—certainly not the small amount he could have spared—and none of his meager possessions would make a suitable gift. He descended the stairs, apologizing for Jōtarō's rudeness and attempting to return the mask.

The widow, however, said, "No, the more I think of it, the more I think I'd be happier without it. And he does want it so badly. . . . Don't be too hard on him."

Suspecting the mask had some special significance for her, Musashi tried once more to return it, but by this time Jōtarō had his straw sandals on and was outside waiting by the gate, a smug look on his face. Musashi, eager to be off, gave in to her kindness and accepted the gift. The young widow said she was sorrier to see Musashi go than she was to lose the mask, and begged him several times to come back and stay there whenever he was in Nara.

Musashi was tying the thongs of his sandals when the dumpling-maker's wife came running up. "Oh," she said breathlessly, "I'm so glad you haven't left yet. You can't go now! Please, go back upstairs. Something terrible is going on!" The woman's voice trembled as though she thought some fearful ogre was about to attack her.

Musashi finished tying his sandals and calmly raised his head. "What is it? What's so terrible?"

"The priests at the Hōzōin have heard you're leaving today, and more than ten of them have taken their lances and are lying in wait for you in Hannya Plain."

"Oh?"

"Yes, and the abbot, Inshun, is with them. My

husband knows one of the priests, and he asked him what was going on. The priest said the man who's been staying here for the last couple of days, the man named Miyamoto, was leaving Nara today, and the priests were going to waylay him on the road.''

Her face twitching with fright, she assured Musashi that it would be suicide to leave Nara this morning and fervently urged him to lie low for another night. It would be safer, in her opinion, to try and sneak away the next day.

"I see," said Musashi without emotion. "You say they plan to meet me on Hannya Plain?"

"I'm not sure exactly where, but they went off in that direction. Some of the townspeople told me it wasn't only the priests. They said a whole lot of the rōnin, too, had got together, saying they'd catch you and turn you over to the Hōzōin. Did you say something bad about the temple, or insult them in some way?"

"No."

"Well, they say the priests are furious because you hired somebody to put up posters with verses on them making fun of the Hōzōin. They took this to mean you were gloating over having killed one of their men."

"I didn't do anything of the sort. There's been a mistake."

"Well, if it's a mistake, you shouldn't go out and get yourself killed over it!"

His brow beaded with sweat, Musashi looked thoughtfully up at the sky, recalling how angry the three rōnin had been when he turned down their business deal. Maybe he was indebted to them for all this. It would be just like them to put up offensive posters and then spread the word that he'd done it.

Abruptly he stood up. "I'm leaving," he said.

He strapped his traveling bag to his back, took his basket hat in hand, and turning to the two women, thanked them for their kindness. As he started toward the gate, the widow, now in tears, followed along, begging him not to go.

"If I stay over another night," he pointed out, "there's bound to be trouble at your house. I certainly wouldn't want that to happen, after you've been so good to us."

"I don't care," she insisted. "You'd be safer here."

"No, I'll go now. Jō! Say thank you to the lady."

Dutifully, the boy bowed and did as he was told. He, too, appeared to be in low spirits, but not because he was sorry to leave. When it came right down to it, Jōtarō did not really know Musashi. In Kyoto, he had heard that his master was a weakling and a coward, and the thought that the notorious lancers of the Hōzōin were set to attack him was very depressing. His youthful heart was filled with gloom and foreboding.

15

Hannya Plain

Jōtarō trudged along sadly behind his master, fearing each step was taking them closer to certain death. A little earlier, on the damp, shady road near the Tōdaiji, a dewdrop falling on his collar had almost made him cry out. The black crows he saw along the way gave him an eerie feeling.

Nara was far behind them. Through the rows of cryptomeria trees along the road, they could make out the gently sloping plain leading up to Hannya Hill; to their right were the rolling peaks of Mount Mikasa, above them the peaceful sky.

That he and Musashi were heading straight for the place where the Hōzōin lancers were waiting in ambush made absolutely no sense to him. There were plenty of places to hide, if one put one's mind to it. Why couldn't they go into one of the many temples along the way and bide their time? That would surely be more sensible.

He wondered if perhaps Musashi meant to apologize to the priests, even though he hadn't wronged them in any way. Jōtarō resolved that if Musashi begged their forgiveness, he would too. This was no time to be arguing about the right and wrong of things.

"Jōtarō!"

The boy started at the sound of his name being called. His eyebrows shot up and his body became tense. Realizing his face was probably pale from fright and not wanting to appear childish, he turned his eyes bravely toward the sky. Musashi looked up at the sky too, and the boy felt more dispirited than ever.

When Musashi continued, it was in his usual cheerful tone. "Feels good, doesn't it, Jō? It's as though we were walking along on the songs of the nightingales."

"What?" asked the boy, astonished.

"Nightingales, I said."

"Oh, yeah, nightingales. There are some around here, aren't there?"

Musashi could see from the paleness of the boy's lips that he was dejected. He felt sorry for him. After all, in a matter of minutes he might be suddenly alone in a strange place.

"We're getting near Hannya Hill, aren't we?" said Musashi.

"That's right."

"Well, now what?"

Jōtarō didn't reply. The singing of the nightingales fell coldly on his ears. He couldn't shake off the foreboding that they might soon be parted forever. The eyes that had bristled with mirth when surprising Musashi with the mask were now worried and mournful.

"I think I'd better leave you here," said Musashi.

"If you come along, you may get hurt accidentally. There's no reason to put yourself in harm's way."

Jōtarō broke down, tears streaming down his cheeks as if a dam had broken. The backs of his hands went up to his eyes and his shoulders quivered. His crying was punctuated by tiny spasms, as if he had the hiccups.

"What's this? Aren't you supposed to be learning the Way of the Samurai? If I break and run, you run in the same direction. If I get killed, go back to the sake shop in Kyoto. But for now, go to that little hill and watch from there. You'll be able to keep an eye on everything that happens."

Having wiped his tears away, Jōtarō grabbed Musashi's sleeves and blurted out, "Let's run away!"

"That's no way for a samurai to talk! That's what you want to be, isn't it?"

"I'm afraid! I don't want to die!" With trembling hands, he kept trying to pull Musashi back by the sleeve. "Think about me," he pleaded. "Please, let's get away while we can!"

"When you talk like that, you make me want to run too. You've got no parents who'll look after you, just like me when I was your age. But—"

"Then come on. What are we waiting for?"

"No!" Musashi turned, and planting his feet wide apart, faced the child squarely. "I'm a samurai. You're a samurai's son. We're not going to run away."

Hearing the finality in Musashi's tone, Jōtarō gave up and sat down, dirty tears rolling off his face as he rubbed his red and swollen eyes with his hands.

"Don't worry!" said Musashi. "I have no intention of losing. I'm going to win! Everything will be all right then, don't you think?"

Jōtarō took little comfort from this speech. He couldn't believe a word of it. Knowing that the Hōzōin lancers numbered more than ten, he doubted whether Musashi, considering his reputation for weakness, could beat them one at a time, let alone all together.

Musashi, for his part, was beginning to lose patience. He liked Jōtarō, felt sorry for him, but this was no time to be thinking about children. The lancers were there for one purpose: to kill him. He had to be prepared to face them. Jōtarō was becoming a nuisance.

His voice took on a sharp edge. "Stop your blubbering! You'll never be a samurai, carrying on this way. Why don't you just go on back to the sake shop?" Firmly and not too gently, he pushed the boy from him.

Jōtarō, stung to the core, suddenly stopped crying and stood straight, a surprised look on his face. He watched his master stride off toward Hannya Hill. He wanted to call out after him, but resisted the urge. Instead he forced himself to remain silent for several minutes. Then he squatted under a nearby tree, buried his face in his hands, and gritted his teeth.

Musashi did not look back, but Jōtarō's sobs echoed in his ears. He felt he could see the hapless, frightened little boy through the back of his head and regretted having brought him along. It was more than enough just to take care of himself; still immature, with only his sword to rely on and no idea of what the morrow might bring—what need had he of a companion?

The trees thinned out. He found himself on an open plain, actually the slightly rising skirt of the mountains in the distance. On the road branching off toward Mount Mikasa, a man raised his hand in greeting.

"Hey, Musashi! Where are you going?"

Musashi recognized the man coming toward him; it was Yamazoe Dampachi. Though Musashi sensed immediately that Dampachi's objective was to lead him into a trap, he nevertheless greeted him heartily.

Dampachi said, "Glad I ran into you. I want you to know how sorry I am about that business the other day." His tone was too polite, and as he spoke, he was obviously examining Musashi's face with great care. "I hope you'll forget about it. It was all a mistake."

Dampachi himself was none too sure what to make of Musashi. He had been very impressed by what he had seen at the Hōzōin. Indeed, just thinking about it sent chills up his spine. Be that as it may, Musashi was still only a provincial rōnin, who couldn't be more than twenty-one or twenty-two years old, and Dampachi was far from ready to admit to himself that anyone of that age and status could be his better.

"Where are you going?" he asked again.

"I'm planning to go through Iga over to the Ise highroad. And you?"

"Oh, I have some things to do in Tsukigase."

"That's not far from Yagyū Valley, is it?"

"No, not far."

"That's where Lord Yagyū's castle is, isn't it?"

"Yes, it's near the temple called Kasagidera. You must go there sometime. The old lord, Muneyoshi, lives in retirement, like a tea master, and his son, Munenori, is in Edo, but you should still stop in and see what it's like."

"I don't really think Lord Yagyū would give a lesson to a wanderer like me."

"He might. Of course, it'd help if you had an introduction. As it happens, I know an armorer in Tsukigase who does work for the Yagyūs. If you'd like, I could ask if he'd be willing to introduce you."

The plain stretched out broadly for several miles, the skyline broken occasionally by a lone cryptomeria or Chinese black pine. There were gentle rises here and there, however, and the road rose and fell too. Near the bottom of Hannya Hill, Musashi spotted the brown smoke of a fire rising beyond a low hillock.

"What's that?" he asked.

"What's what?"

"That smoke over there."

"What's so strange about smoke?" Dampachi had been sticking close to Musashi's left side, and as he stared into the latter's face, his own hardened perceptibly.

Musashi pointed. "That smoke over there: there's something suspicious about it," he said. "Doesn't it look that way to you?"

"Suspicious? In what way?"

"Suspicious—you know, like the look on your face right now," Musashi said sharply, abruptly sweeping his finger toward Dampachi.

A sharp whistling sound broke the stillness on the plain. Dampachi gasped as Musashi struck. His attention diverted by Musashi's finger, Dampachi never realized that Musashi had drawn his sword. His body rose, flew forward, and landed face down. Dampachi would not rise again.

From the distance there was a cry of alarm, and two men appeared at the top of the hillock. One of the

men screamed, and both spun round and took to their
heels, their arms flailing the air wildly.

The sword that Musashi was pointing toward the
earth glittered in the sunlight; fresh blood dripped
from its tip. He marched directly on toward the hillock, and although the spring breeze blew softly against
his skin, Musashi felt his muscles tauten as he as-
cended. From the top, he looked down at the fire
burning below.

"He's come!" shouted one of the men who had
fled to join the others. There were about thirty men.
Musashi picked out Dampachi's cohorts, Yasukawa
Yasubei and Ōtomo Banryū.

"He's come!" parroted another.

They'd been lolling in the sun. Now they all
jumped to their feet. Half were priests, the other half
nondescript rōnin. When Musashi came into view, a
wordless but nonetheless savage stir went through the
group. They saw the bloodstained sword and suddenly
realized that the battle had already begun. Instead of
challenging Musashi, they had been sitting around the
fire and had let him challenge them!

Yasukawa and Ōtomo were talking as fast as they
could, explaining with broad rapid gestures how Yamazoe had been cut down. The rōnin scowled with
fury, the Hōzōin priests eyed Musashi menacingly
while grouping themselves for battle.

All of the priests carried lances. Black sleeves
tucked up, they were ready for action, apparently set
upon avenging the death of Agon and restoring the
temple's honor. They looked grotesque, like so many
demons from hell.

The rōnin formed a semicircle, so they could

329

watch the show and at the same time keep Musashi from escaping.

This precaution, however, proved unnecessary, for Musashi showed no sign of either running or backing down. In fact, he was walking steadily and directly toward them. Slowly, pace by pace, he advanced, looking as if he might pounce at any moment.

For a moment, there was an ominous silence, as both sides contemplated approaching death. Musashi's face went deadly white and through his eyes stared the eyes of the god of vengeance, glittering with venom. He was selecting his prey.

Neither the rōnin nor the priests were as tense as Musashi. Their numbers gave them confidence, and their optimism was unshakable. Still, no one wanted to be the first attacked.

A priest at the end of the column of lancers gave a signal, and without breaking formation, they rushed around to Musashi's right.

"Musashi! I am Inshun," shouted the same priest. "I'm told that you came while I was away and killed Agon. That you later publicly insulted the honor of the Hōzōin. That you mocked us by having posters put up all over town. Is this true?"

"No!" shouted Musashi. "If you're a priest, you should know better than to trust only what you see and hear. You should consider things with your mind and spirit."

It was like pouring oil on the flames. Ignoring their leader, the priests began to shout, saying talk was cheap, it was time to fight.

They were enthusiastically seconded by the rōnin, who had grouped themselves in close formation at

Musashi's left. Screaming, cursing and waving their swords in the air, they egged the priests on to action.

Musashi, convinced that the rōnin were all mouth and no fight, suddenly turned to them and shouted, "All right! Which one of you wants to come forward?"

All but two or three fell back a pace, each sure that Musashi's evil eye was upon him. The two or three brave ones stood ready, swords outstretched, issuing a challenge.

In the wink of an eye, Musashi was on one of them like a fighting cock. There was a sound like the popping of a cork, and the ground turned red. Then came a chilling noise—not a battle cry, not a curse, but a truly bloodcurdling howl.

Musashi's sword screeched back and forth through the air, a reverberation in his own body telling him when he connected with human bone. Blood and brains spattered from his blade; fingers and arms flew through the air.

The rōnin had come to watch the carnage, not to participate in it, but their weakness had led Musashi to attack them first. At the very beginning, they held together fairly well, because they thought the priests would soon come to their rescue. But the priests stood silent and motionless as Musashi quickly slaughtered five or six rōnin, throwing the others into confusion. Before long they were slashing wildly in all directions, as often as not injuring one another.

For most of the time, Musashi wasn't really conscious of what he was doing. He was in a sort of trance, a murderous dream in which body and soul were concentrated in his three-foot sword. Unconsciously, his whole life experience—the knowledge his father had beaten into him, what he had learned at

Sekigahara, the theories he had heard at the various schools of swordsmanship, the lessons taught him by the mountains and the trees—everything came into play in the rapid movements of his body. He became a disembodied whirlwind mowing down the herd of rōnin, who by their stunned bewilderment left themselves wide open to his sword.

For the short duration of the battle, one of the priests counted the number of times he inhaled and exhaled. It was all over before he had taken his twentieth breath.

Musashi was drenched with the blood of his victims. The few remaining rōnin were also covered with gore. The earth, the grass, even the air was bloody. One of their number let out a scream, and the surviving rōnin scattered in all directions.

While all this was going on, Jōtarō was absorbed in prayer. His hands folded before him and his eyes lifted skyward, he implored, "Oh, God in heaven, come to his aid! My master, down there on the plain, is hopelessly outnumbered. He's weak, but he isn't a bad man. Please help him!"

Despite Musashi's instructions to go away, he couldn't leave. The place where he had finally chosen to sit, his hat and his mask beside him, was a knoll from which he could see the scene around the bonfire in the distance.

"Hachiman! Kompira! God of Kasuga Shrine! Look! My master is walking directly into the enemy. Oh, gods of heaven, protect him. He isn't himself. He's usually mild and gentle, but he's been a little bit strange ever since this morning. He must be crazy, or else he wouldn't take on that many at once! Oh, please, please, help him!''

After calling on the deities a hundred times or more, he noticed no visible results of his efforts and started getting angry. Finally, he was shouting: "Aren't there any gods in this land? Are you going to let the wicked people win, and the good man be killed? If you do that, then everything they've always told me about right and wrong is a lie! You can't let him be killed! If you do, I'll spit on you!''

When he saw that Musashi was surrounded, his invocations turned to curses, directed not only at the enemy but at the gods themselves. Then, realizing that the blood being spilled on the plain was not his teacher's, he abruptly changed his tune. "Look! My master's not a weakling after all! He's beating them!''

This was the first time Jōtarō had ever witnessed men fighting like beasts to the death, the first time he had ever seen so much blood. He began to feel that he was down there in the middle of it, himself smeared with gore. His heart turned somersaults, he felt giddy and light-headed.

"Look at him! I told you he could do it! What an attack! And look at those silly priests, lined up like a bunch of cawing crows, afraid to take a step!''

But this last was premature, for as he spoke the priests of the Hōzōin began moving in on Musashi.

"Oh, oh! This looks bad. They're all attacking him at once. Musashi's in trouble!'' Forgetting everything, out of his senses with anxiety, Jōtarō darted like a fireball toward the scene of impending disaster.

Abbot Inshun gave the command to charge, and in an instant, with a tremendous roar of voices, the lancers flew into action. Their glittering weapons whistled in the air as the priests scattered like bees sprung from a hive, shaved heads making them appear all the more barbaric.

The lances they carried were all different, with a wide variety of blades—the usual pointed, cone-shaped ones, others flat, cross-shaped or hooked—each priest using the type he favored most. Today they had a chance to see how the techniques they honed in practice worked in real battle.

As they fanned out, Musashi, expecting a trick attack, jumped back and stood on guard. Weary and a little dazed from the earlier bout, he gripped his sword handle tightly. It was sticky with gore, and a mixture of blood and sweat clouded his vision, but he was determined to die magnificently, if die he must.

To his amazement, the attack never came. Instead of making the anticipated lunges in his direction, the priests fell like mad dogs on their erstwhile allies, chasing down the rōnin who had fled and slashing at them mercilessly as they screamed in protest. The unsuspecting rōnin, futilely trying to direct the lancers toward Musashi, were slit, skewered, stabbed in the mouth, sliced in two, and otherwise slaughtered until not one of them was left alive. The massacre was as thorough as it was bloodthirsty.

Musashi could not believe his eyes. Why had the priests attacked their supporters? And why so viciously? He himself had only moments earlier been fighting like a wild animal; now he could hardly bear to watch the ferocity with which these men of the cloth slew the rōnin. Having been transformed for a time into a mindless beast, he was now restored to his normal state by the sight of others similarly transformed. The experience was sobering.

Then he became aware of a tugging at his arms and legs. Looking down, he found Jōtarō weeping tears of relief. For the first time, he relaxed.

As the battle ended, the abbot approached him, and in a polite, dignified manner, said, "You are Miyamoto, I assume. It is an honor to meet you." He was tall and of light complexion. Musashi was somewhat overcome by his appearance, as well as by his poise. With a certain amount of confusion, he wiped his sword clean and sheathed it, but for the moment words failed him.

"Let me introduce myself," continued the priest. "I am Inshun, abbot of the Hōzōin."

"So you are the master of the lance," said Musashi.

"I'm sorry I was away when you visited us recently. I'm also embarrassed that my disciple Agon put up such a poor fight."

Sorry about Agon's performance? Musashi felt that perhaps his ears needed cleaning. He remained silent for a moment, for before he could decide on a suitable way to respond to Inshun's courteous tone, he had to straighten out the confusion in his mind. He still couldn't figure out why the priests had turned on the rōnin—could imagine no possible explanation. He was even somewhat puzzled to find himself still alive.

"Come," said the abbot, "and wash off some of that blood. You need a rest." Inshun led him toward the fire, Jōtarō tagging along close behind.

The priests had torn a large cotton cloth into strips and were wiping their lances. Gradually they gathered by the fire, sitting down with Inshun and Musashi as though nothing unusual had occurred. They began chatting among themselves.

"Look, up there," said one, pointing upward.

"Ah, the crows have caught the whiff of blood. Cawing over the dead bodies, they are."

"Why don't they dig in?"

"They will, as soon as we leave. They'll be scrambling to get at the feast."

The grisly banter went on in this leisurely vein. Musashi got the impression that he wasn't going to find out anything unless he asked. He looked at Inshun and said, "You know, I thought you and your men had come here to attack me, and I'd made up my mind to take along as many of you as I could to the land of the dead. I can't understand why you're treating me this way."

Inshun laughed. "Well, we don't necessarily regard you as an ally, but our real purpose today was to do a little housecleaning."

"You call what's been going on housecleaning?"

"That's right," said Inshun, pointing toward the horizon. "But I think we might as well wait and let Nikkan explain it to you. I'm sure that speck on the edge of the plain is he."

At the same moment, on the other side of the plain, a horseman was saying to Nikkan, "You walk fast for your age, don't you?"

"I'm not fast. You're slow."

"You're nimbler than the horses."

"Why shouldn't I be? I'm a man."

The old priest, who alone was on foot, was pacing the horsemen as they advanced toward the smoke of the fire. The five riders with him were officials.

As the party approached, the priests whispered

among themselves, "It's the Old Master." Having confirmed this, they fell back a good distance and lined themselves up ceremoniously, as for a sacred rite, to greet Nikkan and his entourage.

The first thing Nikkan said was, "Did you take care of everything?"

Inshun bowed and replied, "Just as you commanded." Then, turning to the officials, "Thank you for coming."

As the samurai jumped one by one off their horses, their leader replied, "It's no trouble. Thank *you* for doing the real work! . . . Let's get on with it, men."

The officials went about inspecting the corpses and making a few notes; then their leader returned to where Inshun was standing. "We'll send people from the town to clean up the mess. Please feel free to leave everything as it is." With that, the five of them remounted their horses and rode off.

Nikkan let the priests know that they were no longer needed. Having bowed to him, they started walking away silently. Inshun, too, said good-bye to Nikkan and Musashi and took his leave.

As soon as the men were gone, there was a great cacophony. The crows descended, flapping their wings joyfully.

Grumbling over the noise, Nikkan walked over to Musashi's side and said casually, "Forgive me if I offended you the other day."

"Not at all. You were very kind. It is I who should thank you." Musashi knelt and bowed deeply before the old priest.

"Get off the ground," commanded Nikkan. "This field is no place for bowing."

Musashi got to his feet.

"Has the experience here taught you anything?" the priest asked.

"I'm not even sure what happened. Can you tell me?"

"By all means," replied Nikkan. "Those officials who just left work under Ōkubo Nagayasu, who was recently sent to administer Nara. They're new to the district, and the rōnin have been taking advantage of their unfamiliarity with the place—waylaying innocent passersby, blackmailing, gambling, making off with the women, breaking into widows' houses—causing all sorts of trouble. The administrator's office couldn't bring them under control, but they did know that there were about fifteen ringleaders, including Dampachi and Yasukawa.

"This Dampachi and his cohorts took a disliking to you, as you know. Since they were afraid to attack you themselves, they concocted what they thought was a clever plan, whereby the priests of the Hōzōin would do it for them. The slanderous statements about the temple, attributed to you, were their work; so were the posters. They made sure everything was reported to me, presumably on the theory that I'm stupid."

Musashi's eyes laughed as he listened.

"I thought about it for a while," said the abbot, "and it occurred to me that this was an ideal opportunity to have a housecleaning in Nara. I spoke to Inshun about my plan, he agreed to undertake it, and now everybody's happy—the priests, the administrators; also the crows. Ha, ha!"

There was one other person who was supremely happy. Nikkan's story had wiped away all of Jōtarō's doubts and fears, and the boy was ecstatic. He began singing an improvised ditty while dancing about like a bird flapping its wings:

> A housecleaning, oh,
> A housecleaning!

At the sound of his unaffected voice, Musashi and Nikkan turned to watch him. He was wearing his mask with the curious smile and pointing his wooden sword at the scattered bodies. Taking an occasional swipe at the birds, he continued:

> Yes, you crows,
> Once in a while
> There's a need for housecleaning,
> But not only in Nara.
> It's nature's way
> To make everything new again.
> So spring can rise from the ground,
> We burn leaves,
> We burn fields.
> Sometimes we want snow to fall,
> Sometimes we want a housecleaning.
> Oh, you crows!
> Feast away! What a spread!
> Soup straight from the eye sockets,
> And thick red sake.
> But don't have too much
> Or you'll surely get drunk.

"Come here, boy!" shouted Nikkan sharply.

"Yes, sir." Jōtarō stood still and turned to face the abbot.

"Stop acting the fool. Fetch me some rocks."

"This kind?" asked Jōtarō, snatching a stone that lay near his feet and holding it up.

"Yes, like that. Bring lots of them!"

"Yes, sir!"

As the boy gathered the stones, Nikkan sat down and wrote on each one "Namu Myōhō Renge-kyō," the sacred invocation of the Nichiren sect. Then he gave them back to the boy and ordered him to scatter them among the dead. While Jōtarō did this, Nikkan put his palms together and chanted a section of the Lotus Sutra.

When he had finished, he announced, "That should take care of them. Now you two can be on your way. I shall return to Nara." As abruptly as he had come, he departed, walking at his customary breakneck speed, before Musashi had a chance to thank him or make arrangements to see him again.

For a moment, Musashi just stared at the retreating figure, then suddenly he darted off to catch up with it. "Reverend priest!" he called. "Haven't you forgotten something?" He patted his sword as he said this.

"What?" asked Nikkan.

"You have given me no word of guidance, and since there is no way of knowing when we'll meet again, I'd appreciate some small bit of advice."

The abbot's toothless mouth let out its familiar crackling laugh. "Don't you understand *yet?*" he asked. "That you're too strong is the only thing I have to teach you. If you continue to pride yourself on your strength, you won't live to see thirty. Why, you might easily have been killed today. Think about that, and decide how to conduct yourself in the future."

Musashi was silent.

"You accomplished something today, but it was

not well done, not by a long shot. Since you're still young, I can't really blame you, but it's a grave error to think the Way of the Samurai consists of nothing but a show of strength.

"But then, I tend to have the same fault, so I'm not really qualified to speak to you on the subject. You should study the way that Yagyū Sekishūsai and Lord Kōizumi of Ise have lived. Sekishūsai was my teacher, Lord Kōizumi was his. If you take them as your models and try to follow the path they have followed, you may come to know the truth."

When Nikkan's voice ceased, Musashi, who had been staring at the ground, deep in thought, looked up. The old priest had already vanished.

LOOK FOR

MUSASHI
BOOK II

THE ART OF WAR

Musashi sets off on his journey to the great temples of the martial arts—while his old friend, Matahachi, is caught in a spell of idleness and lust in Kyoto. But when word comes of a powerful new swordsman who dared challenge all the lords of Yagyū to battle, Matahachi discovers that it is none other than his old friend. While one man seeks knowledge, the other seeks his lost honor . . . as a smoldering peace is fanned by roving bands of masterless samurai and the threat of a new war!